FRANCIS BACON

Francis Bacon as a boy. Nineteenth-century engraving
of a bust of Bacon made around 1572

Francis Bacon

By Perez Zagorin

PRINCETON

UNIVERSITY

PRESS

Third printing, and first paperback printing, 1999
Paperback ISBN 0-691-00966-X

The Library of Congress has cataloged the cloth edition of this book as follows
Zagorin, Perez.
Francis Bacon / Perez Zagorin.
p.   cm.
Includes bibliographical references and index.
ISBN 0-691-05928-4 (alk. paper)
1. Bacon, Francis, 1561–1626.   2. Philosophers—
Great Britain—Biography.   I. Title.
B1197.Z34   1998
192—dc21   97-41404

This book has been composed in Baskerville

The paper used in this publication
meets the minimum requirements of
ANSI/NISO Z39.48-1992 (R1997)
(*Permanence of Paper*)

http://pup.princeton.edu

Printed in the United States of America

3   5   7   9   10   8   6   4

For man is but the servant and interpreter of nature: what he does and what he knows is only what he has observed of nature's order in fact or in thought; beyond this he knows nothing and can do nothing. For the chain of causes cannot by any force be loosed or broken, nor can nature be conquered except by being obeyed.

—Francis Bacon, *The Great Instauration*

The human understanding is no dry light, but receives an infusion from the will and affections; whence proceed sciences which may be called "sciences as one would wish." For what a man had rather were true he readily believes.

—Francis Bacon, *The New Organon*

. . . the sovereignty of man lieth hid in knowledge. . . .

—Francis Bacon, *The Letters and Life of Francis Bacon*

I don't follow or share your way of conceiving the historical problem as the determination of a curve by points. I think that that applies only to what is done and over. . . . But unless the future contains genuine novelties, unless the present is really creative of them, I don't see the use of time at all.

—William James to Henry Adams, 9 February 1908

CONTENTS

PREFACE

During the writing of this book about Francis Bacon, it was often in my mind that the end of the twentieth century and with it the beginning of the new millennium lay close ahead. This awareness may be ascribed in part to the effect of Bacon's own influence, for time and the future occupied an important place in his thought. His writings referred frequently to time. He called truth the daughter of time. On occasion he compared time to a river that carries along light and superficial things in its flow while things weighty and solid sink to the bottom and are lost. He criticized the veneration of past time and antiquity, arguing that the moderns have exceeded the past in their knowledge and observations of the world. More than anything else he saw time as a dimension of existence pointed toward the future, bearing in its womb the seeds of novelty and progress and preparing to bring forth a renewal of knowledge and the sciences for the betterment of the human condition. He named the chief project of his intellectual life "The Great Instauration" to signify his belief in the coming of a new era of knowledge in the investigation of nature whose noble fruits would be the work of time. This project of Bacon's, conceived almost four hundred years ago, was formulated as a solitary undertaking at the inception of the scientific revolution of the seventeenth century and the subsequent era of technological progress that was among the latter's consequences. One of the main reasons Bacon still deserves close study is his importance in human civilization as a prophetic thinker who, standing at the threshold of the modern period, perceived some of the possibilities inherent in the development of science and its technological application, who devoted great intellectual effort to devising ways of assuring scientific progress, and whose imagination gave him some intimation of the role science might play in creating what he envisaged as the future kingdom of man.

Bacon's, however, was a universal intellect whose interests embraced many fields. He was not merely a philosopher but spent an active life as a lawyer, political man, and statesman. While the reform of knowledge and renewal of natural philosophy was his highest priority as a thinker, he also reflected and wrote much about religion, morals and human conduct, politics, the workings of the mind, language and communication, poetry, myth, history, and law. The varied aspects of his work have been discussed in articles and monographs by many scholars, and numerous writings exist that seek to explain his work on science. During the past forty years some outstanding historical studies concerned wholly or principally with Bacon's scientific thought have appeared. I refer particularly to Paolo Rossi's *Francis Bacon: From Magic to Science*, Lisa Jardine's *Francis Bacon: Discovery and the Art of Discourse*, and Antonio Pérez-Ramos's *Francis Bacon's Idea of Science and the Maker's Knowledge Tradition*, all of which have shed much light on his natural philosophy. Graham Rees has also made significant contributions to the understanding of Bacon's science, while Brian Vickers is another leading Bacon scholar who has written widely about his view of rhetoric, language, and other topics.

What has not been available to present-day readers, students, and scholars, however, is a reasonably comprehensive and up-to-date history of Bacon's mind that presents a broad survey and analysis of the whole range of his ideas in their historical context. With regard to the correct understanding of his conceptions concerning the theory and method of science, there is still work to be done. In addition, there are the further aspects of his thought, which to date have mostly been treated separately in specialized accounts. The principal purpose of this book, therefore, is to provide a unified discussion and examination of Bacon's work, achievements, and characteristics as a thinker and philosopher both with respect to science and in the other areas to which he devoted himself. It begins with a sketch of his life and political career focusing on the features most relevant to the development of his thought. The following two chapters, which are the longest, examine his philosophy and his theory of science in their relationship to his project for the reconstruction of knowledge and the promotion of scientific progress. The remaining chapters deal with the other subjects in which he was deeply interested, including morals, politics, language, law, and history. Throughout this book I have striven not only to convey an integrated understanding of Bacon's conceptions in various domains but to enable the reader to gain an acquaintance with his many writings.

I have had Bacon on my mind ever since I first read his *The Advancement of Learning* and the seven volumes of Spedding's great *The Letters and Life of Francis Bacon Including All His Occasional Works* one summer in the National Library in Florence well over thirty years ago. This book is thus the product of an enduring interest in Bacon as both a man and a philosopher. It has likewise grown out of the interest I have taken from the time I was an undergraduate in the problems connected with epistemology, and later on, in those related to the philosophy and history of science. I am fully aware of the obstacles anyone must face who proposes to present a balanced study of the scope of Bacon's thought, and I do not flatter myself that I have succeeded in surmounting them all. The philosopher Thomas Hobbes, who was once Bacon's scribe or secretary for a brief period, formulated very well the essential problem the historian encounters who proposes to write about someone like Bacon:

> Though words be the signs we have of one another's opinions and intentions, yet, because the equivocation of them is so frequent according to the diversity of contexture and of the company wherewith they go . . . it must be extreme hard to find out the opinions and meanings of those men that are gone from us long ago, and have left us no other signification but their books; which cannot possibly be understood without history enough to discover those aforementioned circumstances, and also without great prudence to observe them.

Fully aware of the import of Hobbes's statement, I have tried my best, nevertheless, to make Bacon intelligible as a thinker of his time and to bring out the richness, variety, and greatness of his work. In English culture, Bacon's lifetime saw the appearance of Shakespeare's plays, poems, and the famous first folio edition of his works in 1623.

It also witnessed the publication in 1611 of the new English translation of the Bible, the Authorized or King James Version. After these two, whose effects on human minds and feeling are beyond calculation, there come in order of influence and importance some of the writings of Bacon. His major significance in European intellectual history and the history of science is defined by the fact that he is the first English thinker who must be noticed in the histories of modern philosophy and the first English philosopher to occupy a prominent place in the history of modern thought about science.

In studying Bacon's writings, I have relied almost entirely on the indispensable nineteenth-century edition of his collected works, which was conceived and executed by James Spedding with the help of his collaborators, Robert L. Ellis and Douglas D. Heath. I have also made extensive use of Bacon's letters and miscellaneous writings, the historical documents, and the commentaries contained in Spedding's biography and edition of his correspondence and papers. Spedding was a most intelligent, honest, learned, and painstaking historian to whom all students of Bacon owe an enormous debt. The Clarendon Press has recently initiated a new edition of Bacon's works, but until this is completed, anyone intent on investigating his thought will continue to depend on Spedding's collection. In recent decades, a number of previously unknown manuscripts by Bacon have come to light and been published. Better versions of a few of his known works have also been discovered. Although these additions to the Bacon corpus are most welcome, none of them modifies or alters our understanding of his philosophy.

In concluding this preface, I wish to express my warm thanks to the Shannon Center for Advanced Studies at the University of Virginia, which appointed me a Fellow and thereby greatly facilitated my work. I am also obliged to the Corcoran Department of History at the University of Virginia for extending me its hospitality as a Visiting Scholar.

This book is dedicated to my two young grandsons, Edmund and Oliver Zagorin, who will grow into youth and manhood in the new century and millennium. Although the portents for the future are very mixed, my hope nevertheless is that their generation will live to

see the furtherance of Bacon's vision of the use of science for the
relief and improvement of the human estate in a world more peace-
ful and secure than the one that awaited an earlier generation born
around the years when the twentieth century began.

REFERENCES AND ABBREVIATIONS

A̲ʟʟ references to *The Works of Francis Bacon* are to the edition by James Spedding, Robert L. Ellis, and Douglas D. Heath, which was published in the United States in fifteen volumes (Cambridge, Mass., 1863). The previous English edition of Bacon's *Works* by the same editors was published in seven volumes (London, 1857–61). Because there are great differences between the volume and page numbers of Bacon's writings in these two separate editions, I have done my best to make my references as specific as possible in order to facilitate the location of quotations and citations by readers who use the English edition. In all of the references to the *Works*, I give not only the volume and page numbers but also, in contrast to the practice of many authors on Bacon, the title of the particular work cited. For several of his writings, I give the book and chapter numbers as well, and in the case of *The New Organon*, the number of the aphorism in lowercase Roman numerals.

Tʜᴇ following abbreviations are used:

AL	Francis Bacon, *The Advancement of Learning*
DA	Francis Bacon, *De Dignitate et Augmentis Scientiarum*; used also for the English translation, *Of the Dignity and Advancement of Learning*
DNB	*The Dictionary of National Biography*, ed. Leslie Stephen and Sidney Lee, 22 vols. (Oxford University Press, 1964–65)
Farrington	Benjamin Farrington, *The Philosophy of Francis Bacon* (Liverpool: Liverpool University Press, 1964)
LL	James Spedding, *The Letters and Life of Francis Bacon, Including All His Occasional Works*, 7 vols. (London, 1890)

NO   Francis Bacon, *The New Organon*
Works   *The Works of Francis Bacon*

FRANCIS BACON

1

Introduction: Bacon's
Two Lives

FRANCIS BACON lived two separate but interconnected lives. One was the meditative, reserved life of a philosopher, scientific inquirer, and writer of genius, a thinker of soaring ambition and vast range whose project for the reconstruction of philosophy contained a new vision of science and its place in society. The other was the troubled, insecure life of a courtier, professional lawyer, politician, royal servant, adviser, and minister to two sovereigns, Elizabeth I and James I, who from early youth to old age never ceased his quest for high position and the favor of the great. It was the first of his two lives that brought Bacon the lasting fame for which he strove, and established his claim to the permanent interest of posterity. The second, however, absorbed a large part of his time and energy, pitting him against rivals in a continual competition for office and power, diverting him from pursuing some of his most cherished intellectual goals, and forcing him to leave his main philosophical enterprise fragmentary and unfinished. Moreover, although he was in many ways the most intelligent English statesman of his generation, better equipped than any other to advise a ruler, his political life was a failure. Despite all his efforts, he never attained the kind of influence in government he needed in order to give effect to his ideas and was always obliged to submit to the direction of lesser minds.

Bacon was very conscious of the split between his two lives and the disharmony they imposed on his existence. He sometimes applied to himself the sorrowful words of Psalm 19 in the Vulgate version, "Multum incola fuit anima mea" ("My soul was a stranger"); and in a prayer he composed in 1621 after his condemnation for corruption in his office as lord chancellor, he confessed that he had made poor use of the gifts God had granted him, misspending his talents "in things for which I was least fit, so as I may truly say, my soul hath been a stranger in the course of my pilgrimage."[1]

Despite such expressions of regret, Bacon was irresistibly attracted to politics and would never willingly retire into a private existence. The contrast between his two lives as philosopher and politician, and certain of his traits and actions as a public man, have made his complex personality an enigma to many. Noting the curious mixture of elements in his mental composition, Lytton Strachey felt compelled to put the question, "Who has ever explained Francis Bacon?"[2] Another scholar has commented that "even to the keenest minds Bacon is ultimately an impenetrable mystery."[3] Even Lord Macaulay, who with his customary self-confidence presumed in a famous essay on Bacon that he understood him thoroughly, was perplexed by the contradictions he perceived between Bacon's greatness as a thinker and his baseness as a man.[4] Because politics was so important to Bacon, no account of his philosophy can be adequate that fails to consider certain aspects of his personal history and political career and the character they reveal. This is essential not only for the insight it provides into the human being and his experiences that are present in his writings, but no less for its relevance in helping us to understand some of his ideas. What follows is accordingly a brief and selective biographical sketch discussing chiefly those features of his life that may shed light on his thought.[5]

Bacon came by his aspiration to acquire power in the royal service as a natural inheritance from his father, Sir Nicholas Bacon, a lawyer, statesman, privy councillor, and for over twenty years until his death England's highest judge as Queen Elizabeth's lord keeper of the great seal. Born on 22 January 1561, Francis was Sir Nicholas Bacon's younger son by his second wife, Ann Cooke. Besides his brother Anthony, three years his senior, Francis had a number of siblings stemming from his father's first marriage. He was also related to the Cecil family, whose head, Sir William Cecil, Lord Burghley, the queen's principal minister, was his uncle by marriage. Royal officials of exceptional ability, the two brothers-in-law Nicholas Bacon and William Cecil were recently arrived members of the English governing class. They were part of an administrative elite and new service aristocracy that had taken shape under the Tudor monarchy, particularly since the later period of Henry VIII's reign following England's break with the Catholic Church. Possessing long experience in government, they had risen to the highest positions under Queen Elizabeth and also founded landed families. With influential connections like these, Bacon might reasonably have looked forward to a successful career of his own in the crown's service.[6]

Bacon manifested his extraordinary intellectual powers very early in life. In his boyhood, the queen was impressed by his precocity and wit and called him the young lord keeper. At the age of twelve he was sent to Cambridge University where he stayed for about two and a half years. In 1576 he was admitted to Gray's Inn, of which his father was an eminent member, destined for the study of law. In the same year, in order to broaden his education and fit him for state affairs, his father arranged for him to be part of Sir Amias Paulet's embassy to France. He remained abroad for nearly three years and was in Paris when the news of his father's death in February 1579 obliged him to return home. The loss of his father significantly affected his future prospects. Sir Nicholas, owing apparently to inadvertence and delay, had neglected to make any provision for him in his will. Bacon was thus left without independent means and forced to earn his living. Law was his chosen profession; but as his chaplain, secretary, and earliest biographer, Willam Rawley, wrote, "His heart was more carried after the affairs and places" of state.[7] Lacking any considerable income following his father's death, he continued his legal studies at Gray's Inn. In 1582 he was admitted as an utter barrister and four years later became a bencher and thus eligible to plead in the courts at Westminster. During this time and subsequently, however, his chief aim was to obtain a position in the crown's service. As early as the fall of 1580, therefore, he sought to enlist the patronage of his uncle Lord Burghley on his behalf in a suit of some kind to the queen.[8] Although nothing came of this suit, his main objective thenceforth was to gain office and rise at court.

In 1581, at the age of twenty, he was elected for the first time to the House of Commons for the Cornish borough of Bosinney.[9] This event marked the commencement of his public career. He was a member thereafter of all the successive parliaments of Queen Elizabeth's reign, the last in 1601, as well as of all but one of the parliaments of James I, taking an increasingly active part in business and acquiring a growing reputation for his knowledge and his ability as a speaker.[10] Meanwhile, he pursued his quest for advancement, but without any tangible result.[11] Probably with the aim of bringing his opinions before the queen and her council, he wrote two papers on public affairs at this period, both circulated only in manuscript during his lifetime. The first in 1584 was a letter of advice to Queen Elizabeth concerning her foreign and domestic enemies. In essence it was an acute, well-informed political analysis covering various features of England's international and internal situation. Regarding religious dissidence at home, where the government was faced with the joint problems of Catholic disaffection and Puritan agitation against the established church, Bacon cautioned against the undue persecution of Puritan ministers, pointing out how useful they were as preachers in the battle against popery. He likewise counseled against the too severe treatment of Catholics, recommending that they be discouraged but not driven to desperation. In considering these matters, he used the phrase "reason of state" to indicate his standpoint.[12] The second paper, composed around 1589, dealt with the controversies in the English church between the Puritan Nonconformists and the ecclesiastical authorities. Bacon's approach to this subject was moderate and evenhanded. While expressing his reverence for the bishops' calling, he rebuked them for various faults, including their refusal of needed reforms and their harsh and unjust treatment of Nonconformity. On the other side, he was also critical of the Puritans for some of their opinions and practices, and called their demand for "parity and equality of ministers . . . a thing of wonderful great confusion." In the course of his discussion he referred to Machiavelli without naming him, quoting a passage from the Italian author's *Discourses on the First Ten Books of Livy*.[13] Both of these papers were unusual productions, especially for a man still in his twenties and without an official position. Penetrating and thoroughly objective, they looked at the issues involved in a wholly political light.

In 1589 Bacon was granted the reversion to the clerkship of the Council in the Star Chamber, a position yielding sixteen hundred pounds yearly. Procured for him by Burghley, it was the sole office he was destined to obtain under Queen Elizabeth. As it was given him only in reversion, however, it could not become his until its present occupant vacated it, an event for which he was obliged to wait nearly twenty years, while in the meantime it brought him nothing.[14] Conscious of his great powers and eager to play a role in affairs, he saw himself still without advancement as he entered his thirties. Despite his interest in the theoretical problems of the law, which is reflected in some of his early writings,[15] he did not want to practice law; hence in 1592 he appealed anew to Burghley to help him gain some official position, citing his poor estate and increasing age. With this plea he coupled a statement (to which I shall return in the following chapter) of his "vast contemplative ends" contrasted with his "moderate civil ends," famously adding that "I have taken all knowledge to be my province." If Burghley did not assist him, he said, he would renounce his worldly aims and dedicate himself entirely to an intellectual occupation.[16] His uncle was indisposed, though, to do much for him. His heart was set on promoting the career of his younger son, Robert Cecil, who was rising rapidly in the queen's government, and he regarded Bacon as a possible rival to him.

Bacon had no intention, however, of laying aside his political aspirations. From an early time, moreover, the latter were linked with his philosophical ambitions; for as he wrote a few years later in an unpublished autobiographical fragment, if he gained a high position in the state, he would have the power to command the ability of others to aid him in his intellectual work.[17] Around 1590 or 1591 he became acquainted with the earl of Essex, Queen Elizabeth's new favorite, with whom he soon formed a close relationship. A warrior and a courtier, intelligent, handsome, high-spirited, and generous, the youthful Essex attracted many men to him and gained a strong hold on the queen's affection. Unfortunately, his virtues were accompanied by some serious faults. Essex was impulsive, headstrong, and

sometimes petulant, lacking in sound judgment of situations, quick
to take offense, and eager to triumph over his rivals at court. The
aging queen humored these traits at the same time that she tried to
discipline his temper; but his willfulness and demands for military
commands, offices, and favors to raise his political status at court led
to frequent strains and quarrels with her, which were made up only to
recur. As the 1590s went on, a factional conflict for power developed
between Essex, and his partisans, and the Cecils, Lord Burghley and
Sir Robert Cecil and their followers, which affected the court and
government.[18] It was with this nobleman, five years younger than himself, that Bacon joined forces, doing various things for him, acting
more and more in the capacity of an adviser, and tying his own long-
deferred hopes of political advancement to the earl's fortunes. As
he wrote in his essay "Of Faction," "mean men in their rising must
adhere," an observation that certainly reflected his own situation.[19]
Although he maintained his relationship with the Cecils, it naturally
tended to cool on account of his attachment to Essex. His brother
Anthony, with whom he was on very close terms, likewise allied himself with Essex. Anthony Bacon had lived abroad for almost thirteen
years, mainly in France, as an extremely knowledgeable agent engaged in collecting political intelligence for the English government
through his many foreign connections. Back in England, he entered
Essex's service in 1593 in the role of a foreign secretary, using his
intelligence sources to provide the earl with the best foreign information to enhance his influence in the government.

In the parliament of 1593, Bacon made the serious mistake of pro-
voking the queen's displeasure by obstructing a bill to provide new
taxes. The government, financially very hard-pressed by the costs of
England's war with Spain, was asking Parliament for an exceptional
money grant of three subsidies payable in only three years. While
Bacon did not oppose this amount, he argued in the House of Commons for spreading its payment over six years lest the tax set a dangerous precedent, breed popular discontent, and lay too heavy a burden
on the country. When he learned of Elizabeth's anger at his conduct,
he wrote explaining himself to Burghley, whom he told that he spoke
his conscience, and asked to intercede to restore him to the queen's
favor.[20] As Bacon's tactics in the political arena were usually carefully

calculated with a view to his own fortunes, his statement that he spoke his conscience was doubtless sincere. This was the last time, though, that he ever took an independent stand in disagreement with authority or allowed his conscience to have precedence over his political interests. Elizabeth never fully forgave his offense. While occasionally employing him thereafter as legal counsel in various sorts of crown business, she was never willing to grant him any regular preferment. Among the tasks he performed for the government in the 1590s was the authorship of a tract in 1592, *Certain Observations Upon a Libel*, a cogent defense of Queen Elizabeth's rule and its felicities written in reply to an attack by a Catholic publicist.[21] He was also called upon to take part in the interrogation of prisoners in the Tower of London suspected of treason and plotting to assassinate the queen. At times during these years and later he was present when torture was used to extract information from suspects.[22]

Throughout this period Bacon was constantly short of money and continually in debt. His dependence on Essex's patronage became more pronounced, since it was mainly to the latter that he now looked to advance his career. In the summer of 1593 the nobleman, who had recently been made a privy councillor, encouraged Bacon to sue for the vacant office of attorney general. In the succeeding competition the Cecils sponsored the solicitor general Sir Edward Coke for the position. This was the first occasion of his rivalry with Coke, an eminent lawyer, which was to figure recurrently in his career for many years thereafter. Essex pressed the queen insistently for Bacon's appointment, staking his reputation on the outcome, but after months of uncertainty she finally chose Coke, who was almost ten years older and more experienced in the law. Essex then tried strenuously to get her to name Bacon to Coke's previous office. Bacon himself also canvassed intensively for the solicitorship, petitioning the queen, begging friends to back him, and seeking the aid of the Cecils, despite his suspicion that they secretly opposed him.[23] In the end, because Elizabeth's displeasure continued to weigh against him, the place went to another. While the issue still hung in doubt, Bacon wrote that he was "weary of asserviling myself to every man's charity," and compared himself to a piece of goods for sale in a shop.[24] The entire episode was an illustration of the degrading accompaniments of court patronage and rivalries, which he was to experience throughout his political life. For Essex, Bacon's rejection was a decided personal defeat. Wishing to compensate him for what he felt was his own failure, the earl generously offered him a gift of land worth eighteen hundred pounds. Bacon accepted it, in part, as he said, because he did not want to practice law, and told Essex, "I do think myself more beholding to you than to any man."[25]

The kind of advice he offered Essex is best seen in the letter he sent him in October 1596 at a moment when the earl was a popular hero at the height of his martial reputation owing to his leadership in the successful English naval expedition against Cadiz the preceding summer. The sequel to a previous conversation, this most private and confidential document, which dealt with Essex's relations with the queen, contains the clearest indication of the close alliance existing between the two men at the time. Indeed, at its outset Bacon expressed his belief that "your fortune comprehendeth mine." The burden of his advice was that Essex must think of nothing else but to "win the Queen," which meant that he must overcome her apprehensions regarding himself by changing his "image." If he did so, Bacon assured him, then he need have no fears of his enemies' attempts to poison her mind against him. At present, however, his opinionatedness and uncontrollable nature, his favor with the people, and his military dependency and ambition made him appear dangerous to her. To remove this impression Bacon recommended a number of stratagems. Essex needed to demonstrate his pliability by yielding to the queen; he should therefore pretend, for example, that he planned a project or a journey or that he favored someone for an office, choosing something she was likely to oppose, and then promptly renounce his idea when she expressed her dislike of it; he should flatter her with speeches that seemed sincere rather than mere formalities; he should shun a popular reputation and use every opportunity to speak in her presence against popularity and popular courses; and he should avoid seeking martial greatness or any military office in the future, opting for other more statesmanlike responsibilities instead.[26] Bacon's counsel reflected a purely instrumental rationality, without a trace of the chivalric sentiment that was part of Queen Elizabeth's public cult in court ceremony and literary works. Its dispassionate judgment of Essex's liabilities and insistence on the importance of modifying his conduct in the queen's eyes was undoubtedly sound. But among the remedies he prescribed, he did not scruple to include hypocrisy and dissimulation, presupposing rather unrealistically, moreover, that the queen would fail to see through these devices. In any event, as an extremely intelligent observer he might have known that a man like Essex was incapable of following such crafty counsels by appearing other than he was.

BACON's connection with Essex spanned the decade of the 1590s, when his political career appeared blocked as he neared the age of forty. In his relationship with others he showed a cool, self-contained temperament rarely given to much affection or to strong passions of any kind. Both love and hatred were apparently equally alien to him. Whether he had any close friends at the time other than his brother Anthony may be doubted. He and Anthony—a chronic invalid whom William Rawley, Bacon's biographer, described as "equal to him in height of wit though inferior to him in the endowments of learning and knowledge"—were greatly devoted to each other.[27] Anthony did everything in his power to assist Francis both with money and in other ways. In 1597 Bacon dedicated to him the first edition of his *Essays*, the contents of which were strongly marked by his experience of political and court life.[28] At Anthony's death in 1601, Bacon inherited from him the estate and manor of Gorhambury, which he made his country residence and to which he was deeply attached.

With regard to his parents, Bacon was permanently influenced by the memory of his father, whom he always admired as a judge and statesman and whose steps he hoped to follow as lord keeper or lord chancellor.[29] Toward his mother, on the other hand, his feelings are less clear. Quite possibly they included a fair amount of hostility and resentment. Lady Bacon, who did not die until 1610 at the age of eighty-two, was a formidable dowager. Given a classical education by her father, Sir Anthony Cooke, tutor to King Edward VI, she was intelligent and strong-willed, a fervent Puritan and warm supporter of Nonconformist ministers.[30] It is therefore significant that Bacon failed to share her religiosity or Puritan zeal; and while he opposed the persecution of Puritan clergy, he did not endorse the sweeping changes in religion and church government at which the Puritan program of reformation aimed. Lady Bacon was continually anxious about the spiritual and moral condition of her two sons. Although she hated stage plays and masques as sinful exhibitions, Bacon nevertheless took an active part in the creation of such spectacles both at court and at Gray's Inn.[31] She never hesitated, moreover, to interfere in her sons' affairs. Bitterly opposed to Anthony Bacon's long absence abroad, where he consorted with Catholic agents in the course of his intelligence work, she was so suspicious of his activities that she even questioned his Protestantism and called him a traitor to God and his country.[32] She complained of Bacon's negligence in religious duties and found fault with some of his friends and servants, like the "proud profane costly fellow" whom he kept, she said, "as a coach companion and bed companion."[33] Scarcely any correspondence survives between Bacon and his mother; yet we may infer his reaction to her dominating ways from a revealing letter Anthony sent her in July 1594. In it he objected for both himself and his brother against her "sovereign desire to overrule your sons in all things, how little soever you may understand either the ground or the circumstances of their proceedings," and further protested that she abandoned her mind "continually to most strange and wrongfull suspicions. . . ."[34]

In attempting to fathom Bacon's personality, we must also deal with the subject of his reputed homosexuality, a matter that Spedding, his Victorian biographer, avoided. According to several writers of the time, Bacon was homosexual. The antiquarian John Aubrey, who admired him greatly and collected a considerable amount of information on his life, reported that he was a "pederast" and that "His Ganimeds and favourites took bribes."[35] The same charge was made by the Puritan and antiquarian scholar Sir Simonds D'Ewes, who, commenting in his autobiography on Bacon's condemnation in 1621 for bribery, mentioned his "great and stupendous vices," of which his "most abominable and darling sin" was his notorious homosexuality.[36] These statements, which came from men a generation or more younger than Bacon who never knew him personally, could only have been a distillation of numerous contemporary rumors that were circulating about his sexual proclivities. As we have seen, his mother voiced strong disapproval of his associations—not only with the man she called his "coach . . . and bed companion," but with others whom she described as "cormorant seducers and instruments of Satan" guilty of "committing foul sin by his countenance. . . ."[37]

One of the men with whom he associated for a time during the 1590s was the rather disreputable Spaniard Antonio Pérez. Formerly the secretary of the Spanish monarch Philip II, Pérez had fallen into Philip's disfavor and fled Spain after escaping from prison and inciting a revolt against the king in Aragon. Having been received in France by Henry IV, he arrived in England in the spring of 1593 with a French diplomatic mission. Here he became friendly with the Bacon brothers and with Essex, who found him to be a valuable intelligence source on Spanish affairs by reason of his many foreign contacts. As a result he entered Essex's service in 1594, lodging in the earl's London house until his return to France the following year. Although he had entry into the highest political circles, the queen and others at court disliked him, and he soon became unwelcome in England. An unsavory character, Pérez was married but nevertheless preferred men, and there are numerous Spanish testimonies to his homosexuality. It is impossible to ascertain the nature of his relationship with Bacon. A homoerotic attraction on his part, however, is implied by a letter from him to Anthony Bacon in which, after mentioning a dinner invitation from Francis, he added that if the latter were a woman he would be like a chaste vestal who feigned modesty, but that he, Pérez, would be the right man for her, because hypocritical women liked to be raped by bold men.[38] Anthony Bacon himself may have been homosexual. Although the fact apparently (and rather oddly) never became known in England, in 1586 he was arrested in France for sodomy while residing in Montauban. Luckily for him, though, because of the intervention of his friend the king of Navarre, the future Henry IV, the charge was dismissed.[39]

The evidence of Bacon's personal life indicates that he was never sexually attracted to women. His closest relationships were exclusively

with men, such as his later warm friendship with Tobie Mathew, sixteen years his junior, whom he first met around 1595.[40] His essays do
not speak highly of either love or marriage and suggest that wise men
should not marry.[41] When he took a wife, it was only or chiefly for her
money. In 1606, at the age of forty-five, after failing in an earlier suit
to win the hand of the wealthy Lady Hatton, he married Alice Barnham, the well-connected daughter of a London alderman.[42] Scarcely
any mention of her occurs in his subsequent correspondence, and it
is possible that they never had sexual relations. Much younger than
he, she was apparently unfaithful, and in his last will, drawn up in
December 1625, a few months before he died, he disinherited her.
Ten days after his death she married the steward of her household.[43]

   Although the question of Bacon's sexual identity will probably always remain a puzzle, the likelihood that he may have been a homosexual is undeniable. If this was the case, it might throw light on certain elements of his labyrinthine personality that are also reflected in
his writings. Homosexuality in England was a statutory crime as well
as a social misdemeanor, and Bacon was always a practitioner of the
art of self-concealment.[44] One of the maxims he included in a collection of sayings dating from around 1594 was the statement "I had
rather know than be known."[45] As part of his worldly wisdom he took
a keen interest in dissimulation and cunning, which he discussed in
several of his works and to whose uses and effects he devoted a couple
of his essays.[46] The same interest may partly explain the lasting impression made upon him by the thought of Machiavelli, for which he
felt a strong admiration. His moral philosophy, in dealing with the
subject of worldly advancement, included observations on the presentation of self and how to turn and shape oneself according to occasion. The subjects of secrecy, esoteric communication, and the techniques of managing people also came into his works. In his personal
relationships with the great and powerful whose favor he desired, his
preferred methods were dissimulation, subservience, and flattery; he
makes this approach especially explicit in some private memoranda
of 1608 that we shall shortly discuss. The trouble with his strategy of
deception and veiling himself, however, was that it must sometimes
have backfired. He may not have fooled those he planned to manipulate; instead, they may have seen through his wiles and been repelled

by them. In consequence, they may have disliked and distrusted him, so that his methods could actually have hindered rather than furthered his career.

BACON's association with Essex reached its turning point in 1599 in the aftermath of the latter's failure in Ireland. The situation in that country had become critical because of the earl of Tyrone's rebellion, which had resisted all the English government's efforts to suppress it. In the spring of 1599 Essex arrived in Ireland at the head of a large army charged with crushing the revolt. His inability to achieve any success against Tyrone, with whom he met privately and weakly negotiated a truce, led to his disgrace and fall. His ineffectual actions in Ireland aroused the displeasure and suspicion of the queen, and when, in order to plead his case with her directly, he suddenly returned home at the end of September contrary to her command, he was committed to house arrest. Following months of close confinement, he was tried by a special commission in June 1600 for offenses connected with his conduct in Ireland and suspended from his offices. Later in the summer he was released from custody but continued to be banished from the court and the queen's presence. During the next months, as he brooded gloomily over his treatment and grievances, he became convinced that he was the victim of a plot by his enemies who meant to destroy him. In February 1601, after failing in a sudden, desperate attempt to incite a revolt in London against the court, he was executed as a traitor.[47]

Before Essex went to Ireland, Bacon advised him to take an interest in Irish affairs and later also predicted that he would obtain success and honor from his Irish command.[48] Upon his disgrace, however, Bacon drew away from him. While hoping that the fallen favorite might yet be restored to his former position, and endeavoring to conciliate the queen on his behalf, he nevertheless made sure above all to distance himself from Essex in Elizabeth's mind. Accordingly, he participated in the proceedings of the special commission that tried Essex for his actions in Ireland, and coldly wrote him afterward that there were some things he loved much better than he loved the nobleman, such as the queen's service, honor, favor, and the good of his country.[49] Subsequently, when Essex was put on trial for treason,

Bacon played an important role in his prosecution as one of the crown's lawyers. Sweeping aside his denials, he accused the earl of a premeditated plot to overthrow the queen; he protested, too, against the latitude the court allowed Essex in the defense of his great and notorious treasons. More than this, he urged him to confess to being a traitor and declared that he, Bacon, had spent more time in vainly studying how to make the earl a good servant of the queen and state than he had done in anything else.[50]

After the execution of Essex and those convicted with him, Bacon received twelve hundred pounds from the fines levied on the defendants whose lives were spared. Concerning this grant he commented, "The Queen hath done somewhat for me, though not in the proportion I hoped."[51] He also drafted the official statement that the government issued describing Essex's treasons.[52] In 1604, following James I's succession to the throne, he published an apology defending his involvement in the condemnation of Essex. A survey of his relationship with Essex and his part in the latter's trial, this document was intended as an answer to the "common speech" and the opinion of some of Essex's supporters and his own friends that he had been "false and unthankful" to the earl. His main claim was that he had acted in performance of his "duty and service to the Queen and state; in which I would not shew myself false-hearted nor faint-hearted for any man's sake living."[53] Although an able piece of argument, his apology was not entirely free of factual misrepresentation and of statements inconsistent with things he had said in his earlier dealings with Essex.[54] It is difficult to deny that his participation in the latter's prosecution was highly questionable, a sign of moral coarseness and a deficient sense of personal honor. No doubt, throughout their relationship he had always made clear to Essex that he owed his supreme loyalty and obedience to the queen. Nevertheless, he was under great obligations to the earl, who had treated him with exceptional generosity and consideration and made strenuous efforts to advance his career. He must also have known that in spite of Essex's tragic folly, which had led him to the scaffold, the latter was not a premeditated traitor who had schemed to depose the queen. Self-respect and a sense of decency should therefore have made him refrain from assisting in the earl's destruction. Had he done so, he would very likely have become the renewed object of the queen's anger. This was something a morally more courageous and less complacent man might have been willing to risk. Instead, and not for the last time, he chose the path of opportunism in the hope of enjoying the queen's favor, though it meant ingratitude and the betrayal of friendship.

WITH Essex's disappearance, Bacon resumed his quest for patronage by trying to strengthen his ties to his cousin Sir Robert Cecil, who for some years had been in a powerful position at court as a privy councillor and secretary of state to the queen. Writing to Cecil in April 1601, he said deferentially that he regarded him "as one that ever I found careful of my advancement," a statement that was certainly not true.[55] In fact, despite the two men's observance of an outward cordiality, there never existed any real warmth or friendship between them. Upon the queen's death and James I's accession in March 1603, Cecil became the new sovereign's principal minister. Seeing the inauguration of a new reign as a fresh opportunity to advance himself, Bacon at once wrote the king to offer his services. He also asked several friends to commend him to James and reiterated his devotion to Cecil, whom he called "the personage in this state which I love most."[56] Having begged Cecil to procure him a knighthood, he was knighted in July 1603 in a single ceremony with a crowd of three hundred other men who likewise received the title. The next year the king, in acknowledgment of the services Bacon had rendered in the parliament of 1604 in connection with the proposed union between England and Scotland, gave him the office of learned counsel with a sixty-pound annual pension.[57] Beyond this minor post and small emolument, though, his efforts for promotion bore no fruit. When the place of solicitor general fell vacant in October 1604, it was bestowed upon another. As he retrospectively described his situation at the time, his official career was "at a stop" and his reputation diminished by "continual disgraces, every man coming above me."[58] In June 1607, however, after petitioning the king, Lord Chancellor Ellesmere, and Cecil, now earl of Salisbury, for whose aid he appealed in very humble terms, he was at last made solicitor. This appointment was the first rung of the ladder on which he eventually mounted over the next ten years to the highest legal office in the kingdom. It was worth about a thousand pounds per annum; and combined with the money he gained through his marriage and the income derived from the clerkship of the Council in the Star Chamber, which finally reverted to him in the following year, it enabled him to relieve himself of his acute financial difficulties.[59]

Amidst all the vicissitudes thus far described, and during the free time left him by his legal, parliamentary, and other duties, Bacon diligently continued his investigations in philosophy. Besides a number of writings that he left unpublished, in 1605 he brought out one of his most important treatises, *The Advancement of Learning*, dedicated to James I. In the present chapter, however, we are concerned not with his philosophic life but with his personal history as a political man and the revelation it affords of certain aspects of his mind and character.

For the latter purpose, the private memoranda that he set down over several days in July 1608 are particularly illuminating. These notations, which he termed *Commentarius Solutus*, drawn up solely for his own guidance and intended for no other eyes but his own, were so personal in nature that Spedding, Bacon's editor, worried whether it was proper to make them public even 350 years later.[60] The subjects with which they dealt were very varied, constituting a review of Bacon's situation, plans, and resolutions over a range of matters domestic, financial, professional, medical, literary, intellectual, parliamentary, and political. Some of them touched on his philosophic and scientific projects and the support he sought for them. Once or twice he mentioned his mental state, as in an allusion to recent symptoms of "melancholy" and fears of "present peril," which passed away on the following day.[61] Included also were a number of reminders and observations that offer a striking glimpse of his schemes for self-advancement. These focused mainly on ways of displaying his merits and of ingratiating himself with King James and powerful personages at court. He stressed the need of maintaining access to the king and told himself to attend sometimes at the latter's repasts in order "to fall into a cowrse of famil[iar] discowrs" with him. He should likewise foster the belief in the king's Scottish servants and ministers that he was well-affected toward the Scots. He should make use of the weakness and poor performance of his rival in office, the attorney general Sir Henry Hobart, in order to set off his own abilities.[62] He should provide the earl of Suffolk with "ornam[ents] for publike speaches" and let him know that if he, Bacon, were to be made lord chancellor, he would show the earl great reverence.[63] To gain the favor of Henry Prince of Wales, he should make much of certain men connected with the prince.[64] Generally, he resolved "To have particular occasions, fitt and gratefull and contynuall, to mainteyne pryvate speach with . . . every great persons," sometimes drawing them together, and to do this "specially in publike places and without care or affectation."[65] The propitiation of his cousin Salisbury, who had recently been appointed to the great office of lord treasurer, figured prominently in Bacon's calculations. He aimed to "insinuate" himself so as "to become pryvie" to Salisbury's estate, and "To corresp[ond] with him "in a habite of naturall but nowayes perilous boldness, and in vivacity, invention, care to cast and enterprise (but with dew caution . . .). . . ." He advised himself as well to take care at the council table to support Salisbury's motions and speeches.[66] At the same time he also entertained the thought of succeeding Salisbury as chief minister by, as he put it, amusing the king and prince with "pasty[me] and glory." What he seems to have meant by this was to propose that the king should strive to make the island of Britain the seat of a great monarchy in the West that would civilize Ireland, colonize the wild parts of Scotland, and annex the Netherlands. These last observations, which occurred in a section of the memoranda concerned with policy, were tied in with other comments and recommendations on political topics. What emerges from them is Bacon's notion of linking his own fortune to the prospect of empire by persuading the king that he could be the glorious founder of a golden age: "Perswad the K[ing] in glory, Aurea condet saecula."[67]

The parts of these memoranda relating to his career in government and the court cast light on the most secretive and tortuous side of Bacon's personality. Writing exclusively for himself, he frankly avowed his political ambitions and the cunning designs by which he proposed to realize them. In this context he regarded other persons purely as means he could exploit to attain his own ends. His object was to aggrandize himself by craft, flattery, and displaying himself in the best possible light. To Salisbury, James I's principal minister, he would be submissive and demonstratively loyal, striving to get on the closest terms with him.[68] To the king he would hold out a seductive vision of glory that would gain the royal favor and possibly enable him to supplant Salisbury. Needless to say, Bacon's tactics did not succeed. Although he rose during the following decade to the position of lord chancellor, he remained a secondary figure politically, always subject to more powerful men; and when he eventually suffered public disgrace, it was chiefly because the king did nothing to support him.

Bacon held the post of solicitor general for over six years, representing the crown during this period in a number of important cases. Upon Salisbury's death in May 1612, he promptly petitioned for higher office. In draft letters to the king citing his long record of service, he asked to be removed to "business of state" and did not hesitate to disparage Salisbury's abilities as minister.[69] Underneath his subservience there can be no doubt that he had always harbored a bitter resentment and dislike of Salisbury, who had continually hindered his advancement. The following year he was successful in his suit to be made attorney general, after telling the king that he was already fifty-two years old and still waiting for further preferment.[70]

The next and final stage of his political career was dominated by his connection with Sir George Villiers, later duke of Buckingham, who emerged after 1615 as James I's new and all-powerful favorite. The recipient of a stream of gifts, offices, and titles, Buckingham became the paramount influence in the court and government with a virtual monopoly over the dispensing of royal patronage. Bacon fastened himself to the favorite by obsequiousness and flattery, tendering him occasional advice and using him as an intermediary in approaching the king for promotion. In February 1616 he obtained through him the king's promise of the next appointment to the lord chancellorship. In an expression of gratitude for this favor, he pledged Buckingham his eternal fidelity, declaring, "I am yours surer to you than my own life. . . . I will break into twenty pieces before you have the least fall."[71] Soon afterward he solicited Buckingham's backing to be made a privy councillor in order, he said, to serve the king better. Following several such requests, his suit was granted in June 1616, and he became a member of the privy council.[72]

Bacon cultivated Buckingham assiduously to keep in his good graces. He drew up the latter's patent of nobility when he was elevated to the peerage and sent him detailed advice on public affairs.[73] In March 1617, upon the retirement of the then lord chancellor, Bacon was immediately designated to replace him as lord keeper of the great seal, the same office his father had held under Queen Elizabeth. For this promotion he offered profuse thanks to Buckingham, without whose endorsement he would not have received it, and vowed him daily service and honor.[74] Yet his relations with the favorite did not always go smoothly. Later that year he overreached himself in officiously attempting to dissuade Buckingham from arranging a marriage between the latter's brother and the daughter of Sir Edward Coke, Bacon's old rival. Since the king and Buckingham were equally set on the match, his interference aroused the strong annoyance of both. At first he tried to justify his actions, only to be rebuffed and accused of unthankfulness. At last, seeing that he was in danger of loss of favor, he was forced to abase himself by apologizing and making his submission to Buckingham, who then interceded to reconcile him with the king. His final word in the affair was a grateful letter praising Buckingham's magnanimity and goodness and containing renewed pledges of devotion.[75] These sentiments could hardly have expressed his true feelings; and as this incident indicates, it was one of the tragedies of Bacon's life in politics that he was compelled to humble himself repeatedly to men like Buckingham in order to survive in the world of the court.

Having made amends to Buckingham, he continued his rise. At the beginning of 1618 he was appointed lord chancellor, and this was followed in the summer by his promotion to the peerage under the title of Lord Verulam. Three years later he was raised to the rank of Viscount St. Alban.[76] These honors were underscored by the fact that during Queen Elizabeth's reign no one had ever held the office of lord chancellor and no lord keeper had been ennobled. He was now sixty years old, and with these promotions he attained the summit of his social ambition and the highest professional eminence as a lawyer. His fall, nevertheless, was not far off.

As the presiding judge of the Court of Chancery and nominal head of the judiciary, Bacon aimed to set an exemplary standard in the performance of his responsibilities. In many respects he did so. Yet throughout his tenure he received repeated communications from Buckingham requesting his favor in behalf of particular parties in litigation. In addition, he was lax enough to follow the custom of accepting gifts from suitors to his court. At the meeting of Parliament in the early months of 1621, the House of Commons launched an attack on royal grants of monopoly, financial peculation, and corrupt officials, in which Bacon was accused of bribery. His longtime enemy, Sir Edward Coke, in whose dismissal from a judgeship in 1616 he had been instrumental and who was now a member of Parliament, was one of the leaders in the campaign against him. He was not a disinterested opponent of Bacon, nor were some of the others who attacked him. As additional charges accumulated, his case was referred to the House of Lords for investigation. During these troubles neither the king nor Buckingham, who himself was guilty of corruption, intervened to help him; they preferred to let him be sacrificed as a scapegoat to appease the parliament's anger. His own view of his situation was that even though he had taken gifts from litigants, he had never allowed this to influence his judgment in particular cases. In several instances he had even delivered judgment against the persons who had given him money. Nonetheless, he realized that his conduct had made him vulnerable and that appearances were against him.[77] A sick and broken man, he decided to submit before trial and confess his guilt. In May the House of Lords sentenced him on the charge of corruption to a forty-thousand-pound fine, imprisonment during the royal pleasure, and incapacitation from ever holding state office, sitting in Parliament, or coming within the verge of the court, which in effect meant banishment from London.[78]

The king dealt with him leniently in regard to these penalties. He was required to serve no more than three or four days in prison, his fine was essentially remitted, and in due course he received a partial pardon. He had always lived extravagantly and made ample use of credit; now, however, his loss of office reduced him to such financial straits that he was forced to beg the king and Buckingham for means of subsistence. He also pleaded for the latter's good offices to gain release from the ban against coming within the verge of the court. Buckingham was eager to buy York House, Bacon's London residence in which his family had lived during the years his father was lord keeper. When he signified his unwillingness to sell it, the duke was offended and began to treat him with great coolness. In despair, Bacon begged for the recovery of Buckingham's friendship, and in March 1622 he reluctantly agreed to part with York House, whereupon he was given his freedom to come within the verge of the court.[79]

In the aftermath of his fall, Bacon took comfort in comparing his fate to that of Demosthenes, Cicero, and Seneca, all of whom had suffered a similar political calamity in their careers.[80] He also gave the following sorrowful description of his position: "I find in books . . . that it is accounted a great bliss for a man to have Leisure with Honour. That was never my fortune; nor is. For time was, I had Honour without Leisure; and now I have Leisure without Honour."[81] Even while occupying the office of lord chancellor, he had managed in 1620 to publish the *Novum Organum,* his principal contribution to the renewal of philosophy. After 1621, in the five years of life remaining to him, he made remarkably productive use of his enforced leisure. His numerous writings during this short period included such considerable works as the enlarged Latin version of *The Advancement of Learning,* a new and substantially expanded edition of his *Essays,* the *History of the Reign of King Henry the Seventh,* and *New Atlantis.* Yet notwithstanding his engagement in these demanding tasks, he was dissatisfied with his condition and continued to solicit the king for public employment. He petitioned in vain to be appointed provost of Eton College and kept recommending himself as a political adviser to Buckingham, whom he told that he had seen and read so much that "few things which concern states or greatness, are new cases unto me."[82] Although his sentence disabled him from ever sitting in Parliament, he nevertheless tried unsuccessfully to be permitted to resume his place in the House of Lords in the parliament of 1624.[83] Whatever hopes he may have entertained after his fall that he might sometime return to public life thus remained unrealized. He died a disgraced man and private subject on 9 April 1626, leaving his "name and memory," as he stated in his will, "to men's charitable speeches, and to foreign nations, and the next ages."[84]

In the essay "Of Great Place," which was included in the second, 1612 edition of his *Essays* and also appeared in the third edition of 1625, Bacon gave what was in effect an epitome of his entire political career. The words he penned there described exactly the precarious nature of success in the courts of princes and the drawbacks and burdens that accompanied high state office:

> Men in great place are thrice servants: servants of the sovereign or state; servants of fame; and servants of business. So as they have no freedom; neither in their persons, nor in their actions, nor in their times. It is a strange desire, to seek power and to lose liberty: or to seek power over others and to lose power over a man's self. The rising unto place is laborious; and by pains men come to greater pains; and it is sometimes base; and by indignities men come to dignities. The standing is slippery, and the regress is either a downfall, or at least an eclipse, which is a melancholy thing.[85]

When he wrote these lines and reviewed them again in 1625, he was surely thinking of himself and his own experience. His observation taught him that political life was a form of servitude, yet he pursued it avidly and relinquished it very unwillingly. Bacon was never a detached philosopher contemplating the human or natural world from a haven of serene seclusion. His political career, with its many frustrations, disappointments, and constant dependency on more powerful men, left deep traces on his personality. It also had a significant effect in shaping his outlook on man and society, giving to his thought in this domain its extreme worldliness, its markedly prudential character, and its preoccupation with success and the creation of one's own fortune.

2

Philosophy and the Reconstruction of Knowledge: The Genesis of Bacon's Project

WHEN Bacon wrote in 1592 that he had "vast contemplative ends" and had taken "all knowledge to be my province," he did not exaggerate.[1] In the course of his work he concerned himself with virtually every intellectual domain and type of inquiry. The number of disciplines and subdisciplines in his time was far smaller than it was to become in later centuries. The boundaries between some disciplines were then either nonexistent or differently located, and disciplinary barriers and specialization were also much less developed. In particular, science, meaning chiefly what we understand today as the natural sciences, was not set off or distinguished from philosophy. Bacon's era, moreover, was one of great polymaths who felt no difficulty in spreading their labors over a diversity of fields. An encyclopedic approach to knowledge remained possible and was still practiced by some thinkers. Bacon was nonetheless probably unique even among his most learned contemporaries in the range of subjects he investigated and discussed. In philosophy, metaphysics, logic, epistemology, philosophy or theory of science, philosophy of mind, and ethics or moral philosophy all fell within his purview. In the sciences, which would have been classified in his day as natural philosophy, physics, chemistry, biology, physiology, astronomy, meteorology, acoustics, hydrography, and botany were among the interests to which he devoted a part of his efforts. He was likewise deeply interested in medicine, in psychology, in music, and in rhetoric or the study of modes of communication and the persuasive use of language. In addition to all these areas, his mind embraced a broad portion of what we now call the human or social sciences. Besides being a practicing lawyer, politician, and historian, he was a theorist of law and jurisprudence, of government and politics, and of history. Living in an age of religious conflict in which the Protestant Reformation remained an active force, he was also inevitably concerned with religion, the church, and, if only negatively, by attempting to define its limits, with theology. Perhaps the only discipline that lay largely outside his ken was mathematics. Even the above list, with the great variety of phenomena and the many different branches of knowledge it encompassed, does not exhaust the inventory of subjects that found a place in the corpus of Bacon's writings. For he was also intensely interested in inventions, in the crafts and mechanical arts, and in the practical operations of different kinds of craftsmen for what they enabled him to learn about natural processes.

Within the broad horizon of Bacon's thought, however, certain questions, problems, and aims were uppermost in the sense that they constituted the basis of his primary and most ambitious intellectual project. This project consisted of the reconstruction and hence renewal of philosophy as a form of inquiry, chiefly in relation to natural philosophy. Succinctly stated, the goal of this reconstruction was twofold: first, the achievement of a systematic, continual progress of knowledge in all the sciences of nature and the discovery of its secrets; second, the many-sided improvements and benefits in the condition of human life Bacon believed would ensue from such a progress. The means to this goal would be the reformation of the methods of investigating nature by the introduction of a new logic of discovery or procedure for acquiring and testing scientific knowledge.[2]

This summary description of Bacon's principal project, which centered on the renewal of natural philosophy, will be elaborated upon in what follows. I ought first to note, however, the opposite view that has been expressed in a recent study of Bacon's work. According to B.H.G. Wormald, Bacon had two programs, not one. The first was concerned with the world of nature. The second, which derived from the old Greek injunction "Know thyself," dealt with human beings in their social and political aspects and hence with history, moral philosophy, and politics or civil science.[3] Wormald holds that Bacon ranked his second program as coequal in importance with his first, and therefore concentrates his book on a detailed examination of Bacon's ideas about history, politics, and morals. Although we should not underestimate the amount of thought or significance Bacon gave to these latter subjects, this view of his priorities is a misconception. It is belied by *The New Organon* or *Novum Organum*, published in Latin in 1620 as the second part of the uncompleted *Great Instauration* (*Instauratio Magna*), which Bacon planned over many years as his chief contribution to the growth of knowledge. In this late treatise, which he subtitled *True Directions concerning the Interpretation of Nature* (*Indicia Vera de Interpretatione Naturae*), he presented what he intended as a definitive formulation of the basic features of his philosophy. Its preface declared that what he proposed by his method was to "establish progressive stages of certainty." He claimed to have laid out "A new and certain path for the mind to proceed in," and defined his objective as the opening of "a new way for the understanding," one never known or tried by the ancients. With his own philosophy he contrasted others then in use, leaving no doubt of their inferiority in extending the frontiers of knowledge. He invited the collaboration of those who sought not pretty and probable opinions but certain and demonstrable knowledge and wished to penetrate beyond the outer courts of nature into her inner chambers.[4] It is evident that in Bacon's mind the project of developing a philosophy capable of multiplying knowledge and discovery by a true interpretation of nature was his highest, most cherished aim and that to this enterprise other intellectual pursuits were secondary.[5] It was also this part of his work, of course, that formed the most lasting and important portion of his intellectual legacy.

Bacon held that next to religion philosophy was of all subjects the worthiest and most important.[6] While well-nigh universal in his interests, he was invariably a philosopher in dealing with any question. On whatever particular study he happened to concentrate, he also constantly reflected on the principles and methods it involved in order to improve them. His approach to knowledge was largely theoretical, synthetic, and in some measure systematic. Although he assigned great importance to the collection and establishment of facts in what he called natural histories, what he most sought as the capstone of knowledge were general principles, axioms, and causes, analogies and patterns, the universal and the necessary. In addition to being a philosopher, however, he was a very conscious, highly gifted literary artist. He wrote, of course, in both English and Latin. He had an easy command of Latin, in which he composed many of his works and which until at least the earlier eighteenth century remained the universal language of philosophy, learning, and scholarship for any author who desired an international audience. In English his mastery of style and exceptional power of imagination made him one of the greatest of prose writers. His English works stand out by the originality and sharpness of the memorable images he invented to convey his ideas and by the perspicuity and compacted weightiness of many of his expressions. Thinker and artist, reason and imagination, were inseparably fused in Bacon and put their combined stamp on everything he wrote.

His intellectual formation drew on a great diversity of sources, many of which are obscure and others doubtless no longer recoverable. The ascertaining of these sources and the influence they may have exerted on his mind is one of the foremost problems in attempting to reconstruct and understand his thought. He read vastly, but as his library was dispersed not long after his death without any list of its contents surviving, there is no way of knowing what books he collected. His education and subsequent study, however, made him acquainted with the leading philosophic schools and thinkers of antiquity from the pre-Socratics onward. He was likewise familiar with ancient medical and scientific writers such as Hippocrates, Ptolemy, Galen, and Pliny the Elder, and with the poets and mythology, the orators and moralists, the historians and political writers of the ancient world.[7] Except for Bruno and Kepler, whose work he probably did not know,[8] his writings mentioned or discussed many noted modern philosophers and scientists, among them Ficino, Paracelsus, Copernicus, Tycho Brahe, Agrippa, Cardano, Patrizi, Telesio, Campanella, Ramus, Gilbert, and Galileo. The occult sciences, too, were a part of his mental world, and he was a student of astrology, alchemy, and natural magic, subjects that in his day were not divorced from natural philosophy. He was widely acquainted with European travel literature and with recent and contemporary foreign authors, including Machiavelli, Guicciardini, Commines, and Montaigne. As a learned lawyer and practicing historian, he had a knowledge not only of the legal and historical literature of his own country but of the Roman law. In addition to all these sources that helped affect the direction of his interests, there was the influence of the Protestant religion and the Bible, to which he was exposed from earliest childhood. One of the works he quoted most frequently in his writings was the biblical proverbs of Solomon.

To obtain a better understanding of Bacon's philosophical project, we might helpfully regard it as an extended attack upon what I shall call, with a certain looseness, the old regime of knowledge. By the latter I mean a number of values, assumptions, attitudes, and beliefs that were a heritage of classical antiquity, Christianity, medieval Scholasticism, and of several strains in recent Renaissance thought as well. The old regime of knowledge revered the past, especially the culture of Greece and Rome, and was very respectful of its authority. Its highest ideal was contemplative rather than active. It had no realization of the transformative potentialities of science. It took no interest in innovation and discovery and their deliberate promotion. It did not possess the idea of progress either mental or material. As an intellectual reformer, Bacon set out to combat and supplant the old regime of knowledge with a new philosophy. Of course, as innovators inevitably do, he continued to carry with him varied baggage from the past. He was nonetheless unparalleled among contemporary philosophers in his strong consciousness of modernity and its possibilities, his understanding of the meaning of progress and faith in its prospects, and his attempt to create a novel way of thinking that would be fruitful in revealing the hidden processes of nature.

To achieve his purpose, he was obliged to undertake both a critical and a constructive task. The critical one was to expose and analyze the barriers to intellectual and hence to material progress stemming from the old regime of knowledge and also, as he came to perceive, from certain error-breeding propensities of the human mind. One of the things this involved was a critique of various aspects of the philosophical tradition and the prejudices of the learned. The constructive task was to propound a fresh method of discovery to guide the mind in investigating nature, which would replace the older modes of doing natural philosophy. Among other difficult problems, this entailed the treatment of induction and a justification of the claims he made for it. He was far more successful in the first of these tasks than in the second. In the latter, despite the brilliant perceptions and perspectives in which his writings abound, he fell far short of his goal.

Three closely interlinked thoughts or motives lay at the origin of Bacon's philosophy: the rejection of Aristotle; the conviction that the proper object of philosophy in seeking truth must be *scientia operativa* or a science productive of works for the relief and improvement of human life; and the belief in the necessity of a new method aimed at discovery that would achieve a vastly enlarged knowledge of nature. Bacon traced his lifelong dislike of Aristotle back to the time he was a student at Cambridge less than sixteen years of age, when he decided that the Greek thinker was good only for disputations and barren in the production of works for human betterment.[9] A discourse in praise of knowledge, which he composed in 1592, contains one of his earliest statements of how the command over nature could endow the life of man with infinite conveniences and achieve things that kings could neither obtain by force nor buy with treasure.[10] A short autobiographical fragment dating from around 1603 also indicates the genesis of his philosophy. It declared his belief that he was born for the service of mankind and that no benefit conferred on human beings could be as great as the discovery of new arts and endowments for bettering human life. After explaining that his aim was truth to be followed thereafter by works, he defined the first step toward this end as "the interpretation of nature rightly conducted" in an ascent leading to general propositions. To this he added that it was needless to look for precedents for his plan because there were none.[11]

From Bacon's earliest to his latest works there is a great deal of continuity in regard to these three motivating conceptions of his philosophy, as well as in a number of the ideas associated with them. In a very general sense his entire natural philosophy might be described as the quest for a method; and nearly all of his philosophical writings prior to 1620 tend to be related or to point forward to his goal of "The Great Instauration," the name he gave his project for the reconstruction of knowledge, a part of which was devoted to an explication of this method as the true interpretation of nature. Nor was it by accident that in *The New Organon*, Bacon identified such an interpretation with "regno hominis" or "the kingdom of man," thus resuming one of the basic concepts of his philosophy from its inception.[12]

BACON AND THE PHILOSOPHICAL TRADITION

At the time Bacon came to maturity, Aristotle and Plato divided the sovereignty of the intellectual world between them. A religious type of Christian Platonism and Neoplatonism in a syncretism with Hermetic and various other spiritualistic doctrines formed the basis of the philosophy of Marsilio Ficino, Giovanni Pico della Mirandola, Francesco Patrizi, and other Renaissance thinkers, while Aristotle dominated the curriculum of the universities and exerted the strongest influence on logic and natural philosophy. Well-known humanist scholars and university teachers such as Leonardo Bruni, Pietro Pomponazzi, Agostino Nifo, Jacopo Zabarella, Francisco Suárez, John Case, and many more, treated morals, politics, and metaphysics on Aristotelian principles and composed commentaries on the philosopher's works on logic, natural philosophy, and other subjects.[13] More than those of any other thinker, Aristotle's ideas in a number of areas, especially logic, metaphysics, and the study of nature, constituted the basic and indispensable background, the point of both orientation and resistance, of Bacon's own thought. On occasion he praised certain of Aristotle's conceptions, and he could not help registering the influence of the latter, whose writings had done so much to define the nature and shape the course of Western philosophy in so many domains, even while he fought to overthrow it. Yet despite this fact we need not suppose that he was a very profound student of Aristotle.[14] Although he knew Greek, it is unclear in which language he was accustomed to read the philosopher. Throughout his writings he quotes Greek authors much more often in Latin than in Greek; and because the fifteenth and sixteenth centuries witnessed a flood of Latin translations and commentaries on Aristotle's works, it is quite likely that he generally used some of these rather than the Greek originals.[15] He probably first encountered Aristotle while studying dialectics at Cambridge. During the earlier sixteenth century this subject, the innovation of humanist educators and reformers of logic, replaced the complex and sophisticated Scholastic logic and old dialectics formerly taught in the medieval universities, gaining for itself in due course a central position in instruction in all the arts and sciences. The manuals of dialectical method such as the young Bacon would have used contained a simplified version of Aristotle's logic and concentrated on discourse, the art of finding and organizing information and arguments for the purpose of exposition and practical persuasion. This aim, which sought neither certainty nor new knowledge, was probably the cause of his low opinion of dialectics and also one of the reasons that he considered Aristotle better for disputations than for discovery.[16]

The poet and critic Coleridge, a thinker who expressed the highest regard for Bacon's genius, once observed with regret that the latter's "studied depreciation" of Aristotle and the ancients, together with his "silence, or worse than silence," concerning the merits of his own contemporaries, was the least attractive side of his character. But in palliation of this fault, Coleridge also pointed out that as Bacon was the "founder of a revolution scarcely less important for the scientific . . . world than that of Luther's for the world of religion and politics," it was necessary to make allowances for his heat of protestation, vehemence of hope, and strong awareness of novelty.[17] One must keep this judgment in mind when reviewing Bacon's largely negative estimate of Aristotle and the philosophical tradition. It should be remembered, moreover, that Bacon was far from the only thinker of his time who dissented from and combated the influence of Aristotle; for the sixteenth century witnessed the appearance of a host of intellectual rebels who proclaimed their opposition to Aristotle's teachings and authority from a number of different standpoints. Among them were the German Paracelsus, the Frenchman Ramus, and the Italians Telesio, Patrizi, Bruno, Campanella, and last of all Galileo, who as a scientist helped deliver the deathblow to Aristotelian physics and metaphysics. Of all these anti-Aristotelians, though, Bacon stands out as perhaps the most radical in his attempt to end the Greek philosopher's ascendancy and as the most self-consciously modern in the claims he advanced in behalf of a new kind of natural philosophy that left Aristotle behind.

It was Bacon's habit to revise his work continually and to experiment repeatedly with different ways of communicating his ideas.[18] This explains the existence of a series of his writings, mostly in Latin and the majority left unfinished, all of them dating from the first decade or so of the seventeenth century, which provide valuable insight into the evolution of his philosophy. The only two of the lot that he published in his lifetime were the English *The Advancement of Learning* in 1605, a magisterial discussion of the whole field of knowledge covering much else besides natural philosophy, and the Latin *De Sapientia Veterum* (*The Wisdom of the Ancients*) in 1609, an attempt to convey aspects of his ideas by means of the interpretation of a number of Greek myths. In part these various compositions represent stages or preliminary versions of his project. The earliest of them, *The Masculine Birth of Time* (*Masculus Partus Temporum*), an unpublished fragment from about 1602–3, contains what is apparently the first mention of "The Great Instauration" in its subtitle, *The Great Instauration of Human Dominion over the Universe*.[19] The word "Masculine" in the main title seems to be explainable as a sexual metaphor for the generative power Bacon attributed to his philosophy. Another of these works, written about 1606–7 and also unpublished, *Outline and Argument of the Second Part of the Instauration* (*Partis Instaurationis Secundae Delineatio et Argumentum*), includes the first sketch of the six-part division of *The Great Instauration*.[20] Several of them, beginning with *The Masculine Birth of Time*, also make reference to one of Bacon's most significant concepts, his doctrine of the idols of the mind, those fallacies obstructing the progress of knowledge, which later received definitive treatment in *The New Organon*.[21] All of these writings are packed with penetrating thoughts and challenging observations that shed light on essential themes and concepts of Bacon's philosophy as it developed.

Opposition to Aristotle and other outstanding names in the philosophical tradition figures in most of them, although on this subject

Bacon's tactics varied from outright condemnation to more temperate evaluation.[22] He was convinced, however, that the superstitious veneration of antiquity was a major obstacle to progress and that unless Aristotle's supremacy were overthrown, no better philosophy such as his own could make its way into other minds. In the unpublished *The Refutation of Philosophies* (*Redargutio Philosophiarum*) dating from about 1606–7, he directed a polemic at a number of philosophers, primarily Aristotle, but Plato as well. Deploring the self-imposed servitude to the ancients, he depreciated the limited knowledge possessed by the Greeks, who were not only unacquainted with large parts of the world but like children in their ignorance of the past and of natural philosophy. He appraised Aristotle as a contentious, superficial thinker ambitious for unchallenged intellectual supremacy, who tried to construct a world out of mental categories and whose metaphysics and physics contained more of dialectics than of the voice of nature. Aristotle, he said, tried to provide verbal solutions to every problem without attaining any real knowledge. He failed to seek knowledge of nature from unfettered experiment or a broad impartial survey of experience, instead exhibiting experience carefully schooled, confined, and selected to justify his pronouncements. Plato came in for criticism for his lack of interest in natural philosophy and for corrupting the study of nature with theology through his doctrine of ideal forms just as Aristotle had corrupted it with dialectics. Bacon took an unorthodox view of Greek philosophy, moreover, in estimating some of the pre-Socratics as superior to both Plato and Aristotle. In this and other writings he praised a number of the former, particularly the atomist Democritus, for their greater penetration of nature owing to their devout reliance on experience. Coming nearer his own time, he pointed to the futility of the medieval Scholastics, who devoted their acute intellects to finespun trivialities void of any use. He also censured alchemy and natural magic for their baseless speculations and their errors, delusions, and deceits. Although granting that alchemy had endowed human life with some discoveries of value, he thought that it had done so by accident, not because of the worth of its ideas. Apropos of the pretenses of both these sciences, he made the striking comment that "the mark of a genuine philosophy is that its explanations take the mystery out of things" ("Quem admodum autem philosophiae proprium est, efficere ut omnia minus quam sint admiranda videantur propter demonstrationes"). He blamed philosophers for making their own ignorance the standard of the possible; by affirming out of pride that what they do not know lies beyond the limits of the knowable, they promote an artificial and unjustified despair about the possibility of knowledge and its capacity for works.[23]

Similar reflections on the failure of existing philosophies to increase knowledge occur in a somewhat longer Latin work of about the same date, *Thoughts and Conclusions on the Interpretation of Nature, or A Science Productive of Works* (*Cogitata et Visa de Interpretatione Naturae, sive de Scientia Operativa*). Here, amid various strictures, Bacon noted the inability of "Aristotle's oracle," the syllogism, to cope with the obscurity and subtlety of nature, even though it might be useful in dealing with subjects based on opinion, like ethics and politics. He contended that the principles Aristotle postulated, such as matter and form or privation and substance, were merely words, and that his logic had corrupted the philosophy of nature. One of the main theses of this treatise, as of others of Bacon's writings, was that works are an essential accompaniment of a real natural philosophy and a vital confirmation of its knowledge claims. "The rule of religion," he said, "that a man show his faith by his works, holds good in natural philosophy too." He contrasted the stagnation of philosophy with the progress of the crafts, citing in this connection an example he frequently used that had become a commonplace in the sixteenth century, namely, the invention of printing, gunpowder, and the mariner's compass, which had changed the face of the world in learning, warfare, and navigation. Spurning the reverence for antiquity, he argued that it was the modern age that was in actuality the older in years and experience and that it would be a disgrace for mankind if "the bounds of the intellectual globe should be restricted to what was known to the ancients." In one of his favorite sayings, frequently repeated in his writings, he observed that "imagined plenty is one of the causes of real poverty," adding that "both craft knowledge and book learning look great but on examination are found to be small."

Stressing the need of a philosophy of discovery, he pointed to the
failure of the logicians or dialecticians ("dialectici") to achieve anything of this kind. He expressed strong hopes, however, about the
prospects of knowledge if minds were provided with the right equipment and method. Having noted the fact that the arts and sciences
were divided into the empirical and the rational, he desiderated a
union of the two, of empiricism and rationalism or reason and experience, as the foundation of a new philosophy that would give rise to
works. To the same end, he recommended the establishment of a
great storehouse of facts collected from natural history and the mechanical arts, and the development of a new kind of induction for the
purpose of discovery.[24]

During the later sixteenth century skepticism established itself as a
significant philosophical school with many converts owing to the revival and popularization of the writings of Sextus Empiricus and Di-
ogenes Laertius, which together with Cicero's *Academica* were among
the chief sources of ancient skepticism.[25] Bacon, however, never took
the skeptical challenge to knowledge seriously as a philosophy. He
lumped the skeptics with those who "promote a deliberate and artificial despair as regards the acquisition of knowledge and the possibility of action." By making a "cult of the incomprehensibility of nature,"
they condemn mankind to eternal darkness.[26] He did not see epistemology as a significant problem or worry much about the errors of
the senses or the various other grounds for doubting the very possibility of knowledge that the skeptics proposed. Instead, he was convinced and simply took it for granted that all the impediments to
knowledge, including the fallibility of the senses, could be overcome
by the intellect furnished with the proper helps and method for dealing with the subtleties of nature.[27]

A commitment to materialism was another basic feature of his philosophy. He pictured reality in its ultimate character as body or matter, and also expressed a strong attraction to atomism in his earlier
writings. In *Thoughts on the Nature of Things* (*Cogitationes de Rerum Natura*), a short unpublished piece in Latin written before 1605 that
contains speculations on bodies, the vacuum, and motion, he observed that the atomic doctrine of Democritus is either true or serves

usefully for demonstration; and further, that "without supposing an atom," one must find the great subtlety of nature hard to understand. He also considered motion as the fundamental principle of things, maintaining that only the study of motion, by showing how bodies come together and how they change, could lead to works.[28] A further noteworthy aspect of his scientific speculations was his claim, contrary to the traditional and widely held view, that no physical difference existed between the celestial and sublunary worlds. In an unpublished Latin tract of around 1612, *A Description of the Intellectual Globe* (*Descriptio Globi Intellectualis*), he described the divorce between heavenly and earthly things as a "dogma," "figments," and "superstitions," seeing that a great number of the same phenomena occur in both the heights of the heaven and the depths of the earth. He was critical of Aristotle's opinion that the substance of the heavenly bodies is unlike the substance of bodies below, as well as of the related belief that the former are eternal and the latter corruptible. On this topic he affirmed that "the best hope and security for the study of celestial bodies" lay in the discovery of "physical reasons" ("physicis rationibus") to explain "those appetites of matter which no diversity of regions or places can distract or dissever."[29] In the same composition he also discussed the Copernican hypothesis that the earth and other planets revolve around the sun as the center of the universe. Reviewing some of the arguments pro and con on this disputed subject, he remarked that Copernicus did not care what fictions his speculations introduced into nature as long as his calculations worked out. Though in the end he refrained from offering any definite opinion on the truth or falsity of the Copernican theory, it is evident that he felt considerable reservations about its likelihood. And in fact, throughout his life he rejected the new Copernican picture of the universe, with its requirement of the daily and annual rotation of the earth, because he regarded it as no more than a mathematical construction to account for planetary motions and was never convinced of its physical truth.[30]

The constant emphasis Bacon placed upon works and the necessity of an operative science signaled one of his most decisive breaks with the philosophical tradition. For him the philosopher or inquirer is no longer merely a beholder, a pure knower, or only an interpreter of nature; he is an active agent compelling nature by his intervention to do his bidding, who measures his success in adding to knowledge by the production of works. It was evident to Bacon that if the natural philosopher understands causes, then he should be able to meet the test of practice and bring about purposeful effects in the actions of nature. In one of the most significant contributions to Baconian studies in many years, Antonio Pérez-Ramos argues that Bacon's idea of science was rooted in the maker's knowledge tradition or what is also called the theory of maker's knowledge.[31] According to this theory, cognition and construction are connected in such a way that knowing and making, *verum* and *factum* (where knowing means an apprehension of the truth), are interchangeable. This entails that to know or understand X (including its cause and inner structure) is identical with being able to make X, or explain how X is made, or reproduce X. A standard illustration of this concept comes from mathematics, where the geometer, for instance, is said to have a perfect knowledge of geometrical truths because he creates them himself, his science being entirely an intellectual construction dependent on his own definitions. While adumbrations and statements of the theory of maker's knowledge may be found in classical antiquity, it first acquired major importance as an epistemological thesis only in the thinking of a number of early modern philosophers. The most prominent example is the earlier-eighteenth-century Neapolitan philosopher Giambattista Vico, who based his entire theory of knowledge on the principle of the equivalence of *verum* and *factum* and attempted to demonstrate its application to the human sciences of history, philology, mythology, and anthropology. The same constructivist principle also played a considerable role in the epistemological reflections of Hobbes and Locke, both of whom regarded maker's knowledge as the most complete and certain kind of knowledge.[32]

According to Pérez-Ramos, the theory of maker's knowledge is present as an ideal-type or regulatory principle underlying Bacon's concept of science.[33] By equating science with dominion over nature, Bacon, he holds, was proffering a constructivist criterion of knowledge that viewed effective practice, the capacity to manipulate nature in the production of works, as the sole guarantee of scientific truth. Nowhere in his writings, though, does Bacon ever discuss or even mention the theory of maker's knowledge. It is likewise significant that while Vico expressed the highest admiration for Bacon, whom he regarded as one of four exemplary authors (the others being Plato, Tacitus, and Grotius), he never showed any sign of perceiving in Bacon's philosophy the constructivist principle he himself promulgated in the thesis of the identity of *verum* and *factum*.[34] So far as it may be part of his philosophy, therefore, it is, as Pérez-Ramos is obliged to admit, at most a tacit assumption never explicitly stated.[35] Nonetheless, this need not prevent us from agreeing that its constructivism can provide us with a helpful perspective on Bacon's image of science.

Hence, in speaking of works, as he so often did, what made them essential for him as a natural philosopher besides their possible benefits to human life was their connection with truth. This comes out very clearly in *Valerius Terminus*, another of his unpublished earlier treatises written around 1603, one of the few in English, in which he discussed the question of determining the truth of claims to knowledge in the interpretation of nature. Here, as in subsequent writings, he took the position that neither antiquity, authority, commonly held notions, the willing consent of the mind, the internal coherence of propositions, inductions without contradictory instances, or the reports of the senses could provide infallible evidence of truth. The sole test he considered acceptable was "the discovery of new works and active directions not known before," and this only in cases where facts and particulars "induce an axiom or observation, which axiom ... discovereth and designeth new particulars." Such a test is a proof of truth, he explained, "not because you may always conclude that the Axiom which discovereth new instances is true, but contrariwise you may safely conclude that if it discover not any new instances it is vain and untrue." These statements fall well short of the theory of maker's knowledge, because they definitely fail to identify truth in natural philosophy with the production of works. At the same time, though, they consider works to be a basic criterion of truth, with the further proviso that an axiom that fails to predict new particulars or lead to the discovery of works is surely false.[36]

BACON AND THE OCCULT SCIENCES

Throughout all of Bacon writings on natural philosophy early and late runs the vision of a science that commands nature by means of art and compels it to give up its secrets. This was a vital part of what he meant by *scientia operativa* or a science capable of works. One of his metaphors of nature was the mythical Proteus who changed shapes at will, and he called the arts "the bonds of nature" because, like Proteus, nature had to be "forced by art to do that which without art would not be done."[37] This activist approach to knowledge was shared by the contemporary occult sciences, which were also intent on operations and practical ends, and therefore indicates the formative presence of such studies as natural magic and alchemy in the development of Bacon's thought. The extent of his involvement with these studies cannot be determined; but as Paolo Rossi was the first to show clearly, Bacon was indebted to them in certain respects even though he pronounced them gravely deficient.[38]

The concept of the secrets of nature was itself a legacy of the mystical and spiritualistic currents increasingly prevalent in the philosophy of the later Greco-Roman world, which became less and less distinguishable from religion with the passage of time. Among its several sources were the Neoplatonism of late antiquity and the Hermetic literature of the first to third centuries of the Christian era. Neoplatonist spiritualistic philosophers were concerned with magic, while Hermeticism looked upon knowledge as an arcane wisdom derived from Egypt and the semidivine Hermes Trismegistus in the remote past, a spiritual revelation bestowing insight into the occult forces of nature and enabling their exploitation by magical means. Many books on the secrets of nature appeared during the Middle Ages and the Renaissance, absorbing the minds of philosophers like Francis Bacon's namesake, the thirteenth-century monk Roger Bacon, who was deeply interested in natural science. This was the matrix for the emergence of natural magic, which aimed at the manipulation of nature by art to achieve wonderful and beneficial effects. Natural magic was regarded as distinct from the dangerously harmful black magic condemned by both the Catholic and Protestant churches, in which the practitioner relied on the cooperation of demons to effect his ends. The most influential Renaissance thinker to expound the theory of natural magic was the Florentine Platonist Marsilio Ficino, the third book of whose treatise *De Vita* (1489) contained a description of various magical techniques of harnessing astral and occult powers to attain good health and long life.[39] In Bacon's day one of the best-known writers on natural magic was the Neapolitan nobleman Giambattista Della Porta, whose most widely read work, *Magiae Naturalis, sive De Miraculis Rerum Naturalium Libri IIII* (1558), was frequently reprinted and translated over the following century. The premise of natural magic was that nature with the help of art could be imitated, improved upon, and used for human benefit. Della Porta was especially concerned with explaining extraordinary phenomena; he was also interested in experiments and in the technical processes of the crafts. Like other occult philosophers, he conceived the universe as a vast system of hidden correspondences and of sympathies and antipathies between things, hierarchically ordered and ruled by God through celestial intelligences, the planets, and the stars. His theory of natural magic postulated form in its union with matter as the cause of nature's productions. In trying to expose nature's hidden actions and qualities, his chief purpose was to imitate and manipulate nature in order to produce marvels.[40]

That the influence of natural magic was an important factor in leading Bacon to connect knowledge with power and to base his natural philosophy on the necessity of works seems quite probable. At the same time, however, he completely rejected the claims and presuppositions of natural magic in various critical remarks in his earlier writings, and especially in *The Advancement of Learning*, where he associated it with astrology and alchemy as sciences that were more the product of imagination than of reason. While admitting that its ends were noble, he refused credence to its experiments and ridiculed its "superstitious conceits" concerning nature's hidden sympathies and antipathies. Denying that it was a true natural magic, he judged it incapable of works because it lacked the understanding of forms essential to perform operations upon nature.[41] To provide such an understanding was one of the foremost goals that he sought in his logic of discovery.[42] Although sympathetic to the aspirations of natural magic, his own philosophy differed markedly from the latter by its

consistent materialism, its critical empiricism, and its concentration
on a reformed induction, and also went far beyond it in seeking an
investigative procedure that would establish a connection between
particulars and axioms and thus lead to a plenitude of works.[43]

Bacon was likewise affected by the alchemical tradition, an inextri-
cable mixture of science and pseudoscience incorporating various
sorts of magical, mystical, and spiritualistic doctrines in its theory and
practice. The alchemists regarded man as the interpreter and servant
of nature; and as Rossi has plausibly suggested, Bacon could have
derived this concept from them, although his natural philosophy
gave it a new and much larger significance.[44] Like the alchemists, he
was interested in the analysis, separation, and reduction of chemical
substances, the conversion of one substance to another, and even in
the possibility of producing gold through transmutation.[45] His comments on alchemy, nevertheless, are usually negative, and he speaks
of it in *The Advancement of Learning* as based on error, deceit, and
impostures.[46] He considered that the alchemists were mere empirics,
addicted to a vain, unproductive philosophy based on a few limited
experiments and rising to no higher intellectual plane than that of
the mechanical arts.[47] These criticisms referred especially to the controversial German physician Paracelsus and his disciples, who were
the main representatives of the alchemical tradition in the sixteenth
century. The Paracelsians promulgated a recondite philosophy combining chemistry, medicine, magic, and religion, which included
such ideas as the close physical and analogical connection between
the macrocosm and man as microcosm, the belief in the signatures of
celestial bodies on the plant and animal kingdoms, and the theory of
the three principles of sulphur, mercury, and salt as the active forces
in nature that constituted the basic ingredients of things.[48] Bacon
occasionally mentioned Paracelsus in his writings, but nearly always
unfavorably, describing him as someone who exalted the power of
the imagination to the same position as the power of wonder-working
faith. Of the "ancient opinion" that man is a microcosm, "an abstract
or model of the world," he commented that Paracelsus and the alchemists had fantastically exaggerated this notion, as though there could
be found in man correspondences and parallels with everything, including stars, planets, and minerals, that exists in the great world.[49]

He was willing to concede, though, that the alchemists in their futile search for gold had sometimes hit on worthwhile inventions and experiments. He also acknowledged that the Paracelsian triad of sulphur, mercury, and salt was not completely useless and did bear "some relation to things."[50]

In attempting to understand Bacon's relationship to the occult sciences, we must also note the attraction to esotericism that he shared with them to some extent. The devotees of the occult sciences were addicted to secrecy. They thought of themselves as possessors of an esoteric higher knowledge that needed to be reserved and hidden from the multitude lest they misuse it, and which was therefore to be imparted to only a limited number of chosen minds. The penchant for secrecy, with its deliberate obscurity as well as its possible resort to dissimulation to preserve an arcane knowledge from exposure, was widely characteristic of the astrologers, alchemists, Hermeticists, physicians, and practitioners of natural magic who sought to gain dominion over the forces of nature with the help of magical means.[51] Despite the fact that Bacon basically viewed science as a public, collaborative, and progressive enterprise, his earlier writings expressed a frequent interest in the esoteric principle of withholding higher truths from the unworthy. This proclivity corresponded closely to the strategy of indirection, concealment, and dissembling that, as I have shown in the preceding chapter, he strove to follow in advancing his political career. In *Valerius Terminus* (1603), whose subtitle, *Of the Interpretation of Nature: with the Annotations of Hermes Stella,* seems to imply some Hermetic association,[52] he spoke of a manner of transmitting knowledge "by publishing part and reserving part" or of publishing in a way that "shall not be to the capacity nor taste of all, but shall as it were single and adopt [the] reader." When he discussed different modes of delivering knowledge in *The Advancement of Learning,* one of those he mentioned was "the enigmatical method," which was designed to prevent "the vulgar capacities from being admitted to the secrets of knowledges, and to reserve them to selected auditors, or wits of such sharpness as can pierce the veil." He knew, of course, that this method lent itself easily to fraud and deceit, and he pointed out that although the ancients had used it, it had later been disgraced "by the impostures of many vain persons who have made it as a false light

for their counterfeit merchandises. . . ." Nevertheless, this fact did
not cause him to repudiate it. It was not to be laid aside, he declared
in *Valerius Terminus*, but used "both for avoiding of abuse in the excluded, and the strengthening of affection in the admitted." In *Of the
Interpretation of Nature Proem*, an unpublished fragment of 1603 containing autobiographical remarks on his project, he reflected on
whether to keep back some knowledge as private and fit only for selected minds. In the confidential memoranda written to himself in
1608, he also raised the question of secrecy in connection with the
publication of his writings.[53] The fictional speaker in *The Refutation of
Philosophies*, echoing a very Baconian sentiment, tells his disciples that
"every man of superior understanding in contact with inferiors wears
a mask," and accordingly advises that they should keep the new philosophy he is expounding for when they deal with nature, while using
the traditional philosophy "to deal with the populace."[54] In Bacon's
utopian tale *New Atlantis*, the "Fathers" of the great scientific foundation, Salomon's House, are practitioners of secrecy.[55] Because of
some of Bacon's statements on this subject, his editor James Spedding felt obliged to pose the question of whether he wished to keep
some parts of his philosophy a secret. After reviewing the evidence
from different passages in Bacon's writings, he concluded that while
Bacon was not in favor of secrecy, he did want to direct his work to fit
and receptive minds to avoid the misconstruction and abuse of his
ideas.[56] This conclusion, from which there is no reason to dissent,
shows that even as an intellectual reformer and critic of the occult
sciences, Bacon continued to feel a lingering allegiance to the principle of esotericism as a way of safeguarding his philosophy from incomprehension or misuse by the hostile or unworthy.

Philosophy and Religion

Bacon's design of reconstructing natural philosophy entailed far-
reaching expectations for relieving and elevating the human condition: expectations that contrasted profoundly with the cool realism
and pragmatism of his outlook and actions in the political realm. The
view of science contained in his earlier writings included an extraor-

dinary hopefulness and idealism that at times became positively utopian. From the holy marriage of the mind with things themselves he foretold the appearance of what he called in *The Masculine Birth of Time* a blessed race of heroes who would overcome "the immeasurable helplessness and poverty of the human race."[57] In keeping with this perspective, he defined the main end of knowledge as nothing less than

> the restitution and reinvesting (in great part) of man to the sovereignty and power (for whensoever he shall be able to call the creatures by their true names he shall again command them) which he had in his first state of creation. And to speak plainly and clearly, it is a discovery of all operations and possibility of operations from immortality (if it were possible) to the meanest mechanical practice.

He then modified this statement a little by acknowledging that the curse God had pronounced on fallen man could not be removed in two respects: first, that in the light of eternity vanity must be the final result of all human efforts; second, that human power would still have to be exercised through labor mental and physical, and that there might be limits to the potentialities of knowledge that were actually realized. But even with these qualifications, he insisted that a world of unknown sciences and inventions remained to be attained; and in behalf of this prospect he applied to his own era the biblical prophecy in the Book of Daniel 12:4, "Many shall pass to and fro, and science shall be increased." And it should be noted that although the Authorized Version renders this passage as "knowledge shall be increased," Bacon preferred the word "science."[58]

Such statements suggest that Bacon dreamed at times of reversing the consequences of original sin and restoring humanity through the power of science to its pristine condition before the Fall. It is thus no wonder that he envisaged his project as the entrance to the kingdom of man. This very hopeful outlook on human regeneration was at odds with the religion of the age and his own Calvinistic heritage. It defied the essential pessimism inherent in the Christian doctrine of mankind's primal transgression and lasting punishment in this world,[59] a doctrine that pictured earthly existence as condemned to

suffer under the burden of the curse God had laid upon Adam and
Eve and their descendants, as the result of which human beings' faculties were corrupted, their nature damaged or depraved, and their
free will impaired, if not lost.[60] Bacon's faith in what would eventuate
from the renewal of natural philosophy ran counter to this picture; it
implied a quite different vision of the human prospect. His choice of
immortality as an example in this connection is especially striking.
Probably he never believed that men might someday become immortal. He did take a deep interest, though, in the prolongation of life,
a matter to which he gave persistent attention. One of his unpublished treatises on natural philosophy, *The Ways of Death, the Postpone-
ment of Old Age, and the Renewal of the Vital Powers* (*De Viis Mortis, et de
Senectute Retardanda, atque Instaurandis Viribus*) dealt with this subject.[61] In 1623 he published on the same subject *The History of Life and
Death* (*Historia Vitae et Mortis*), which was intended as a contribution
to the third part of *The Great Instauration*.[62] Both of these works contained, together with other speculations, a theory of fluid, intangible
vital spirits in bodies as the principle of life and the basis of longevity.
In a statement prefixed to *The History of Life and Death*, Bacon stressed
the extreme profit and importance of the subject, observing that although Christians longed for the land of promise, "yet meanwhile it
will be a mark of God's favour if in our pilgrimage through the wilderness of this world, these our shoes and garments (I mean our frail
bodies) are as little worn out as possible."[63] In the enlarged 1623
Latin version of *The Advancement of Learning*, which Bacon issued as
one of the parts of *The Great Instauration*, he also discussed the means
to the prolongation of life, describing this as the "noblest object of
medicine."[64] He returned to the same subject once again in his final
writing, *New Atlantis*, whose conclusion was followed by a list of great
works (*magnalia*) for human use, the first items of which consisted of
"the prolongation of life, the restitution of youth in some degree, the
retardation of age, the curing of diseases counted incurable, and the
mitigation of pain."[65] These were among the humane goals associated with Bacon's project, goals hardly in accord with the orthodox
Christian understanding of what humanity's earthly lot must inevitably be on account of mankind's disobedience of God's command and
expulsion from paradise.

In explaining the historical reasons for the backwardness of natural philosophy, Bacon always assigned a large importance to the role of religion.[66] He noted, for example, that ever since the establishment of Christianity divinity had received the greatest support and attracted the efforts of most minds, while science had been the most neglected and least pursued of all disciplines. He likewise observed that "in superstition and blind immoderate zeal natural philosophy has found a troublesome and intractable enemy."[67] Reflections of this kind made it inescapable for him to define the relationship of religion both to natural philosophy and to his own project. He was forced to confront this problem in order to safeguard philosophy from religious incomprehension and animosity as well as to defend his own aims against the appearance of irreligious pride and presumption. Among his earlier writings he first discussed the subject in the unfinished *Valerius Terminus* of 1603, whose opening chapter explained the limits of divine and human knowledge,[68] and then more fully in *The Advancement of Learning* of 1605, his biggest work prior to *The New Organon*. At its beginning he attempted to refute "the zeal and jealousy of divines," who claimed that the original temptation leading to the Fall was the excessive aspiration to knowledge; for knowledge puffed men up, making them forget their dependence on God in their contemplation of and inquiry into secondary causes.[69] His mention of this charge was not simply an invention. The Puritan clergyman and Cambridge University teacher William Perkins, for example, one of the foremost English theologians of the later sixteenth century, not only stigmatized excessive intellectual curiosity as sinful, but even named it as a cause of witchcraft. The curiosity he referred to, which had likewise been the cause of the Fall, was a "discontentment" of the mind that made a man aspire to search out the things God would have kept secret, and therefore led him "to attempt the cursed art of Magicke and Witchcraft, as a way to get further knowledge in matters secret and not revealed, that by working of wonders, hee may purchase fame in the world, and consequently reape more benefit by such unlawfull courses, than in likelihood he could have done by ordinary and lawfull meanes."[70] While Perkins's condemnation of intellectual curiosity might apply particularly to witchcraft as well as to the practitioners of magic among the occult sciences, it was not irrelevant to a project like Bacon's, which probed the secrets of nature and looked to works for human benefit as the principal fruit of scientific knowledge. Replying to an indictment of this sort, he declared that it was not "the pure knowledge of nature" that caused the Fall, but rather the proud desire to know good and evil, by which man would make himself his own lawgiver independent of God's commandments. He went on to explain that God had framed the human mind "as a mirror or glass capable of the image of the universal world and joyful to receive the impression thereof. . . ." God had accordingly barred no part of the world from man's inquiry or invention, and there was no danger in even the greatest knowledge as long as it was carried with charity. Countering the claim that too much knowledge of philosophy inclined men to atheism, he asserted that while a little superficial knowledge might lead that way, greater knowledge drew the mind to religion and made it realize the connection between secondary causes and God as the first cause. It was impossible, he held, that man could "search too far or be too well studied in the book of God's word or in the book of God's works," that is, in either divinity or philosophy. But he added the significant caution that these two kinds of learning should be kept separate and never mingled or confounded.[71] In the essay on atheism included in the second and third editions of his essays, he declared that God's existence was manifest in his ordinary works and that contemplation of the chain of secondary causes brings the mind eventually to belief in God and providence. Atheism, he maintained, degraded human nature by denying mankind's spiritual kinship with God, while only belief in God enabled human nature to exalt itself above its frailty.[72]

Bacon thus consistently justified the Faustian pursuit of knowledge and limitless investigation of nature as in no way either contrary or harmful to religion. Chiefly, nevertheless, he was concerned, in order to promote the progress of natural philosophy, with maintaining a strict separation between it and religion so that neither impinged upon the other. He developed this point further in *The Advancement of Learning* in a discussion of the differences distinguishing the three kinds of philosophy—divine, natural, and human—relating respectively to God, nature, and man himself. The first, which he also called natural theology, was the knowledge of God that might be gained through contemplation of his creatures. Such knowledge, he thought, could show the omnipotence and wisdom of God's works but not his image; nor could it attain to truth in matters of faith, since these lay beyond reason. His conclusion was that men should not "attempt to draw down or submit the mysteries of God to [their] reason," as divine philosophy had too often done. And he warned in addition of "the extreme prejudice which both religion and philosophy hath received and may receive by being commixed together; as that which undoubtedly will make an heretical religion, and an imaginary and fabulous philosophy."[73] He put the same thesis even more forcefully in the unpublished *Thoughts and Conclusions on the Interpretation of Nature.* Here again he deplored the damage inflicted on natural philosophy by religious zeal and superstition and condemned the former's mixture with theology, while affirming at the same time that next to the word of God, natural philosophy was "the loyal handmaid of religion, for religion reveals the will of God, natural philosophy his power."[74]

There are certain Baconian scholars who claim that Bacon was secretly irreligious but dissembled his unbelief.[75] His writings, however, contain no clue or statements to substantiate this view. The distinction he assumed between faith and reason was a very old one, common to many Christian philosophers. Certainly it need not have implied any doubt of the supernatural truths of the Christian religion as known through revelation. Nowhere, as far as I have been able to discover, did he ever hint that he had concealed in any of his writings an esoteric message of unbelief directed to a sophisticated, discerning reader. Moreover, as Paul Kocher pointed out in his study of Elizabethan science and religion, Bacon's attitude was typical of the English thinkers of his time who took an interest in science. All of them held that religion and science should be kept separate and also that the two were complementary to one another. In answer to clerical warnings about the dangers of "curiosity," they responded as Bacon did that God had made nature and the physical world to be the object of man's knowledge.[76] Intent on the advancement of natural philosophy for human betterment as his foremost object, Bacon worried about the power of religious hostility and fanaticism to block its progress. He recorded, for example, how among the Greeks "those who first suggested to men's untutored minds that thunderbolts and storms had natural causes were condemned for impiety." Similarly, some of the early Christian fathers persecuted cosmographers "who on clear evidence which no sane man would reject today, claimed that the earth was a sphere and therefore inhabited at the antipodes. . . ."[77] To defend natural philosophy against such adversaries, he insisted that unless it was segregated from theology, both would be corrupted, while also offering assurance that the two were not in conflict and that natural philosophy did not vainly seek to penetrate divine mysteries but rather endeavored to know God's creatures and works.[78]

As for Bacon's personal religion, I have found no reason to question the sincerity of his Christian professions. Religious piety is one of the notes of Baconian science. The preface and plan of his *Great Instauration* included a fervent prayer imploring God's blessing on Bacon's work as a means of endowing "the human family with new mercies."[79] Among his occasional writings were translations of seven of the Psalms, which he published in 1624 with a dedication to his friend the deeply devout poet George Herbert.[80] The thoughts contained in *Religious Meditations* (*Sacrae Meditationes*), a short collection of reflections published in 1597 in company with the first edition of his *Essays*, were unexceptionably orthodox.[81] For the clearest statement of his religious convictions, one must turn to his unpublished confession of faith written prior to 1603, which expressed beliefs he could just as well have held throughout his life. They included faith in an eternal, almighty, all wise, and all good creator God and in the three persons of the Trinity. Of this confession Spedding said that "the entire scheme of Christian theology—creation, temptation, fall, mediation, election, reprobation, redemption"—underlay it, defining for Bacon the limits of the province of human speculation. The confession contains no indication that he accepted the Calvinist doctrine of predestination and the denial of human free will, although it does state that among the generations of men God had "elected a small flock" through which to express the riches of his glory. It is also noteworthy that in speaking of the creation of heaven and earth, he declared that God had given them "constant and everlasting laws, which we call nature" and which are "nothing but the laws of the creation. . . ." Following the creation these laws were "to govern inviolably till the end of the world. . . ." He qualified this point, however, by noting that God's dealing with spirits is not part of nature and the laws of heaven and earth, but is reserved to the law of his secret will and grace in the work of redemption; moreover, that God may break the law of nature by miracles, which he never performs except in regard to the work of redemption.[82] If this confession of faith may be taken at face value, it shows that Bacon was a genuine Christian, although it is equally evident that his mind was overwhelmingly secular in its interests and that in his reflections as a Christian philosopher he was far more concerned with the advancement of scientific reason and the improvement of mankind's welfare in this world than with religion and the destiny of the immortal soul.

THE PROBLEM OF METHOD

I have previously remarked that in a very general sense Bacon's philosophy centered on the quest for a method. In the history of Western thought the notion of method is most commonly associated with Descartes. One of the latter's earliest works, *Rules for the Direction of the Mind* (1628), laid great stress on the necessity of a method to investigate the truth of things, while his subsequent *Discourse on Method* (1637) gave classic expression to the attempt to propound a method for the guidance of thought that would establish a foundation of absolute certainty for both the existence of God and a number of fundamental truths about the world.[83] Well before Descartes, however, method was a subject of widespread interest among sixteenth-century philosophers, and to none more so than to Bacon, who saw in it the key to certain knowledge and the renewal of natural philosophy. To grasp the distinctiveness of his view of method and to understand his personal terminology in dealing with it, we must take note of the etymology and meaning of this concept in the philosophy of Bacon's era.

The term "method" derives from the Greek *méthodos*, which signified among other things a way of inquiry, method, or system. For Aristotle it meant both a reasoned way of inquiry and a disquisition or disputation. In Greek philosophy it was often associated with *techné*, meaning an art or technique of making something in accord with rational principles. Thus Aristotle began his *Nichomachean Ethics* with the proposition that "every art (*techné*) and every type of inquiry (*méthodos*) . . . is thought to aim at some good."[84] Transliterated into Latin, the Greek term became *methodus*. Classical Latin authors, however, seem rarely to have adopted this word of Greek origin, preferring instead synonyms such as "ratio" and "via." Cicero, a model of Latin prose, sometimes used the former to mean a system, method, or procedure, and joined it with the latter as "ratio et via" when referring, for example, to the method of teaching something like the art of oratory.[85] Among the Latin equivalents for the Greek *méthodos* listed in Stephanus's great Greek thesaurus are "via," "ratio," "argumentum," and "ratio et via docendi et discendi," this last designating a method of teaching and learning.[86] Fifteenth- and sixteenth-century Latin translators of the works of Aristotle and other Greek philosophers tended to avoid the Latinized *methodus* as unclassical. Hence in rendering the Greek term *méthodos*, they chose words like "doctrina," "disciplina," "disputatio," "via," and "ratio docendi."[87] Apart from Latin usage, however, by the sixteenth century the word "method" had also entered the English and other vernacular languages, in which one of its principal meanings was a systematic arrangement, order, or procedure, a leading sense it still retains.[88]

In sixteenth-century philosophy the concept of method was employed chiefly in connection with dialectics and logic, both of which dealt with types of reasoning: the latter with demonstrative inference, the former with the art of discourse, that is, the finding, organization, and presentation of information and probable arguments. In this context, "method" was generally taken to refer to a way of imparting knowledge or teaching a subject and to the systematic disposition and ordering of a sequence of propositions or precepts in an art, as well as to forms of logical demonstration and proof relating to causes and effects. Hardly ever did it signify a procedure or mode of inquiry aiming at the discovery of new knowledge of nature.[89]

In his influential dialectics textbook, *Erotemata Dialectices* (1547), the Protestant reformer and humanist educator Philipp Melanchthon gave the following definition of method, which he attributed to the Greeks:

> Method is an acquired aptitude, to wit a science or an art making a way according to a certain plan; that is, it discovers and opens a way as if through places blocked and made impassable by thorns, because of the confusion of things, and produces material pertinent to a subject and sets it out in an orderly fashion.[90]

Not dissimilarly, Thomas Wilson, a leading English authority on logic and rhetoric, described method in his logic textbook as "the maner of handelinge a single Question and the readie Waie how to teache and sette forth any thyng plainlie and in order, as it should bee, in Latin Methodus." Another English writer on the subject, Abraham Fraunce, stated in a manual of logic for lawyers that "Methode hath only to deale with the ordering and setling of many axioms."[91] In his well-known philosophical lexicon published in 1613, the German Rudolf Goclenius declared that "methodus" is commonly understood to mean "any system of teaching . . . or the order of a whole art . . . whereby the parts of the art are explained."[92]

This appears to have been the usual understanding of the concept of method held by sixteenth-century philosophers. A significant exception, however, was constituted by those thinkers and disciples of Aristotle, especially at the University of Padua, who also conceived of method as a type of demonstration leading to the discovery of causes or effects. Of these the most prominent was the Paduan philosopher Jacopo Zabarella, an Aristotelian purist and the foremost sixteenth-century commentator on Aristotle's logic. In *De Methodis* (1578), a treatise devoted to method, Zabarella clearly differentiated *ordo*, the orderly presentation of the subjects relating to a discipline, from *methodus* in the strict sense as a way of reasoning from the known to the unknown. Influenced chiefly by the conception of science and logic of scientific explanation set forth in Aristotle's *Posterior Analytics*, he attached little value to induction and based scientific method on the primacy of the syllogism and two kinds of demonstration. The first of these was the compositive method ("methodus compositiva"), which inferred an unknown effect from its proximate known cause; the second was the resolutive method ("methodus resolutiva"), which inferred an unknown cause from one of its effects. These two methods, which depended on the arrangement of the terms of the syllogism, demonstrated either that something is a fact ("demonstratio quia") or the reason why it is a fact—that is to say, the reasoned fact ("demonstratio propter quid").[93] For Zabarella they were all that were needed to achieve the aims of natural philosophy by providing a complete knowledge of principles and their effects.[94] Although it has been suggested that Zabarella's writings on logic and method must have formed part of the background to Bacon's thoughts concerning the investigation of nature, he never referred to the Italian commentator or gave any indication of having known or studied his writings.[95] In any case, the latter's confinement of the method of discovery to syllogistic demonstration would have been regarded by Bacon as wrongheaded and cripplingly restrictive. Besides providing no place for the interrogation of nature by experiment—what Bacon called "nature vexed"—or for the testing of theories, it dealt, as did Aristotle's own science, only with the most observable and ordinary phenomena of nature, not with its subtle and invisible actions. So far as natural philosophy was concerned, this approach was thoroughly discordant with Bacon's conception of a process of inquiry and logic of discovery, which downgraded the syllogism as an instrument and looked to a systematic, critical empiricism and to induction ascending to axioms as the essential means to the growth of scientific knowledge.

In the extensive sixteenth-century discussions that took place over method, a pivotal figure and the most controversial and influential of philosophers was Peter Ramus, who made method the linchpin of his system of ideas. A critic of Aristotle and Scholasticism, a contentious educational and intellectual reformer at the University of Paris, he helped to popularize the absorption of logic into dialectics as an art of discourse that had been initiated by fifteenth- and sixteenth-century humanist innovators like Lorenzo Valla, Rudolph Agricola, and Melanchthon. Ramus sought a simplified logic that lent itself to what he deemed the natural and most rational arrangement of a subject. As did Agricola and other predecessors, he divided dialectic into two parts, invention and judgment, the first dealing with topics (the categories or mental places for finding different types of arguments and facts), the other, which included logic, with the assembling and judging of what invention had made available. Method as he conceived it applied to any discourse, discipline, or subject. He defined it as a disposition among a number of things by which the first in respect to conspicuousness (meaning its generality and clearness) was put in the first place, the second in the second place, the third in the third, and so on; and thus, he stated, "there is an unbroken progression from universals to singulars," and "one proceeds from antecedents entirely known to the declaration of unknown consequents."[96] With respect to logic he laid down three axioms or rules adapted from Aristotle's *Posterior Analytics*, which he considered essential in the formulation of the principles of every science. These required that the predicate of a proposition stating such principles should be necessarily true (i.e., inherent in the definition of the subject), universally true (i.e., true of every single instance of the subject), and convertible (i.e., the proposition's converse must also be true). A further aspect of his method was its implementation through the use of dichotomies, the division and subdivision of any subject into a continuous series of dichotomous classifications, starting with its most general features and branching down to its most specific ones. These dichotomies, graphically illustrated by diagrams, became a familiar feature of many of the books, whatever their subject might be, that reflected the influence of Ramus's doctrines. All this constituted Ramus's famous "single method," which according to his view supplied the key to all knowledge and the teaching of all arts.[97]

What Ramus propounded as method was highly successful in providing teachers with an efficient means of instruction and in helping students to develop orderly habits of thought so as to learn a subject systematically. At best, however, it could serve only for the organization of knowledge and discourse; as an instrument for the discovery of new truths in natural philosophy it was useless. Bacon had read Ramus, of course, and made several allusions to him in his earlier writings. Most negative was his comment in *The Masculine Birth of Time* describing him as an ignorant begetter of compendia who squeezes and tortures things by his method until they become arid and barren.[98] In *The Advancement of Learning* he spoke favorably of the rules Ramus had required for the framing of propositions, but again criticized his method, describing his device of dichotomizing as "the canker of Epitomes."[99]

This last statement occurred in a survey of the diversities of method that Bacon included in book 2 of *The Advancement of Learning*. What stands out with striking clarity throughout this survey is that he understood the term "method" to refer exclusively to what he called "tradition," his designation for the delivery or transmission of knowledge. Although he reviewed the various methods of delivering knowledge, nowhere did he use this word in connection with discovery. Instead he limited its meaning exclusively to the presentation and transmission of knowledge.[100] He reiterated the same view in *De Dignitate et Augmentis Scientiarum*, the expanded 1623 Latin version of *The Advancement of Learning*. Here he associated the word "methodus" entirely with "sermo" or discourse, defining it generally as the doctrine concerned with the transmission of knowledge.[101]

Bacon's persistent refusal to regard "method" as an instrument of discovery is best explained by the place it occupied in contemporary dialectics. In the latter, as has been remarked, the concept of method was not related to the growth of knowledge or the attainment of certainty. It pertained solely to discourse, argument, and the disposition and exposition of the probable or already known. This was the sense, therefore, in which Bacon generally understood the word. From the same point of view he also maintained in *The Advancement of Learning* that as commonly conceived, invention, one of the two main parts of dialectic, was incapable of adding to knowledge. Discussing invention, he pointed out that the word signified two very different things: it could mean either the invention of arts and sciences or that of speeches and arguments. The first kind of invention, he stated, was altogether deficient and lacking, because the syllogistic logic that it utilized could not invent new arts and sciences and simply took on trust the axioms and principles of those that existed. This kind of invention, resting on the common notions of things, was helpless in natural philosophy, since it could not grasp the subtlety of nature and its operations. As for the invention of speech and arguments, this, according to Bacon, was not properly invention at all; "for to invent is to discover that we know not, and not to recover . . . that which we already know. . . ." Nevertheless, he expressed his willingness to retain the conventional name "invention" for the latter, provided it was taken to mean "the readiness and present use of our knowledge, and not addition or amplification thereof."[102]

Bacon's observations in *The Advancement of Learning* on the current conceptions of method and invention constituted a negative judgment on the inadequacies and limitations of dialectics in the philosophy of his time.[103] Accordingly, when he came to write *The New Organon*, a work composed in Latin, he refrained from using "methodus" to describe a method of discovery. The word occurs only five times in this treatise, usually with an unfavorable connotation. Thus he speaks critically of the "method" ("methodum") of those who have dealt with and transmitted the sciences, and similarly of the "methods" ("methodos") of the medieval Schoolmen. Once, in commenting on the need for a greater abundance and a different kind of experiments, he says that an entirely different "method, order, and process" ("methodus, ordo, processus") must be introduced for cultivating and advancing experience.[104] On the other hand, when alluding to his own method and its goal of achieving certainty and a new understanding of nature, he prefers the term "ratio" or sometimes both "ratio" and "via."[105] He therefore distinguished between "methodus" as understood in dialectics and "ratio" as the method of discovery he sought to expound in his own philosophy.

THE ADVANCEMENT OF LEARNING

As a philosopher Bacon was highly attentive to the problem of how best to present his thoughts. A conscious literary artist and student of communication, he dedicated his entire life, as Brian Vickers has rightly said, to the task of persuasion.[106] His attitude toward antiquity and attack on the philosophical tradition were an affront to the old regime of knowledge and a defiance of many prejudices. To obtain a favorable hearing for his ideas and support and patronage for his project were thus objectives that he kept constantly in mind. One of the rationalizations he gave for his political ambitions and pursuit of office was that if he rose to a position of honor in the state, he would have a greater command of the ability and industry of others to assist him in his work.[107] This work, the renewal of natural philosophy, was in its full dimensions a far-reaching enterprise, necessitating investigators, libraries, laboratories, and research institutes. In the private memoranda he wrote to himself in 1608, he spoke of his design to secure a place in which to command "wyts and pennes" and then proceeded to list a number of scientific aims. These included the procurement of a history of experiments and observations in all the mechanical arts; the payment of pensions to four persons to search out the materials for this history; the founding of a college for inventors, a library, and a collection of engines; financial allowances for travelers, experiments, intelligence, and correspondence with foreign universities; and the provision of furnaces, vaults, terraces for "Insolacion," and work houses of all sorts.[108]

Since a revitalized science in Bacon's vision of it required such large resources, it was natural that he should have looked for material assistance to the monarchy itself. *The Advancement of Learning* was accordingly addressed to King James I with a fulsome dedication praising his great erudition, wisdom, and virtue. This work, which gathered up many of the themes of his thought, was one of the very few of his earlier philosophical writings that he decided to publish. Most of the rest remained unfinished; but he may also have felt about a number of them that they were too uncompromisingly polemical in their treatment of prevailing beliefs and the philosophical tradition to be suitable for general publication. *The Advancement of Learning* was his most comprehensive philosophical statement prior to the appearance of *The Great Instauration*. That he wrote it in English indicates pretty clearly that it had the practical purpose of making his ideas known to a comparatively wide audience of native readers. Its tone was on the whole studiedly moderate, in contrast with that which we find in some of his unpublished writings. The value he attached to it is proved by the fact that he later decided to incorporate it in an expanded Latin version as one of the parts of *The Great Instauration*. James I, the recent inheritor of the English throne, was a well-educated man of literary and scholarly tastes whom Bacon might with reason have expected to show some response to his work. The king, however, had an old-fashioned mind, and neither then nor later did he express any comprehension of or interest in Bacon's philosophy.[109]

Of the *Advancement*'s two books, the first was a defense of learning against its detractors; the second, nearly three times as long, presented a classification and survey of the different branches of knowledge with the purpose of assessing their condition and deficiencies.[110] This classification differed from traditional classifications of knowledge such as Aristotle's in its basic principles.[111] Bacon did not hierarchize the sciences or parts of knowledge, nor did he give primacy to the theoretical and contemplative over the practical disciplines. He considered the several branches of philosophy (natural, moral, and civil or political), as well as other kinds of intellectual activities, to belong to a single, interrelated world of knowledge. Practice and the uses of knowledge constantly occupied his mind in connection with every discipline. Above all, he attempted not only to present a comprehensive outline of the various divisions of knowledge but to point out which parts of learning were neglected or deficient and in need of improvement or radical reform. At the work's conclusion, Bacon justly described it as "a small Globe of the Intellectual world."[112] Since its range was encyclopedic, containing a treatment of numerous other subjects besides natural philosophy, I shall deal here only with the parts that pertain most directly to his conception of philosophy and to his own project. Those parts that relate to the further aspects of his thought will be the subject of discussion in later chapters.

In book 1, Bacon set himself to refute various criticisms of learning, following which he took notice of several "distempers" and errors in learning that he believed had contributed to its discredit. The first, which he called "delicate learning," he attributed to the humanists and their literary affectations. These were the students of classical antiquity and texts who preferred style over substance and eloquence of language in imitation of ancient authors to weightiness of matter and depth of judgment. The second distemper was "contentious learning," which referred to the medieval Scholastics, their minds in thrall to Aristotle and occupied with useless subtleties and controversies, whose method of handling knowledge by framing objections, refutations, solutions, distinctions, and further objections upon every proposition bred only verbal points and niceties. These he likened to spiders laboriously spinning their webs of learning, admirable for the fineness of the thread but of no substance or profit. The third distemper was "fantastical learning," involving credulity and imposture, which he saw exemplified especially in the sciences of astrology, natural magic, and alchemy. The "theories" and "practices" of these sciences he declared to be pervaded by error and vanity that their professors deceitfully strove to hide by their "enigmatical writings" and other devices to preserve the credit of their impostures.[113]

Bacon's account of the distempers of learning was, of course, less than fair or impartial in its judgments. His estimate of Scholastic philosophy, for example, hardly did it justice, although his opinion was shared by other leading seventeenth-century thinkers as well as by Protestant reformers who blamed the Scholastics for corrupting religious truth with the profane philosophy of Aristotle. Pervading his discussion, however, is a view of philosophy as a rigorous and independent inquisition after truth. He complained of the "overmuch credit given unto authors in the sciences" as one of the main causes of these disciplines' failure to progress. Just as water could rise no higher than its source, he asserted, so knowledge derived from Aristotle and exempted from liberty of examination would never rise higher than knowledge of Aristotle.[114]

From these broad distempers Bacon passed on to some other errors of learning. They included such failings as the extreme addiction either to antiquity or to novelty and men's undue reverence for their own minds, which drew them away from experience and the observation of nature to concoct things out of their own reason and conceits. But the greatest of all errors, he maintained, was the misconception of the chief and ultimate end of knowledge. Reviewing the various motives for pursuing knowledge, whether to satisfy curiosity, or for ornament and reputation, or for victory in argument, or for wealth, he declared that its true purpose was to provide a "rich storehouse, for the glory of the Creator and the relief of man's estate." What would most exalt and dignify knowledge, he considered, would be the closer unification of contemplation and action than had hitherto obtained, so that "knowledge may not be as a curtesan, for pleasure and vanity only, or as a bond-woman, to acquire and gain for her

master's use; but as a spouse, for generation, and fruit, and comfort."[115] These feminine analogies for knowledge are striking, culmi-
nating as they do in the image of the intimate union of marriage with
progeny as the symbol of a science productive of works. As his words
indicate, Bacon did not look upon knowledge from a narrowly utilitarian standpoint. The end to which he dedicated the achievements
of the human intellect was also moral insofar as it served religion and
the welfare of mankind by showing through discoveries in natural
philosophy the greatness of God's works.

The *Advancement*'s second book began with remarks addressed directly to the king, reminding him that the support of learning with
buildings, libraries, endowments, and sustaining institutions was a
princely work. In this connection Bacon drew attention to the shortcomings and need for reform in colleges and universities. All of
them, he commented, were "dedicated to professions, and none left
free to arts and sciences at large," with the result that they contributed little to the progress of "fundamental knowledges." Lecturers in
educational foundations were inadequately paid and were not the
best men. Resources in these institutions, such as furnaces, engines,
and other instruments, were lacking for the performance of scientific
experiments. The traditional university curriculum, moreover, was
outdated and required change. Bacon was specifically critical of the
teaching of logic and rhetoric to immature young students, who were
unready for these subjects and turned them into sophistry and affectation. He also observed that learning would benefit "if there were
more intelligence mutual between the universities of Europe than
now there is." All these reflections make it clear that his project for
the reconstruction of knowledge necessarily implied substantial
changes in education, and they foreshadow the scientific and research institutions he was later to depict in his portrait of an imaginary commonwealth, the *New Atlantis*.[116]

After these preliminaries, Bacon commenced his "general peram-
bulation of learning" by dividing learning into three basic categories
(history, poetry, and philosophy), corresponding respectively to the
three faculties of the human understanding (memory, imagination,
and reason).[117] Within the different species of history he included the
history of nature, comprising the history of creatures, of marvels, and

of arts. He found the second of these deficient, as no satisfactory collection existed of the works of nature in their departure from its ordinary course of productions and motions. This subject, he noted, was filled with fabulous reports and frivolous impostures; and while marvels might be conceded to exist if there were assured evidence for them, he displayed his consistent naturalism in the comment that "it is not yet known in what cases, and how far, effects attributed to superstition do participate of natural causes. . . ."[118] The history of arts—that is, of "Nature Wrought or Mechanical"—was also deficient, a fact he attributed to the prevalent intellectual and social disparagement of mechanical matters as vulgar and without dignity. Contesting this attitude, he held that a "History Mechanical" was of the utmost importance to a true natural philosophy. Not only would it exhibit the ingenious practices of all trades and suggest observations arising from them, but it would provide a greater illumination of causes and axioms than had yet been attained. This was because nature's actions and variations "cannot appear so fully in the liberty of nature as in the trials and vexations of art."[119] In a statement such as this lay the rationale for the importance Bacon always ascribed to experiment as the way to determine what nature can accomplish when forced out of its ordinary course by art. The insistence on the essential value of craft knowledge and processes for the understanding of nature was a fundamental Baconian tenet that he reiterated throughout his work. It broke with the disparaging view of such knowledge as inferior compared with the soaring but unconfirmed speculations of philosophy and reflected his aspiration to achieve a science capable of works.

The Advancement of Learning reserved its lengthiest discussion for philosophy, which Bacon classified into divine philosophy, natural philosophy, and human philosophy or humanity. Concerning the first, his main care, as I have previously pointed out, was to maintain the need for its separation from the other two lest their mixture submit the mysteries of God to reason and thereby generate both a false religion and an imaginary philosophy.[120]

Proceeding to natural philosophy, he defined its two divisions as inquiry into causes and production of effects, or speculative and operative, also termed natural science and natural prudence. His conciliatory tactics are evident in his statement that he desired to depart as little from antiquity in his terminology and opinions as was consistent with truth and the proficiency of knowledge.[121] "Natural Science or Theory," the first of these divisions, consisted of physics and metaphysics, and in his treatment of these two disciplines lay the focal point of his philosophy of science. At the outset he was at pains to distinguish metaphysics from "prima philosophia" or "first philosophy," with which it had usually been identified since Aristotle's time. Criticizing the ill-assorted things that were commonly consigned to "primitive" or "first philosophy," he defined the latter's proper scope as the universal categories of thought and the basic axioms of logic shared by all of the different parts of philosophy and the special sciences. Metaphysics, on the other hand, was a branch of natural science. Like physics, it was concerned with causality; but whereas physics occupied itself with the variable and particular causes of things, to metaphysics pertained their general and constant causes. Otherwise stated, physics dealt with material and efficient causes, metaphysics with formal and final causes.[122] These two pairs are identical with Aristotle's well-known doctrine of the four types of causes, which Bacon adopted and assigned respectively to the domains of physics and metaphysics as the basis for the explanation of all natural phenomena.[123] In metaphysics, formal cause, which entailed the investigation of forms, was the key to explaining the essential nature of something and what determines it to be what it is. Connected with it, therefore, was the notion of form, which reveals itself in *The Advancement of Learning* as one of the fundamental concepts of Bacon's natural philosophy. Like the four sorts of causes, form was another Aristotelian concept of enduring importance in Western philosophy and of which Bacon tried to develop his own materialist version. He recorded only to dissent from "the received and inveterate opinion that the imagination of man is not competent to find out essential forms or true differences." The discovery of the forms of substances was possible, he believed, and stood as the highest object of knowledge. He does not state how this discovery is to be accomplished. What his discussion at this point shows, however, is that he understood forms to be the primal and most general properties of matter inhering in differing combinations in many different things and thereby determining the latter's distinctive natures. Thus he points out that it would be useless to search for the forms of a lion, an oak or gold, or even of air or water. On the other hand, to inquire into the forms of sense, of vegetation, of colors, of weight and lightness, heat and cold, "and all other natures and qualities" would be like investigating the letters of an alphabet, which are few in number but of which all words are compounded.[124]

This part of metaphysics, according to Bacon, the discovery of the "simple forms" or "essences" of which "all creatures do consist," was deficient and incapable of attainment by existing methods. He regarded it as the most excellent part of knowledge because it led to the highest degree of generality, abridging "the infinity of individual experience as much as the conception of truth will permit. . . ." It could also "enfranchise the power of man unto the greatest liberty of works and effects." In comparison with the possibilities of operations created by the knowledge of forms, physics was much more limited and could only imitate the ordinary course of nature. Physical explanations of the greatest scope and productive of the largest variety of works were therefore the supreme objective of Baconian science.

In keeping with this view, he visualized natural philosophy as a pyramid with three levels. At its base were the empirical particulars collected by natural history. The second level consisted of physics and its knowledge of material and efficient causes. The third level, closest to the top, was metaphysics, the understanding of forms. Above all these and at the apex stood the "Summary Law of Nature," the work "which God worketh from beginning to end." Although confident that the human intellect could ascend to the pyramid's third level, he confessed of the last and highest kind of knowledge residing in the mind of God that "we know not whether man's inquiry can attain unto it."[125]

On final causes, Bacon had much less to say. His chief point was to emphasize the prevailing error of introducing the final causes of metaphysics into the inquiry into "real and physical causes," which belonged to physics. He suggests that statements like "the skins and hides of living creatures are to defend them from extremes of heat and cold," "clouds are for watering the earth," or "the leaves of trees are to protect the fruit" are no more than pseudoexplanations when offered as a substitute for physical causes. Plato, Aristotle, Galen, and others, he maintained, were often guilty of this error; and though granting that final causes might be true in their own province, he held that their intrusion into physics had arrested the progress of discovery and done great harm to science.[126]

Bacon also offered a cursory appraisal of the place of mathematics in natural philosophy. He classed it with metaphysics, because in dealing with number or quantity as a form of things it is the most abstracted and separable from matter. While he recognized the practical utility of mathematics, his comments indicate no awareness of its vital importance in the investigation of nature. The latter was a fact well understood by contemporary scientists like Kepler and Galileo, the latter of whom declared that the grand book of the universe was written entirely in the language of mathematics, and that no one could comprehend it without a knowledge of this language.[127]

In the *Advancement*'s treatment of causal inquiry as the first division of natural philosophy, Bacon concentrated on formal, efficient, and material causes while giving short shrift to final causes. He was convinced that a knowledge of forms would yield the deepest truths about the actions of nature and facilitate the widest range of applications, including the invention of many new things. All that he said on this subject, however, was purely programmatic and promissory. It held forth a prospect, outlining what needed to be done, but furnished no details about the means to achieve this desired knowledge. Nor was he completely successful in explaining what forms are. There can be no doubt that throughout his work on science he was engaged in a continual struggle with the problem of forms. *The Advancement of Learning* makes evident the great significance this concept held for him as a crucial part of natural philosophy, which was later also to occupy a major place in *The New Organon*.

The second division, containing the operative part of natural philosophy in Bacon's classification, was natural prudence, which he dealt with very briefly. In it he included the occult sciences of natural magic, astrology, and alchemy. As we have already seen, none of these disciplines came near to meeting his standards for the growth of knowledge, and he dismissed them all as occupied more with fictions than with the truths of nature.[128]

The remainder of the *Advancement* was devoted to human philosophy, which embraced the different parts of human beings' knowledge of themselves. During this discussion, Bacon also touched on a few topics relevant to natural philosophy and the epistemology of the sciences. Thus, speaking of logic as one of the intellectual arts related to invention or discovery, he pointed to its defects in the investigation of nature. Induction as currently practiced, based on the simple enumeration of some particulars without contradictory instances, was merely conjecture; hence it was unable to discover the general principles of the sciences. This was the reason the latter were filled with ungrounded and dogmatic theories actually scornful of particulars. But even if some principles or axioms had been rightly induced, the syllogism could not generate workable "middle principles" because the subtleties of nature were too great to be captured by words and propositions that were no more than tokens of "popular notions of things." These failures, according to Bacon, were what persuaded some philosophers to become skeptics, distrusting the senses as deceitful, denying the possibility of certain knowledge, and concluding that human knowledge extended only to appearances and probabilities. Needless to say, he opposed this view. Insisting that the senses aided by instruments were sufficient to report truth, he claimed that the problems of knowledge were due to the weakness of the intellectual powers and the inadequacy of their methods in collecting and concluding upon the reports of the senses. He ended his remarks on this subject with the promise that "if God give me leave," he would propound something in the future concerning discovery in the sciences.[129]

Another of the intellectual arts he touched upon was judgment, in which he identified certain profound fallacies of the human mind that had been entirely overlooked by philosophers. This was his earliest published analysis of the idols of the mind, one of his most significant conceptions. At this point he terms them "false appearances," but a marginal Latin note in the text refers to them as "idolis animi humani, nativis et adventitiis" ("idols of the human mind innate and acquired"). In the unpublished work in English *Valerius Terminus,* written prior to the *Advancement,* he called them "idols" and "fictions."[130] Their importance lay in the fact that their effects extended beyond particular errors to the entire warping and misdirection of the understanding; for rather than reflecting things as they are, the mind is "like an enchanted glass, full of superstition and imposture, if it be not delivered and reduced."

He listed three categories of such false appearances. The first, "the root of all superstition," was due to the general nature of the mind, which liked affirmatives better than negatives and was apt to see uniformities and analogies where none existed. This explained why human beings constantly generalized on the basis of a few positive instances, simply overlooking countervailing negative examples, and also why mathematicians, despite the evidence of the heavens, constantly strove to reduce the movements of all celestial bodies to perfect circles. Bacon succeeded in identifying here a deep, persisting inclination to anthropomorphism in men's unrectified perceptions of the world. It was incredible, he observed, "what a number of fictions and fancies" the supposed similarity between human actions and the operations of nature and "the making of man a common measure" had introduced into natural philosophy.

The second kind of false appearances arose from the peculiarities of each individual's nature and habits. In this respect, humans resembled the benighted inhabitants of the cave in Plato's famous parable, their vision dimmed by its shadows. So "our spirits," according to Bacon, are enclosed "in the caves of our own complexions and customs," causing infinite errors and vain opinions unless corrected by examination.

The third of these false appearances was the product of confusions of language, which bred disputes over words. Although people believed that they governed their words, the latter shot back at them like the Tartar's bow, entangling and perverting the judgment of even the wisest.[131]

The *Advancement*'s account of these three classes of fallacies as major sources of human misconception and irrationality is the germ of the fuller, definitive treatment of them Bacon later included in *The New Organon*. Summarizing his view of them in the former work, he admitted that man's understanding could never be entirely free of their effects, as they were inseparable from human nature. By identifying them, however, he felt he had provided cautions against them "which doth extremely import the true conduct of human judgment."[132]

At the conclusion of his discussion of philosophy, he expressed high hopes for the future of knowledge. Persuaded that recent developments like the art of printing favored the progress of truth, he predicted that his own era would surpass that of Greece and Rome in learning. Of his own personal contribution he offered only a modest estimate, comparing it to the sounds musicians make when tuning their instruments in order to play sweet music afterward. So likewise he had been content "to tune the instruments of the muses" for others who could play better.[133] This appraisal of himself as one who undertakes the preliminary labor in behalf of those to come was a standard trope that he frequently used to define his relationship to the project of reconstructing knowledge that he had at heart.

BACON AND CLASSICAL MYTH

Among the parts of knowledge surveyed in *The Advancement of Learning* was "poesy," in which Bacon distinguished a type of "allusive" or "parabolical" poetry, one of whose uses was to veil the mysteries of religion, policy, or philosophy in parables or fables.[134] These remarks foreshadowed his publication in 1609 of *The Wisdom of the Ancients* (*De Sapientia Veterum*), an interpretation of the allegorical meaning of thirty-one classical myths that included among its different subjects an exposition of aspects of his natural philosophy. Written in Latin, this was the first of his books to gain him a European reputation. It was popular enough to be reprinted during his lifetime and to be translated into English and Italian.[135] Its dedications to his cousin the earl of Salisbury and his alma mater Cambridge University emphasized that it was a work of philosophy whose aim was to provide some help toward the difficulties of life and the secrets of the sciences.[136] *The Wisdom of the Ancients* was another of Bacon's experiments in the presentation of his ideas to make them acceptable to his audience.[137] In choosing myth interpretation as a vehicle for this purpose, he was operating in a venerable tradition. Since the time of the Greeks, philosophers and literary men had sought for hidden meanings in the myths of pagan antiquity. Plato had charmed his readers by his use of myths to expound some of his teachings. Dante, Boccaccio, Chaucer, and other medieval authors turned them into moral and religious allegories. The fifteenth-century Platonist Giovanni Pico della Mirandola was merely one of many Renaissance thinkers and men of letters who believed that pagan myths contained esoteric Christian truths and divine mysteries cast in obscure form to prevent their profanation by the vulgar. Numerous handbooks of mythology appeared during the era of the Renaissance, which related and commented on the stories of the gods and supernatural beings of Greco-Roman religion and literature. One of the most popular, which served Bacon as an important source, was *Mythologiae* (1551) by Natalis Comes. Comes regarded all of these stories as philosophy presented in the guise of fables. He shared the widespread opinion that philosophy began as a primitive wisdom that came to Greece from Egypt, where it had originated with Egyptian priests who, to keep their knowledge of sacred doctrines secret from the multitude, allowed it to be transmitted in the form of myths.[138]

Bacon demonstrated the suppleness of his mind and the creativeness of his imagination in the artistry with which he depicted the allegorical meaning of some of the great classical myths. What is uncertain, though, is how he regarded these myths. Did he consider them to be authentic repositories of a primordial wisdom or rather an appealing device for propagating his own doctrines? Referring to these stories in *The Advancement of Learning*, he suggested that the fables came first, while the morals perceived in them were a later accretion. Nevertheless, he left open the question as to whether the fables and fictions of the poets were designed only for pleasure or as symbols possessing a further hidden import. Discussing the subject again four years later in the preface to *The Wisdom of the Ancients*, he noted how pliant fables could be in yielding whatever meaning one wished to draw from them. Despite this reservation, however, he advanced the opinion that the fables of the ancient poets contained "from their very beginning a mystery and an allegory"; and though conceding that he might be enthralled by reverence for the primitive age, he said he could not help believing that the meaning of these stories had been designed and intended from the first.[139]

Bacon's earlier writings thus proposed two alternative theories of pagan myths. One was skeptical or noncommittal respecting their original allegorical significance. The other credited them with containing profound truths that their ancient authors purposely concealed in parables or fables. In an effort to account for this difference, Paolo Rossi argued in his study of Bacon's thought that the latter changed his view of the classical myths, replacing the skeptical position taken in *The Advancement of Learning* with a firm belief in their original allegorical character in *The Wisdom of the Ancients*.[140] Such a shift of attitude, for which no clear evidence exists, appears to me improbable. A more likely explanation of the difference is that in *The Wisdom of the Ancients*, Bacon professed his faith in the original truth of myths in order to add credibility to his own interpretation of these stories. An unnoticed proof of his continuing skepticism is the statement I have previously quoted from the preface to this work in which he speaks of his "reverence for primitive antiquity" ("captus veneratione prisci seculi").[141] That this sentiment could not have been sincere is evident; for we know how strongly he believed that reverence for antiquity was one of the greatest obstacles to the progress of knowledge; and we know, too, that he often depreciated the Greeks for their ignorance of both nature and history. In *The Refutation of Philosophies* he also refers with considerable skepticism to the idea that the fables of the poets contained a hidden knowledge dating back to remote ages.[142] *The Wisdom of the Ancients* should most probably be read, therefore, as an ingenious literary exercise in which, by adopting the view that the ancient myths were profound allegories, he sought to expound and recommend his own philosophy. He himself actually allowed for the possibility of this interpretation by stating in his preface to the work that even if one wished to believe that the fables were made for no definite purpose other than pleasure, they would still be useful "as a method of teaching, whereby inventions that are new and abstruse and remote from vulgar opinions may find an easier passage to the understanding."[143]

The pattern Bacon followed in *The Wisdom of the Ancients* was first to tell the story of each myth and then explain its meaning. The myths pertaining to natural philosophy embraced a number of themes. In "Pan," one of the longest, the god Pan is construed as representing universal nature. His sisters were the Fates, who stand for the chain of natural causation drawing all things after it. He is hairy as an allusion to the rays that all bodies emit, his beard having the longest hair because the rays of celestial bodies operate from the greatest distance. He was the god of hunters, and when Ceres successfully hid herself from the other gods, it was he who found her, an indication that the discovery of things like grain which are useful to life should be expected not from abstruse philosophies but from wise experience and universal knowledge of things. Pan married the nymph Echo, who was alone fitted to be the world's wife, since true philosophy faithfully echoes the world and is written at the world's own dictation.[144] In "Orpheus," another allegory about philosophy, Orpheus's singing to propitiate the infernal powers in order to regain his wife from Hades is taken to signify the work of natural philosophy in restoring everything corruptible and conserving bodies in their existing state. This can be effected only by the exquisite adjustment of the parts of nature to produce a state analogous to the harmony and perfect modulation of Orpheus's lyre.[145]

Bacon made the fable of Cupid into a figurative expression of his belief in atomism and materialism. Cupid was Love, the oldest of the gods, who stands for the natural motion of the atom, the unique force that constitutes all things out of matter. Just as he had no parent, so the atom, similarly, has no cause, its motion being, next to God, the cause of causes that brings the particles of matter together to produce all the variety of nature. Cupid is pictured naked as a sign of the nakedness of the primary particles of things, in contrast to compounds, which can be considered as masked and clothed. He is a child because atoms, the seeds of all things, are tiny and remain in perpetual infancy. His attribute of archery points to the atom's virtue of acting at a distance, which is like the shooting of an arrow.[146]

The story of Proteus furnished another allegory of materialism as well as an indirect reference to experiment. In Bacon's exposition, the old herdsman and prophet Proteus, who knows the past, present, and future, represents matter, the most ancient of all things except for God. Like Proteus in his changeableness, matter will transform itself into strange bodies if any skillful servant of nature should vex and drive it to extremes.[147]

The longest myth in *The Wisdom of the Ancients* was that of Prometheus, which Bacon recounted as an allegory of mankind's position in the universe and the advance of science. Prometheus created man from a mixture of clay and the parts of different animals and brought him the gift of fire. He thus symbolizes Providence, whose special work is man, the center of the world and composite of all things. Later on men fell to complaining to Jupiter against both Prometheus and fire. Jupiter approved their action, however, as it showed that they were not satisfied with their condition or their own nature. Bacon could have been describing himself in his comment that those who abound in complaints about nature and the arts are much more useful and modest than those who are complacent about what they possess and believe that the sciences are perfect, for it is the former who are perpetually stimulated to new discoveries. The fable's moral, criticizing complacency in regard to knowledge, afforded him an occasion for repeating one of his frequent sayings that "opinion of plenty is one of the greatest causes of want" ("opinionem copiae inter maximas causas inopiae reponi"). In Prometheus's crime of attempting the chastity of Minerva, Bacon discerned a symbol of the offense of transgressing the boundary separating the senses from faith and of failing to distinguish between things divine and human, thereby begetting a heretical religion and a fabulous philosophy. The relay race of burning torches instituted in Prometheus's honor alludes to the perfection of the arts and sciences, which comes not from the swiftness of any single person but from a succession of inquirers.[148]

Touching the arts and nature, Bacon derived a lesson from the myth of Atalanta. Despite her superior speed, she lost her race against her suitor Hippomenes, who craftily diverted her from her course by casting golden apples along the way that she paused to pick up. This shows that though art in the person of Atalanta is far swifter than nature in accomplishing its ends, it commonly fails to reach them because it turns aside from its legitimate course owing to a desire for profit and lucre. Hence art has failed to outstrip nature and remains subject to her like the wife to the husband.[149] With regard to the arts, Bacon also took note of their misuse in his interpretation of the myth of Daedalus, the great artificer who devised, along with many wonderful works, a number of wicked inventions such as the labyrinth of the cruel Minotaur. Although human life was greatly indebted to the arts, from them had likewise come instruments of death such as poisons, guns, and other engines of destruction. Bacon's conclusion, however, was that the mechanical arts could be made to serve for good as well as harm and were powerful enough "for the most part to dissolve their own spell."[150]

Bacon used the famous myth of the sphinx to set forth an image of science. Like the sphinx, which was the wonder of the ignorant, science could be called a monster, many-shaped in allusion to the variety of matter it encompasses. It, too, has wings, because its discoveries fly quickly around the world. Its sharp claws are its arguments and axioms, which grip the mind and will not release it. It is lofty and sublime, placed on a mountaintop from whence it looks down upon ignorance. As the sphinx did, it poses hard questions and riddles about man and nature. The reward for solving these riddles is power: in the case of nature, command over bodies, medicines, mechanical forces, and infinite other things, which is the proper end of a true natural philosophy.[151]

Although Bacon owed some of the elements of his interpretations to previous mythographers like Natalis Comes, he retold all of these tales in his own original fashion, felicitously extracting from them metaphors and symbols of his concepts of nature and science. The classical myths attracted him strongly as a medium for rendering philosophy more vivid and approachable. He introduced several of the same fables again in the longer Latin edition of *The Advancement of Learning* as well as in a late uncompleted work in Latin that reiterated his praise of Democritus and the pre-Socratics, his fundamental naturalism, and his commitment to materialism.[152] *The Wisdom of the Ancients* was the ingenious creation of a thinker-artist who used these myths as a means of placing literature in the service of philosophy.

3

The Great Instauration

*T*he *Great Instauration* (*Instauratio Magna*), published in 1620, represented the culmination of Bacon's efforts to achieve a decisive advance in man's knowledge of nature through the renewal and reconstruction of philosophy. Included in the same volume with it as a separate work was the *The New Organon* (*Novum Organum*), his most important treatise on the theory of science and the investigation of nature. *The Great Instauration* was dedicated to James I, for whose assistance in furthering the advancement of philosophy Bacon again appealed. In a brief section entitled "Plan of the Work," he made public for the first time the full scope of his project. As he summarized its contents, *The Great Instauration* was to contain six parts:

1. a survey of the divisions of the sciences and the existing state of knowledge;

2. a description of the new logic of discovery to make possible the true interpretation of nature and the attainment of works;

3. a natural history embracing the phenomena of the universe to supply the materials and foundation for philosophy;

4. a "ladder of the intellect" furnishing examples of inquiry and invention in order to illustrate the application of the Baconian method;

5. an account, for temporary purposes only, of the discoveries Bacon himself had made, not according to the rules of his method but merely through the ordinary use of the understanding; these discoveries he called "forerunners or anticipations," and as they were

not obtained by means of the true kind of interpretation, he was careful to state that he did not hold himself committed to them;

6. finally, as the most important part to which all the others were subordinate, an exposition of the new philosophy as established by inquiry, in which the twins of human knowledge and power would truly meet in one ("Itaque intentiones geminae illae, scilicet Scientiae et Potentiae, vere idem in coincidunt"). Of this last part Bacon said that its completion exceeded both his strength and his hopes, but that he had made a beginning toward its ultimate achievement.[1]

Conceived on a vast scale, *The Great Instauration* remained an unrealized dream, as was indeed inevitable. *The New Organon,* published with it, was designed to be its second part. The first part on the division of the sciences was declared lacking in the original 1620 volume, but in 1623 Bacon issued *De Dignitate et Augmentis Scientiarum,* the expanded Latin version of *The Advancement of Learning,* to fill the gap. Appended to the 1620 edition of *The New Organon* was a short work, *A Preparative towards a Natural and Experimental History (Parasceve ad Historiam Naturalem et Experimentalem),* which was meant to serve as a contribution to the third part on natural history. In addition, before his death Bacon published several other treatises related to this part, and he also left some fragments of works pertaining to other parts. Besides the last part, however, which he called beyond his power, parts 3, 4, and 5 were never brought near completion. *The Great Instauration* thus survives in truncated form, its plan a monument to the far-flung intellectual vision and ambition inspiring Bacon's project.[2] Yet in spite of this failure, what he succeeded in accomplishing toward it, especially in *The New Organon,* fully merited the encomium the poet Abraham Cowley bestowed upon him later in the century in a verse epistle to the Royal Society. Cowley hailed him as the liberator of philosophy who, like Moses,

> led us forth at last;
> The barren wilderness he pass'd,
> Did on the very border stand
> Of the bless'd Promis'd Land,
> And from the mountain top of his exalted wit,
> Saw it himself, and shew'd us it.

The Great Instauration, a very short and purely programmatic work
serving as a prelude to the accompanying *The New Organon,* reiterated
a number of the major themes from his earlier writings: his claim of
the unique and solitary character of his project, which no one had
attempted before; his criticism of the stagnation of the sciences; his
hope of restoring the commerce of man's mind with things to its
original and perfect condition, if possible; his aim of achieving the
regeneration of the sciences by the introduction of a superior
method of investigating nature; his belief that he has established a
true and lasting marriage between the empirical and rational faculties; his avowal that the true end of knowledge is the benefit of human
life and that the increase of natural light poses no threat to religion;
his conviction that he strives by his labors to lay the foundation not of
any sect or doctrine but of human utility and greatness.[3]

Pervading *The Great Instauration* and *The New Organon* is a very
marked consciousness of innovation and modernity. It was, of course,
not unusual for authors of Bacon's time to speak of newness in connection with their scientific work. Noteworthy examples are Kepler's
Astronomia Nova of 1609; Galileo's *Discorsi e demonstrazioni mathemati-
che intorno a due nuove scienze* of 1638; and Pascal's *Expériences nouvelles
touchant la vide* of 1647.[4] In *The Great Instauration* and *The New Organon,* however, an awareness of novelty and of opening an entirely
untraveled road for the human mind is exceptionally strong. The
Latin noun, "instauratio" and its related verb "instauro" meant both
renewal and restoration. In the Vulgate Bible, the term occurs in connection with the repair and rebuilding of the house of the Lord. It
may well be that in using this word, Bacon was implying an analogy
between his own project and the renovation of Solomon's temple.[5] In
the conception of his work as a great instauration, the motif of innovation is much more prominent than that of restoration. The proemium of *The Great Instauration* declares that in view of the previous
record of man's failure in the inquisition of nature, it was necessary
to begin anew on a better plan and attempt the total reconstruction
of the sciences, arts, and human knowledge. Again, in the preface
Bacon says that a way must be opened for the human mind altogether
different from any yet known.[6] The title of *Novum Organum* or *The
New Organon* also speaks for itself. "Organum," Latinized from the

Greek *órganon*, signifies an instrument, engine, or tool; the *Organon* was likewise the title given to that portion of Aristotle's philosophy comprising his six treatises on logic. By calling his own book *The New Organon*, Bacon was implicitly claiming to have superseded the old Aristotelian logic with his new instrument or method of investigating nature. The Italian scholar Marta Fattori, who has compiled a lexicon of *Novum Organum*, has found that the word "novus" (new) occurs in its pages 109 times. It is used in a strong sense and linked to "inventio" or the discovery of new works and sciences.[7] The consciousness of the modern and of bringing forth the new is also closely associated in *The New Organon* with Bacon's opposition to reverence for the ancients and his belief in the progress of knowledge. In a paradoxical reversal of language, he argues, as he had also done in earlier writings, that the old age of the world is the true antiquity and that the latter attribute therefore belongs to the present rather than to the ancient world. The present is accordingly riper in experience and knowledge; and as truth is the daughter of time, so it is necessary to throw off the enchantments of authority and antiquity that have held mankind back from progress in the sciences ("a progressu in scientiis detinuit").[8] *The Great Instauration* and *The New Organon* as its centerpiece must therefore be regarded as foretelling the advent of a new era in humanity's intellectual evolution in which Bacon's new logic of discovery would lead to "the command of nature in action" and the unity of human knowledge and power in the production of works.[9]

THE KINGDOM OF MAN, THE CRITIQUE OF DOCTRINES, THE PURGING AND PREPARATION OF THE MIND

The New Organon is a synthesis and further development of Bacon's earlier thoughts and a presentation of his method of discovery by induction. As his description of the second part of *The Great Instauration* states, it exhibits "the art of interpreting nature and of the truer operation of the intellect."[10] Although he says there that his method is equally adaptable to all sciences, including even ethics, politics, and various mental operations, *The New Organon* deals entirely with its application to natural philosophy.[11] Divided into two books, the treatise is written as a series of aphorisms, a form of expression whose virtues Bacon had extolled in *The Advancement of Learning* as especially suited to the delivery of knowledge by reason of its requirement of depth and also because its broken, disjunctive character invited further inquiry rather than mere acceptance.[12] *The New Organon* is not totally aphoristic, however; while it contains many observations that stand out by their compressed force, some of its discussions tend to become quite discursive.

The two books of which *The New Organon* consists both bear the title, "Aphorisms concerning the Interpretation of Nature and the Kingdom of Man." Despite its dramatic import, the latter phrase, which now appears for the first time in Bacon's writings, has been generally ignored by students of his work.[13] It is of the utmost significance, however, as a symbol of the basic orientation of his thought.

What did he mean by the kingdom of man? In their context, these words seem to allude to the *entrance* to the kingdom of man and signify that his reconstruction of philosophy constitutes this entrance. What they point to is the prospect of using scientific knowledge for the vast amelioration of humanity's condition to the extent of making the world the kingdom of man. In the religious society to which Bacon belonged, they could not help also standing in tacit contrast to the kingdom of God in which the faithful Christian placed his ultimate hope. Without in the least detracting from the object of this hope, Bacon was positing alongside of it another kingdom, that of life on this earth of which man would be the sovereign. Indeed, in one place he even goes so far as to liken "the entrance into the kingdom of man, founded on the sciences," to the entrance into the kingdom of heaven.[14]

Bound up with the concept of the kingdom of man is the image of man *The New Organon* projects. Man is seen in it as both a knowing and an active subject who investigates nature in order to master it. The first aphorism of the work depicts man as at once "the servant and interpreter of nature," who "can do and understand so much and so much only as he has observed in thought or fact of the course of nature. . . ."[15] The human understanding must therefore conform to nature's course or laws in order to control it. In this relationship obedience and domination are totally intertwined; hence Bacon never tires of insisting that "nature to be commanded must be obeyed" ("Natura enim non nisi parendo vincitur"). Only in this way can "human knowledge and human power meet in one."[16] To release man's potential to achieve the union of knowledge and power is the supreme object of Bacon's philosophy, and this, when achieved, would be synonymous with the kingdom of man.

The first book of *The New Organon* is occupied chiefly with the criticism of reigning philosophical doctrines and systems. It also includes an extended discussion of the idols of the mind and frequent comments on the defects of current methods of inquiry and their causes. All this serves as an introduction to the exposition in the second book of the new method of discovery. Bacon considers this prior critique therapeutically essential. It represents a necessary "purging" of the understanding to render the latter "cleansed" and receptively prepared for the discussion to follow.[17] He nonetheless denies any wish to destroy the existing philosophy, arts, and sciences. These, he grants, have their function in supplying material for disputations and ornaments for discourse, and they should continue to be used for this purpose.[18] With this condescending judgment, professing compromise and coexistence, he defines the relationship between his own philosophy and the one then current that he was proposing to supersede.

A materialist and a realist in the modern, philosophical meaning of the term, Bacon had no doubt that the world and nature existed independently of the mind. It followed that thought and language must give a true representation of the world if they are to qualify as knowledge. Some such assumption, implying a correspondence theory of truth, underlay his unfavorable opinion of the current logic. The preface to *The Great Instauration* reiterated his oft-expressed belief that this logic, though properly applied to civil business and the arts dependent on discourse and opinion, lacked the subtlety needed for dealing with nature. In the plan of the instauration he criticized logicians for relying on the syllogism and neglecting induction, the only way to penetrate nature.[19] *The New Organon* amplified this objection by focusing upon the inability of the logic then in use—which was, of course, Aristotle's—to make scientific discoveries or invent new sciences.[20] Enumerating what he diagnosed as the syllogism's flaws, he pointed out that it was never applied to the first principles of the sciences, which it simply accepted as given, with the result that both these principles and the intermediate axioms deduced from them remained uncertain. Moreover, its propositions were too hastily abstracted from facts or things and based merely on common ideas ("notiones") that were no match for the subtlety of nature. Hence, while the syllogism might compel assent to a proposition, it failed to grasp or master things. More specifically, he argued that fundamental logical and physical concepts employed in the syllogism, like substance, quality, act, and essence, or heavy, light, dense, rare, element, matter, form, and others, were all unsound and ill defined.[21] Besides the faults of the syllogism, he blamed the existing mode of inquiry for its habitual practice of jumping at once from the senses and particulars to the most general axioms. The right way, on the other hand, thus far untried, would be to derive axioms from sense perception and particular facts in a gradual ascent, arriving at the most general axioms last of all.[22]

By axiom ("axioma") Bacon here and elsewhere appears to mean any kind of general proposition, whether constative, causal and explanatory, or predictive.[23] One of his requirements in scientific investigation as an alternative to the verbalism and futility he imputed to the syllogism was that empirically well confirmed lower-level generalizations should precede and provide the foundation for higher-level ones. The "manner of discovery and proof," he stated, "according to which the most general principles are first established, and then intermediate axioms . . . tried and proved by them, is the mother of error and curse of all the sciences."[24] He likewise maintained that the axioms current in natural philosophy were based on limited experience and a small number of particulars and simply framed in such a way as to cover the latter. If a contrary instance should then come to light, the usual response was to preserve the axiom by some frivolous distinction, whereas the proper procedure would have been to correct the axiom itself.[25] Bacon termed the practice of hasty, premature generalization from a few familiar instances "anticipations of nature." Just because they gained assent so easily, anticipations prevented scientific progress, and he distinguished them from the "interpretation of nature," whose axioms were methodically gathered from many varied facts.[26]

Remarks like some of those above may make it seem that in his insistence on a systematic, critical empiricism as the foundation of axioms, Bacon overlooked the importance of theories and hypotheses in the guidance of scientific inquiry and ignored the need for a principle of selection in the collection of particular facts. As I shall point out further on, however, this impression would be quite misleading; for when his strictures against the prevailing methods of natural philosophy are viewed in the full context of his procedural precepts and observations in *The New Organon*, it will be seen that he recognized the place of theories in the practice of science.

When he looked at the received systems of philosophy, Bacon reiterated the disparaging assessment of his preceding works. Only a small number of the older Greek thinkers like Anaxagoras, Leucippus, and Democritus won his praise for their rigorous pursuit of the knowledge of nature.[27] To the skeptics' despair of the senses and doubts of the possibility of attaining truth, he gave a short dismissal. Contrasting his own approach with theirs, he explained that his aim was not to destroy the authority of the senses and understanding, but to equip them with helps for overcoming error.[28] Of the Greeks, to whom mankind owed most of its science, he commented that they were greatly given to disputations, a type of activity most adverse to the search for truth. Plato and Aristotle resembled the Sophists in making philosophy disputatious and a subject for contending sects. Aristotle, seeking to provide answers to every question and reign supreme over all other philosophers, corrupted natural philosophy with his logic, introduced many false views and pointless distinctions, and bent experience into conformity with his preconceptions instead of investigating the truth of things. Pythagoras, Plato, and other writers mixed philosophy with superstition and theology through doctrines such as abstract forms and final and first causes. In any case, the Greeks in general knew little of history or the different parts of the world. They were ignorant of the existence of innumerable nations in climates and regions they imagined uninhabitable. In comparison with them, the modern age possessed a far greater knowledge of the globe and an infinite stock of experience. Bacon's conclusion from all these reflections was that nothing great could be expected from the existing schools of philosophy.[29]

The high point of the first book of *The New Organon* is its analysis of the idols of the mind, an endeavor to uncover the deep-seated causes of misconception and irrationality that bar the way to truth. This was a larger, more fully developed treatment of a subject Bacon had discussed in several of his previous writings, notably in *The Advancement of Learning*. His Latin term, "idola," from the Greek *eídola*, did not mean false gods but phantoms, fictions, fallacies, delusive images, and what he called false ideas ("notiones falsae").[30] His examination of the idols stands out as his most significant and original contribution to the philosophy of mind, with little if any precedent in the work of prior thinkers. In a comparison with Aristotle, he explained that the doctrine of the idols was to the interpretation of nature what Aristotle's refutation of sophisms was to ordinary logic.[31] Whereas the latter's *Sophistical Refutations* dealt purely with logical fallacies, however, Bacon's discussion extended far more widely to the different mental, psychological, and socially engendered dispositions and naive beliefs responsible for systematic distortion and error.

He named four classes of idols that beset the mind.

1. Idols of the tribe ("idola tribus"): these were founded in human nature itself, being common to the whole human race, and caused men to regard the universe according to their own measure and as an analogy to themselves.

2. Idols of the cave ("idola specus"): these were the errors peculiar to the individual, each of whom dwells in his own cave, arising from his own personal traits, rearing, and variety of impressions.

3. Idols of the marketplace ("idola fori"): these were the misconceptions bred of human intercourse and the use of language, whose confusions generated innumerable sterile controversies and vain fancies.

4. Finally, idols of the theater ("idola theatri"): these were the offspring of the false dogmas of philosophers, false demonstrations in logic, and false principles and axioms in the sciences, which, like stage plays, generated fictions and unreal worlds.[32]

He next went on to describe the effects of the idols. Regarding those of the tribe, he pointed to the many errors to which the human understanding is innately prone. Such is its supposition of greater order and regularity in nature than can actually be found; its perception of fictitious analogies and parallels, despite the many phenomena in nature that are singular and distinctive; its tendency, once an opinion has been formed, to adhere to it in the face of contrary evidence with the help of continual rationalizations; its attraction to affirmative instances in preference to negative ones, even though the negative instance has the greater force in the establishment of axioms; its disposition, because of the mind's restlessness in always seeking something prior in the order of nature, to fall back upon final causes that, however satisfying to human nature, have no relation to the universe.[33]

All these errors were traceable to the inveterate anthropocentrism with which human beings project onto nature and the world the patterns of their own instinctual thinking. Bacon carried his analysis further, however, in the observation that the intellect, far from being a "dry light," is strongly affected by the will and passions. The consequence is the creation of "wishful sciences" ("ad quod vult scientias"), for what someone wishes were true he is also much more ready to believe. Moreover, the passions infect the understanding in ways that are innumerable and often imperceptible.[34] Another trait of the intellect is its inclination to reify abstractions by attributing substance and reality to things in flux. Rather than inventing abstractions about nature, however, Bacon maintains that it would be better to dissect it, a task that requires the study of matter in its configurations and laws of motion and action.[35] In this revealing comment he underscores his methodological commitment to the principle of analysis and the reduction and separation of bodies and phenomena into their smallest constituent elements as the royal road to scientific knowledge. But of all the aberrations due to the idols of the tribe, he emphasizes that the greatest result from the dullness and deceptions of the senses, which are weak and erring when left to themselves. On this account, many subtle things fail to strike the senses, like the imperceptible changes in the parts of substances or the working of spirits enclosed in tangible bodies. He observes, however, that a truer interpretation of nature could be obtained with the help of appropriate instances and experiments, for in these the senses would judge only the experiment, while the latter would determine the point of nature in respect to things themselves.[36]

Turning next to the idols of the cave, he mentioned several examples of peculiarities due to the individual that led the mind astray. Some people become attached to particular sciences and speculations that they mix with their own fancies. Thus Aristotle enslaved natural philosophy to his logic and the chemists invented a philosophy based on a few experiments. There are likewise those who are better at noticing the differences between things, which they carry to excess, and others who are guilty of the same excess in the perception of resemblances. Similarly, some minds feel an extreme admiration for antiquity, others an extreme love of novelty, both of which attitudes are injurious to the sciences. As an antidote to these idols, Bacon proposed the salutary rule that every student of nature should be especially suspicious of anything his mind seizes upon and embraces with satisfaction.[37]

The most troublesome of the idols, according to Bacon, was the third kind, those of the marketplace, the product of the duplicities of language. Generally framed to the capacities of the vulgar, words fail to follow the true lines and divisions of nature. Learned men engage in empty disputes over words and names, and even definitions of natural and material objects cannot cure this evil, since they, too, consist of words that beget other words. Names deceive by naming things that do not exist, like Fortune, Prime Mover, Planetary Spheres, and similar fictions. In the case of names of things that do exist, they are often confused and ill defined owing to inept abstraction. Hence a word like "humid" is applied to very different things in different senses, so that in one sense fire can be humid, in another sense dust, and in still another sense glass. While one might remove misconceptions arising from the names of fictitious things simply by rejecting the false theories on which they are based, Bacon thought that there were other confusions caused by the misuse of names that were more deeply rooted and much harder to expel.[38]

The last class of idols, those of the theater, came into the mind from false systems of philosophy and bad rules of demonstration. Whether these philosophies belong to the Rational school, which brings meditation and ingenuity of wit to bear on a small amount of uncritically accepted experience; or to the Empirical school, which builds whole systems on the slender basis of a few experiments; or to the Superstitious school, which mingles theology with philosophy to the detriment of each, all of them are strongholds of these idols of the theater.[39] No less so are the vicious demonstrations used in logic and the sciences in passing from the senses and things to axioms and conclusions. Bacon noted their failure to correct the faults and deceptions of the senses; their use of confused, indefinite notions ill drawn from the senses; their reliance on a bad kind of induction that uncritically posits principles of the sciences through simple enumeration without employing exclusions and solutions and separations of nature;[40] and finally, their mode of discovery and proof whereby they first establish the most general principles and then deduce and prove lesser axioms by them. He promised a fuller discussion of this subject in the second book but does point out that experience is by far the best demonstration and that the current methods of experiment are very poor and thus incapable of leading to the discovery of true causes and axioms.[41]

In scrutinizing the idols of the theater, Bacon had said in passing that his own method ("ratio") of discovery tended to equalize all intellects, leaving little to differences in strength and acuteness of mind; and he compared it to drawing a perfect circle or a straight line with a compass or a ruler, which was easy to do, as against drawing them by hand, which demanded great steadiness and practice.[42] It is hard to see why he should have made such an implausible claim, unless perhaps to gain support for his project. His statement indicated in any case how much he tended to underestimate the difficulties of scientific advance. At times it would appear that he regarded his method as a recipe almost anyone could apply successfully irrespective of ability.

In *The New Organon* Bacon spoke of the idols as fallacies to be renounced and purged. He does not convey any sense in this work that some of them might be inexpugnable.[43] Nowhere does he belong more surely among the inaugurators of the scientific revolution than in his examination of the idols. His critique of the failures and aberrations of intelligence under their sway is one of the foremost reflections of his and his philosophic successors' effort to clear the way for the ascendancy of scientific reason. On one of the most famous etchings of his *Caprichos*, Goya inscribed the motto "The sleep of reason breeds monsters."[44] The monsters Bacon attacked in the idols were not only indigenous traits of the mind; they were animism, anthropocentrism and anthropomorphism, unreal abstract entities, and human delusions and wish projections that make the cosmos a reflection of their own image and desires. While he wished to equip the mind to master nature, he sought at the same time to separate the mind from its naive, spontaneous operations, to assist it to overcome its prejudiced suppositions and beliefs, and to gain for it an objective rationality, an impersonal standpoint, as an essential prerequisite for the advancement of knowledge.

Still engaged in the task of purgation, *The New Organon* devoted the rest of its first book to a discussion of the signs and causes of bad philosophy and poor science, interspersed with comments on the character and promise of a new method in natural philosophy. Most of this material is carried over, occasionally verbatim, from earlier writings. Among the signs of bad philosophy, observable in nearly all the Greek thinkers and their heirs, was the failure to produce works for human benefit, works or fruit being the most certain and noble evidence of truth. Another sign was lack of progress, for while things founded in nature grow, bad philosophy merely varies in opinion without advancing. Still another was the complaints by philosophers of the subtlety and obscurity of nature, by which they made their own inability in discovery a calumny upon nature.[45]

Bacon offered a broad historical and sociological explanation of the causes for the retardation of philosophy and the sciences. It is doubtful whether any other contemporary thinker could have matched the scope and sophistication of his account of why the knowledge of nature had failed to progress. The causes he cited included the influence of Christianity, which for centuries had led the best minds to neglect natural philosophy for theology and religious controversies; ignorance that the true goal of the sciences was the endowment of human life with new discoveries and powers, and lack of a method to attain this goal; disdain for experiments as illiberal and an impairment of the dignity of the human mind; reverence for antiquity and complacency about discoveries already made, although nearly all were old; superstition and blind religious zeal, ever the enemies of natural philosophy, plus clerical fears that a deeper investigation of nature would be a profanation of sacred mysteries; the character of schools and universities, which discouraged all departures from conventional learning and denounced any dissent from approved authors. But beyond these causes, the one to which he accorded the greatest weight was that "men despair and think things impossible" when they reflect on the obscurity of nature, the deceits of the senses, the infirmities of judgment, the difficulties of experiments, and the brevity of life.[46]

To counter the arguments of despair, he proffered arguments of hope through the rectification of past errors. It was a hope that lay entirely in the rebirth of the sciences, which meant building them afresh on the basis of regularly ordered experience.[47] This new kind of science capable of progress would consist of features he had often discussed. It would combine the rational and experimental faculties and rest on what he called "learned experience" ("experientia literata"), a comprehensive, carefully ascertained natural history of both natural species and the mechanical arts, arranged in tables of discovery to facilitate inquiries into particular subjects. It would perform many experiments, giving priority to experiments of light, which serve to discover causes and axioms, rather than experiments of fruit.[48] In order to establish axioms, it would need a different form of induction from any previously employed: one that would discover and prove first principles and all middle and lesser axioms, as well as analyze nature by a process of elimination that took account of a sufficient number of negative instances before coming to a conclusion on affirmative instances. Bacon claimed that this kind of induction presented the greatest hope, although he conceded that its achievement would be hard and demand more labor than had ever been expended on the syllogism. A point of special significance concerning the establishment of axioms by induction was his

requirement that they must extend beyond the particulars from
which they were derived; they should be "wider and larger," he stipu-
lated, so as to indicate new particulars that served to confirm them.[49]
This statement is one of a number suggesting quite clearly that
Bacon's understanding of an axiom included the concept of a theory
or hypothesis to be tested and corroborated by its prediction and
discovery of new facts and observations.

The New Organon's first book concluded with a further exposition of
the author's aims in the part still to come. The discussion included a
candid admission that the natural history and tables of discovery he
had produced thus far were not sufficiently copious or verified to
serve the purposes of a legitimate interpretation of nature. He felt
sure, nevertheless, that whatever errors they contained were small
and easily corrected.[50] He emphasized that he was in quest of the
causes of common things generally neglected, such as the causes of
weight, of the rotation of the heavenly bodies, of heat, cold, light,
hardness, softness, liquidity, solidity, and the like. To the objection
that his inquiries might appear unprofitably subtle, he replied that
first and foremost he wanted experiments of light, not fruit; by revealing the knowledge of simple natures, light or truth would draw whole
troops of works in its train and disclose the sources of the noblest
axioms.[51] Here and elsewhere it is noticeable how often Bacon found
in the image of light his best symbol for the beauty and value of
knowledge and truth. In a further aphorism he observed that in the
knowledge of nature "truth and utility are the very same things"
("Itaque ipsissimae res sunt . . . veritas et utilitas"), and that "works
themselves are of greater value as pledges of truth than as contributing to the comforts of life."[52] The linkage of truth to utility in this
statement should not create puzzlement about how Bacon understood the relationship between the two. He was neither a utilitarian
nor a precursor of utilitarianism. As he frequently stressed, the truth
in natural philosophy was also productive of works. In that sense truth
and utility were inseparably joined. Conceptually, however, they were
distinct. Thus he was generally consistent in holding that truth was
the primary value of scientific inquiry, which opened the way to operations, while the latter were among the evidences of truth. He repeated his belief in the primacy of truth in the next-to-last aphorism

in the first book. Just as the beholding of light was more excellent and beautiful than its many uses, "so assuredly the very contemplation of things as they are, without superstition or imposture, error or confusion, is itself more worthy than the fruit of all inventions."[53]

Truth and works, the increase of knowledge and the mastery of nature, were the twin poles within which Bacon's philosophy revolved. "I am building in the human understanding," he declared, "a true model of the world, such as it really is, not as man's reason would like it to be." He proposed to dispel "those foolish and apish images of the world" that men's fantasies had created in philosophical systems. Recounting how much European civilization owed to past invention and discovery, he avowed his ambition "(if ambition it can be called) to establish and extend the power and empire of the human race over the universe."[54] Yet at this point he paused to utter a significant caution: his recognition that his precepts were capable of improvement and that "the art of discovery may advance as discoveries advance."[55] It was thus not as the final or definitive word but as the inauguration of a new stage in an ongoing process of inquiry that he envisaged his personal contribution to philosophy.

THE INTERPRETATION OF NATURE: FORMS AND INDUCTION

The main subjects of *The New Organon*'s second book, which is nearly twice as long as the first, are forms and induction. It presents an explanation of forms as the key to the understanding and control of nature, and it demonstrates the true inductive method by applying it to the form of heat. Knowledge of forms gained by induction constitutes Bacon's art of the interpretation of nature. At the end of the work he said that his organon dealt with logic, not philosophy, its purpose being to teach how to dissect nature and discover the virtues and actions of bodies and their laws grounded in matter. From this we must understand that he was not professing to offer any actual discoveries in natural philosophy but intended his discussion as a manual of scientific procedure.[56] To fill out his account of induction, he also presented further directions for its use in investigating different phenomena in an elaborate treatment of what he described as "prerogative instances." According to a statement in book 2, *The New Organon* was also planned to include a number of additional topics as helps to induction and the interpretation of nature. These do not appear, however.[57] The work in its published form was not completed, therefore, coming to a sudden end with the close of the second book.

Before we approach the specifics of Bacon's ideas on the method of science and induction in *The New Organon*, a few preliminary remarks are necessary to remove several misunderstandings. While Bacon's reputation as a philosopher of science stood very high in the seventeenth and eighteenth centuries, and was still considerable during the Victorian era, it has declined greatly since then. Twentieth-century philosophers and scientists, who, of course, evaluate his methodological precepts in the light of their own theory of science, usually judge his work quite negatively, mainly because of their belief that the centrality he gave to induction reflected a deep misconception of how science operates. The dominant view among philosophers today is that reasoning in the natural sciences proceeds in accord with the hypothetico-deductive method, which consists of framing hypotheses inspired by empirical data, from which observational predictions and consequences are deduced that can be tested and falsified. Hypotheses that are successful in surviving tests and resisting falsification assume the status of accepted scientific propositions, theories, or laws subject to subsequent revision or even displacement. For allegedly failing to realize the crucial function of theories or hypotheses, and for mistakenly believing that the knowledge of nature advances by induction—systematic experiment, observation, the accumulation of facts and particular instances that generate axioms—Bacon is convicted of incomprehension of the true method of the natural sciences. This view of his errors has become something of a commonplace in the twentieth century and has been stated by various philosophers of science such as Morris R. Cohen, Bertrand Russell, Karl Popper, Peter Medawar, Mary Hesse, and others. The criticism of Popper, in particular, as the foremost modern opponent of inductivism in science, has been especially influential in helping to discredit Bacon as an antitheoretical inductivist.[58]

These adverse judgments rest in some cases on nothing more than a superficial acquaintance with Bacon's work. Thus, as other writers have shown and as will be made evident below, Popper was mistaken in supposing that the doctrine underlying the Baconian theory of induction was the primacy of the repetition of positive instances as the justification for the acceptance of a theory or universal law; for Bacon always rejected simple enumeration or repetition of instances as the basis of induction, insisting instead upon elimination and other refinements as prerequisites of an inductive conclusion.[59] Similarly, it is simply not true, as I have already remarked and will presently point out again, that he was ignorant of the need for theories and hypotheses in scientific research.[60]

In addition to these considerations, however, critics of the misconceptions and errors of Bacon's philosophy of science are often quite unhistorical in their failure to take account of the intellectual conditions in which his thought concerning the investigation of nature developed. In the sixteenth century, and before science had become institutionalized, there was not available to him any community of practicing scientists, any living, continuous tradition of successful scientific activity, nor any exemplary body of scientific research from which he might have drawn guidance for his reflections.[61] There was, of course, the discussion of scientific method in the writings of a number of philosophers at the University of Padua, such as Nifo and Zabarella, but either he did not know their work, since he never mentions it, or he regarded it rightly as an expression of the Aristotelianism to which he was opposed. Although he was acquainted with Galileo's discoveries with the telescope and explanation of the tides, and with his countryman William Gilbert's ingenious experiments with the magnet, he was critical of Gilbert's theories, and in any case, neither of these working scientists could have served him as a model.[62] In the main, Bacon, despite the extent of his reading and studies, worked quite alone in natural philosophy. Anyone who trawls through his correspondence will find little trace of profitable exchange with other thinkers interested in the natural sciences. His own writings on natural philosophy, moreover, received little helpful criticism or comments during his lifetime.

Again, with respect to induction, it is usually not realized how little he had to go on in attempting to improve it. Aristotle's logic had discussed induction or *epagogé* as a form of reasoning that involved the passage from particular judgments to a general or universal one. He devoted only a small amount of attention to it, though, allowing it much less importance than he gave to the syllogism and demonstration. It was not for him, moreover, a way of proceeding from the known to the unknown but rather, among other things, the means by which the mind could intuitively perceive or come to know a general proposition not attainable by demonstration through a process of abstraction from a number of particular instances or facts.[63] Medieval and Renaissance authors on logic did not extend induction beyond its limits in Aristotle's writings. Sixteenth-century dialectics, which was oriented toward rhetorical presentation and persuasion, treated induction solely as a means of imparting knowledge and as a form of argument establishing a general conclusion by the enumeration of particular cases. For Zabarella, on the other hand, who was one of the ablest students of Aristotelian logic, induction was inferior and ancillary to the syllogism, its main role being the collection of particulars in order to furnish a general principle that would serve in demonstration.[64] None of Bacon's predecessors or philosophical contemporaries conceived of induction as a research procedure and method of discovery that could add to the knowledge of nature. He was therefore forced to work out for himself, in connection with his critical empiricism, how the logic of induction could be reformed so as to serve as an instrument of progress in the natural sciences.

A further point concerning induction that unhistorical modern critics of Bacon's scientific method easily forget is that he knew of no reason to doubt the validity of induction in establishing the empirical generalizations and scientific axioms he desiderated in natural philosophy. He was not cognizant of the celebrated "problem of induction" that stemmed from the philosopher David Hume's skepticism about causation. From Hume's argument that belief in causation and the laws of nature had no better foundation than mere regular association or conjunction between singular past events from which no logical inference to necessary connection and universal propositions was possible, it followed that no valid conclusions about any causal or other necessary and invariant relationship between events or facts could ever be derived from inductive premises. This meant that observational evidence about the behavior of natural phenomena, even under controlled experimental conditions, provided no logical justification or proof of the truth of scientific theories, laws, and predictions. Hume's reasoning seemed to put the rationality of science in question and has been more responsible than any other factor for the influence of deductivism in the contemporary philosophy of science.[65] Unaware of the considerations Hume advanced, Bacon always believed in the reality of causal necessity and the efficacy of induction to yield certified general propositions and causal laws. He assumed that if based on critically tested evidence joined with successive elimination of negative instances, induction could generate the certain knowledge of forms that he equated with the laws of nature; and since he also constantly emphasized the importance of works in natural philosophy, he would have taken the ability of scientific axioms to lead to works as clear support and confirmation of their truth.

Bacon opened his second book with an analysis of form that at times is very obscure. I think it may be possible, though, to obtain at least an approximate idea of what he meant by form as the chief object of scientific inquiry and the essential means of manipulating nature.[66] He explained that he used the word because it was common and familiar.[67] It was indeed a term with a long history in Western thought, a portmanteau concept containing deposits of the metaphysics of Plato, Aristotle, and the medieval Scholastics. For all of these, form was related in some manner to causal agency as that which determined or constituted the distinctive being, nature, or ordered structure of different things. It might be, as it was for Plato, the supremely real eternal ideas or abstract universals defining the essence of fleeting sensible things; or it might be, as it was for Aristotle, the causal principle of individuation that imparts to unformed matter the different identities of which the multiplicity of things consists.[68] There can be no doubt that it was very largely from Aristotle that Bacon derived the conception of form as an essential part of scientific explanation.[69] His own understanding of form, however, was differentiated from that of his predecessors by his materialism, his adherence to a strict principle of physical explanation, and his consistent integration of form with the ability to carry out operations.

He began his discussion with the broad thesis that the task and purpose of human power is "to generate and superinduce a new nature or new natures on a given body," while the task and purpose of human knowledge is "to discover the form, or true specific difference, or nature-engendering nature, or source of emanation (for these are the terms that come nearest to a description of the thing) of a given nature." The successive phrases he included here as synonyms of form all serve to denote that form is what causes, structures, and defines the distinctive natures of which bodies consist.[70] In several subsequent aphorisms he identifies form with the physical cause or law governing the actions of individual bodies, and contrasts it with material and efficient causes. Whereas to know the latter, he points out, is to know only particular causes in particular substances, as, for instance, the cause of a nature like whiteness or heat in certain things, the knowledge of forms embraces the unity of nature in the most dissimilar substances. This makes it possible to do things never yet done, which the vicissitudes of neither nature, accident, nor laborious experiment could ever have achieved. The discovery of forms "therefore results in truth in contemplation and freedom in operations," in short, in the unity of knowledge and power.[71] Hidden in this thought, although beyond the author's ken, is the foreshadowing of inventions like electric light, engine-driven vehicles, the camera, telephone, radio, synthetic fibers and materials, electronic devices, and all the other innumerable productions of science and technology that never existed in nature but which are created from the knowledge of its laws, or what Bacon called forms, and their application to different properties.

Bacon then goes on to treat forms as identical with the rules of operation that act universally and with certainty of result in introducing any nature on a given body. A form and a given nature invariably imply each other, and the form is inherent in the nature. Thus when the form is present, so is the nature, and the converse is likewise the case.[72] This appears to suggest, in language other than Bacon's, that one of the meanings of form is that it is the necessary and sufficient cause of any nature; hence to discover the form of a particular nature is to discover the necessary and sufficient cause of the latter's production.[73] Most frequently he refers to forms as synonymous with the "fundamental," "universal," and "eternal laws of nature" ("naturae ... leges fundamentales et communes," "leges fundamentales et aeternas"). In his fullest formulation he says that "when I speak of forms, I understand nothing other than those laws and determinations of pure actuality, which govern and constitute any simple nature, such as heat, light, weight, in every kind of matter. . . . Thus the form of heat or the form of light is the same as the law of heat or the law of light" ("eadem res est forma calidi aut forma luminis et lex calidi sive lex luminis").[74] Principally, therefore, it would appear that form signifies the physical law that is the cause of any nature inhering in a body and that brings this nature into being. The knowledge of forms prescribes the rules and directions for an operative science by which natures can be freely and with certainty introduced into different bodies to join with other natures in new combinations. In this knowledge, joining truth and contemplation with action, lies the infinite possibility of works.[75]

The allusions in the foregoing passages to the laws of nature and of particular phenomena suggest that Bacon may have been among the earliest, if not the first, of Western philosophers to give to the concept of a law of nature the meaning it came to acquire in the natural sciences. When he refers to law in defining forms, it seems to be detached from any association with a divine lawgiver, providential design or oversight, or teleological purpose. Nor has it the normative character of the venerable idea of natural law as a permanent moral standard that was a legacy of ancient Stoicism to medieval thinkers and was thence transmitted to legal and political philosophers like Hooker and Grotius, who were Bacon's contemporaries. In *The Advancement of Learning* he had spoken of "the summary law of nature" as "the work which God worketh from the beginning to the end," and doubted that the human mind could know it.[76] Here the concept had seemed to combine the attributes of regularity in the realm of nature with God's supreme ordering of the universe. In *The New Organon*, however, the theistic background is missing, and the laws of nature are the physical laws, causes, and regularities grounded in matter and motion that describe and explain the structure and changes of bodies due to forms.[77]

While for Bacon forms are correlated with specific natures, he nowhere tells us what a nature is. In an earlier work, however, he distinguished "secondary" from "original," "radical," and "formative" natures,[78] while *The New Organon* often mentions "simple natures." Hence we may gather that a nature is a primary or ultimate physical property or quality that can combine with other such natures in particular bodies and that also defines the latter. Accordingly, he describes a body as "a troop or collection of simple natures"; and taking gold as an instance, he lists some of its simple natures as yellow, heaviness to a certain weight, ductility, fixity, fluidity, and so forth. One who knows the forms of these simple natures can superinduce them onto another body and transform it into gold. There is not the slightest hint in this example that he has alchemy in mind, though perhaps its ghost lurks somewhere in the background; he is thinking only of how an axiom of this kind can generate a substance identical with gold from the forms of its constituent natures.[79]

Bacon envisages two classes of axioms, one containing the basic and primary knowledge of the forms of simple natures, the other comprising axioms pertaining to what he called latent process and latent configuration. Latent process describes the manner in which simple natures interact to produce the innumerable compound bodies and effects found in the ordinary course of nature; it is what accounts for the generation of substances like the different minerals, plants, and animals, and of phenomena like nutrition and voluntary motion in animals and humans. Latent configuration describes the structure of simple natures in any compound body or phenomenon. He attached very great importance to the discovery of both of these, since "no one can endow a given body with a new nature, or . . . transmute it into a new body, unless he has attained a competent knowledge of the body so to be altered or transformed." He also emphasizes the extreme difficulty of such discovery, because, as their names imply, latent process and latent configuration are highly subtle, hidden, and largely invisible. They can be known, therefore, only by means of reasoning and true induction with the aid of experiments.[80] He expressed confidence that the analysis of compound bodies would lead, not to atoms, but to "real particles." This comment reveals that he had ceased to believe in atomism for the reason, as he explains, that it falsely assumes the existence of a vacuum and the unchangeableness of matter.[81] His mention of "real particles" would seem to indicate that he considered simple natures as diverse arrangements of these particles. Of the two categories of axioms, Bacon, in conformity with his earlier classification of knowledge in *The Advancement of Learning*, assigned those concerned with the investigation of the forms of simple natures to metaphysics, while those involving the investigation of efficient causes, latent process, and latent configuration belonged to physics. He left no doubt that form was much the more important because it incorporated the "eternal and fundamental laws" of nature, whereas the latter dealt only with nature's "common and ordinary course."[82]

Taken generally, Bacon's concept of form presents certain distinctive characteristics that should be underlined. First, it is wholly interwoven with and inseparable from the knowledge of operations; scientific understanding and technical implementation are aspects of a single cognitive enterprise. Second, it constantly presupposes the difference between what nature does by itself and what nature can be made to do through human intervention and the application of scientific knowledge; the major purpose of Baconian natural philosophy is to produce innovations of which nature unaided is incapable. Third, it postulates the existence of many unobservables, for that is what simple natures are, and sets itself the task of identifying them and the laws explaining their action. Fourth, axioms pertaining to forms function in Bacon's science not only as explanatory or causal laws but as theories that give rise to experiments and testable predictions of new facts and effects. This last point is restated at the conclusion of the discussion of forms, when he observes that his directions for interpreting nature contain two parts, one showing how to educe axioms from experience, the other how to deduce and derive new experiments from axioms. The second of these is further evidence of his understanding that theory was essential in the pursuit of scientific inquiry.[83]

Having posited forms as the main object of knowledge in natural philosophy, Bacon next explained the way to investigate them by

"true and legitimate induction, which is the very key of interpretation."[84] Nothing he said on this subject can be understood unless it is
borne in mind that the method he outlines was chiefly designed to
avoid the simple enumeration of positive instances which he considered the vitiating flaw of induction in the past and in current use. Of
this sort of induction, he had stated earlier in *The New Organon* that its
conclusions were precarious and always in danger from a contradictory instance, and that it continually generalized from too few facts
and only from those close at hand.[85] We must therefore regard Baconian induction as his attempt to overcome these faults. We ought also
to keep in mind that the result he expected from the right kind of
induction in natural philosophy was certain knowledge, and that he
believed such knowledge to be possible. He expressed no recognition, so far as I have been able to see, that general conclusions about
unobserved cases drawn by inductive reasoning from premises about
the observed are never certain and always remain fallible.[86]

To illustrate how induction should be carried out, Bacon chose the
investigation of the form of heat as an example in the first part of his
discussion. The method proceeded through several steps in order to
arrive by a process of analysis, separation, and elimination at the form
sought. For this reason it can be described as eliminative induction.[87]
The first step was to draw up a "table of presence" containing a number of affirmative instances of heat in a variety of bodies. He listed
twenty-seven such instances, including the sun's rays, flame, boiling
liquids, and the like.[88] This was followed in the second step by a "table
of absence" designed to identify the possible negative instances, that
is, cases that were counterparts akin to the instances in the first table,
but in which heat was absent or its presence uncertain. Thus neither
the rays of the moon or stars are hot, nor is liquid hot in its ordinary
state.[89] Some of the data in this table had to be tentative, for as Bacon
pointed out at the beginning of his exposition, a prerequisite of induction was a natural and experimental history of ascertained facts.
As this history did not exist, he sometimes recommends experiments to determine whether the negative instances hold or not—for
example, the construction of a powerful burning-glass to test whether
the rays of the moon can be caught and collected to produce any
degree of heat.[90] The third step was the compilation of a "table of

degrees or comparison in heat," which examined the increase or decrease in the presence of heat in the instances contained in the other
two tables. ". . . since the form of a thing is the very thing itself," he
explained, it necessarily followed that nothing "can be taken as the
true form unless it always decreases when the nature in question decreases, and in like manner always increases when the nature in question increases."[91]

With these tables at hand, induction then went on to perform a
dissection or separation by eliminating the several natures not found
in some instances in which the given nature, heat, is present; or that
are found in some instances in which the given nature is absent; or
are found to increase or decrease in some instance when the given
nature acts in the opposite manner. After these exclusions and rejec-
tions had been made, there would remain as the residue "a form
affirmative, solid and true and well defined." He offered a number of
examples of this process of exclusion of different natures from the
form of heat, such as the rejection of light and brightness on account
of the fact that the rays of the moon and other heavenly bodies except
for the sun were not hot. Pursuing the interpretation, he next established from the tables that the nature of heat appeared to be constantly and invariably associated with motion; and from thence after
further inductions he arrived at the conclusion that the form, cause,
or true definition of heat is "a motion, expansive, restrained, and
acting in its strife upon the smaller particles of bodies." This definition also gave a rule or direction for operations by prescribing that
the way to generate heat in a body is to excite and manipulate a dilat-
ing or expanding motion in it.[92]

Bacon stated that "true induction" was based on a "process of exclusion" which remained incomplete until it arrived at an affirmative
conclusion. He recognized, however, that his demonstration using
the form of heat was imperfect. One of the main reasons for this, as
he pointed out, was that exclusion involved the rejection of simple
natures "and if we do not yet possess sound and true notions of simple natures," the process of exclusion could not be accurate. In the
case of his tables, he confessed that some of the notions of simple
natures they contained were vague and ill defined.[93] Owing to this
shortcoming, as well as to his lack of the reliable data a natural and

experimental history would have provided, he knew that his inquiry into the form of heat could not be complete or certain. In acknowledgment of this fact, he described his attempted induction from the three tables as merely a "permission" he had given his intellect, a "first vintage," and "a beginning of interpretation."[94] What these expressions imply, I think, is not only the provisional character of his investigation but that it included some speculations and conjectures in arriving at its conclusion.[95]

As a sequel to his inductive quest for the form of heat, Bacon devoted the remainder of *The New Organon* to some further suggestions for the conduct of a true and perfect induction. Twenty-seven in number, they were termed "prerogative instances" because of their special evidential usefulness in prosecuting an inquiry into the form of a simple nature.[96] We need not discuss these prerogative instances beyond noticing a few aspects. Throughout his survey of them Bacon mentioned many observations of natural phenomena, reports of experiments, and proposals for experiments to elucidate various facts. One of the instances, entitled "instances of the fingerpost," pertained to cases in which a "decisive," "commanding," or what we might also call a crucial experiment could resolve an uncertainty about the cause of a simple nature. He cited a number of examples of unexplained phenomena for which experiments of this kind might be devised.[97] In another prerogative instance, where he referred to the products of the crafts and human arts, he mentioned "matters of superstition and magic," which he treated purely from the standpoint of natural causality. Despite their being buried in a mass of falsehood and fable, he suggested that they should be looked into, "for it may be that in some of them some natural operation lies at the bottom; as in fascination, strengthening of the imagination, sympathies of things at a distance, transmissions of impressions from spirit to spirit no less than from body to body. . . ."[98]

In one of *The New Organon*'s most eloquent similes, Bacon compared empiricists to ants, who "only collect and use," and rationalists to spiders, "who make cobwebs out of their own substance." With these two insects he contrasted the bee, who both gathers its material from garden and field and "transforms and digests it by a power of its own." The business of philosophy, he said, is to imitate the bee;[99] and

in the method of discovery he presented in his treatise he strove to do
so by showing how the power of the mind could digest the evidence
it derived from natural history and experiments and transform it
into a knowledge of forms and the mastery of nature. Bacon intended
his organon to be both innovative and a lasting contribution to the
renewal of philosophy. Its concentration on a logic of discovery, its
continual insistence on the importance of operations, and its preoccupation with induction set its ideas in systematic opposition to the
philosophic tradition. What it propounded, however, was less a con-
frontation with this tradition than a radical departure from it. So
widely did he diverge from its fundamental assumptions that he felt
he shared no common ground with it at all. In consequence he took
the position in *The New Organon* that earlier philosophy lacked the
basis upon which to challenge his doctrines, "there being no use for
confutations when the difference is upon first principles and very
concepts and even upon forms of demonstration."[100] This was not an
attempt to evade criticism but a declaration of the profound incom-
patibility he perceived between his own ideas and those of existing
philosophical systems.

Grand in ambition, a work of great intellectual power, *The New
Organon* was nevertheless a failure; an honorable failure, to be sure,
but still a failure in its endeavor to create a method of discovery, a
task whose difficulty Bacon seriously underestimated. The imperative
for his reform of induction could well have come from his much
pondered insight that the mind is more attracted by positives than
negatives, but that "in the establishment of any true axiom, the negative instance is the more forcible of the two."[101] By devising an eliminative type of induction, he imagined that he had found a way to
dispose of all negative instances before coming to an affirmative conclusion. He failed to see that no inductive conclusion, however well
supported, could be made invulnerable against the future possibility
of falsification by a contradictory instance. If he committed the error
of supposing that eliminative induction guaranteed the exclusion of
negative instances, this was because, as his nineteenth-century editor
Ellis pointed out, his entire method depended on the assumption
that there was a limited and probably small number of simple natures
of which all bodies were compounded and whose forms could be

identified and distinguished from one another.[102] He did not state, though, what a simple nature is; and he admitted that some of his notions of simple natures were not well defined. He failed to demonstrate that only a limited number of simple natures existed; and even if the latter proposition were true, he could not tell how many there were or whether all of their relevant properties were brought into consideration in any particular induction. All of these flaws undermined his claim to have established a logic of discovery that would yield a certain knowledge of forms and the laws of nature.[103]

The widespread false impression that Bacon was a pure and naive empiricist whose method consisted of a large amount of fact collecting devoid of theoretical guidance, based on the supposition that the facts would speak for themselves in pointing to a generalization that would fit them, should be dispelled by a very little reflection on his concept of induction. The eliminative induction he described in *The New Organon* involved the continual interrogation of nature and seeking answers to the questions posed. At each step the natural philosopher is conscious of what he wants to know and tries to devise ways to obtain this knowledge. The inquiry is never undirected. The questions put to nature raise further questions. Some of the questions are like hypotheses that suggest experiments, which is the reason for the many experiments Bacon proposed in his treatise. Some of the answers obtained become axioms. These in turn act as theories that point to further lines of investigation, permit deductions of new facts, generate hypotheses, and also lead to experiments. Bacon gave a precise formulation of the constant interaction between theory and experiment in his logic of discovery in the following passage of *The New Organon*:

> . . . my course and method, as I have often clearly stated . . . is this,—not to extract works from works or experiments from experiments (as an empiric), but from works and experiments to extract causes and axioms, and again from those causes and axioms new works and experiments, as a legitimate interpreter of nature.[104]

A recent writer on Bacon's philosophy of science has characterized this method as the "hypothetico-inductive method," in virtue of the function performed in it by hypotheses or theories.[105] This is an apt description, to which an alternative might be the "theoretico-inductive method." Both convey the essence of Baconian experimental science as a fusion of reason and critically sifted experience in pursuit of the laws of nature and the production of works.

NATURAL HISTORY

Natural history, which constituted part 3 of *The Great Instauration*, occupied, as we have seen, a position of major importance in Bacon's theory of science as the foundation of a progressive natural philosophy. Its task was to furnish the materials for induction to operate upon; unless it did so, his logic of discovery could not be fully implemented. That was why he included in the same volume with the *The New Organon* a short treatise, *A Preparative towards a Natural and Experimental History (Parasceve ad Historiam Naturalem et Experimentalem)*, written to serve as a guide to the creation of a natural history.[106] This work was not itself a natural history but a set of instructions for how to compile one. Although he left *The New Organon* unfinished by failing to take up a number of subjects he had promised to include, he did not use the final years of his life to remedy this omission.[107] Instead, he concentrated his efforts in natural philosophy on the third part of the instauration by writing several natural histories. It may well be, and is indeed more than likely, that he found the completion of *The New Organon* beyond his strength. In addition, though, he also explained that "my Organon, even if it were completed, would not, without the Natural History, much advance the Instauration of the Sciences, whereas the Natural History without the Organum would advance it not a little. And therefore I have thought it better and wiser by all means and above all things to apply myself to this work."[108] Accordingly, in 1622 he published the book from which the above passage is quoted, *Natural and Experimental History for the Foundation of Philosophy (Historia Naturalis et Experimentalis ad Condendam Philosophiam)*, which contained *History of the Winds (Historia Ventorum)* together with very brief introductions to five more natural histories that he promised would appear successively over the following months. Of these, *History of Life and Death (Historia Vitae et Mortis)* was published in 1623. A second title, *History of Dense and Rare (Historia Densi et Rari)*, was published in 1658, more than a quarter-century after his death. The other three natural histories were never published. Besides these and some remaining fragments, he also wrote one more natural history in English but with the Latin title *Sylva Sylvarum*, meaning a collection of collections, which covered a miscellany of subjects and was posthumously published in 1627.[109]

Bacon's natural histories range over a great mass of phenomena and are filled with facts, pseudofacts, reports and proposals of experiments, inferences, speculations, explanations, and questions for further investigation. The materials in them came from his own observations and much more from the writings of other authors ancient and modern.[110] We are concerned, however, not with the detailed substance of these histories but with their rationale and principles and the light they throw on his natural philosophy.

The intention behind them is entirely clear. They were never conceived as indiscriminate collections of facts but were strictly related to a purpose. Bacon always distinguished three states or manifestations of nature: nature in its "free" or "ordinary course" as it usually operates; nature forced out of its ordinary course by "the violence of impediments" and "the insubordination of matter"; and nature "constrained and manipulated" by human art. Corresponding to this threefold division, the natural histories were supposed to treat of the liberty, the errors, and the bonds of nature. The data they gathered were to supply the primary material for natural philosophy and true induction. They were also to be subordinated to a single end, the formation of axioms. Bacon stated that a natural history of this kind was a new thing, not thought of by ancient authorities like Aristotle, Theophrastus, Dioscorides, and Pliny the Elder, who had compiled natural histories.[111]

He laid down a number of precepts for such a history. Superfluities, for example, were to be excluded. The natural history should contain nothing philological like antiquities, citations of authors, and scholarly disputes. No controversies were to be admitted unless of very great moment. Everything should be recorded concisely and in the plainest language. All superstitious stories and experiments of ceremonial magic were to be rejected, while experiments of natural magic should not be accepted unless first severely sifted.[112] He wished

the natural history to be "made to the measure of the universe," encompassing the divisions of nature and the history of arts and experiments in which nature is changed by man.[113] Among his other
specifications was that everything in the history dealing with bodies in
nature should as far as possible be numbered, weighed, measured,
and defined; and he mentioned examples of several different subjects for which quantitative data were needed, like the exact revolutions and distances of the planets and the specific gravities of
metals.[114] In addition, his rules strongly recommended the inclusion of questions to stimulate further investigation and proposals for
new experiments on particular subjects of inquiry.[115] When doubtful
statements were admitted, they were to be identified as such. The
natural history, because it was the book of God's works, had to be
compiled with religious care as if every particular were delivered
upon oath.[116]

   In Bacon's concept, the compilation of a natural history was directed by questions and experiments. It was to be a selective accumulation of information varied enough to exhibit nature in its three
different states and controlled by the aim of facilitating induction
and the formation of axioms. It would have been a fruitless endeavor,
however, had he not held the belief mentioned earlier that the universe contained only a small number of simple natures and their
forms to be discovered. The fundamental rationale of the natural
history grew out of this assumption, which allowed him to think that
the materials collected in the history would provide all the instances
needed for a complete induction. In *A Preparative towards a Natural
and Experimental History*, he stated that once such a history was in existence, "the investigation of nature and all sciences will be the work of
a few years."[117] This conclusion was due to the same assumption of a
limited number of forms and natures, leading him to greatly underestimate the time scale and difficulties involved in scientific inquiry.
If not for this assumption, moreover, he could not have listed among
the subjects he promised to treat in *The New Organon*, though it was
finally omitted, "the limits of investigation, or a synopsis of all natures
in the universe."[118] Also related to it is the fragment of a work, *The
Alphabet of Nature* (*Abecedarium Naturae*), a reflection of his conception of such an alphabet as an exhaustive summary of the natures or

forms that combine in all bodies as letters do in language to make up the infinite variety of words and sentences.[119]

Bacon proposed many subjects for treatment in natural histories. *A Preparative towards a Natural and Experimental History* contained a catalog of 130 titles he wished to see undertaken. They dealt with the heavens, the earth, animals, plants, minerals, metals, and man. Well over half pertained to man and the crafts, extending to such subjects as histories of sleep, dreams, blood, medicines, vision, music, foods, excrements, spittle, urine, pleasure, pain, hair, wax, sugar, salts, dyeing, weaving, basket making, pottery, and mathematics.[120] It is hard to understand how he imagined that the materials in these histories could be synthesized, winnowed, and reduced for scientific use. The histories nevertheless served as the empirical and evidential foundation his theory of science required. Even within the limitations inherent in the ordinary methods of investigation then current, he believed they would be useful in advancing knowledge. For his logic of discovery, however, they were indispensable, and he was convinced that with the help of the facts they supplied to aid induction and the formation of axioms, natural philosophy would make giant strides in both truth and operations.[121]

DE AUGMENTIS

According to Bacon's plan, the first part of *The Great Instauration* was to be a general survey of the divisions of the sciences and the present state of knowledge. As this part was not included in the 1620 edition of *The Great Instauration,* he tried to supply its omission by the publication three years later of *De Dignitate et Augmentis Scientiarum* (*Of the Dignity and Advancement of Learning*), a translation and expansion of his earlier English treatise *The Advancement of Learning. De Augmentis,* as I shall refer to it, which like its predecessor was dedicated to James I, consisted of nine books compared with the *Advancement*'s two.[122] The parts most relevant to natural philosophy are contained mainly in the third and fifth books. In these Bacon did not substantially revise any of his previous views concerning the divisions and the subject matter of the sciences. He developed and added to some of them, however, and we should therefore notice certain of his comments in order to see their bearing on the conception of philosophy and the investigation of nature set forth in *The Great Instauration*.

Among the divisions of physics discussed in *De Augmentis* were astronomy and astrology. Bacon pronounced astronomy deficient in several respects. He regarded as absurd, for instance, the beliefs that the heavenly bodies move in perfect circles and that the region beyond the moon differs from that beneath it. His main objection to astronomy in its current state, however, was that it presented merely the exterior of the heavenly bodies—that is, their number, position, motions, and periods—without explaining their interior or physical reasons ("rationes physicae"). By means of such reasons, and with the help of astronomical hypotheses ("hypothesibus astronomicis adjunctis"), he argued that it should be possible to produce a theory ("eruatur theoria") that not only satisfied the phenomena but made clear the substance, motion, and influence of the heavenly bodies as they truly are. He held that the theory of the earth's daily rotation, a part of the Copernican heliocentric hypothesis, was false; but what he chiefly criticized in astronomical science was its neglect of the pursuit of physical causes in order to busy itself instead with mathematical demonstrations and observations that showed only apparent motions and the fictitious machinery to account for them, not the real causes and truth of things. The issue of whether astronomy should present a true physical description of the movements of the heavenly bodies or a mathematical scheme for saving the observed phenomena was an old one that had been discussed by ancient and medieval thinkers. There was accordingly nothing new in Bacon's objection that saving the phenomena was not enough, and that what was needed was an accurate account of the heavenly bodies' actual motions. In taking this position, however, he placed the stress on physical causes in order to bring astronomy into closer relation with physics. If it did its proper job, he held that it would be the noblest part of physics; for once the imaginary divorce between superlunary and sublunary things was set aside and study directed to the universal appetites and passions of matter throughout the cosmos, it would be possible to gain knowledge both of the phenomena of the heavens and of the lower world as well. This kind of science, which he wished to see developed, he named Living Astronomy.[123]

Looking at astrology, he described it as so full of superstition that it contained practically nothing that was sound. He was willing, nevertheless, to accept it as a science linked to physics, but only insofar as it conformed to reason and evidence ("ratio et evidentia rerum"). Among the astrological doctrines he rejected were horoscopes, the distribution of houses, and the notion that the exact positions of the stars and planets at any hour had a fatal influence on human affairs. Except for the sun's heat and the moon's magnetic effect on the tides and sea, he maintained that the power of the heavenly bodies over the natural world was slight, affecting things only in large numbers, not individuals, and the more tender kinds of bodies like air and spirits, as well perhaps as metals and other subterranean substances. Nor did the stars exert any fatal necessity; at most they could incline, not compel. He conceded, though, that the heavenly bodies might manifest other influences than heat and light, but these would have to operate through causes investigated by physics. He desired astrology to give up most of its traditional conceptions and become a "Sane Astrology" that would study the rays of the planets and stars in their conjunctions and carry out many other observations. It would also make predictions of recurring natural phenomena like comets, floods, droughts, and earthquakes, and of greater revolutions in civil matters such as migrations of peoples, seditions, and wars. It might likewise be cautiously applied to predictions of singular events, and with even greater circumspection to the choice of favorable times for undertaking certain things. To sum up his assessment, he insisted that all astrological doctrines must meet the test of physical principles founded in matter and the motions of bodies or else be discarded. Along with this condition, he required the exclusion from astrology of celestial magic, the superstition that the favorable position of the stars could produce an effect by impressing itself upon seals, metals, or gems.[124]

The connecting thread in Bacon's treatment of astronomy and astrology was its pervasive naturalism and concentration on physical causes. Astronomy was to forsake fictitious mathematical contrivances for the discovery of the true motions of the heavenly bodies and their causes. In the case of astrology, while not entirely denying the possibility that it could make predictions, he considered it tenable only if it rectified its methods, jettisoned its superstitions, and became a genuine branch of physics grounded in a common materialism and search for the physical explanation of celestial influences.

In *De Augmentis* Bacon reiterated the distinction he had previously made between physics and metaphysics. To the former he assigned the inquiry into material and efficient causes, to the latter the inquiry into forms or formal causes and final causes.[125] It is therefore of considerable interest that in a letter of 1622 to an Italian natural philosopher who had asked about his method, he attributed a much wider significance to physics. There he said that "when a true physics has been discovered, there will be no metaphysics. Beyond the true physics would be nothing but divinity."[126] It is hard to know how to interpret this statement in the light of his other remarks on the subject; but if he believed that a true physics would at some time displace metaphysics, it confirms once more how deeply committed he was to the principle that the sole way of understanding nature was by physical reasons and explanations.[127]

From the same standpoint, *De Augmentis* criticized the inclusion of final causes, which should be left to metaphysics, in physics. Bacon did not conceal his skepticism about final causes in his complaint that they had replaced the inquiry into physical causes to the great detriment of science. He praised the natural philosophy of Democritus because it "removed God and Mind from the fabric of things" and assigned the causes of particular things "to the necessities of matter without any intermixture of final causes. . . ." While denying that he intended to call divine providence into question, he curtly relegated final causes to the realm of speculation with the comment that the inquiry into them "is barren and like a virgin consecrated to God produces nothing."[128]

De Augmentis also envisaged the rehabilitation of natural magic, a subject toward which Bacon had always expressed considerable reservations. To restore it to the ancient and honorable reputation it had lost, he classified it with metaphysics as the science that applies the hidden knowledge of forms to the production of wonderful operations to reveal the wonders of nature. He distinguished it, however, from the contemporary natural magic with its faith in occult properties, sympathies and antipathies, and other speculations that had nothing to do with the truths of nature. The latter, a degenerate science based like alchemy and astrology on imagination and credulity, begot only empty hopes and specters that divert men from the investigation of true causes. By incorporating natural magic into the science of forms and their application, he hoped to reestablish its credit.[129]

Related to *De Augmentis*'s appraisal of natural magic was its brief discussion of divination and fascination, subjects that fell under one of the divisions of human philosophy dealing with the faculties of the soul. Bacon perceived two kinds of divination, artificial and natural; the first made predictions from external signs and tokens, the second by discerning the inward presentiments of the mind. He appeared to accept that by withdrawing into itself in sleep, ecstasies, or visions, the mind could have premonitions of things to come. Similarly, it might receive an illumination from the foreknowledge of God or spirits. Bodily abstinence was conducive to both these kinds of natural divination. Fascination, on the other hand, was the power of the imagination to act upon another body. Here he noted that Paracelsians and disciples of natural magic had exaggerated this power to the point of crediting it with miracles. Its more probable explanation, he thought, was that impressions and communications could pass from spirit to spirit, since the spirit is beyond all other things quick to act and soft and tender to be acted upon. This was only one of the many places in which Bacon talked of spirits, and I shall consider later in this chapter what he meant by the idea. He dissociated the power of fascination, however, from ceremonial magic and its use of rites, charms, amulets, and the like, to fortify the imagination through contacts with evil spirits. That he gave any credence to ceremonial magic and its employment of evil spirits is doubtful, seeing that when speaking of it in connection with astrology, he dismissed it as a superstition. Nevertheless, he stated that even if ceremonial magic were to refrain from inviting the aid of spirits, its purpose was to gain by a few easy observances the fruits that God had commanded man to attain by labor. On this account, because it violated God's ordinance to sinful mankind that "in the sweat of thy brow shalt thou eat," he condemned it as unlawful.[130]

In the fifth book of *De Augmentis*, which dealt with logic and its four divisions, Bacon returned once again to the deficiencies of the current syllogistic logic that made it unable in his view to serve as a method of discovery of new arts and sciences. At this point he introduced a discussion of the conduct of experiments in natural philosophy that contained his longest treatment of this subject. His remarks harked back to several aphorisms in *The New Organon* that used the phrase "learned experience" ("experientia literata") to denote the right way to manage experiments for the discovery of new things of service to human life.[131] *De Augmentis* amplified this characterization by considering learned experience as an important aid to discovery, despite its inferiority to induction and the interpretation of nature. Not a part of philosophy or capable of generating axioms, it was essentially a sagacity or skill in experimenting that drew on experiments already performed to devise further experiments with the aim of yielding new knowledge. Bacon defined eight classes of methods of experiments, reviewing each one in detail to illustrate how it might add to knowledge. One class, for example, called variation in experiment, consisted of producing variations on the matter, subject, and efficient cause in previous experiments; thus silk and other materials could be tried instead of linen in the manufacture of paper, or successful grafts already made on cultivated trees tried on different species of wild trees, or a lead ball of a certain weight that had been dropped from a height and its fall timed could be changed for a ball of greater weight in order that it might be determined whether the increased quantity increased the speed of the downward motion. Collectively, these several categories of experiments, a major ingredient of Bacon's critical empiricism, constituted a guide to systematic scientific inquiry, an array of procedures for manipulating and exploiting experience to produce new effects and possibly discoveries. Because literate experience did not give rise to axioms, however, Bacon placed it well below his new organon. Yet he stressed that such experiments could provide instruction even when they were unsuccessful, and he saw them as a part of his enterprise of promoting experiments of light, which, as he had often said, were of greater value than experiments of fruit.[132]

The last subject in *De Augmentis* that should be noted for its relevance to Bacon's natural philosophy is the importance it gave to the framing of questions in the process of inquiry. He took up this matter in connection with invention, one of the divisions of logic. For him, invention in logic or dialectics had always possessed two different meanings; the first was the conventional one of the discovery of arguments, while the second and much more significant one was the discovery of new sciences. Having commented on the deficiencies of the traditional logic in the latter kind of invention, he also gave some attention to the discovery of arguments, which included the provision of particular topics relating to a subject. Of such topics he observed that they were useful not only in argumentation with others but also in private reflection by suggesting both what to affirm and what to ask. ". . . a faculty of wise interrogating," he stated in this connection, "is half a knowledge"; moreover, "the fuller and more certain our anticipation is, the more direct and compendious our search." Particular topics were accordingly of great value, especially when combined with the matter of the different sciences. As an instance of a particular topic, he selected the subject of heavy and light, proposing a set of nineteen "articles of inquiry," each aimed at eliciting information on an aspect of the phenomenon of heaviness and lightness in the actions of bodies. The answers to many of the questions would have necessitated the performance of experiments. Questions like these, we should recall, were a regular feature of Bacon's natural histories. Those he used in this example were probably intended for a natural history of heavy and light that he had promised to publish but which never appeared. At the conclusion he declared that particular topics were so important in natural philosophy that he planned to devote a separate work to them, summing up his view in the trenchant observation that "we are masters of our questions, though not of the nature of things."[133]

In his well-known book *The Idea of History*, the English philosopher R. G. Collingwood referred to Bacon as one of the great masters of the "Logic of Questioning" and described his theory of experimental science as based on a logic of question and answer.[134] There is a good deal of truth in this characterization; and, as I have previously suggested, it should be obvious that the thinker who regarded particular topics in the manner described above was by no means a simpleminded empiricist. Bacon always conceived of natural philosophy as a form of research that was oriented by the questions it asked at the

outset, and in which questions likewise set the course of further investigation in order to achieve the desired end of the formation of
axioms. This process was central to his conception of experimental
philosophy, and no account of the latter can be adequate that fails to
give this fact its due significance.

SPIRITS, BODY, WORLD PICTURE

In the preceding discussion I have noted in passing Bacon's occasional allusions to spirits. Not only do many mentions of spirits appear throughout his writings on natural philosophy, but also scattered among them are statements intimating or outlining a broad
picture of the world or universe. References to these subjects occur in
his earlier works as well as in some that were intended for *The Great
Instauration*. Among the earlier writings shedding light on his conception of spirits and his world picture is a short, unfinished treatise,
*The Ways of Death, the Retarding of Old Age, and the Restoration of the Vital
Powers* (*De Viis Mortis, et de Senectute Retardanda, atque Instaurandis Viribus*), first published in 1984 from a newly discovered manuscript. Its
editor, Graham Rees, has described this work, which dates from
1611–12, as the most important text of Bacon's in natural philosophy
to be published since the seventeenth century.[135] *The Ways of Death* is
closely related in content to *History of Life and Death*, one of the natural histories assigned to part 3 of *The Great Instauration*. Other works
touching upon Bacon's notion of spirits include *Theory of the Heaven*
(*Thema Coeli*), a short composition dating from about 1612; remarks
in several of the other natural histories, especially the last, *Sylva Sylvarum*; and occasional passages in *The New Organon* and *De Augmentis*.
In his introduction to *Ways of Death* and a number of articles, Rees has
given the fullest account of Bacon's world picture and the place that
spirits occupy in it.[136]

If one is to grasp Bacon's idea of spirit, it helps to understand his
ideas about body. His underlying thought is that matter or body is all
that exists in nature. Matter cannot be annihilated, and the amount
of it in the universe remains always the same. All entities are bodies
because they all consist of matter. Some bodies, however, are tangible
and accessible to sight, while many others are highly subtle, invisible,

and not discernible by any of the senses. Spirits are bodies of the latter kind. They are nothing else, he explained in *Sylva Sylvarum,* "but a natural body, rarified to a proportion, and included in the tangible parts of bodies, as in an integument." Moreover, they "are in all tangible bodies whatsoever, more or less; and they are never (almost) at rest; and from them and their motions principally proceed arefaction, colliquation, concoction, maturation, putrefaction, vivification, and most of the effects of nature. . . ."[137] It is worth noting in passing that Bacon's idea of spirit in these remarks was not unlike that held at the end of the century by Sir Isaac Newton, who explained gravitation and certain other phenomena as due to "a certain most subtle spirit which pervades and lies hid in all gross bodies, by the force and action of which the particles of bodies attract one another."[138] Elsewhere Bacon said that spirits are present in all tangible bodies, whether the latter are living or lack life.[139] Again, in an implied dissent from other philosophical views and referring to spirits in the upper parts of the earth, he declared that "spirit is not a virtue, energy, entelechy, or some foolishness of that kind, but a body thin and invisible, yet having place, dimension, and real."[140]

Thus for Bacon spirit was not something immaterial such as a soul, nor did it imply any sort of dualism entailing the existence of a spiritual realm separate from the universe of matter. He recognized, of course, that human beings possessed an immaterial rational soul which is of divine origin and imparted by God; and he consigned the knowledge concerning this soul in man to religion, not philosophy.[141] Spirit, however, was a physical reality, an intangible, invisible body whose action upon other bodies is explainable by physical causes. With respect to bodies, he sometimes spoke of them as having perception, consents, and aversion. ". . . all natural bodies," he observed, "have a manifest power of perception," instanced in such things as the magnet's attraction of iron, the rays of light deflected from a white surface, and animal bodies that assimilate what is useful to them and expel what is not. By this manner of language he was not attributing purposes or occult powers to bodies but describing the fact that bodies react to each other, "since no body when placed near another either changes it or is changed by it, unless a reciprocal perception precedes the operation." For this reason he concluded that "perception [is] everywhere." It was essential, however, to distinguish the simple perception belonging to all bodies from sensibility or feeling, which many bodies lack. He deplored philosophers' failure to understand the difference between simple perception and sense and the extent to which the first could exist without the second. It was their ignorance on this point that had led some ancient philosophers to imagine that "a soul was infused into all bodies without distinction," because they could not conceive "how there could be motion . . . without sense, or sense without a soul."[142]

In a similar manner, he alluded in *The New Organon* to consents and aversions ("consensus," "fuga") as diverse relationships between bodies that often lay deeply concealed. There were consents and aversions, for example, between chemical substances based on their rarity, density, and latent configurations. A very general consent was the kind that existed between primary bodies and their supporting conditions and aliments. Hence one needed to ascertain in what climates and earths and at what depths the various metals are generated, and in what soil the different trees, shrubs, and herbs thrive best.[143] Bacon took care to dissociate the metaphors he applied to bodies from the fanciful belief in occult properties and sympathies and antipathies that were part of natural magic and which he called "corruptions of philosophy."[144] When we read his reflections on fascination, the power of imagination, and the transmission of spirits, we need to do so in the light of the physicalist naturalism and materialism that were basic principles of his philosophy. His consistent tendency was to treat all such phenomena as the actions, attributes, and capacities of bodies operating as physical causes and effects.

In *Sylva Sylvarum*, whose final section included a discussion of the transmission of spirits and the force of imagination, his naturalistic and frequently skeptical attitude is unmistakable. While cautioning that the failure of such operations should not necessarily cause them to be disbelieved, he also warned that they should not be too easily credited when they succeed, since they often do so through the effect of autosuggestion on the "imaginant." Thus if a man carries a planet's seal, a ring, or other talisman in the faith that it will help him to

obtain something he strongly desires, this belief in itself will make
him much more active, industrious, and persistent to achieve his end.
One should therefore not mistake the cause of these operations and
"rashly . . . take that for done which is not done." In the case of witchcraft, too, men should not readily accept witches' confessions nor the
evidence against them, for witches themselves are imaginative, often
believing "they do that which they do not," while people, being cred-
ulous, easily impute accidents and natural operations to witchcraft.[145]
Bacon reviewed various kinds of operations involving alleged transmission of spirits and the ability of the imagination to influence other
bodies, and also proposed experiments to test these phenomena. Unless he could perceive a possible physical explanation for them, he
was inclined to doubt their existence. Accordingly, he commented
that "the experiments which may certainly demonstrate the power of
imagination upon other bodies are few or none," and gave it as his
general view that "these effects of imagination upon other bodies
have . . . little credit with us. . . ."[146]

In *Theory of the Heaven* Bacon presented a sketch of his world picture or what he called a "theory of the universe." Summarized in its
barest outline, it rested on the assumption that two kinds of matter
made up the universe, the one gross or tangible bodies, the other fine
or pneumatic bodies. Pneumatic bodies consisted of either air or
flame. The earth and nearby heavens were the region of the gross
bodies, while the upper heavens were the region of pneumatic bodies
of which the stars and interplanetary ether or atmosphere were composed. In between the two lay a third, intermediate region in which
the two kinds of bodies mingled. In the air close to the earth, where
grosser bodies and their effects predominated, flame lasts only mo-
mentarily and then perishes. In the middle region, where the air begins to be cleared of the exhalations of the earth, flame acquires a
certain duration. In the third region beyond the moon, it ceases to be
extinguishable, and further out it grows stronger still, reaching its full
intensity near the sun and undergoing various changes in its proxim-
ity to the different planets. Among other things, Bacon maintained
that air and flame were distinctly different bodies, that space is filled
with either airy or flamey natures, and that the moon is neither watery

nor solid but a body of slow and weak flame. He also offered a number of opinions regarding planetary and celestial motions, one of which was that the heavens revolved approximately every twenty-four hours around the earth in a direction from east to west.[147]

There was also a chemical aspect to this theory of the cosmos, which, as Rees has amply shown, was adapted from Paracelsian sources. Of the well-known Paracelsian triad of sulphur, mercury, and salt, Bacon discarded salt but considered the other two as basic, describing them as "the most primaeval natures," "the most original configurations of nature," and the "two enormous tribes of things which occupy and penetrate the universe." Each of the two formed a separate "quaternion," comprising itself and three other entities to which it was allied. Thus sulphur was associated with subterranean bodies, with oil and oily inflammable substances, and with fire both in the earth's region and among the stars. Mercury was also present in subterranean bodies but was associated with water and nonflammable substances, with air in the region of the earth, and with the interplanetary ether.[148] Touching upon this pair of quaternions in *The New Organon*, Bacon said that they represented one of the most general consents in nature, there being a consent among sulphur, oil, greasy exhalations, flame, and perhaps the body of a star, and also among mercury, water and watery vapors, air, and perhaps the pure intersidereal ether.[149]

The Ways of Death and *History of Life and Death* add further details showing the place of spirits in this theory. On this subject one of Bacon's main sources was the Italian philosopher Telesio, whose principal work, *De Rerum Natura Iuxta Proprium Principia*, was published in its final form in 1586. According to Bacon's understanding, the spirits that inhabit all tangible bodies were either vital or lifeless spirits. Lifeless spirits, which are cold and akin to the substance of air, are discontinuous and separated from one another by the grosser parts of the bodies that surround them. Vital spirits, which are hot, are continuous and akin to the substance of flame, and some are branched, permeating their adjoining bodies by threadlike channels, while others have a cell from which various channels diverge and which has its main location in the brain. Lifeless spirits reside in inanimate, inorganic bodies; members of the plant and vegetable kingdom contain vital spirits that branch; animals contain vital spirits, either branching in the case of the lowest animals, or with cells that become larger in the higher animals and man. Both kinds of spirits, however, coexist in all living bodies. Bacon traces various differences in bodies to the quantity and diffusion of their spirits and other factors. To these two classes of spirits as "agents and workmen" he attributed all the functions and processes of bodies. Vital spirits, which are tender, warm, or fiery, constitute the principle of life and strive to remain in their tangible bodies. They are in constant conflict with lifeless spirits, which seek to escape from their containing bodies and unite with air, and which ultimately conquer the vital spirits by wearing away the bodies in which they reside. All of Bacon's proposals for prolonging life are aimed at the strengthening and conservation of the vital spirits in the human body.[150]

There is, of course, something fantastic about this world picture with its two great chemical families, its three zones of gross and pneumatic bodies, its account of celestial bodies and motions, and its analysis of the action of the vital and lifeless spirits inhabiting bodies. Derived from various sources, an eclectic mixture of assumptions, conjectures, observations, hypotheses, and inferences, it is a strictly physical theory that proposes in principle an explanation of a great variety of phenomena. The essential question, though, is how this theory, devoid of empirical foundation, is related to the rest of Bacon's natural philosophy. Referring to its conception of the two kinds of spirits and the principle of life, Ellis, the main editor of Bacon's philosophical writings, called it a "speculative physiology" and further observed that Bacon had failed to indicate either the reasons for believing it or the kind of evidence that might establish the existence of spirits.[151] Rees, whose erudite studies have examined its details most closely, describes the entire theory as a "speculative philosophy," which is exactly right. Going beyond this characterization, however, he makes the misleading suggestion that Bacon may therefore have had two philosophies, not one, the first being his inductive method, the second a speculative system that apparently violated his most cherished methodological principles. Accordingly, he asks why Bacon should have bothered to write *The New Organon* when he already possessed what he considered to be a substantive natural philosophy. In Rees's further discussion of the subject, though, some of his own citations from Bacon show plainly that this question is quite beside the point.[152] Whatever the inconsistencies into which Bacon may have inadvertently fallen, we have no reason to attribute to him the deliberate incoherence of concurrently propounding two separate and contradictory philosophies. His speculative doctrines were not independent of the main body of his natural philosophy but subordinate to it; moreover, he explained clearly enough what their status was.

In *The New Organon*, he declared, with probable reference to some of these doctrines, that on certain subjects and in incomplete form he possessed results that he considered more true and certain than those presently accepted, and that these were designed for the fifth part of *The Great Instauration*. According to the latter's plan, this part was to consist of "anticipations, or forerunners of the new philosophy."[153] Hence it was here, as Rees has noted, that Bacon's speculative philosophy was to have its place.[154] The essential feature of this part 5 was its tentative, provisional character. It was, Bacon said, "for temporary use only. . . ." Consequently, it was to include only the things he had discovered, proved, or added, not by means of "the true methods and rules of interpretation," but by the ordinary use of his intellect such as others customarily employ in inquiry and discovery. These results were therefore to serve only as a refreshment or way station of the mind on its journey to more certain conclusions. He also wished it to be understood that because these doctrines were not discovered or proved by the true form of interpretation, he did not consider himself bound by them.[155] What all this tells us is that in *The Great Instauration* Bacon left himself a conceptual space for the presentation of insights and theories whose provisional character he admitted but that he held to be nearer the truth than others currently accepted, even though not the fruit of induction. This explanation leaves no doubt that he did not promulgate two rival philosophies. His speculative philosophy or world picture was a subsidiary portion of his science, of much lower standing than his main project of a logic of discovery and its expected results; a forerunner superior, he was convinced, to received notions, but nevertheless temporary and possibly to be superseded by a more certain knowledge.[156]

CONCLUSION

As a philosopher, and particularly in his approach to natural philosophy, Bacon's thought exhibits a fundamental consistency and continuity. No ruptures or sharp deviations are visible in his mental history. The preoccupations with which he began his intellectual life were still prominent at its end. His critical reaction against Platonism and Aristotelianism was part of the earliest phase of his thought; so likewise was his opposition to the veneration of antiquity, his belief in the need for an operative science, and his aim of contributing to the reconstruction and renewal of philosophy. His project of a great instauration of philosophy originated no later than the beginning of the seventeenth century and probably sooner. Maturing over many years, when it finally took shape in the publication of *The Great Instauration, The New Organon, De Augmentis,* and several ancillary natural histories, it remained uncompleted and far short of its goal. Bacon had no illusions on this score, seeing himself as the precursor and herald of those to come who he hoped would carry further and reap the fruits of the work he had begun. During the whole period of his activity as a philosopher, aside from the last five years of his life following his fall from power, he was always employed in the profession of law, political tasks, and the service of the monarchy. It is a marvel that he succeeded in pursuing his studies and observations in so many different fields, writing so prolifically, and accomplishing as much as he did.

His motives in focusing upon the renewal of natural philosophy were both intellectual and moral. Of his intellectual motives, looking to the growth of truth in the knowledge of nature, the perfection of a logic of discovery, and the creation of an operative science, we have said enough. The moral motive, however, requires emphasis. It was a humanitarian motive, difficult though it may be to reconcile this with his personal self-seeking in politics and the counsels of prudence and expediency for worldly advancement that marked other parts of his thought. In the letter he wrote Lord Burghley in 1592, which spoke of his "vast contemplative ends" and hope of reforming knowledge, he termed his motive "philanthropia," love or care for mankind.[157] Later, in the essay on goodness published in his *Essays*, he gave the word "humanity" as a synonym for "philanthropia," its meaning "the affecting of the weal of men," which he described as the greatest of all the virtues and dignities of the mind.[158] His pity for the miseries of mankind, his insistence that the improvement and benefit of human life is the true end of knowledge, the relationship he perceived between the renewal of philosophy and the inception of kingdom of man—these were all direct reflections of the humanitarian motive underlying Baconian science.

For Bacon knowledge brought power, and the science he desired was inseparably linked with the conquest and mastery of nature. There is an enormous irony in the fact that this objective, which in his mind was designed to promote human welfare, should have become a cause of odium and the main reason for the opprobrium often attached to his name in our time. As Anne Righter has justly commented, Bacon could never have guessed that he would be considered as the architect of the twentieth century's dilemmas or that "his efforts to establish the Kingdom of Man would come to be regarded as destructive by precisely those generations that inhabit it." Far from appearing as the Moses of Cowley's adulatory poem who showed the way to the Promised Land, he is now often seen, as she points out, as the false prophet leading mankind to the "wilderness of materialism."[159] To present-day environmentalists and ecologists, he is one of the foremost evangelists of the disastrously mistaken belief that nature and the creation are ordained for man's benefit and rule, from which has sprung the ever growing modern exploitation, pollution, and devastation of the earth.[160] Some philosophers have associated him with the miscarriage of the Enlightenment's project in behalf of reason and progress, to which they have ascribed such negative consequences as the unlimited expansion of human power, the tyranny of technology over men, and the relentless rationalization of every aspect of human existence.[161] Historians in search of the roots of modernity, and disillusioned by its results, claim to discern in Baconian science an extreme dehumanization, even a negation of life, and an authoritarian will to domination and control.[162] To those feminist theorists who look upon modern science as an oppressive male construction, Bacon was a misogynist whose program of subjugating nature is indistinguishable from the rape of the female, and whose conception of experiment and the interrogation of nature was taken from the torture chamber and the prosecution of witches.[163]

This indictment reflects a huge misunderstanding as well as a grave injustice. It is a doctrinaire misjudgment due to gross anachronism and to irrational hostility and fear of science. Those who criticize the aim of mastering nature to which Bacon's science aspired either forget or are ignorant of what his world was like. In that world, human beings were extremely liable to disease, physical suffering, and early death. Average life expectancy in sixteenth- and seventeenth-century Western Europe was probably not much over thirty years of age. Infant mortality was very great, averaging around 20 to 25 percent per thousand births. Populations were afflicted by recurrent bubonic and pneumonic plague and other epidemic diseases. Physicians were nearly helpless to diagnose or treat illness and to alleviate pain. Cities were unhealthy from poor sanitation and danger of infection. Food supply was precarious and regularly affected by scarcity and dearth due to periodic harvest failure. Local famine and starvation were not uncommon. Preindustrial economies were subject to widespread unemployment, underemployment, and chronic poverty. Heavy labor was essential to the performance of many different kinds of work. The gap in standards of life between rich and poor was enormous, and as much as a third of the population may have lived at a subsistence level.[164]

Such was Bacon's world, which lasted well down into the eighteenth century and then began to change with accelerating rapidity into the very different modern world we have come to know. It was also the world of the old regime of knowledge, which Bacon helped to overthrow and whose demise was accomplished by seventeenth-century philosophy and science and the subsequent European Enlightenment. When Bacon made the mastery of nature the aim of a revitalized natural philosophy, together with the enlargement of truth he also hoped for the betterment of life through new discoveries and inventions that would lighten mankind's burdens and provide it with hitherto unknown conveniences. When he strove to learn how to prolong life and postpone old age, he had the same end in view. It makes no historical sense, therefore, to blame him for the undesirable and unintended consequences that ensued from science's effort to understand and control nature for human purposes and needs. He had no way in his world of conceiving the idea of living in balance with the environment that inspires the modern conservationist and ecologist; and he had no great reason to fear that the mastery of nature would breed serious threats and dangers for mankind. He could not know or foresee the multifarious effects that the technological application of science would produce, and should not be held responsible for those that have proved harmful. Beyond these considerations, what is simply ignored in the criticism of Bacon is the enormous intellectual achievement that modern science represents and the benefits it has brought humankind in the form of great new knowledge and improved well-being. And one might venture to add that should the world succeed in coping with its present environmental problems, it will do so, not by opposition to or rejection of science, but by the intelligent and humane use of science coupled with the existence of a public and governments capable of making sensible decisions about the application of science and its limits.

Bacon gave remarkable expression to his scientific utopianism, as we may call his vision of the possibilities of science, in the fictional *New Atlantis*, an unfinished composition written toward the end of his life and published posthumously in 1627. This work belongs to the genre of utopias or ideal commonwealths, whose authors depict, either seriously or playfully, the world as they think it ought to be. *New Atlantis* also intimates some of Bacon's political ideas, which will be discussed in the following chapter; but as he left it, in its incomplete state, what it chiefly describes is a humane society directed in part by benevolent philosophers, in which science and scientific research play a dominant role. The mind or focal intelligence of this society is Salomon's House, also called the College of Six Days Work, which is nothing less than a great research institution, a scientific establishment endowed with facilities for pursuing far-flung investigations into all the secrets of nature. The Fathers or Elders who administer it are natural philosophers and experimentalists who can perform many kinds of operations. Some of the inspiration for the things they do may have come from Bacon's acquaintance with the activities of craftsmen and inventors like the two foreign practitioners Cornelis Drebbel and Salomon de Caus, who, while working in England in the early seventeenth century, produced various ingenious devices and experimented in applied science with steam power, submarines, and different kinds of industrial processes.[165] The purpose of Salomon's House, as one of its Fathers explained it, is Bacon's most memorable summary of the true scope and significance of his own project: "The end of our foundation is the knowledge of causes, and secret motions of things, and the enlargement of the bounds of human empire, to the effecting of all things possible."[166] The same Elder gives an account of the resources for research that Salomon's House possesses. They include deep caves, high towers, great lakes both salt and fresh; wells, fountains, and baths; houses in which to produce imitations and demonstrations of meteors, snow, rain, and other natural phenomena; orchards and gardens with a variety of soils; parks and enclosures of beasts and birds; breweries, bakeries, and kitchens to make various drinks and other consumable substances; pharmacies, mechanical arts, and many kinds of furnaces; rooms for the study of light, vision, and color; collections of precious stones, minerals, and magnets; houses to investigate sounds, smells, and taste; engines and instruments to reproduce all sorts of motions. Salomon's House was a great collection of laboratories for the performance of experiments, the supply of data for natural histories, and the making of new discoveries. It was the dream of a Faustian experimental philosopher who had taken all knowledge for his province. It was likewise a picture of science as an organized, collaborative enterprise and transformed into a great social institution. Finally, it was also, no doubt, an example of the abundance of resources and facilities Bacon imagined science might have at least partially at its disposal if it were to succeed, as he had hoped in his vain appeals to James I, in gaining the patronage of kings to support and subsidize its labors. It was fitting that the *New Atlantis,* as his final work, should embody an image that was in some ways prophetic of a world in which science was to become a great power in shaping humanity's course.

One of the most distinctive features of Bacon's philosophy was the attention it gave to the history of science and to the conditions that promoted and retarded the advancement of the knowledge of nature. In this sense the inherent tendency of Bacon's thought was historical and sociological.[167] We need not say that he was an accurate or impartial historian of philosophy: his prejudice against Aristotle and medieval Scholasticism is obvious, and he was ignorant of the interest taken by medieval philosophers in the study of nature, such as the work done by a number of thinkers in the Universities of Paris and Oxford in the fourteenth century in physics and the theory of motion. Nevertheless, his approach was essentially historical when he sought to delineate the changes in Greek philosophy between the pre-Socratics and their successors or the adverse effects of the triumph of Christianity upon the investigation of nature. It was both historical and sociological when he pointed to the limitations in the Greeks' knowledge of nature and the globe, and to the importance of recent inventions and geographical discovery in opening new prospects for the progress of knowledge. There is an evident sociological dimension in his emphasis on the value of studying the crafts and their technical processes, and his explanation of philosophers' neglect to do so because of the predominant attitude in the ancient world and later European society of contempt for manual labor as base and degrading. The same is true of his discussion of those of the idols of the mind that are socially engendered through education, human intercourse and language, and the influence of philosophical systems. In the treatment of the varieties of historical writing in *The Advancement of Learning*, he deplored the lack of a history of learning and of the different kinds of knowledges that would describe and explain the causes of their flourishings, decays, and changes.[168] Keenly aware of the need for a historical view of the vicissitudes and course of knowledge, he was among the first thinkers to see philosophy and science as an integral part of the history of civilization and to recognize the significance of understanding the intellectual and social conditions of the development of knowledge.[169]

Much ink has been spilled over the question of Bacon's relationship to the scientific revolution of the seventeenth century. In his

Philosophy of the Inductive Sciences (1840), William Whewell, one of the foremost nineteenth-century historians and philosophers of science, felt no doubt that Bacon stood in the front rank as a scientific innovator. Calling him one of the founders and the "supreme Legislator of the modern Republic of Science," Whewell wrote that "if we must select some one philosopher as the Hero of the revolution in scientific method, " then "beyond all doubt Francis Bacon must occupy the place of honour."[170] Twentieth-century historians of science have expressed a much more qualified judgment. E. J. Dijksterhuis in his classic *The Mechanization of the World Picture* observed that Bacon "did not make a single positive contribution to science" and that "his method of scientific research was never really applied either by himself or by anyone else and consequently never produced any result." He also emphasized, as other scholars have done, that Bacon failed to appreciate the importance of the mathematical treatment of science, which even in his own lifetime had begun to achieve such great triumphs. The most Dijksterhuis could find to record in Bacon's favor was the inspiring influence he exerted in stimulating the progress of science in England and elsewhere.[171] Alexandre Koyré, another leading historian of early modern science, ruled Bacon out of the scientific revolution altogether because he was an empiricist, whereas the change that dominated the major advances of science in the seventeenth century was its mathematization and the geometrization of space in the work of men like Galileo, Descartes, and Newton.[172] A modification of this negative judgment was presented by Thomas S. Kuhn in his noteworthy essay "Mathematical versus Experimental Traditions in the Development of Physical Science." Starting with the fact that science was not one but many, Kuhn identified the existence of two distinct scientific traditions. The first, that of the classical sciences based on mathematics and comprising astronomy, geometry, optics, statics, and harmonics, flourished from antiquity down to the sixteenth century as a recognized cluster of disciplines and then underwent a radical reconstruction during the scientific revolution. The second tradition was that of experimental science with roots in the crafts, including the study of heat, electricity, magnetism, phenomena of life, and chemistry, which emerged in the seventeenth century and involved a new kind of empiricism based on the experimental manipulation of nature. Kuhn associated this latter cluster of sciences with Bacon and observed that although Baconianism contributed little to the classical sciences, it gave rise to a number of new scientific fields exemplifying a new kind of experimental method.[173]

Kuhn's account helps somewhat to restore Bacon to a deserved position in the history of the scientific revolution from which Koyré would have expelled him. To grasp the true measure of Bacon's significance, however, we must look beyond the technical history of science to the realm of scientific ideas, philosophy, and organization. If Bacon did not make a single positive scientific discovery, his opposition to the old regime of knowledge and the authority of the past was nevertheless crucial in the development of science. A vital aspect of his philosophy was its reasoned arguments to show the great new possibilities that existed for the progress of knowledge of nature. This became one of the principal factors in helping to bring about a major change in the climate of opinion by the end of the seventeenth century, a change highly favorable to the growth and practice of science. His depiction of Salomon's House in *New Atlantis* helped to inspire the formation and the experimental aims of later scientific societies, most notably the Royal Society of London established in 1662. His exposure of the causes of intellectual error and their remedies may stand alongside Descartes's rules of method as a major effort to show how the mind ought to proceed in its quest for truth. Although his own attempts at discovery bore no fruit, he must be credited in his critical empiricism and his concentration on the conduct of experiments, and on eliminative induction, with going a considerable way toward the understanding and statement of the principles of scientific research and inductive procedure that are an essential part of all work in the natural sciences.[174] As one historian of science has explained, "Bacon's emphasis on experiment did shape the style of science. So strongly did it do so that the term 'experimental science' has become practically a synonym for 'modern science,' and nothing so clearly differentiates post-seventeenth-century science from that of the Renaissance, or of Greece, as the role of experiment."[175]

According to Koyré, one of the two essential features of the scientific revolution was the destruction of the old conception of the cosmos, which meant that the world ceased to be thought of as a finite,

hierarchically ordered and qualitatively and ontologically differentiated whole. Instead, it was seen as an open, indefinitely large or infinite universe united only by its fundamental constituents and the laws
of nature, in which heaven and earth and all their parts were placed
on the same ontological level; and this in turn implied the disappearance from scientific thought of all considerations based on value,
perfection, harmony, meaning, and aim, none of which could have a
place in the new ontology.[176] Most of these principles, as we have
seen, were adumbrated or explicitly stated in Bacon's philosophy. His
strict demarcation of theology from natural philosophy was intended
to free the positive sciences from the detrimental effects of religious
zealotry and superstition. His disparagement of final causes in scientific explanation involved the abandonment of teleology with all its
religious implications of purpose and value in natural phenomena.
His theory of the universe represented a clear break from the long-
dominant concept of the great chain of being with its gradations of
value at different levels of existence. He rejected any qualitative distinction between the earth and the heavens, considering all phenomena as subject to a uniform causality and the laws of nature. As the
ultimate component of things he postulated first atoms and later a
particulate kind of matter. The world for him consisted therefore of
body or matter, whose configurations and motions and their causes
were the subject of natural philosophy. The spirits that he believed to
exist in all tangible bodies were themselves body behaving in accor-
dance with natural laws. In one form or another, nearly all of these
ideas entered into the new image of the universe in the course of the
seventeenth century. Thus it is pointless to deny or minimize the importance of Bacon's role in the scientific revolution, to which, when
the latter is seen in the broadest perspective, his philosophy made a
seminal and visionary contribution.

1. Francis Bacon as a boy. Colored terra-cotta bust, probably by an Italian artist, made around 1572. Reproduced from the original at Gorhambury House by kind permission of the Earl of Verulam.

2. Francis Bacon's father, Sir Nicholas Bacon. Colored terra-cotta bust, probably by an Italian artist, made around 1572. Reproduced from the original at Gorhambury House by kind permission of the Earl of Verulam.

3. Francis Bacon's mother, Lady Ann Bacon. Colored terra-cotta bust, probably by an Italian artist, made around 1572. Reproduced from the original at Gorhambury House by kind permission of the Earl of Verulam.

4. Francis Bacon as a young man of eighteen. Miniature by Nicholas Hilliard, inscribed with Bacon's age, the date 1578, and the motto "Si tabula daretur digna, animum mallem" (If I could only paint his mind). Reproduced from the original at Belvoir Castle by kind permission of the Duke of Rutland.

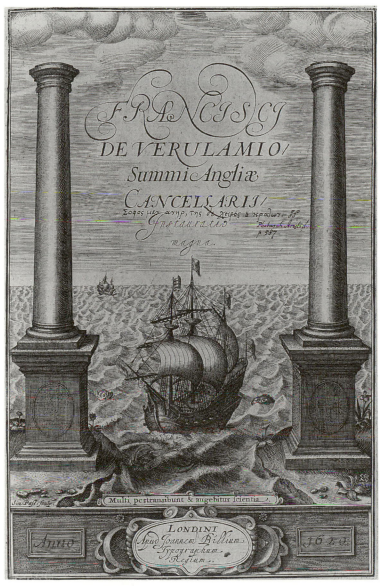

FRANCISCI
DE VERULAMIO,
Summi Angliæ
CANCELLARII,
Instauratio
magna.

Multi pertransibunt & augebitur scientia.

LONDINI
Apud Joannem Billium
Typographum
Regium.

Anno

1620.

5. Frontispiece of Bacon's *Instauratio Magna* (*The Great Instauration*), 1620, symbolizing the ship of knowledge returning through the Pillars of Hercules from its voyage of discovery in unknown seas. The Latin motto below is taken from the prophecy in the Book of Daniel 12:4: "Many shall run to and fro, and knowledge shall be increased." This engraving was made by Simon van de Pass, a Dutch artist working in London. Reproduced from the original edition by kind permission of the Folger Shakespeare Library.

APHORISMI
DE INTERPRETATIONE
NATVRAE,
ET REGNO HOMINIS.

APHORISMVS
I.

 Omo *Naturæ minifter, &
Interpres, tantum facit, &
intelligit, quantum de Na-
turæ Ordine re, vel mente,
obferuauerit, nec amplius
fcit, aut poteft.*

II.

*Ec manus nuda, nec Intellectus fibi permiffus,
multùm valet; Inftrumentis & auxilijs res perfi-
citur; quibus opus eft, non minùs ad intellectum, quàm
ad manum. Atque vt inftrumenta manûs motum aut*

E 2   cient,

6. The first aphorism of the first book of Bacon's *Novum Organum* (*The New Organon*), 1620: "Man, as the servant and interpreter of nature, can do and understand so much and so much only as he has observed in fact or in thought of the course of nature; and beyond this he neither knows anything or can do anything." Reproduced from the original edition by kind permission of the Folger Shakespeare Library.

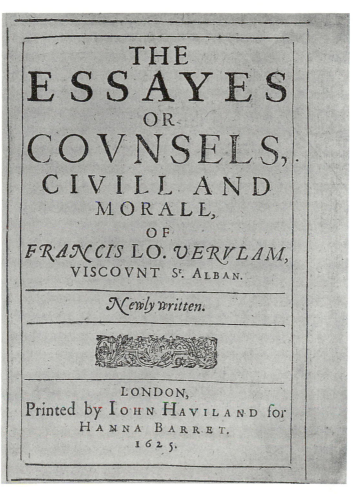

THE
ESSAYES
OR
COVNSELS,
CIVILL AND
MORALL,
OF
FRANCIS LO. VERVLAM,
VISCOVNT St. ALBAN.

Newly written.

LONDON,
Printed by IOHN HAVILAND for
HANNA BARRET.
1625.

7. Title page of the 1625 edition of Bacon's *Essays*, the last edition to be published in Bacon's lifetime. This work has never been out of print, and his essays remain the best-known writings of this kind in the English language. Reproduced from the original edition by kind permission of the Folger Shakespeare Library.

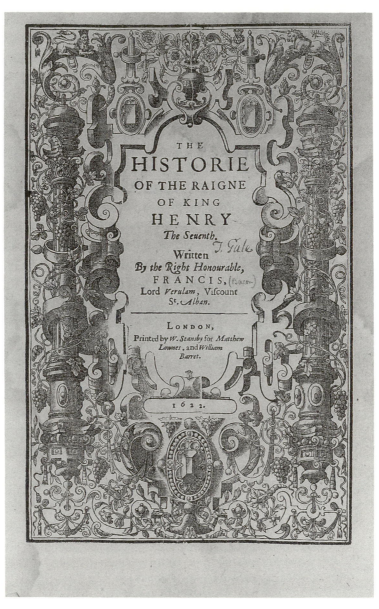

THE

HISTORIE
OF THE RAIGNE

OF KING

HENRY
The Seuenth.

Written
By the Right Honourable,
FRANCIS,
Lord *Verulam*, Viscount
S.t *Alban.*

LONDON,
Printed by *W. Stansby* for *Matthew
Lownes*, and *William
Barret.*

1 6 2 2.

8. Title page of the first edition of Bacon's *The History of the Reign of King Henry the Seventh* (1622). Bacon's portrayal of Henry VII and his government is one of the foremost English historical works of the seventeenth century and influenced generations of historians. Reproduced from the original edition by kind permission of the Folger Shakespeare Library.

The right Honble, Francis Lo: Verulam, Viscount Sct Alban. mortuus 9 Aprilis,
Anno Dni. 1626. Annoq, Aetat 66.

9. Engraving of Bacon from his *Sylva Sylvarum*, published in 1627, the year following his death. The portrait was the work of the Dutch artist Simon van de Pass. Reproduced from the original edition by kind permission of the Folger Shakespeare Library.

10. Bacon as lord chancellor, eighteenth-century copy by an unknown artist of an earlier portrait at Gorhambury House. Reproduced by kind permission of the National Portrait Gallery, London.

11. Tomb effigy of Bacon in St. Michael's Church, St. Albans, by an unknown sculptor. Photographed from an electrotype copy. The monument was erected by Bacon's friend, admirer, and creditor, Sir Thomas Meautys, who married Bacon's niece and inherited the Gorhambury estate. In his last will Bacon said that he bequeathed his "name and memory . . . to men's charitable speeches and to foreign nations and the next ages." Reproduced by kind permission of the National Portrait Gallery, London.

4

Human Philosophy: Morals
and Politics

Moral Knowledge and *Vita Activa*

Bacon was not a moralist in the particular sense that he looked upon the world of man primarily as a scene of the conflict between good and evil; but his experience in the dangerous, intensely rivalrous world of the Elizabethan and Jacobean courts made him a keen student of human nature, its varieties, permutations, and disguises. In his capacity as a longtime royal servant, adviser, and minister, politics and problems of power between men and between states were never far from his mind. These interests were transmuted into philosophical reflections in various of his writings that touched upon human conduct, ambitions, and the ends of life. The plan he laid out for *The Great Instauration* made no provision for the inclusion of moral philosophy, politics or political theory, historiography, or several of the other subjects he dealt with in some of his works. In *The New Organon*, it is true, he did not limit the inductive method to natural philosophy but stated that it was equally applicable to all of the sciences, including ethics and politics.[1] He never attempted, though, to give effect to this sweeping claim, which thus remained no more than an untried theoretical possibility. Bacon's moral and political reflections were therefore independent of his natural philosophy and must be understood in terms of their own principles.

In his threefold division of philosophy, human philosophy c• humanity was described as a separate part whose subject was mankind's

knowledge of itself. This encompassed man in his individual and social aspects—man "segregate" and man "congregate"—and compre-
hended both moral and civil philosophy.[2] Bacon discussed moral philosophy in each of his two surveys of knowledge, *The Advancement of
Learning* of 1605, and its expanded Latin version of 1623, *De Augmentis*, which are substantially alike in their treatment. He also commented on moral questions in his *Essays*, as well as in several other
writings.[3] These sources enable us to gain an understanding of his
moral viewpoint and its presuppositions.[4]

His approach to moral philosophy was preeminently practical,
looking invariably to use. One of his chief accusations against traditional moral teaching in philosophy was that it painted fine pictures
of goodness and the virtues without showing how to attain them. He
connected moral knowledge not only with reason but with the will,
which, moved by the passions, can mistake a false for a genuine good.
This branch of knowledge accordingly had two parts: one, "the exem-
plar or platform of the good," described the nature of the good; the
other, "the culture or georgics of the mind," prescribed the rules for
accommodating the will to the good.[5] To establish the nature of the
good, he invoked an axiom derived from "first philosophy." The latter consisted of the prior logical and conceptual principles common
to all the sciences. One such principle, as formulated in physics, specified that "whatever is preservative of a greater form is more powerful
in action." When applied to morals and politics, it affirmed that
"whatsoever contributes to preserve the whole state in its own nature,
has greater power than that which benefits only the particular members of that state."[6] This axiom accordingly defined the moral good.
Bacon pointed out that everything is imbued with an appetite both
toward its individual or self-good and toward the good of the whole of
which it is part. The latter, however, is the greater and worthier "because it tends to the conservation of the more general form." In
human beings, the desire for the common good is more strongly en-
graved unless they are degenerate. He did not try to defend this de-
batable claim but noted that the exaltation of the good of all over
private and particular good is in complete harmony with the Christian religion and the law God gave to mankind. With the help of this
principle, he then undertook to resolve what he termed "some of the

most important controversies in moral philosophy," discussed by
Aristotle, the Stoics, and other thinkers.[7]

The first question he addressed was the famous one of whether the
active or the contemplative life was superior. Aristotle had considered the contemplative life of the philosopher the highest for man;
but Bacon, needless to say, decided in favor of the active life, which
could exert itself for the good of all, whereas the contemplative life
placed its goal exclusively in personal well-being. Another question
was whether happiness lay, as the Epicureans believed, in pleasure
and tranquillity of mind. He rejected this view as well on the ground
that it took account only of private repose and contentment, not the
good of society. A third question was whether happiness was to be
found, as the Stoic philosopher Epictetus thought, solely in the things
within men's power, lest in seeking for more they expose themselves
to disturbance and the blows of fortune. Bacon also opposed this
conception, of course, maintaining that to strive for good and virtuous ends for the public, even if one should fail, brought more happiness than to gain everything one could want for one's private benefit.
He likewise dissented from the opinion that philosophers should
avoid perturbations of mind and the occasions that create them. Instead, he held that they should help men to shape a course of life in
which, conscious of their duties to society, they could endure and
overcome the greatest perturbations and temptations.[8] Regarding individual good, he pointed out that it could be active or passive, hence
striving either to conserve or to increase and perfect what it valued.
Even in this case, however, where self-good alone was involved, he
praised its active form as higher and more worthy. Critical of philosophies that preached abstention and renunciation, he characterized
their counsels as "the precaution of cowardice and pusillanimity."
Looking at the common good, which referred to society, he equated
it with duty—both the duty every person owes as a member of the
community, and the particular duties incumbent on individuals in
their different ranks, vocations, and professions. He expressed the
further opinion that for honest and virtuous men to discharge their
duties, they needed to know and understand evil, because without
this knowledge their virtue would be sheer ignorance, and they would
be incapable of correcting the wicked or seeing through their malice.

On this account he declared his appreciation of Machiavelli, whose writings "openly and unfeignedly . . . describe what men do, and not what they ought to do."[9]

Bacon's moral philosophy thus began with the strongest possible commendation of the active life of engagement in the world on behalf of the common good as the best and worthiest life for the individual. It also approved the moral realism of Machiavelli and urged the need of acquaintance with evil as essential to virtue. His endorsement of the *vita activa* placed him in the long tradition of thinkers such as Cicero, whose moral doctrine gave priority to men's social duties to others and to their country. It likewise reiterated one of the major themes of Renaissance civic humanism, which ascribed great value to the active life of man as a citizen and participant in the commonwealth.[10] At the same time it ran directly counter to the particular Stoic doctrines that equated the best life with *apatheia* or a state of indifference to external circumstance and with *otium* or a private existence of leisure and freedom from public responsibilities. It was no less opposed to the Christianized neo-Stoicism of Bacon's time advanced by such influential writers as the humanist scholar Justus Lipsius, who advocated a privatistic ethic of neutrality, withdrawal, and avoidance of involvement in public affairs.[11] It might also be seen in part as a rationalization of Bacon's own political ambitions and long years devoted to the royal service. It is clear, too, that it had a close affinity with his conviction that the main end of knowledge should be the improvement of human life.

After clarifying the nature of the good, Bacon proceeded to consider the culture of the mind or the means of acquiring virtue. To attain this kind of knowledge, in which he found moral philosophy deficient, he believed that each person needed to make a self-accounting in order to determine which ends were in his power and which were not. This could not be done without an understanding of the varied characters, dispositions, and passions of human beings; and as the best source for this purpose he recommended the works of historians and poets, which show character in action. The aim of such an inquiry would be to gain "an accurate dissection of minds and characters" and learn the secret dispositions of particular men in order to frame better rules for training the mind.[12] He then took note of some of the factors that affect the will and appetites and thereby influence the individual's morals—factors like custom, habit, education, imitation, praise and reproof, books, company, and the like. Choosing custom and habit for special treatment, he presented several precepts or exercises of the mind designed to aid in the development of virtuous habits. His last suggestion on this score was that the most effective means of acquiring virtue was to choose good and virtuous ends that lay within one's power and pursue them resolutely throughout life. He perceived the highest expression of this disposition in the charity taught by the Christian faith as a virtue that comprehends all virtues.[13]

With these truisms, he concluded his treatment of the culture of the mind and that part of human philosophy concerned with the individual apart from society. Despite his complaint of the limitations of earlier moral philosophy, there is little that is distinctive or original in his own remarks on the formation of virtue. The importance of training and habits in building a virtuous character was a standard point in classical moral philosophy and a major theme in Aristotle's *Nichomachean Ethics*, the greatest ethical treatise of the ancient world. It is noticeable, however, that Bacon's conception of the moral good was not especially rooted in Christianity, even though he was at pains to emphasize its accord with the Christian faith and the virtue of charity. The ethic he propounded was fundamentally secular and autonomous in its character and social and collective in its purpose, a conclusion based on reason that he claimed to derive from the axiom of first philosophy regarding the priority of the preservation of the whole over that of its particular members.

CIVIL KNOWLEDGE AND THE ARCHITECTURE OF FORTUNE

Bacon's classification of learning had separated moral from civil knowledge, and when he passed from the first to the second, he descended from the ideal plane of his previous dicussion to the spotted reality of common life. While moral philosophy strove to imbue the mind with internal goodness, civil knowledge looked only to external goodness, which sufficed for society.[14] It is not easy to follow his reasoning on this point, since his conception of the common good as the criterion of individual virtue and morality surely involved men's actions in society. Nevertheless, by equating civil knowledge with external goodness, which might also be construed as the show or appearance of goodness, he was able to focus on a subject that had always absorbed him, the techniques of self-presentation and advancement in life.

Civil knowledge, according to Bacon, comprised three topics: knowledge of conduct, of negotiations or affairs, and of governing or the commonwealth. To these three corresponded three kinds of wisdom: wisdom in behavior, in business, and in government. To conduct, which he considered had been well handled by other authors, he gave only brief attention, dwelling largely on the necessity of the proper management of facial expressions, gestures, and speech, and of preserving an easy dignity without affectation.[15]

Negotiation received a more extended treatment. It included two divisions, doctrine concerned with scattered occasions and with advancement in life. Observing that hardly anything had been written on wisdom in business, Bacon chose as an illustration of the doctrine of scattered occasions thirty-four of the sayings of Solomon from the biblical Book of Proverbs, which he quoted one by one with the addition of a short explanation. These proverbs were repositories of wise experience which he applied to various contingencies and problems that could occur in life. Their subjects included relationships with princes and superiors, the management of servants, poverty and prodigality, domestic discord, the choice of friends, adaptation to people and circumstances, and so forth. The lessons in living he drew from them were those of an unillusioned mind intent on seeing things as they are, not cynical, but deeply aware of the treacheries of human nature and of the limits, insecurities, and risks attendant on human affairs. For the knowledge of scattered occasions he especially recommended Machiavelli's *Discourses* on Livy, as well as biographies and collections of letters that yielded insight into all manner of transactions large and small.[16]

The other part of negotiations, which concerned advancement in life, addressed the subject of wisdom for oneself. This was a very specific sort of knowledge, he noted, quite different from the wisdom required to advise others, and consisted of the wisdom of foresight into one's own affairs. Bacon found it pointed at in two Roman proverbs, "The wise man fashions his fortune himself" ("Sapiens fingit fortunam sibi"), and "Everyone is the maker of his own fortune" ("Faber quisque fortunae propriae"). Although admitting that these sayings might seem impolitic or arrogant, he justified them as sound and right provided they were taken not as expressions of insolence and pride but as a spur to industry, resolution, and strength of judgment. This knowledge, which he considered untreated in books, he called "the architect of fortune" or "doctrine of advancement in life," adding that its acquisition was very difficult, since it was as hard to be a "true politician as to be truly moral."[17]

Throughout his career Bacon had thought continually about the methods for rising in life. "Ambitus," the Latin word he used for "advancement" in *De Augmentis*, also meant a solicitation and canvassing for office. This is what he himself had done ever since his early years when he had entreated the patronage of his uncle Lord Burghley in order to obtain employment in Queen Elizabeth's government. That he should couch advancement in terms of the architecture of fortune was no accident. Fortune and its effect on human life was an enduring theme in Western thought, meditated on by Roman historians and moral philosophers, Christian theologians such as Augustine, and Renaissance humanists. The extent of fortune's sway over individuals and history, its relationship to fate and whether it was subject to God's providence, and the qualities and devices best suited to secure its favor: these were perennial questions.[18] Fortune's role might be discussed in the context of politics and large historical events or in relation to the personal fate of individuals. Machiavelli, whom Bacon admired and frequently quoted in *De Augmentis*, had written a chapter on fortune in *The Prince*, showing how princes and men intent on winning or retaining power could master fortune by bold action and adaptation to the times.[19] Bacon's father, Sir Nicholas Bacon, used to repeat the Latin saying that everyone makes his own fortune, only to point out that most men marred theirs.[20] In his *Essays*, Bacon discussed fortune in a separate essay, which first appeared in the 1612 edition and again slightly enlarged in the edition of 1625. Here, quoting the Roman proverb, he declared that "chiefly, the mould of a man's fortune is in his own hands." In another observation, he commented that it was an unfortunate trait to be too honest, and that extreme lovers of their country or their masters were never fortunate because they placed their thoughts on others rather than on themselves.[21]

In *The New Organon* Bacon had described fortune as one of the idols imposed upon the mind by words, and as a fiction corresponding to no reality.[22] Doubtless he was thinking then of fortune as a personified force ruling over human affairs; and it may be remembered that for the Romans, Fortuna was a goddess, and that the Christian philosopher Boethius had depicted her as a wanton power whose revolving wheel arbitrarily raised men up and cast them down. But though he regarded fortune in this sense as nonexistent, it is clear that when it was understood as the various accidents that can decisively further or frustrate men's plans and projects, fortune and its control was a subject he considered worthy of serious deliberation. In beginning his discussion of it in *De Augmentis*, he stated that "as an instrument of virtue and merit," fortune "deserves its own speculation and doctrine."[23] This doctrine is what he attempted to provide in the several precepts that followed.

Bacon's treatment of the architecture of fortune was in essence a concise disquisition on the arts of self-advancement. His point of view was quite objective and largely devoid of moral judgment until the end, when he introduced some pious comments to give a virtuous turn to his preceding remarks. The historical examples he cited were mainly figures from Roman history like Caesar, Pompey, Augustus, and Tiberius, while Cicero and Tacitus were two of the authors he quoted most. Although in the main he appeared to have political advancement in mind as the matter at stake, his observations were plainly intended to apply to some of the other worldly prizes men might seek.

His first two and perhaps chief precepts focused on the importance of being able to see deeply into the people one had to deal with and of knowing one's self. To attain the former, one needed information on their natures, desires, and aims, their habits, weaknesses, advantages, and disadvantages, their friends, factions, patrons, and clients, their enemies and competitors; one also needed to know about their particular actions, who had supported and opposed them, and their results. Knowledge of men could be obtained from their faces, expressions, words, acts, dispositions, ends, and the reports of others. While outward deportment might deceive, certain subtle motions of the eyes, mouth, face, or gesture could reveal the hidden mind. Few people, moreover, were so skillful in dissembling as not to be detected, nor so true to their secrets and concealed purposes as not to betray them in one way or another. Counterdissimulation could also be effective in eliciting secret thoughts and feelings, in accord with the proverb "Tell a lie, and find the truth." The surest key, though, to unlock the minds of others, Bacon advised, was by searching and thoroughly understanding their natures and character or their intentions and ends; simple and weaker people could best be interpreted by their natures, the wiser and more reserved by their ends. In the case of princes, they were best read through their natures, because, standing at the summit of human desires, they did not usually have fixed ends to which they constantly aspired. Further means for knowing others included discretion in both speech and secrecy, using liberty in speaking to provoke the same in others, and secrecy as the occasion required. It was also essential to develop a watchful and ready habit of mind so as to remain alert to every possibility.[24]

The environment Bacon seemed to presuppose in all these recommendations was a fiercely competitive one of different human types and marked by ambition, concealment, secrecy, and dissimulation. It was a world of many obscure signs whose meaning had to be deciphered by those who aimed to prosper in it. Its nearest embodiment was the royal court in which Bacon had gathered almost all the experience that underlay his reflections on fortune and self-advancement.

Next to the knowledge of others came the knowledge of one's self, which was vitally important, Bacon thought, both as a rule of wisdom and for its special relevance to politics. Self-knowledge required that men make a careful survey of their abilities, virtues, failings, and disadvantages and determine how far their nature and manners agreed with the state of the times. If the accord between the two was close, they could allow their dispositions greater scope and freedom; if it was not, they had to be more cautious and reserved. They needed to consider whether their nature was adapted to their professions and course of life in order to choose what was fittest for themselves. They needed also to judge how they compared with their equals and rivals who were competing for the gifts of fortune, and to make sure that they chose friends and dependents suitable to their own nature. In picking examples on which to model themselves, they must be careful to select those appropriate for them; otherwise their attempt at imitation would be vain.[25]

But essential as self-knowledge was, Bacon emphasized that it was insufficient unless a man likewise knew how to exhibit himself to best advantage, to disclose himself, and to turn and shape himself according to occasion. It was therefore an important attribute of wisdom to be able to display gracefully and skillfully one's virtues, merits, and fortune, which one might do without arrogance or arousing distaste, while prudently concealing one's vices, defects, misfortunes, and blemishes. He mentioned several ways that one's virtues could be shown, as well as some precepts for covering up defects. With respect to the disclosure of one's self, he proposed a wise middle course in revealing or concealing one's designs. Secrecy and dissimulation could be useful, but the latter also bred errors that could ensnare the dissembler himself. As for adaptation to occasions, the main thing he stressed was the need to make the mind obedient to opportunities and circumstances. One had to know how to change when occasions changed, and "nothing [was] more politic than to make the wheels of the mind concentric and voluble with the wheels of fortune."[26]

In this last advice the resemblance and indebtedness to Machiavelli's view is evident. In *The Prince* and elsewhere the Italian writer had argued that political success depended above all on adaptation to the time; fortune favored those who conformed to and altered with circumstances rather than opposing them.[27]

Besides the means to know one's self and others, Bacon propounded some additional precepts on the architecture of fortune that included a warning not to row against the stream, plus the advice that one preserve a way out when engaging in an enterprise. At two points he alluded to Machiavelli. The first concerned wealth as a means to enlist fortune. On this, after cautioning that the importance of wealth should not be exaggerated, he quoted Machiavelli's dictum that the true sinews of war were not money but a people's military valor; by the same token, he maintained that the true sinews of fortune were also not money but a man's wit, courage, audacity, resolution, and industry. The second point concerned the moral character of the precepts he had given. Terming them "good arts," he said that for "evil arts" one needed to go to Machiavelli's principles that one should cultivate the appearance of virtue without practicing it and that men are best controlled by fear. He rejected such principles as a "corrupt wisdom," and while granting that fortune might sometimes be advanced more quickly with their help, opined that "it is in life, as it is in ways, the shortest way is commonly the foulest and muddiest, and surely the fairer way is not much about."[28]

Bacon concluded his account of the architecture of fortune in *De Augmentis* with some final religious reflections in behalf of virtue and against the use of wicked arts.[29] Despite his rejection of Machiavelli's immoral standpoint, he had much in common with him. He shared the Florentine theorist's instrumental approach to human affairs and his calculated appraisal of means. No less than the latter did he insist on accommodation to times and circumstances as the pathway to success. Moreover, it is not easy to be convinced of his entire sincerity in disavowing the methods with which Machiavelli's name was identified. The goal of advancement in life, for which he designed his precepts on the architecture of fortune, was not in itself a moral one. Nor need it have had anything to do with the common good that he took as his moral standard for individual conduct. In the advice he gave to those who aspired to rise, he recommended masking and role-playing, the manipulation of others, and a dissimulation that could easily become outright dishonesty. We find numerous instances of these methods in the advice contained in the private memoranda he set down for his own guidance in 1608, which have been discussed in the first chapter. A wisdom of expediency and opportunism seemed to occupy a larger place in his doctrine of the architecture of fortune than did morality. Despite his references to religion, the ideas Bacon associated with civil knowledge were thoroughly worldly in their concentration on personal success and self-aggrandizing ends. If here he also envisaged a kingdom of man, it was one in which men adept in the arts of advancement in life competed for advantage, power, and the gifts of fortune.

Moral Perspective in Bacon's Essays

To do justice without partiality to Bacon's moral position, however, we need to take account of his other statements pertaining to the subject that are part of his *Essays*. A consideration of the latter is essential to the comprehension of both his moral and his political beliefs. At present we are concerned only with the first, and I shall look at some of his essays with this object in view. The *Essays* is Bacon's most popular work, reprinted thirteen times during his life and in many later editions. First published in 1597 as a small collection of ten essays, it went through two further editions in 1612 and 1625 in which the treatment and contents were continually expanded and developed. The third edition of 1625 was a substantial book containing fifty-eight essays, including twenty new ones, on a wide diversity of subjects.[30] A number of those added to the later editions were very likely intended, as R. S. Crane showed many years ago, to supply gaps in the knowledge of certain subjects that Bacon had noted in *The Advancement of Learning*.[31] The essays have been variously interpreted. One scholar, Karl R. Wallace, saw them as an attempt to apply the inductive method to moral problems.[32] Another, Stanley E. Fish, has striven to explain them as an exemplification of Bacon's scientific and critical approach to knowledge, and hence written in a manner designed to create a continuous experience of unsettlement, perplexity, and uncertainty in his readers in order to incite them to inquire further.[33] More recently, Robert K. Faulkner has argued that Bacon gave the essays a concealed order to further their covert purpose of insinuating various ideas subversive of received beliefs and values as part of his revolutionary plan to prepare the way for a progressive new political and social order.[34] None of these readings seems to me plausible or genuinely supported by the essays themselves; the last one in particular is lacking in evidence and wholly improbable.

The essays are generally persuasory and positive in tone rather than exploratory or tentative, exhibiting their subjects in several different aspects and using various literary devices to make their point.[35] Where they diverge from common opinion, Bacon does not disguise the departure. Their character and purpose were clearly indicated in the title of the 1625 edition: *The Essayes or Counsels, Civill and Morall.* The posthumous Latin translation issued in 1638 by William Rawley, Bacon's chaplain and secretary, was entitled *Sermones Fideles sive Interiora Rerum*, signifying the work's intention to penetrate to the inside of things. In his dedication of the 1625 edition to James I's favorite, the duke of Buckingham, Bacon said that the essays "come home to men's business and bosoms," which again conveys their essential character.[36] They are in the main practical discourses on worldly matters, and while they have no logical order or unity of content, they may be read in part as a further treatment of the architecture of fortune that Bacon had previously discussed in *De Augmentis*. Some of the essays deal with policy for princes and men in high position, others with serious intellectual questions like truth and atheism, and still others with subjects like gardens, buildings, and masques. A number, however, are written from the viewpoint of those seeking advancement in life. Bacon proffers concise advice and judgments on civil business, situations, conduct, and the weighing of character and motives. The work's appeal is due to the pragmatic intelligence and knowledge informing its observations, which are expressed in a style employing striking images, apt examples and quotations, and pithy aphorisms. Of course, exemplary moral sentiments may be found in the essays. The one on goodness, for example, exalts goodness as "[the greatest] of all virtues and dignities of the mind." The essay on envy condemns this particular vice as "the vilest affection, and the most depraved." The essay on unity in religion is in part an argument for moderating religious controversies and refraining from persecution.[37] Many of the essays, on the other hand, are concerned with effectiveness rather than morality and are notable for the same realistic quality that Bacon praised in Machiavelli: that is to say, they deal with men as they are and not as they ought to be.

Let us look at the essay "Of Negotiating" as an example. It is a succession of packed sentences showing the reader how to deal with someone in a piece of business. Among other advice, the observation "It is better dealing with men in appetite, than with those that are where they would be," indicates the desirable position in a negotiation; the other party should be hungry to obtain what you have to offer. The concluding portion explains the way "to work" another party, that is, to get him to serve your interest. "If you would work any man, you must either know his nature and fashions, and so lead him; or his ends, and so persuade him; or his weakness and disadvantages, and so awe him; or those that have interest in him, and so govern him."[38] What is pictured here is not immoral but simply the average morality of the world, in which it is permissible and expected of you to try to manipulate and get the better of someone.

Assumed throughout the essays is the hierarchic social and political order of the age based on gradations of status determined by birth, wealth and landed property, titles of honor, profession, and office. "Of Negotiating," discussed in the preceding paragraph, may be taken in conjunction with several other essays expressive of Bacon's views on related themes grounded in this type of society and its politics centered in the monarch's court and government. "Of Followers and Friends" dispenses advice on the right sort of followers to have. It avers that the most honorable following consists of those who look to advance themselves by virtue and merit. This point is immediately modified, though, in the statement that "to speak truth, in base times active men are of more use than virtuous." In a preceding essay on friendship, Bacon had extolled the great benefits to be derived from this relationship. "Of Followers" tells us, however, that "there is little friendship in the world," least of all between equals, and the kind that does exist is mostly "between superior and inferior, whose fortunes may comprehend the one the other."[39] Bacon would thus have it that friendship is generally based more on material interest than on affection.

"Of Suitors," which follows next, focuses on the prosecution of suits and petitions for preferment or some kind of favor. Bacon notes the variety of motives men have in pursuing suits and points out that the latter are often undertaken by "corrupt" and "crafty minds." He recommends the usefulness of secrecy when one is pressing a suit, but especially emphasizes the importance of timing as the main factor: "Timing, I say, not only in respect of the persons that should grant it, but in respect of those which are like to cross it."[40] A succeeding essay, "Of Faction," discusses the best way to act with regard to factions. Bacon's opinion is that "mean men, in their rising, must adhere; but great men, that have strength in themselves, were better to maintain themselves indifferent and neutral." He also notes that when adhering to a faction, one is usually best advised to do so moderately in order to remain acceptable to those of another faction.[41] The last essay in this group, "Of Ceremonies and Respects," examines self-presentation and the great advantages to be gained by good form. It stresses the value of naturalness and ease over artificiality and excessive formality, and says in reference to giving compliments that "there is a kind of conveying of effectual and imprinting passages amongst compliments, which is of singular use, if a man can but hit upon it." Among other comments is the observation that "to apply one's self to others is good, so it be with demonstration that a man doth it upon regard and not upon facility."[42]

All of these essays are concerned with prudential expedients and instruction in appearances in the pursuit of self-interest. They may be thought of as giving effect to the statement in the essay "Of Fortune" that "chiefly, the mould of a man's fortune is in his own hands."[43] Two other essays should be noticed that likewise discuss such expedients. The first, "Of Cunning," is not an endorsement of cunning; on the contrary, at the outset it calls the latter "a sinister or crooked wisdom" and states that "there is a great difference between a cunning man and a wise man. . . ." The essay goes on, nevertheless, to describe a some specimens of cunning that Bacon had noted. One, for instance, is that "when you have anything to obtain of present despatch, you entertain and amuse the party with whom you deal with some other discourse; that he be not too much awake to make objection." Another stratagem, in case a man wants to stop a business he expects someone to propose with a good chance of success, is "to pretend to wish it well, and move it himself in such sort as may foil it." The essay presents various particulars of this kind, not omitting the suggestion that "a sudden, bold, and unexpected question doth many times surprise a man, and lay him open." Such devices Bacon terms "the small wares and petty points of cunning," and he says that it would be good to list them all, since "nothing does more hurt in a state than that cunning men pass for wise." By imparting them, though, he has made them available to anyone who wishes to practice them.[44]

Dissimulation, the subject of the second essay, was not an unusual one for Bacon to have chosen. As I have shown elsewhere, the licitness of dissimulation had been discussed since antiquity by moral theologians and casuists, and its use in politics and religion was widely noted and debated in the sixteenth and seventeenth centuries.[45] Dissimulation was often considered one of the foremost characteristics of courts and courtiers, and Bacon had commented on its prevalence in politics and the courts of princes.[46] It was also a prominent theme in the literature devoted to reason-of-state of which Machiavelli was the most famous exponent. His *The Prince* was notorious for the opinion that rulers were not obliged to keep faith when it was contrary to their interest, but should know how to be great dissemblers in order to disguise their faithlessness.[47] Montaigne discussed dissimulation, and so did the influential neo-Stoic scholar and philosopher Lipsius, who approved its use by rulers for public ends.[48] The context in which Bacon treats it is that of political maneuver and advancement.

The essay opens with the striking thought that "dissimulation is but a faint kind of policy or wisdom," and that it takes a strong mind and heart to tell the truth and do it. For this reason, "it is the weaker sort of politics that are the great dissemblers." To those of keen judgment, however, who can discern what things should be disclosed and what kept secret, and to whom and when, the habit of dissimulation is a hindrance. Only where this quality is lacking must a man be a dissembler as "the safest and wariest way in general." Bacon also notes that the ablest men have generally been frank and open, with a reputation for veracity, so that when they saw the need for dissimulation, they could use it almost invisibly while preserving the opinion of their good faith. All these observations were in substantial accord with the judgment of Machiavelli, who never commended dissimulation as a habitual policy but held that the astute political man will know the occasions when it is necessary to break faith and how to dissemble in doing so.

The essay next distinguished "three degrees of this hiding and veiling of a man's self." The first is "closeness, reservation, and secrecy," which makes it impossible to determine what a man is. The second is "dissimulation," in which a man acts in a manner calculated to show that he is other than what he is. The third is "simulation," in which a man feigns and pretends to be what he is not. In reviewing these three strategies, Bacon emphatically approves the habit of secrecy as both politic and moral. Secrecy draws confidences from others; moreover, it is a great weakness in a man to discover and betray himself. Toward dissimulation his attitude is somewhat noncommittal, and he points out that it is usually necessary as an accompaniment of secrecy. As for simulation, he pronounces it culpable and impolitic "except . . . in great and rare matters"; otherwise it is a vice arising out of a natural falsity and fearfulness.

The dubiety of dissimulation and simulation does not prevent him, however, from assessing their advantages and disadvantages. On the advantage side, they are good for lulling opposition to sleep and for surprise, they enable one to reserve a retreat in a failing undertaking, and they help to discover others' minds. Of their disadvantages, the greatest is that they deprive a man of trust and belief, among the principal instruments of action. In conclusion, Bacon opines that the best combination of these practices is to enjoy a reputation for openness, to preserve secrecy by habit, to employ dissimulation when needed, and to possess the power of simulation if there is no other remedy.[49]

Bacon's handling of this subject is to some extent an exercise in equivocation. While secrecy is strongly recommended, dissimulation is not totally endorsed nor simulation completely reprehended. The reader is instructed that all of them are resources and that the latter two are permissible or necessary in certain circumstances. The moral standpoint is only faintly present in this essay, if it is not a mere camouflage. Truth telling, trust, and candor are regarded as means, not intrinsic values in human relationships or politics. To get on best in the world, one must know when to be and not to be truthful. Bacon admires most of all the strong, capable man who rarely needs to dissemble, but he also reveals his own penchant for self-concealment in his belief that secrecy is a cardinal part of wisdom.[50]

His distrust of men and rather cynical opinion of friendship are matched by his negative view of love. In his essay "Of Love," he could find nothing good to say about this elemental human feeling, which he regarded chiefly as an irrational passion responsible for much mischief in life. Great spirits and great business, he declared, have no room for love. Of the lover who kneels in adoration before his beloved, he spoke with contempt. In his considered judgment, it was impossible to love and be wise. If one could not avoid love, then his advice was "to sever it wholly from [the] serious affairs and actions of life," because once it came into conflict with business, it prevented men from being "true to their own ends."[51]

Bacon's discussion of advancement in life and coping with fortune did not entirely ignore moral principles. In the essay entitled "Of Wisdom for a Man's Self," he criticized those who were too great lovers of themselves, maintaining that one should "divide with reason between self-love and society." Wisdom for a man's self, he said, can be a "depraved thing" resembling "the wisdom of rats," who will be sure to leave a house "before it fall." The rule he proposed was "to be so true to thyself, as thou be not false to others, specially to thy king and country."[52]

Notwithstanding such occasional qualifications, however, the essays as a whole convey the unmistakable impression that he was more intent on the means men could employ to attain their ends than on the worthiness of the ends themselves. Scholars have often noted that the amoral standpoint implicit in many of his comments closely resembles that of Machiavelli, whose influence it in part reflects.[53] I shall return to the relationship between Bacon and Machiavelli later in this chapter when discussing the former's politics.

There is a definite and unresolved paradox, though, in Bacon's moral attitude. When he contemplated individuals apart from society, he found their foremost virtue to be a concern for the common good as their standard of action. At this point his view remained in accord with the humanitarian *philanthropia* that actuated his natural philosophy and search for an operative science. On the other hand, when he looked at men as they interacted in society, his standpoint became largely one of moral neutrality in which he considered them in the same objective spirit as he did other phenomena of nature. He saw them then as self-centered creatures incessantly competing for the goods of position and power, and he ministered to their desires by the methods he recommended. These methods had in common the aim of deciphering others' motives and of controlling, deceiving, and making use of people for one's own personal interest and ambitions. Bacon never showed any recognition of the discord between the humanitarianism of his natural philosophy and the concentration on self-interest that pervaded parts of his human philosophy. And this concentration is consistent with all that we know of his own political life and struggle for advancement, which reveal him as morally rather obtuse, lacking in strong human feeling for most people, and not exceptionally scrupulous or sensitive in his choice of means for getting on.

The value he attributed to secrecy may help account for the attention he gave to secret writing or ciphers, a topic included in *De Augmentis* as part of his treatment of the transmission of discourse. There he discussed and included examples of several kinds of ciphers. The purpose for which he considered them was mainly political or governmental, connected with the need to preserve the secrets of princes. The subject led him to recall that he had invented a cipher himself while in Paris as a youth, which he thought still worthy of use; and he lamented that because of the "unskillfulness of secretaries and clerks in the courts of kings . . . the greatest matters are commonly trusted to weak and futile ciphers."[54] I think it can hardly be questioned that secrecy held a powerful fascination for Bacon. This could have been due in part, as I have suggested earlier, to the need to conceal his homosexuality, if indeed he was homosexual, as contemporary report indicated. Whatever the reason, it seems to have corresponded to a proclivity in his own nature for what he described in his essay on dissimulation as the "hiding and veiling of a man's self," which was likewise reflected in the precepts he gave for advancement in life.

POLITICS, POLICY, POWER

Among the divisions of civil knowledge mapped out in *De Augmentis* was one dealing with empire and government. Empire in this context signified not an imperial state with colonies but rule, dominion, or state power. From his discussion of this subject, however, Bacon first excluded certain unnamed matters on which he said he must be silent because they pertained to the *arcana imperii*, or secrets of state. Throughout his political writings he was always aware that certain aspects of government were unfit for public exposure. What he left himself for consideration, therefore, were the three arts of government dedicated to the preservation, the prosperity, and the expansion of dominion. As he estimated that the first two had already been well handled, he addressed himself solely to the last in the form of a short treatise on the extension of empire, followed by another on universal justice that, in fact, was mostly concerned with English law.[55]

Both of these disquisitions, which constituted the sum of his discussion of government in *De Augmentis*, were highly practical in character; and this pragmatism, which likewise pervaded his treatment of moral knowledge, was typical of everything he wrote about civil knowledge or politics. Although much has been written about his politics, Bacon never produced a general political philosophy or theory.[56] His works say very little about the origin and nature of political society, the grounds and limits of political obligation, or the rights and duties of sovereigns and subjects. He speaks hardly at all of the law of nature as a standard of reason by which to measure the actions of rulers or governments and the justness of positive law. He makes no attempt to delineate the nature of justice, nor do his political discussions assume as their essential background and normative framework the principles of the great chain of being and a cosmic moral order within which human society and the body politic have their place as parts of a great organic whole. These principles were virtual commonplaces in much of the political philosophy of the sixteenth century and still retained some of their power in the century that followed.[57] They expressed an idealistic, Christian vision that found its fullest realization in the work of Bacon's contemporary Richard Hooker, whose *Of the Laws of Ecclesiastical Polity* was the greatest and most comprehensive treatise of political philosophy produced by an English thinker during the Tudor era. Intended primarily as a defense of the English church, Hooker's is a masterly work in its learning and range of subjects, its deep reflection, and its acute insights and worldly knowledge. To compare Bacon's political writings with it, however, is to see that they simply ignored the all-embracing philosophical conceptions of law and the great chain of being that informed Hooker's thought.[58]

Bacon's thought on politics was focused largely on actual problems of government and law. It dealt mostly with the constitution and functioning of the English government and with subjects like the preservation of stability, the making of war, and the expansion of dominion. To a great extent it was occupied with policy and the enhancement of governmental efficiency and power. He was close in spirit to Machiavelli, whose writings were a strong and diffuse influence in his political reflections. In several recent discussions of Bacon's political thought, Markku Peltonen has argued interestingly that it is best understood as belonging to the tradition of classical humanism and republicanism. In justification of this view he adduces Bacon's indebtedness to Machiavelli, himself a republican; the priority he assigned to the public good as the criterion of virtue; his preoccupation with civic greatness; and his conviction, shared with Machiavelli, that it was not riches but the military valor of an arms-bearing people that enabled a nation to be strong and victorious in war. Peltonen also points to the fact that some of Bacon's ideas exerted considerable influence upon James Harrington, the foremost English republican theorist of the seventeenth century.[59] While it is no doubt true that Bacon possessed certain affinities with classical republicanism, it is nevertheless quite misleading to place his political thought within the republican tradition. He was emphatically a monarchist and was dedicated as a political man, lawyer, and judge to upholding the king's hereditary authority and prerogatives against attempts to restrict them. Much more significant than classical republicanism in the shaping of his political outlook was the dominant English constitutionalist tradition that regarded England's polity as an exemplary combination of high royal power and liberty under law. This tradition provided the basic framework of his political thought within which the conceptions he derived from republicanism were subsumed. The chief value to him of the latter was their relevance in indicating possible ways by which a country could become a great imperial state. As an independent mind he took from Machiavelli only that which he found useful. He would not have wished to be considered a disciple of the Italian thinker, from whose evil arts he dissociated himself in *De Augmentis*. He doubtless also had Machiavelli in mind in a remark addressed in 1624 to the future King Charles I that "I will never set politics against ethics; especially for that ethics are but as a handmaid to divinity and religion."[60] Nevertheless, his attitude toward Machiavelli was rare, if not unique, among his contemporaries in that it was completely devoid of prejudice or hostility. He quoted or referred to the Italian writer without apology, alluding often to his wisdom or authority.[61] He was as keenly interested in effective government as Machiavelli was, as much concerned with questions of power, and strove no less persistently to be a political realist. Although he said that he would not set politics against ethics, he assuredly did not give ethics priority or prominence in his political observations.[62]

Among the things he found most congenial in Machiavelli was the latter's manner of using historical examples and parallels to derive political instruction. At the beginning of his *Discourses*, Machiavelli asserted that his treatment of politics, based on the examination of cases taken from histories from which lessons for action could be drawn, was a new way never tried before.[63] Bacon attached great value to this method, which was, one might say, an aspect of his empiricism. In *De Augmentis* he referred to it as "that which Machiavelli most wisely and aptly chose for government; namely, observations or discourses upon histories and examples." He also recommended "histories of times" as "the best ground for . . . discourses on government."[64] This was the pattern he himself followed in much of his discussion of political topics.

The comparatively few general statements that Bacon made on kingship and government tended to occur in connection with practical questions and in a context of legal reasoning and argument. One such context was *The Case of the Post-Nati of Scotland*. In this case, among the most important to be heard by the judges during the reign of James I, Bacon as solicitor general appeared as a successful counsel for the crown. At issue was whether the king's Scottish subjects born after his succession to the English throne in 1603 were also, by virtue of this fact, naturalized subjects in England. In the course of his pleading Bacon stated that hereditary monarchy was the only natural form of government, whereas all the other kinds took their existence from preceding laws. Monarchy originally arose when a number of families submitted themselves to a single line, an arrangement "grounded upon nature," although afterward perfected and formalized by means of law. Relying on old, well-tried analogies, he likened monarchy to the father's rule over his wife, children, and servants, to the shepherd's rule over his flock, and to God's government over the

world, "whereof lawful monarchies are a shadow." From these considerations he drew the conclusion that "there be precedents and
platforms of monarchies, both in nature and above nature," and that
while "other states are creatures of law . . . this state only subsisteth by
nature." For this reason he claimed that allegiance and obedience to
hereditary monarchs antedated all laws and were as natural as children's obedience to fathers. As a correlative to this view, he argued
further that subjects in England owed their allegiance not to the law,
the crown, or the kingdom, but to the natural person of the king.[65]

Bacon's involvement in the law also led him into scattered reflections on the nature of sovereignty, the contract of government, and
the power of the people. He had a clear concept of sovereignty as the
supreme power and source of law in the state that was not subject to
law itself. In some aphorisms pertaining to law and justice, he stated
that supreme bodies and lawmakers could not bind themselves to
repeal or change laws because that would be in contradiction to their
supremacy. "Supreme power" could, however, transfer, diminish, or
extinguish itself by granting some of its powers to other organs or by
its incorporation in another state. He also pointed out that although
power may originally have been in the people, once the latter had
transferred this power to government, it could not revoke its gift; the
government then held power by the same right that the people originally had. Nevertheless, another aphorism declared that if a government commits great abuses in violation of the common good, the
people may then reinvest itself with its former power. Bacon based
this possibility on the validity of the principle of *salus populi*, that the
safety and well-being of the people takes precedence over all laws.
Concerning the authority of laws, he held that even bad laws create a
civil obligation though not a moral one, and that subjects owe not
active but passive obedience to unjust and wicked laws and have no
right to resist with arms, even if injured by an iniquitous law.[66] Elsewhere, and looking at England, he conceived that Parliament—
which, of course, included the crown as its head—was the sovereign
power. In his *History of the Reign of King Henry the Seventh*, referring to
a well-known piece of legislation in which Parliament prohibited itself from making a future law on a certain subject, he commented
that such an act was futile, because "a supreme and absolute power

cannot conclude itself . . . no more than if a man should appoint or declare by his will that if he made any later will it should be void."[67]

Much more indicative of the character of his political interests were his numerous discussions relating to the state, government, and war. In these the mental climate was one of political expediency and the utilization of political reason and knowledge to assess means and goals. Some of these discussions appear among the interpretations of classical myths included in *The Wisdom of the Ancients* that he perceived as political allegories. His account of the myth of the river Styx, for example, in whose name the gods swore their most inviolable oaths, applied this fable to the observance of treaties. Echoing Machiavelli, he pointed out the weakness of compacts between princes even when they were sealed by the sanctity of oaths; ambition, greed, and the license of power could always find plausible pretexts to justify and veil bad faith. The only true assurances of faith, therefore, were necessity, which is "the god of the powerful," community of interest, and danger to the state.[68] In the myth of Perseus, an allegory of war, he discerned several rules for a war of conquest. The first was that the choice for conquest should not necessarily be a neighboring nation but rather one whose subjugation would yield the greatest profit, following the example of the Romans, who acquired some of their eastern provinces before they had subdued all of Italy. A second rule was to depict the cause of war as honorable and just in order to obtain the support of the people, soldiers, and allies. A third rule was to pick the kind of war that had definite goals and could be decisively carried through and finished.[69]

Other myths offered Bacon a range of matter for political observations and lessons. He took the stories of Icarus and of Scylla and Charybdis to refer to moderation or the middle way. From them he deduced the striking conclusion that while the middle way was good in morals, it was questionable in politics and to be used with caution and judgment. If one had to perish by the sins of either excess or defect, then excess was preferable because in it "there is something of magnanimity. . . ."[70] This view appears closely allied with his strong endorsement of the active life and the pursuit of one's ends even at the risk of failure.

The myth of Diomedes, who attacked and wounded the goddess Venus, was a parable of the folly and peril of religious zeal and conflicts, which breed such terrible hatreds that even pity is banished.[71] The story of the fierce and brutal Cyclops, who murdered Aesculapius at Jupiter's order and was then slain by Apollo, showed how kings first use cruel and bloody ministers for harsh and odious tasks, then gain acclaim by destroying them to appease popular anger.[72] His treatment of this fable closely resembled the similar episode related in Machiavelli's *The Prince*, in which Cesare Borgia, after employing the cruel Ramiro d'Orco to establish his authority in the Romagna by a reign of terror, then had him executed to dissociate himself from his hated minister.[73]

The myth of the monster Typhon, who was killed for making war on Jupiter, had rebellion as its theme. As Bacon expounded it, kings and their kingdoms are properly like man and wife; but sometimes a king becomes a tyrant and provokes his subjects to rise against him. Rebellion is nourished by the innate depravity and malignant disposition of the common people, resulting in infinite calamities, although able kings can recover their power.[74] Bacon's attitude to the *plebs*, or common people, here and elsewhere is generally disparaging. In contrast to Machiavelli, whose *Discourses* praised the *popolo* for its constancy and devotion to liberty, he pictures the common people as filled with malice toward rulers and inclined to revolt.[75]

Nowhere did Bacon find occasion for more trenchant political analyses than in some of his essays, which in their incisiveness and clarity are like little works of political art. I shall cite a few instances only, of which the first, "Of Empire," discusses some of the problems of governing from the standpoint of kings, who, "being at the highest," "have few things to desire, and many things to fear." The treatment is enlivened as usual by historical examples English and foreign and ancient and modern. The chief theme is that the policy of princes in recent times has been one of "fine deliveries and shiftings of dangers when they are near [rather] than solid and grounded courses to keep them aloof." Bacon especially wished, therefore, to inculcate the necessity of foresight, always recognizing, of course, that "the difficulties in princes' business are many and great." The

essay goes on to survey the possible quarters from which dangers can
arise and must accordingly be guarded against. One is the ambition
of neighboring princes for the acquisition of territory or the engross-
ment of trade. In connection with such threats, he delivers the judgment that "there is no question but a just fear of an immediate danger, though there be no blow given, is a lawful cause of war." Another
danger is domestic, stemming from royal wives or children. There
may also be dangers from churchmen who are too powerful or independent, and from greater and lesser nobilities. In the case of merchants, it is risky to tax them too heavily lest it harm the country's
trade. As for the common people, they present little danger unless
headed by great and powerful leaders or provoked by interference
with their religion, customs, or livelihoods. Finally, soldiers can be
dangerous if kept in a body and accustomed to donatives, but the
ruler can avoid this danger by dispersing them under several com-
manders and not giving them gifts. Amidst the abundant political
intelligence conveyed in this essay, one comment in particular strikes
deep by its exceptional insight. It follows just after Bacon has remarked on how hard and rare it is to keep "the temper of empire."
He then observes that "certain it is that nothing destroyeth authority
so much as the unequal and untimely interchange of power pressed
too far, and relaxed too much." This illuminating sentence contains
the essence of an entire explanation of certain kinds of revolutions in
which repressive regimes that embark upon a policy of liberalization
unleash by their concessions explosive forces and discontents that
lead to their overthrow.[76]

Another of the essays, "Of Counsel," is full of weighty advice on
how kings should use and manage counsels and councillors to best
advantage. Bacon regarded good and faithful counsel as of the utmost importance to government, and he presents a searching analysis
of the subject with comparisons to practices in the French and Spanish monarchies. His discussion concludes with the shrewd remark
that when presiding in council, a king should "beware how he opens
his own inclination too much in that which he propoundeth; for else
counsellors will but take the wind of him, and instead of giving him
free counsel, sing him a song of *placebo*."[77]

The essay "Of Sedition and Troubles" stands out as an acute little treatise on revolutions, their causes and remedies. Bacon's era witnessed a large number of revolutionary civil wars that shook the greatest monarchies and provided him with ample material for his reflections. He took note of the different signs that preceded "tempests in state," observing generally that "when any of the four pillars of government are shaken or weakened (which are Religion, Justice, Counsel, and Treasure), men had need to pray for fair weather." His list of the causes and motives of sedition could be applied to all or most of the rebellions of his time. It included innovations in religion, taxes, alteration of laws and customs, violations of privileges, and "whatsoever, in offending people, joineth and knitteth them in a common cause." Among the remedies he recommended against rebellion, one was prevention, the removal of its material causes such as "want and poverty" in the state by means of constructive economic policies designed to promote trade, manufactures, and agriculture. These last comments may be said to fall into the category of political economy, and Bacon's political vision certainly embraced the economy in presupposing a paternalistic government that regulated economic activity both to preserve stability and to increase the state's power and wealth. Hence, as another of the remedies against sedition, he urged the use of good policy to assure that "the treasure and monies in a state be not gathered into few hands. For otherwise a state may have a great stock and yet starve. And money is like muck, not good except it be spread." A government could do this, he believed, by suppressing or strictly controlling "the devouring trades of usury, engrossing, great pasturages, and the like."[78]

Throughout his political observations, it is noticeable that his approach to problems is never unduly abstract. Writing out of a broad experience of government and extensive historical knowledge, he brings to his discussion a constant sense of the realities with which government must deal. Accordingly, when considering a subject like the remedies against sedition, he says, characteristically, that "there may be some general preservatives, whereof we will speak; as for the just cure, it must answer to the particular disease; and so be left to counsel rather then rule."[79]

The longest of all of Bacon's essays was "Of the True Greatness of Kingdoms and Estates," which dealt with the expansion of empire, a subject that long preoccupied him as a political thinker, minister, and statesman. He inserted a Latin translation of this essay in *De Augmentis* in the section on civil knowledge as an illustration of one of the arts of government and included the original English version in the 1625 edition of his *Essays*.[80] His interest in the expansion of empire was reinforced by the influence of Machiavelli, whose *Discourses* distinguished between republics that merely preserve the status quo and those like Rome that become great by extending their dominion.[81] He shared Machiavelli's assumption that states were power entities ever under actual or potential threat from other powers; and having given considerable attention to analyzing the foundations of the power of states, he was convinced that England's and Britain's destiny lay in expansion.

The germ of the essay on the true greatness of kingdoms lay in an earlier uncompleted treatise of 1608 entitled "Of the True Greatness of the Kingdom of Britain." In the confidential memoranda Bacon wrote to himself in that year, he mentioned this treatise among a list of items concerned with policy. The same list also included the idea of persuading the king that Britain could become the seat of a great monarchy in the West of which he would be the founder.[82] It seems likely that "Of the True Greatness of the Kingdom of Britain," which Bacon addressed to James I, was intended to present this prospect to the monarch. This fragmentary treatise is of interest in several respects. Although written as an inducement to Britain's expansion, it also frequently refers to the "state" or "estate," terms it used interchangeably. It seems evident from such expressions that besides particular forms of government, Bacon recognized the existence of the state as such, an entity conceived as the embodiment of sovereign power typifying the nature of any independent polity. He likewise referred to "reason of estate," by which he meant a judgment grounded upon the state's interests.[83] The main point of the treatise was to prove that Britain was eligible to be a great power. By Britain, it had especially in mind, of course, the recent bond established between England and Scotland in consequence of the accession of the Scottish king, James VI, Queen Elizabeth's successor, to the English

throne as James I. Bacon argued that largeness of territory was not
necessary for expansion and could even be a liability in some cases.
What counted most for expansion was military virtue. As did Machiavelli, whose name he invoked, he denied that money constituted the
sinews of war; the iron of the sword would always overcome gold, and
"the records of all times" concurred that "valor" predominated over
"treasure." He cited the prowess of Britain's people, its favorable position as an island commanding the sea, and the substantial resources
of the English crown as elements of strength. Before coming to an
abrupt end, the treatise also contended that a state could best support a war if its wealth were widely distributed, as shown by the Dutch
and their ability to sustain the enormous charges of their revolt
against and conflict with Spain.[84]

The later essay "Of the True Greatness of Kingdoms and Estates"
was a pure meditation on reason-of-state whose central theme was the
primacy of military power. It dealt with expansion generally, making
only an occasional allusion to Britain, although its application to the
latter was undoubtedly part of its purpose. Pointing out how difficult
it was to estimate correctly a state's real power and forces, Bacon gave
the highest importance to its capacity for war, which required a war-
like people above all else. Like Machiavelli, he disparaged reliance on
mercenaries, arguing that a state must look to its own subjects to be
good and valiant soldiers if it wished to achieve greatness. Several of
his observations examined the social and economic preconditions of
military strength. A people could not be valiant and martial if exces-
sively burdened with taxes. Moreover, taxes "levied by consent of the
estate do abate men's courage less," a proposition in support of which
he cited the excises in the Dutch republic and the subsidies in England, which were granted by Parliament. He thus took the view that
some measure of political freedom made for a spirited people and
was thus a prerequisite of military superiority. He also maintained
that it was incompatible with greatness for a state to have too many
noblemen and gentlemen, the reason being that their large numbers
abased the common people and made them servile and unfit for
military service. In proof of this opinion, he pointed to the contrast
between England and France; although much smaller in territory
and population, England had been an overmatch for France in war

because its "middle people make good soldiers, which the peasants of France do not." By "middle people" he referred to small independent farmers, freeholders, and yeomen, who "had such a proportion of land . . . as may breed a subject to live in convenient plenty and no servile condition."

To be fit for empire, Bacon believed that a state should also be liberal in naturalizing foreigners. As the example of Sparta proved, a handful of people could not sustain wide dominion. On the other hand, the greatest instance of the correct policy was Rome, which in building its empire gave naturalization not only to cities but sometimes even to whole nations. Everything hinged, however, on success in war, and hence the principal instruction in the essay was that "above all, for empire and greatness, it importeth most, that a nation do profess arms as their principal honour, study, and occupation." The Romans, Macedonians, and other peoples of the ancient world had been nations of this kind, and so afterward were the Goths, Saxons, and Normans for a time. In modern Christian Europe, though, only the Spaniards qualified as a nation dedicated to arms. The latter characteristic also required a willingness to go to war on any just occasion or the pretense of one. Neither the natural or the political body, according to Bacon, could be healthy without exercise. He did not hesitate, therefore, to recommend foreign war as a necessary exercise to keep the body politic in health; "for in a slothful peace . . . courages will effeminate and manners corrupt." Some brief reflections followed on the advantages of commanding the sea, which he called "one of the principal dowries of this kingdom of Great Britain." The essay ended with a reiteration of its judgment that the policies it described could bring greatness to the states and kingdoms that adopted them, adding the rather pessimistic note, however, that "these things are commonly not observed, but left to take their chance." This last statement probably sprang from Bacon's years of disappointment as a royal adviser in which he failed to gain acceptance of his main ideas.[85]

"The True Greatness of Kingdoms and Estates" is remarkable for its fidelity to Machiavelli's spirit and teaching. Looking solely to the interests of the state, it integrated history with policy to fashion an argument explaining what made states great and how they could extend their empire. Predominance was the end, superiority in war the essential means, and the statesman's chief task was the promotion of measures that contributed to the state's power.

The position he took in this essay and in the preceding "The True Greatness of the Kingdom of Britain" was one that also guided his policy statements and recommendations as a public man and minister. He was strongly in favor of the political union between England and Scotland that James I was eager to achieve after he came to the throne but which was blocked by the opposition of the English parliament. In Bacon's view, anything that brought the two neighboring countries closer together was an addition to England's strength. In 1607 he delivered a speech as a member of the House of Commons advocating the grant of naturalization to the king's Scottish subjects. Several times during this address he explained that he founded his arguments on "reason of state." Following Machiavelli's practice, he bolstered his case with numerous historical examples to prove the benefits of extending naturalization, and he also referred to the Italian writer by name when quoting his maxim (one of Bacon's favorite sayings) that the true sinews of war were not money but the arms of valiant men.[86] In replying to the fear that if the Scots were naturalized, they would flock to settle in England in overwhelming numbers, one of his answers was that a foreign war was a good way to make use of an excess population. Bacon invariably thought as an imperial statesman and always kept war in mind as a possible instrument of policy. He urged his fellow M.P.'s to "refer our counsels to greatness and power, and not quench them too much with considerations of utility and wealth." The conclusion of his speech, which contained passages identical with those in the unfinished treatise "Of the True Greatness of the Kingdom of Britain," held forth the prophetic prospect that England united with Scotland would grow into one of the greatest monarchies the world had ever seen.[87]

Consistently in favor of the expansion of Britain's dominion, on questions of war and peace Bacon's attitude was entirely determined by considerations of *Machtpolitik*. This is well illustrated by the document he wrote in 1624 addressed to Prince Charles, the heir to the throne, on the subject of a war with Spain. Catholic Spain, which had been England's foremost enemy since Queen Elizabeth's time, was still the preponderant European power in the earlier seventeenth century. As a belligerent in the Thirty Years War, which began in 1618, it had been instrumental in the Catholic conquest of the Palatinate in Germany and the expulsion of its Protestant prince, who was James I's son-in-law. Subsequent Anglo-Spanish negotiations for the restoration of the Palatinate had proved fruitless, and by 1624 the two states were on the verge of hostilities. It was at this juncture that Bacon offered his strategic appraisal of the situation in support of a war.

While recognizing that offensive wars for religion were "seldom to be approved or never," he contended that a war against Spain would be defensive and for just cause. Its grounds were the recovery of the Palatinate and Spain's long-standing attempts to subvert England's Protestant religion and government. A preventive war based on justified fear, even if fought on the enemy's territory, was no less defensive in character, he claimed, than resistance to an actual invasion; and this would be especially true in the case of Spain, which constantly aspired to new conquests and to universal monarchy. As he examined what he called "the balance of forces between Spain and us," he did not doubt that England was Spain's match. Recounting the numerous reverses England had inflicted on Spain during their war in Queen Elizabeth's reign, not least the defeat of the great armada in 1588, he estimated that Spain's power was less at present than it had been then. Among the factors he reckoned in this conclusion were that in Britain, England and Scotland were now united under a single ruler and Ireland subdued; France, "able alone to counterpoise Spain," was also united under its valiant king after the civil war of the preceding century; Venice, Savoy, and the cities and princes of Germany were all apprehensive of Spanish ambitions; and the United Netherlands or Dutch republic outnumbered Spain in ships by five to one. Also, Spain was thinly populated and the number of native Spaniards in its armies small, while England, Scotland, Ireland, and the Dutch were a "seminary of brave military people." Spain's dominions, moreover, were scattered and hard to defend. Although its power was sustained by the flow of treasure from its possessions in the Indies, this flow could be cut off by superior naval strength. Together, the maritime forces of Great Britain and the Dutch republic could beat

Spain at sea, and if this were done, then "the links of that chain whereby they hold their greatness are dissolved." He noted, too, that Spain had few allies and numerous causes of difference with almost all other states.[88]

Although he added several more points, this was the gist of his argument in support of war. The reasons he adduced, a calculus of power, led him to decide that Spain was a declining great power whose supremacy was vulnerable to aggressive adversaries. While he recognized the objection that England might be short of financial resources to undertake a war and that wars were "generally a cause of poverty and consumption," he claimed that in the case of Spain, a sea war would likely be "lucrative and restorative," no doubt because of the rich prizes in captured ships and treasure that could be anticipated.[89]

The war with Spain that Bacon advocated came to pass the next year, following Charles I's succession to his father. It lasted until 1630, four years after Bacon's death. His expectations for it, however, were not borne out. Instead of successes, England suffered humiliating military defeats and failed to achieve the restoration of the Palatinate. Moreover, the war was unpopular and incompetently managed, imposing heavy costs and burdens on an unwilling people, which gave rise to considerable political tension and discontent. But if he was a bad prophet with regard to this particular war, his vision was more than accurate in the longer term. By the mid-seventeenth century Spain's decline was evident, while during the later century and the one that followed, Britain, with its far-flung colonies and domination of the sea, acquired a commercial and imperial supremacy that made it into a world power.

THE ENGLISH GOVERNMENT AND CONSTITUTION

In his ideas of statecraft and advocacy of the expansion of Britain's empire, Bacon's thinking was very near to Machiavelli's, whose unmoralized conception of politics entered deeply into his own outlook. An Italian historian of Machiavelli has said that the latter's "predominating mental gift, in which he outstripped all his contemporaries, was his singular power of piercing to the innermost kernel of historic and social facts."[90] This kind of originality was Bacon's as well and constituted an essential part of his political insight. When it came to his understanding of his country's government and polity, however, he was not a Machiavellian but a statesman whose views were largely consonant with law and English constitutionalist tradition.

Bacon's birth in the kingdom's political elite and his long service to the crown made him familiar with the workings of English government and all or most of its problems. He expressed his views on some of the latter in speeches, legal arguments, and statements of advice. We have a memorable picture of his powers as an orator by his friend the poet Ben Jonson, who wrote that "no man ever spoke more neatly, more presly, more weightily, or suffered less emptiness, less idleness in what he uttered. . . . His hearers could not cough, or look aside from him, without loss. He commanded where he spoke, and had his judges angry or pleased at his devotion. The fear of every man that heard him was lest he should make an end."[91] Always ambitious to attain a leading place in government, he dreamed of replacing his cousin the earl of Salisbury as the king's secretary of state and principal minister. Immediately upon Salisbury's death in May 1612, in a letter to the king advancing his qualifications for higher position, he declared that the deceased minister "was a fit man to keep things from growing worse, but no fit man to reduce things to be much better."[92] As this remark indicates, he was something of a reformer. In the functioning of government he was not satisfied to preserve the status quo but desired to make improvements. Almost all the subjects on which he commented were connected with legal, political, and constitutional controversies. His confidential memoranda of 1608 included cryptic allusions to some of the latter, like the following under the heading of "policy": "the bringing the King low by poverty and empty Coffers": "The greatness of the lower hows in parliament": "Limiting all Jurisdictions. More regularity": "Bookes in commendacion of Monarchy mixt or Aristocracy"; "Lawgyver perpetuus princeps"; "Restoring the Church to the trew limits of Authority since Henry 8ths confusion."[93] These notations reflect the domestic political scene and contested issues after James I became king, and provide a clue to a number of the problems that occupied Bacon's mind in that period.

One of the most important of these was the powers of the crown and the nature of the royal office. Connected with it in part was also the question of Parliament's position in the state and its relationship to the crown. Some of Bacon's statements on these subjects were called forth as a result of legal and political challenges to specific exercises of royal authority and by James I's dealings and disputes with his parliaments over different matters. Although a devoted royal servant, neither as a crown lawyer nor as an adviser was Bacon ever a supporter of unrestricted monarchical absolutism. His theory of English kingship recognized in the monarchy both attributes of sovereignty and legal limitations that secured the liberty and property rights of subjects, while perhaps tipping the balance somewhat more in favor of the former than a number of his contemporaries would have accepted. In the reign of James I, Bacon was often in conflict with his old professional rival Sir Edward Coke, a great lawyer and legal scholar who, after being appointed a judge in 1606, took the position that the king's power or royal prerogative was entirely subject to and limited by the law. Because of his clashes with the king over this issue, he was dismissed from the bench in 1616.

Bacon did not disdain characterizations of kingship as divinely derived. His argument in *The Case of the Post-Nati* acknowledged that kings are "sacred" because of "the conformity of a monarchy with a divine Majesty. . . ." The fact that monarchy, unlike other forms of government, had its foundation in nature antecedent to any law enabled him to compare it, as we have seen, not only to the natural authority of fathers but to God's rule over the world, of which it was the image.[94]

The essential constitutional question, however, was how far the crown in its actions was bound by the law. Among his observations on this point were some he made in connection with a case involving a legal attempt to abridge the jurisdiction of the Council in the Marches of Wales, a judicial and administrative offshoot of the king's council established in the fifteenth century by Edward IV. Reviewing the issue of whether the crown, by its sole authority and without Parliament's sanction, could create this institution as a judicial body, Bacon commented that while some of the king's prerogatives were given him by the law, others came to him immediately from God in the same way as did his inheritance of his crown. The extent of the prerogatives that derived from the law, such as related, for example, to the king's revenue, could be disputed and their limits tried in the ordinary courts of justice. But the king also possessed a "sovereign power" that was of a different nature and not subject to legal adjudication. Bacon called the actions that fell within this power "matters of government and not law" that must be left to the determination of the king and his advisers. This power, he held, was necessary to the state to enable it to achieve the purpose of government, which was the preservation of the public and the general good. He went on to point out how monarchies in name could degenerate into aristocracies and oligarchies because of attempts to make the crown and its prerogatives completely accountable to law. Such a process of "limiting prerogatives" in favor of subjects' rights and laws could even lead without its promoters' intention to civil wars.[95]

In the same observations Bacon presented a further formulation of his conception of the king's prerogative, which affirmed that it consisted of a "double power." One was the ordinary power delegated to the king's judges, triable at law, and administered in all the courts of justice. The other power was inherent in the king's person and made him the supreme judge both in Parliament and in all other courts. This power was "exempt from controlment by any Court of Law." It existed so that the king could discharge his responsibility for the public good and safety as the governor of his people. Yet Bacon nevertheless regarded this second power as still basically consistent with the ultimate supremacy of law. Accordingly, he also stated, "God forbid that we should be governed by men's discretions and not by the law. For . . . a King that governs not thereby can neither be comptable to God for his administration, nor have a happy and established reign."[96]

Bacon's conception of the English monarchy, to which he consistently adhered, thus combined the principles of lawful kingship and of sovereignty by distinguishing the dual but conjoined domains of the king's prerogative. He saw the two as complementary, not conflicting. The first assured the subject's private rights, liberty, and the rule of law; the second, in which the king was absolute, was concerned with policy, government, and what he elsewhere also called "matters of estate."[97] Although in the latter domain the king's acts were not controlled by law, it was always presumed that their aim was the public good and benefit of all his subjects. This doctrine of the royal power and its two branches was by no means peculiar to Bacon. It was held quite widely in the earlier seventeenth century and was sometimes applied by the judges in the king's courts to uphold royal policies whose legality had been questioned.[98]

Bacon also directed his attention to the relationship between the crown and Parliament as one of the major problems of government. James I ran into a number of conflicts with Parliament over the extent of its privileges, fiscal issues, and other grievances, which provoked episodes of opposition to his policies by the House of Commons. Bacon regarded harmony between the king and Parliament as a very high priority of effective government and an important factor in the king's reputation abroad. He had, of course, long parliamentary experience, having sat in all of Queen Elizabeth's parliaments since 1581 and in every one of James I's except the last in 1624. In a speech in the Commons in 1610, he described "the King's Sovereignty" and "the Liberty of Parliament" as "the two elements and principles" of the state, each strengthening and supporting the other. "Take away the liberty of Parliament," he pointed out, and "the griefs of the subject will bleed inwards," giving rise to "sharp and eager humours" that could "ulcerate" and "endanger the sovereignty itself." On the other hand, if the king's sovereignty were to "receive diminution or any degree of contempt with us that are born under hereditary monarchy," the state could not function, and "it must follow that we shall be a *meteor* or *corpus imperfecte mistum* [an imperfectly mixed body]; which kind of bodies come speedily to confusion and dissolution."[99]

This statement leaves no doubt that Bacon conceived England's constitution to be a mixed polity blending regal sovereignty with liberty and consent through the respective positions of the crown and Parliament. He worried, though, that parliaments at times exceeded their proper limits by trenching on sovereignty. This was probably what he had in mind in the mention in his memoranda of 1608 of "the greatness of the lower hows in parliament." In a speech prepared as lord chancellor for delivery in Parliament in 1621, he declared that when tendering its advice to the king, Parliament must take care to respect the "Arcana Imperii, and reserved parts of sovereignty," not entering into matters beyond its legitimate limits and competence.[100] Notwithstanding the problems associated with Parliament, he held that it should be summoned regularly both to knit the subjects' affections to the king and as the usual means of relieving the crown's financial needs.[101] He considered it beneath the king's dignity, however, to give royal money needs prominence over other reasons for calling Parliament. In a letter of advice blaming Salisbury for bargaining with Parliament over money, he urged the king to "put off the person of merchant and contractor and to rest upon the person of a King." The importance he assigned to relations with Parliament may be gauged from his statement in the same letter that it would be "a thing inestimable to your Majesty's safety and service that you once part with your Parliament with love and reverence."[102]

Another problem that concerned him was the judiciary's relationship to the crown. One of the main provocations to this problem was the attitude taken as judge by Sir Edward Coke, who while solicitor general and attorney general under Queen Elizabeth and James I had been a defender of the royal prerogative. After becoming a judge in 1606—he was successively chief justice of the Court of Common Pleas and of the King's Bench—Coke strove to hold the crown completely accountable to law and claimed for the judiciary the duty of deciding the limits of the royal prerogative. A venerator of the common law, he saw the judges of the common-law courts as independent mediators between the king and other parties in disputes over the extent of the crown's powers. Owing to his dominant personality and great legal knowledge, he exerted considerable influence on his judicial colleagues in asserting this doctrine.

Bacon's conception of the royal prerogative and the judges' position did not accord with Coke's. During the latter's tenure on the bench, and while Bacon himself was solicitor general and attorney general prior to his elevation to the office of lord keeper presiding over the Court of Chancery, he had some sharp disagreements with Coke over the king's prerogative. While holding a high view of the judges' calling, he did not consider that their position entailed complete independence of the monarchy and its policies. Besides their duty to defend the law and administer justice impartially, they were

also legal advisers to the crown with an obligation to uphold its prerogative and inherited powers. His essay "Of Judicature" contained a
precise statement of his understanding of the judges' role. The larger
part of the essay described the rigorous standards of conduct they
needed to observe in dealing with private suits, lawyers, and em-
ployees of the courts. Only the final section discussed their relationship in what concerned "the sovereign and the estate." This was to
be a close one, based on frequent consultations with the king whenever law and "matters of estate" affected one another. Matters of state
included "not only the parts of sovereignty" but anything that introduced a great alteration, dangerous precedent, or concerned a great
number of the people. "Just laws" and "true policy" could never come
into conflict, he maintained, being like the spirit and sinews of a body
that move together. Invoking a strong biblical simile, he likened
the judges to the lions that supported King Solomon's throne. Joining power with subordination, they were to be "lions, but yet lions
under the throne," ever careful not to "check or oppose any points of
sovereignty."[103]

Throughout his statements concerning the royal prerogative, Parliament, and the judges, Bacon's aim was to have the several parts of
England's mixed constitution work efficiently and harmoniously together in order to contribute to the state's stability and power. His
desire was that the institutions of government should fulfill their traditional functions well. In his *Discourses*, Machiavelli declared that if
states and other composite bodies were to be preserved from decline
and disintegration, they needed to be restored periodically to their
original principles; hence the only way to renovate such institutions
was "to reduce them to their starting points."[104] Bacon held a similar
view, quite possibly indebted to Machiavelli. On one occasion he recommended to the king that the next parliament be "a little reduced
to its more ancient form," in which it would be called "for some other
business of state, and not merely for money."[105] When he argued that
Parliament should refrain from infringing on the king's prerogative,
he was striving to keep it within the bounds it had been made to
observe under Queen Elizabeth. His essay "Of Great Place" included
a general comment on reform and renovation. He advised the man
in high office "to reduce things to their first institution, and observe

wherein and how they have degenerate; but yet ask counsel of both times; of the ancient time, what is best; and of the latter time, what is fittest."[106] These words well sum up his approach to governmental problems as a statesman who was at once conservative, moderate, and liberal in his political attitudes.[107]

The same attitudes are likewise manifest in relation to the problems of the national church, to which he also gave some attention. The English church, of which the king was the head and whose services the law required every subject to attend, was a branch of the state, its task the religious indoctrination and moral supervision of the people. From without, it was assailed by Catholic opponents as heretical and false; from within, by Puritan Protestants who denounced it as insufficiently reformed and called for further changes in its structure and worship. Although he was not devoid of piety, as many of his statements testify, Bacon's chief concern as a political man was that the church should help sustain national unity and stability. He was alive to the dangers of religious zeal, fanaticism, and clerical inflexibility and intolerance in creating internal conflict and disaffection. In his outlook upon religious matters he was an Erastian and *politique* who believed that the church and churchmen needed firm secular and state control.

Early in his career he had written a privately circulated paper surveying the controversies in the Church of England and discussing ways to moderate them.[108] In 1603, immediately upon James I's accession, he sent the new sovereign a paper of considerations for "the better pacification and edification of the church." Noting that time brought degeneration to all institutions, the church not less than the state, it proposed a number of constructive changes to repair what was corrupt or decayed in the church's spiritual functions. Believing that episcopacy best suited a monarchical state, Bacon summarily rejected any suggestion for the elimination of church government by bishops, a reform many Puritans desired. But some of the alterations he recommended were in accord with the wishes of more moderate Puritans and might be seen as a concession or compromise with their position. Thus he would have associated with the bishops the participation of other clergy in the performance of certain of their responsibilities, and he also argued for modifications in the liturgy, ecclesi-

astical discipline, and other matters that had provoked complaint.
While the substance of doctrine and general rules of government
were immutable, he said, God had otherwise left men at liberty to
determine particular forms of church government, hierarchies, rites,
ceremonies, and discipline in accord with time, place, and circumstances. Deploring the bitterness of religious divisions, he outlined a
program of moderate reforms aiming to distinguish religious essen-
tials from indifferent matters and to achieve the widest ground of
unity in the English church.[109]

This document does not seem to have had any effect upon
James I's religious policy. Bacon never abandoned the standpoint
he took in it, however, and the same spirit informed his essay "Of
Religious Unity," which might be read as a definitive statement of his
attitude toward religious division. Extolling peace as the fruit of unity,
he explicitly distinguished unity from uniformity and "points fundamental" in religion from those reflecting merely differences "of
opinion. . . ." It seemed to him that most religious controversies were
useless, the product solely of intellectual ingenuity and a desire for
contradiction. In their desire for unity, he warned that men should
beware of means that "dissolve and deface the laws of charity and
human society." Thus he condemned the propagation of religion by
wars and by bloody "persecutions to force conscience"; and with an
eye to atrocities in his own time like the St. Bartholomew massacre
in France and the Gunpowder Plot in England, he denounced as
unchristian the murder of princes, butchering of people, and sub-
version of states in the cause of religion. Although the essay did not
envisage religious liberty, Bacon's political philosophy and pragmatic statesmanship made him sympathetic to toleration and a conception of unity that left considerable latitude to differing religious
consciences.[110]

UTOPIAN BACON: *NEW ATLANTIS*

In his many political comments and papers of advice, Bacon was invariably a realistic statesman whose mind was set on facts, institutions
and problems of government, and estimates of power. At the height
of his reflections of this kind, he could consider the public good and

Britain's greatness as the true goal of all policy. At least once, though, he raised his eyes above these compelling actualities to speculate on an idealized community for the kingdom of man. In *The Prince*, Machiavelli declared his preference for "the truth of things" rather than "imaginary ones" and therefore refused to discuss "imagined republics which have never been seen or known to exist in reality." [111] Bacon departed from the Italian thinker's point of view by writing *New Atlantis*, in which he presented an imaginary picture of an ideal or an advanced society. Although I have already spoken briefly of this work in the preceding chapter as a scientific utopia, it has some political aspects as well. Never finished, it was one of Bacon's last compositions, published the year after his death. According to his chaplain and secretary Rawley, his purpose in writing it was "to exhibit therein a model or description of a college instituted for the interpretation of nature and the producing of great and marvellous works for the benefit of men, under the name of Salomon's House. . . ." This was the only part he completed, and though he also thought, as Rawley informs us, of including "a frame of Laws, or the best state or mould of a commonwealth," he did not do so because it would have been too long a task.[112] What *New Atlantis* contains, therefore, is a partial relation of an imaginary society with a concentration on the role of science. Its political side is omitted, and the most we can find are a few clues to the latter's character and features.

New Atlantis has been variously and at times most implausibly interpreted.[113] I do not think, however, that Bacon made its meaning deliberately obscure or wished to imply more than the story itself tells us. He used it to embody and illustrate some of the same values and beliefs he had expressed in a number of his other writings; and he did so by inventing a human community that is guided by wisdom and science.

The fable, as Rawley called it, took its name from the mythical island of Atlantis mentioned in several of Plato's dialogues, a lost civilization destroyed by a natural catastrophe. Its story rests on the familiar literary device of European voyagers whose ship, driven far off course in Pacific waters, reached land in the remote, unknown island of Bensalem. Sir Thomas More's *Utopia*, written a century before, relied on an analogous plot to explain how the traveler Raphael Hyth-

loday, while voyaging in the New World, came to know the country
and institutions of Utopia. Although in ages past Bensalem had had
many contacts with the outside world, ever since the destruction of
Atlantis several thousand years ago, other nations had ceased to visit
it, and it remained completely isolated and forgotten.

To the European strangers, the most significant fact about the new
Atlantis, which is named Bensalem, a Hebrew word signifying "son of
peace," is that it is a Christian society whose Christianity is manifested
in an exceptional degree of charity, humanity, kindness, and compas-
sion. After being permitted ashore, the strangers are hospitably received, comfortably accommodated, and generously treated. They
are sent to reside in a House of Strangers whose governor, a Christian
priest, replies to their expressions of gratitude by stating that he
looked only for a priest's reward, "which was [their] brotherly love
and the good of [their] souls and bodies."[114] Responding to their
questions, he relates to them how Christianity and the Scriptures
were miraculously brought to Bensalem soon after Christ's resurrec-
tion.[115] Since we receive no hint of a state church or officially enforced creed in the society, we might guess that Bacon has chosen to
depict Bensalem's Christianity as preeminently a religion of morality
and love that is better practiced in those remote parts than in Christian Europe.[116]

Of Bensalem's social institutions, we are given a description only of
the customs associated with the family and marriage. Families and
the propagation of children are greatly valued as the foundation of
the social order. Every man with thirty living descendants aged three
or older is honored by a solemn feast at the state's expense and receives gifts of money, privileges, and other distinctions. Marriages are
based on complete fidelity. Brothels, prostitution, and courtesans do
not exist, as they do in Europe, nor is there any trace of "masculine
love." Bensalem rejects as gross the practice, noted as having been
mentioned in More's *Utopia*, that allows a couple to look at one another's naked bodies for defects before contracting marriage. Instead, the "more civil way" prevails of permitting each of the pair to
be observed bathing naked by a friend of the other. Although marriage without parental consent is not banned, it is penalized with
a fine. The strangers learn some of these details from a wise Jew,

Joabin, one of a small number of Jews living in Bensalem, whose religion is tolerated. He considers Bensalem the most chaste of all nations and says that "there is nothing among mortal men more fair and admirable, than the chaste minds of [its] people."[117]

The government of Bensalem is not explained. We hear only of two kings in the distant past, one of them a great ruler nineteen hundred years earlier named Solamona, who prohibited the admission of foreigners to avoid novelties and contamination of manners. He observed the requirements of humanity, however, by providing for the relief of distressed strangers who happened upon Bensalem, and permitted them to remain permanently if they desired. Patterning himself on the wisdom of the biblical King Solomon, he established Salomon's House, also called the College of Six Days Work, "the noblest foundation . . . that ever was upon the earth," which is dedicated to "the finding out of the true nature of all things." Although forbidding his people to travel abroad, Solamona ordained that every twelve years a pair of ships carrying three Fellows of Salomon's House should depart on a mission of knowledge. Sailing to other countries but never disclosing their identity, the three were to remain abroad until the arrival of a new mission, and to bring back with them books, instruments, and information on state affairs, arts, manufactures, and inventions. In this manner Bensalem reaped the benefits of communicating with foreigners while avoiding the damage. These expeditions did not go, as those of the Europeans had done, to search for precious metals, spices, silks, or other such commodities but sought instead only for light to aid the growth of knowledge.[118]

The high point of the unfinished *New Atlantis* is the meeting with a Father, or Elder, of Salomon's House. Religious awe surrounds this personage, who arrives in solemn state and is greeted by the people with profound respect. He is the first Father in a dozen years to visit the city where the strangers are staying. In an interview he grants to one of the latter, he explains "for the love of God and man" the character and purpose of Salomon's House. It is a great foundation of scientific research whose aim is the investigation of the "Causes, and secret motions of all things" in order to enlarge "the bounds of Human Empire to the effecting of all things possible." The account that follows is a wish fulfillment of Bacon's desire for the endowment of science by states and kings. It also makes clear that Salomon's House exists not only for the advancement of knowledge but for beneficent and philanthropic ends.

The Father describes the institution's vast resources in laboratories, equipment, artificial climates and environments, and personnel; the great scope of its experiments; and the division of labor among its Fellows in the collecting, devising, and performing of experiments and in the interpretation of nature. Among its buildings are large galleries containing samples of all manner of rare and excellent inventions. Standing in them are also statues of Columbus and of the inventors of ships, gunpowder and ordnance, music, letters, printing, astronomical observations, metalworking, glass, silk, wine, grain, bread, sugar, and other things. The foundation holds daily religious services of hymns and prayers to thank God for his works and implore his aid for its labors and their use for good and holy ends. Periodically the Fathers visit the country's principal cities to make known new inventions, to forecast the threat of diseases, scarcity, and other natural disasters, and to advise the people on how to prevent or deal with the latter.[119]

The Bensalem of Bacon's fiction is such a peaceable, orderly, and law-abiding society that there might seem to be little role for government or coercion. From what we see of its citizens, they appear so contented that they are unlikely to feel much longing for change or improvement, even though the latter was for Bacon the proper end of knowledge. Bensalem has also seemingly eliminated the tension between religion and natural philosophy of which Bacon frequently spoke in his other writings. He had often warned of the harmful effects of religious fanaticism and superstition on the progress of knowledge and had argued for the separation of scientific inquiry from religion in the interests of both. Bensalem appears to represent the realization of this idea. There science itself, in the pursuit of its humanitarian goals, almost resembles a religious vocation, while the Christian religion may have ceased to care about dogma or orthodoxy and become entirely centered on charity and goodness toward others.

Notwithstanding *New Atlantis*'s references to kings, the impression we gain from the work in its unfinished state is that the true authority

in Bensalem is Salomon's House. Bensalem may thus be a utopia
ruled or directed by a philosophical and scientific elite. There is a
noticeable air of mystery about this great foundation that adds to its
fascination. This may have been simply a literary device to make the
fiction more interesting, but it also accords with Bacon's own penchant for secrecy and esoteric knowledge. The latter was based on his
conviction that certain kinds of knowledge could be dangerous if mis-
used or made generally available. The Fathers have certain practices
of concealment. They all take an oath of secrecy. The missions of
knowledge they send out across the seas are secret, too, and never
made known to the countries they visit. While they publish some of
their inventions, others they think unfit to reveal, withholding them
even from the state. Bensalem itself is a reclusive society, kept hidden
from the world. The strangers are not allowed to learn certain things
about it. The Father who relates these facts pertaining to Salomon's
House gives the strangers permission to publish them "for the good
of other nations," confident that Bensalem is so remote that it will
remain "a land unknown."

If Bacon did not intend Salomon's House to be the ruler of his
utopia, he nevertheless conceived it as a kind of veiled power whose
knowledge directs the society to which it belongs. This is the political
vision that informs his *New Atlantis*. Plato's *Republic* described an ideal
commonwealth governed by a class of philosopher guardians. In *New
Atlantis*, Bacon's imagination pictured for the first time a human society in which the collaborative, systematic investigation of nature is a
major institutional activity, which greatly honors invention and technology, and in which science and an elite of scientists occupy a high
or dominant place supported fully by the resources of the state.

5

Language, Law, and History

LANGUAGE: COMMUNICATION, RHETORIC, POETRY

THROUGHOUT Bacon's intellectual life he maintained a constant interest in language and the methods of communicating knowledge, information, and opinion. He made numerous experiments with different modes of imparting his ideas, ranging from courtly entertainments and polemical discourses to formal treatises, aphorisms, essays, interpretations of myths, histories, and utopian fiction. The papers on policy he composed during his political career, like his speeches in Parliament and legal pleadings, were all carefully structured attempts at persuasion. From the age of the Greek Sophists down to Bacon's own time and well beyond, rhetoric, which Aristotle had defined as the art of the persuasive use of language, was an essential ingredient in Western education.[1] Throughout this long period, those who aimed to pursue the active life of the citizen or subject in the service of the commonwealth or prince aspired to acquire the power of eloquence that training in rhetoric could give. Cultivated by Greek orators and the Roman political elite, joined in the Middle Ages with grammar and logic as a part of the liberal arts course in the medieval universities, during the Renaissance rhetoric acquired an enhanced cultural and social prestige because of the widespread preoccupation with Greek and Latin literature. A heightened demand for it was also created by the increasing need of royal states and the Italian republics for officials who spoke eloquently and wrote well in accord with classical standards. As a result rhetoric was considered a necessity in the education of gentlemen, lawyers, religious preachers, literary persons, and anyone ambitious for a career in government.[2] Bacon, like many of his contemporaries, was a student of rhetoric. Besides the numerous modern works English and foreign he might have read on the subject, he was familiar with the major treatments of rhetoric by classical authors, which meant chiefly Aristotle's *Rhetoric*, certain of Cicero's works, and Quintilian's famous *Institutes of Oratory*.[3] His writings attest to his extensive use of the literary devices discussed in rhetorical manuals. In his philosophical and other works he relied continually on *partitio* or division by parts as a basic way of arranging the topics and sequence of his exposition. His prose style included many instances of the figures of speech, not only metaphor and analogy but various others, which were part of the repertoire of classical rhetoric.[4]

As a philosopher Bacon was acutely conscious of the snares and deceptions of language. Among the idols of the mind that systematically delude it he reckoned that the most troublesome were the idols of the forum or marketplace. These were the fallacies of the understanding that sprang from the falsity and misuse of words and names. Instead of reason's governing language, language governed reason and led it astray. Words framed to the capacity of the vulgar failed to register the true divisions of nature. Names did not correspond to reality and endowed fictions and abstractions with a false existence. Abstract concepts were often ill defined and lacking a consistent meaning. Owing to the traps of language, philosophers fell into fruitless verbal disputes.[5] At times Bacon speculated on the possibility of a philosophical grammar that would investigate the relationship between words and things.[6] He believed that in philosophy language must be a true representation of realities. In describing the prerequisites of a proper natural history, he prohibited "all ornaments of speech, similitudes, treasury of eloquence, and such like emptinesses."[7] His insistence that *verba* should stand for *res* and that natural philosophy deal with things themselves was among the causes that contributed to the seventeenth-century discrediting of medieval Scholasticism as a mere hairsplitting verbalism. In spite of his rhetorical skills and distinction as a stylist, what a modern scholar has termed "a distrust of language" was something, at least in the domain of natural philosophy, that Bacon passed on to his seventeenth-century successors who were the pioneers of early modern science in England.[8] This took the form of attempts to purge and reform language so as to make it an instrument of clarity and undistorted representation of nature. John Wilkins, one of the main founders of the Royal Society, upon which Bacon's ideas exerted a seminal influence, hoped to overcome the defects of ordinary language by devising a universal "real character" or "philosophical language" consisting of signs or symbols to stand for words and concepts. In his *Essay toward a Real Character*, published in 1667, Wilkins pointed to the confusion wrought by metaphors and ambiguity of language, which he wished to eliminate from philosophical and scientific discourse. Affirming that "things are better than words as real knowledge is beyond the elegancy of speech," he proposed to introduce a rational language in which names and words would correspond to things themselves. This Baconian aim, along with an interest in linguistic experiments to attain it, was shared by a number of the early members of the Royal Society.[9] The first history of the society, by Thomas Sprat—a semi-official publication issued in 1667, five years after its founding—emphasized the need to reform and correct the excesses of language in natural philosophy. The author described the society's resolve to reject "all the amplifications, digressions, and swellings of style," to restore a primitive purity and brevity of expression, and to require from its members a concise, naked manner of speaking that would bring all things as near as possible to a "Mathematical plainness. . . ."[10] This goal in the use of language was not out of keeping with Bacon's own conception of the prerequisites of communication in philosophy and the investigation of nature.

From the beginning of the Western philosophic tradition the relationship between philosophy and rhetoric was more often than not one of antagonism and disparagement on the part of the former. Most famous for his hostility to rhetoric was Plato, who considered it a corrupt art of persuasion based on opinion rather than knowledge and equally indifferent to truth and justice. The quarrel of philosophy and rhetoric recurred sporadically in the centuries that followed.

Even during the Renaissance, when rhetoric was valued most highly, there were philosophers like the Florentine Neoplatonist Pico della Mirandola who criticized the rhetorician's function and questioned whether eloquence had anything to do with wisdom.[11] The great philosophic innovators of the seventeenth century who came after Bacon were in agreement that rhetoric was an impediment to truth. Despite his humanistic education, Descartes in his *Discourse on Method* expressed disdain for rhetoric, observing that all that was necessary for persuasion was clear and powerful reasoning, not stylistic skills.[12] Hobbes stated that persuasion begets only opinion, not knowledge, and would have excluded metaphors, tropes, and other rhetorical figures from all rigorous search for truth.[13] Locke, whose attitude was the most negative, condemned rhetoric as an instrument of deceit and error whose sole purpose was to insinuate false ideas, excite the passions, and mislead the judgment.[14]

In *The Advancement of Learning*, Bacon described the undue preoccupation with words and style over matter as one of the distempers of learning. While admitting that eloquence might be an adornment to philosophy, he pointed out that it was likely to hinder "the severe inquisition of truth" by giving a too early satisfaction to the mind and thus quench the desire for further search.[15] Notwithstanding these comments, he was not hostile to rhetoric and believed Plato's view of it to be unjust.[16] For him it had a legitimate place in the methods of communication and need not be opposed to reason. His principal treatment of the subject was in *De Augmentis*, the enlarged version of *The Advancement of Learning*, which explained most fully his conception of the nature and function of rhetoric among the divisions of knowledge.

Early in this treatise he proposed a basic classification of the parts of human learning in relation to the three intellectual faculties of memory, imagination, and reason. To these corresponded respectively history, poetry, and philosophy.[17] At a further stage he also distinguished reason and will as the two faculties of the human soul. To the first of these pertained logic, which was concerned with understanding; to the second, ethics, which was concerned with action. Between reason and will stood imagination, a Janus-faced messenger looking to both faculties, bringing to each of them images from the senses, and which not only operated on the two but sometimes usurped authority over them. It was imagination that exerted its dominion in the persuasion resulting from eloquence. When the arts of speech affected men's minds, they could stimulate the imagination in such a way that it became ungovernable and defied reason.[18] Bacon regarded rhetoric, therefore, as particularly bound up with imagination and discussed it chiefly in that connection.

In order to do so, however, he first found it necessary to deal with the logical or rational arts, to one of which rhetoric belonged. Classical treatments of rhetoric had associated it with logic. According to a famous figure of speech cited by Cicero and Quintilian and repeated by Bacon, logic resembled a closed fist, rhetoric an open hand. This simile referred, of course, to the different modes of reasoning each employed, either rigorous or loose.[19] Aristotle viewed rhetoric as a loose kind of logic that attempted to achieve persuasion and proof by such means as enthymemes, induction derived from examples, and arguments of probability.[20] Bacon listed the four logical arts as follows according to the different ends they pursued: inquiry or invention; examination or judgment; custody or memory; and elocution or tradition.[21] In classical rhetoric, invention, which he put at the head of the logical arts, was considered the first of the five parts of rhetoric and the earliest stage in the composition of a speech. Cicero defined it as "the discovery of valid or seemingly valid arguments to render one's cause plausible."[22] Rudolph Agricola and other Renaissance authorities, however, had detached invention from rhetoric and made it one of the two main divisions of dialectics instead, the other being judgment.[23] Bacon followed a similar practice in classifying invention with the logical arts;[24] but as was pointed out in a previous chapter, he gave to the concept of invention a much wider scope by explaining that it referred to two quite different meanings. It could signify either the invention of arts and sciences or that of speech and arguments. The first entailed the discovery of new knowledge, while the second meant only the recapitulation of what was already known.[25] Needless to say, it was the former sort of invention, until then deficient and neglected, that he thought far the more important. The type of induction expounded in *The New Organon* was his contribution to remedying this deficiency and to insuring thereby the progress of discovery in natural philosophy.

Notwithstanding his insistence that invention, properly speaking, was the art of creative innovation, he went on to treat the other kind of invention consisting of the discovery of arguments. This art taught the way to give order to the knowledge the mind already possessed so as to use it in discourse.[26] After dealing with this subject, he went on to the remaining logical arts: the art of judgment, which concerned proofs, demonstrations, and the validity of arguments; the art of memory, which concerned helps and techniques for the retention of knowledge; and the art of tradition, which concerned the delivery or transmission of doctrine.[27] Only with this last did he finally arrive at the discussion of rhetoric itself.

He defined transmission as the art of "producing and expressing to others those things which have been invented, judged, and laid up in memory."[28] It comprised all the arts pertaining to words and discourse. One of these arts, the organ of discourse, covered grammar and different forms of writing, including codes and hieroglyphics. Another, the method of discourse, analyzed the diverse ways of conveying doctrine to hearers or readers. The third, the illustration of discourse, was rhetoric or oratory. Rhetoric for Bacon was thus not identical with transmission but occupied only a limited role as a subdivision of the latter.[29]

He felt that he could curtail his treatment of rhetoric because, as he stated at the outset, earlier authors like Aristotle and Cicero had already given excellent accounts of this discipline and its rules. The art of rhetoric was in his view subservient to the imagination in the same way that logic was to the understanding. Its duty was "to apply and recommend the dictates of reason to imagination" in order "to excite the appetite and will." The government of reason over human actions could be assailed in several ways: by sophisms, which pertained to logic; by tricks of language, which pertained to rhetoric; and by violence of the passions, which pertained to ethics. Rhetoric's purpose, therefore, was to infuse the imagination with images that supported rather than oppressed reason. It needed to create lively pictures of virtue and goodness that could be seen and felt. Bacon likewise observed that while reason and passion both aim at apparent good, passion shortsightedly perceives only the present, whereas reason looks forward to the future and hence to consequences. As the present usually fills the imagination more, reason is vanquished. But when eloquence and persuasion succeed in making things future and remote appear as if they were present, then imagination joins with reason to help the latter prevail.[30]

It will be seen that Bacon's conception of rhetoric rested on a rather crude traditional psychology of discrete human faculties capable of opposition or alliance.[31] By the images it conjured up through its persuasive eloquence, rhetoric could influence the imagination either to sustain or to subvert reason's sway. He would not blame rhetoric for its ability to make the worse side look attractive, any more than he would blame logic for knowing how to make sophisms. Logic dealt with reason as it existed in truth and nature; rhetoric, on the other hand, had to deal with reason as it was planted in the common opinion. Bacon accordingly expressed his agreement with Aristotle's view, which positioned rhetoric between logic on the one side and politics and morals on the other side as a participant in both. While the proofs and demonstrations of logic were universal and the same for everybody, those of rhetoric were obliged to vary with the character of the audience.

These remarks constituted the sum total of Bacon's general reflections on the nature and purpose of rhetoric. It will be seen that the place he assigned it among the methods of transmitting doctrine was quite restricted. It was, as it were, a technical, not a philosophical, discipline, whose job was to affect the imagination. If it did this constructively, as it was supposed to do, then it served as an aid to reason in keeping the passions in order.

The rest of his discussion focused on several techniques of argumentation and persuasion in which he considered that rhetoric was deficient. Termed by him "colors of Good and Evil" and "Antitheses of Things," they were equally relevant to rhetoric and to politics. Colors of good and evil were plausible popular notions of seeming good and evil that were actually sophisms. He illustrated these with a number of examples in which, after stating the proposition, he then showed how it deceives. The first sophism, for instance, affirmed that what men praise and honor is good, while what they dispraise is evil. To this proposition he responded that it deceived in four different ways: by reason of ignorance, because popular judgment was worthless as a test of good and evil; by reason of bad faith, because in praising and blaming, men usually think only of their own interests and do not say what they really believe; by reason of faction, because men tend to exalt those of their own party and disparage their opponents; and finally by reason of natural disposition, because some men being by nature servile adulators and others captious critics, both kinds praise and blame with no regard for truth. In each case the exposure of the sophism provided a refutation when the particular color was used in argument.[32]

Antitheses of things were opposing propositions on a variety of common topics, which could be utilized for persuasion and dissuasion. Thus Bacon listed examples of arguments both for and against honor, nobility, riches, love, envy, temperance, dissimulation, popularity, and many other topics, with reasons stated on either side. He refrained from judging between these arguments but presented them impartially as an arsenal on which to draw.[33] Collections of this kind were to serve as a promptuary or preparatory store essential for speakers and writers, and he recalled the advice of Cicero that orators should have commonplaces ready to hand to use on either side of a question. In these collections Bacon proposed inclusion of all the topics that there was frequent occasion to handle, whether proofs and refutations or persuasions and dissuasions. He likewise recommended the inclusion of lesser things like prepared prefaces, conclusions, digressions, transitions, intimations of what is to come, and excuses, all of which, if skillfully fashioned, could add ornament and effectiveness to speech.[34]

Bacon's interest in such aids to speaking and writing was of long standing. In *De Augmentis* he reported that he had made large collections of sophisms and antitheses in his youth.[35] His first publication, the 1597 edition of his *Essays*, included in the same volume a fragment entitled *Of the Coulers of Good and Evil*, which set forth a number of arguments concerning questions of good and evil together with answers to them.[36] He also habitually made notes of quotations, sayings, phrases, apophthegms, and hints for speaking and gestures that appear among his various writings.[37] All of these notations, intended for his own use as an author, lawyer, conversationalist, orator, court politician, and royal adviser, reveal how intently during his career he studied to master the art of rhetoric and its skills in persuasion. Such collections were typical of the importance attached by educators of the period to the notebook or commonplace book, in which students were advised to record all kinds of useful material from their reading as an essential resource upon which to draw in both writing and speaking.[38]

Bacon's discussion leaves no doubt that he considered morals and politics, where argumentation, persuasion, and opinion held sway, as the special province of rhetoric. But besides the latter, he also devoted much thought to other types of communication whose task was the delivery or transmission of knowledge. Much of what he had to say on this subject is concisely dealt with in *De Augmentis* as a part of the method of discourse, which belonged, like rhetoric, to the fourth of the logical arts.

One of his principal points in respect to the delivery of knowledge was the distinction he laid down between the "magistral" and "initiative" methods, The first, which was essentially a method of authority, was used to teach the crowd of learners and aimed to induce belief; the second, which was directed to initiates in a science, aimed to incite examination and fresh inquiry. While the former occupied itself with existing knowledge, the latter strove for the progress of knowledge. The contrast between these two different approaches to the delivery of knowledge was a fundamental theme of Bacon's philosophy from its beginning. He held that the initiative method was neglected, and associated it with induction, which served not only to convey knowledge but to increase it.[39]

Another distinction that he noted in the transmission of knowledge was that of the exoteric and acroamatic methods, the second a synonym for esotericism. While the two agreed in separating out select auditors from the vulgar, the first employed an open delivery, the second a secret one to convey its doctrine. In a previous chapter I have commented on Bacon's somewhat ambivalent attitude toward esotericism.[40] The appearance of the acroamatic or esoteric method in *De Augmentis,* one of his latest works, indicates that it continued to retain some of its interest for him. Its purpose was to preserve the secrets of knowledge from the vulgar lest they misconceive or misuse it. He recognized, however, that this method had fallen into discredit; because while the ancients had used it with discretion and judgment, many later authors disgraced it by making it into a device for imposture and deceit.[41]

Of the remaining methods of delivering knowledge that Bacon surveyed, I need mention but one more, the important distinction between delivery by aphorisms and by means of a few axioms and observations on a subject. He was strongly in favor of the former, which, as we have seen, was his preferred method in *The New Organon.* His main objection to the use of axioms and observations was that they created an unjustified and deceptive impression of completeness and were much better for implanting belief than for spurring inquiry. Aphorisms, on the other hand, constituted a genuine test of whether a writer was thin and superficial or really equipped with solid knowledge. In order not to be ridiculous, aphorisms had to be made from the heart of the sciences. Omitting everything extraneous, they relied solely on a substantial quality of perceptive observations. Hence only someone amply furnished with the requisite knowledge was capable of writing aphorisms. Moreover, as they were only portions or fragments of knowledge, they invited others to contribute and add something in turn.[42]

As his commendation of aphorisms indicates, for Bacon the method of transmission affected the character of knowledge itself. This conviction is reflected in his striking observation that "knowledge that is delivered to others . . . ought to be insinuated (if it were possible) in the same method wherein it was originally invented."[43] Transmission was not something extraneous or merely a matter of technique but an integral part of the process of inquiry. What especially stands out is his disapproval of a mode of transmission that operated to produce acquiescence and the illusion of completeness. He looked upon knowledge as an open-ended project of discovery and therefore advocated ways of delivery that would incite auditors and students not only to receive it critically but to endeavor by their own further inquiries to promote the growth of knowledge.

There was one other art of language and communication that Bacon included in his survey of the state of knowledge, and this was poetry. Rather than placing it among the methods of transmission, he accorded it an independent position as one of the three principal branches of learning along with history and philosophy.[44] Because of his scientific materialism and effort to demythologize nature and the cosmos, Bacon has sometimes been accused of hostility to poetry and the imagination.[45] Toward imagination itself, it is true, his attitude was somewhat ambiguous on account of its ability as a creative faculty to oppose and elude reason.[46] Since it was "not . . . bound by any law or necessity of nature," he pointed out, it could separate things nature had joined together and join things nature had kept apart, all in accord with the pleasure of the human mind.[47] To their alliance with imagination more than with reason he also attributed the errors of the occult sciences of alchemy, astrology, and natural magic.[48] On the other hand, where it touched religion he noted how imagination could raise itself above reason to become an instrument of divine illumination that entered the mind in the form of similitudes, parables, visions, and dreams.[49] For poetry, moreover, another offspring of imagination, he expressed profound respect, emphasizing both its freedom and its fictive power to create worlds that exceed and transform reality and meet a deep human need.

The three kinds of poetry he discussed in *De Augmentis* were narrative or heroic, dramatic, and parabolical. Narrative poetry seemed to him to resemble history; it made history visible and present but at the same time also exaggerated it beyond probability. In so doing, though, it endowed life with a greater, more ideal character than was possible for history and its narratives to attain, thus adding to the dignity of human nature. Bacon believed that such poetry satisfied the mind's desire for a higher greatness and more manifest order than man could find in the world since the Fall. By imaginatively depicting heroic actions in relation to virtue and vice, and by exhibiting extraordinary events and unexpected vicissitudes, it elevated the mind above the factuality of history and things, conducing thereby not only to delight but to magnanimity and morality. This was the reason, in his view, that poetry was held in honor even in the rudest ages that lacked every kind of learning.[50]

Dramatic poetry, created for the stage, occupied his attention only briefly. What he mainly noted about it was its usefulness in instilling discipline and virtue, a function that he felt the poets of his time had neglected.[51] Of the three kinds of poetry he gave the highest place to parabolical poetry owing to its nearnesss to religion. Consisting of fables, myths, and allegories, it had commonly been used as a means of communication between divinity and human beings. To it belonged the dual and opposite tasks of both teaching and concealment. Good for illustrating knowledge, in ancient times, when the conclusions of reason were yet new and hard to understand, parabolical poetry helped to make them comprehensible and palpable to sense by its fables and similitudes. But it also served the contrary purpose of hiding the mysteries of religion, policy, and philosophy under a veil of allegory. Bacon went on to speculate, as he had previously done in *The Wisdom of the Ancients*, whether the myths of the ancient poets, which were the oldest human writings next to the Bible, contained a secret meaning transmitted from still more ancient times. He did not answer this question in *De Augmentis* other than to suggest that some of them might conceal a mystery. As he held that the philosophical interpretation of the ancient myths was deficient, he wound up his discussion with an exegesis of three of the myths he had already expounded in *The Wisdom of the Ancients*, those of Pan, Perseus, and Dionysus, as allegories of natural philosophy, politics, and moral philosophy.[52]

While his survey of learning did not rate dramatic poetry highly, Bacon found none of the species of poetry deficient. He perceived several kinds of qualities and values in poetry as a distinctive creature of the imagination. First was its didactic role as a medium for teaching virtue and morality. Second was the verisimilitude of its fictions, which made them appear as real as the facts related by history. Third was the ability of its inventions to transcend the limits of reality, raising the mind above the ordinary, delighting it with images of grandeur and ideal order, "accommodating," as he said, "the shows of things to the desires of the mind, not (like reason and history), buckling and bowing down the mind to the nature of things."[53] Last was poetry's function as a repository and illustration of ancient wisdom, by which it gave visible shape to abstract concepts and concealed the mysteries of religion, philosophy, and policy beneath a veil of myth and allegory. Bacon therefore considered poetry to be neither a light diversion nor an inferior sort of learning but a vital expression of the imagination, a vessel of wisdom, and an art of language that ministered to an essential need of human nature.

LAW: LAW REFORM AND JURISPRUDENCE

For more than forty years, amidst his multifarious intellectual occupations and his grand project for the renewal of philosophy, Bacon was engaged in the profession of law. When he completed his legal education at Gray's Inn, he never intended to become merely a successful lawyer in private practice, a prospect he shunned. His ambition was always fixed upon serving the monarchy and public in a legal capacity and as an adviser, minister, and statesman.[54] It was from the perspective not only of a lawyer but of a statesman that he looked upon the law, and he often expressed the view that neither philosophers nor lawyers were the best qualified to write on the law. Philosophers were too abstract and remote from fact, devising imaginary laws for imaginary commonwealths that were inapplicable for use. Doubtless he was thinking in this comment of a philosopher like Plato and his *Republic*. Lawyers, on the other hand, suffered from professional narrowness, being too much attached to the laws of their own country or to Roman or canon law to be able to consider from a broader standpoint what ought to be law. Here he probably had in mind someone like his old professional rival Sir Edward Coke, a great lawyer and legal commentator who could not praise the English common law too highly. It was the statesman, according to Bacon, who was best equipped to deal with law because he best understood the condition of civil society, the well-being of the people, natural equity, the customs of nations, and the different forms of government and was therefore best fitted to determine laws in relation to the rules of policy and natural equity.[55] His own treatment of law, in combining the statesman's political and worldly knowledge with the technical expertise of the lawyer, endeavored to exemplify this standard.

Bacon's legal experience was very varied.[56] In the late 1580s and the 1590s he assisted Queen Elizabeth's ministers as a legal adviser, performing a multitude of tasks including the examination, sometimes by means of torture, of state prisoners suspected of treason. He also appeared as an advocate in major civil and criminal cases and delivered lectures on the law to students and lawyers at Gray's Inn. Later on, under James I, he did legal jobs for the king and then represented the crown successively as solicitor general, attorney general, and finally as lord keeper and lord chancellor presiding over the Court of Chancery and performing other legal duties connected with his judicial office. His writings on law, many of which were first published posthumously, take several forms. Some of them are his arguments in notable cases in which he participated as counsel. Thus *Chudleigh's Case* contained the plea he delivered in 1594 in a civil trial involving the interpretation of the Statute of Uses, an enactment of the utmost consequence in regulating the settlement and transfer of legal estates in land. Similarly, *The Case of the Post-Nati* in 1608 presented his argument as solicitor general in support of the claim that, according to law, Scotsmen born after the accession of James VI of Scotland to the English throne in 1603 were ipso facto naturalized English subjects. Certain of these printed arguments, like *The Case of the Jurisdiction of the Council of the Marches* of 1608 and *The Case of the Writ De Non Procedendo Rege Inconsulto* of 1616, touched significant political and judicial issues and were produced to uphold some aspect of the royal prerogative against legal challenge. Another type of writing was his *Reading on the Statute of Uses*, an exposition and discussion of the statute based on lectures given in 1600 at Gray's Inn.[57] Besides works of these kinds, he also drafted papers concerning the reform of the laws and composed a number of writings of a jurisprudential nature that reflected on the underlying reason of the law and advanced proposals to make the law more rational and just. Of the latter the most important was the example of a treatise on universal justice and equity that he included in *De Augmentis* as the conclusion to his review of civil knowledge and government. Looking at the range and character of his work relating to the law, a great modern historian of English law, Sir William Holdsworth, pronounced him "a more complete lawyer than any of his contemporaries" and a "great juridical thinker" who studied both English law and law in general "scientifically and critically."[58]

Bacon's approach to law was cosmopolitan. While trained and intellectually rooted in the tradition of the English common law, which was an insular system of law based on custom and the precedents of cases adjudicated in the courts, he did not hesitate to draw on the principles of Roman law where he found them useful. Although he devoted little consideration to the venerable conception of the law of nature as a universal norm and source of justice, it formed part of the background of his legal philosophy, and he shared with most lawyers the conviction that English law had some relation to it. "There are in nature," he held, "certain fountains of justice, whence all civil laws are derived but as streams, and like as waters do take tinctures and tastes from the soils through which they run, so do civil laws vary according to . . . regions and governments . . . though they proceed from the same fountains."[59] In *The Case of the Post-Nati* he affirmed that English law "is grounded upon the law of nature" and that because three things "flow from the law of nature"—namely, preservation of life, liberty, and the society of man and wife—the common law likewise favored these things. When arguing that the law of England should favor naturalization, he observed that by the law of nature "all men in the world are naturalized one towards another," all being made by God of one lump of earth and with the same common parents, while it was the civil law and national laws that first introduced the differences of native and alien.[60]

Bacon's earliest work on jurisprudence, written around 1596, was *Maxims of the Law*, a collection of rules or grounds of law gathered out of the scattered body of English law. He conceived these rules to be the reason of the law, the understanding of which would help to make the law more certain. By drawing them up, he explained, he wanted to give light in "new cases and such wherein there is no direct authority"; to confirm the law and "make it received one way" where authorities differed; and to see more deeply into the reason of judgments and ruled cases in order to apply the latter more readily to the

decision of doubtful cases. He called these rules "conclusions of reason" and hence "the laws of laws." He made the further point that it
was unnecessary and preposterous to prove them or support them
with authorities, thereby implying that their rational character was so
evident as to need no argument.[61]

Several previous English jurists had written about the maxims of
the law. Two of the most distinguished were Sir John Fortescue in the
later fifteenth century and Christopher St. German in the reign of
Henry VIII. In his *Praise of the Laws of England* (*De Laudibus Legum
Anglie*), Fortescue declared that there were certain principles or elements called maxims by learned lawyers, out of which all law proceeded as natural things do from matter and form or the sentences of
books from letters. These principles were not known through force of
argument or demonstration but, as Aristotle had said in his *Posterior
Analytics,* by induction through the senses and memory. Despite emphasizing the necessity of learning the principles of any branch of
knowledge in order to understand it, Fortescue did not list or discuss
any of the maxims of the law. St. German's *Dialogue of the Doctor and
Student,* a famous legal textbook, described maxims as one of the six
grounds of the laws of England and stated that they had always been
taken as law, each one being a sufficient authority for itself. What was
or was not a maxim was always to be determined by the judges. He
mentioned a number of such maxims, noting that they could be
known in several ways—by the law of reason, by books of the law, by
records in the king's courts, and by statutes.[62]

Bacon's maxims belonged to a tradition not only of English common law but of classical Roman law as well. Roman jurists had discussed and formulated rules of this kind, and a title about such rules,
"De Diversis Regulis Iuris Antiquae," was incorporated in the *Digest,*
which formed one of the parts of the Emperor Justinian's sixth-
century codification of the law.[63] Although Bacon said that he had
compiled as many as three hundred maxims, he propounded only
twenty-five, which he presented in the form of aphorisms.[64] Each
maxim or rule was given in Latin, followed by an exposition in English of its scope accompanied by examples drawn from cases. The
third rule, for instance, declares that "words are interpreted more
strongly against the one who proffers them" ("Vera fortius accipiun-

tur contra proferentem"). On this he commented that the rule "A man's deeds and his words shall be taken strongliest against himself" is "drawn out of the depths of reason." He then indicated how this rule teaches men to be watchful in their own business and contributes in several ways to peace and quiet in the settlement of disputes. He also pointed out, however, that like all very general rules, it is "but a sound in the air" and hence required directions as to "where it taketh place and where not." The subsequent remarks accordingly described the rule's applications and limitations.[65] Certain of his maxims were taken directly from Roman law.[66] Throughout his discussion, the distinguishing feature, in which he excelled his English predecessors, was the clarity and relative precision with which he explicated and illustrated the nature, qualifications, and limits to these rules and how they constituted a ground of law.

A common misconception among authors who have written about Bacon's work on law is that his legal philosophy was founded on his scientific method and the use of induction. This error is compounded in some of these authors by a second, even bigger misconception, which supposes that Bacon's natural philosophy was actually the product of his legal ideas and experience as a lawyer. Paul Kocher in an essay of 1957 on Bacon's jurisprudence supposed that he intended his inductive method to apply to law, that he strove to make law a predictive science, and that his legal maxims were the same as the middle axioms he sought in the investigation of nature. In Bacon's statement in his *Reading on the Statute of Uses* that he would define the nature of a use by first considering what it was not, Kocher perceived an example of induction proceeding by way of negative instances.[67] Daniel Coquillette's recent survey of Bacon's legal thought, which cites some of the same material that Kocher did, continually assumes that Bacon's jurisprudence utilized the principles of his natural philosophy. He attributes to Bacon's legal arguments the inductive logic described in *The New Organon* and credits him with "the brilliant insight . . . that scientific methods can, and should, be applied to legal study."[68]

An essay by Harvey Wheeler in 1983 went even further than this by claiming that "Bacon's science derived ultimately from his jurisprudence" and that "the novel principles of his scientific method" and

"concept of scientific law" stemmed from "the foundations of his professional calling." Wheeler located the origins of Bacon's "scientific
empiricism" and "new logic of inquiry" particularly in his use of the
case method of ferreting out the maxims or rules of the law from
existing precedents and cases. On this account, he assigned "devel-
opmental priority" to law in the formation of Bacon's scientific
method.[69] Similarly, other authors have imagined that Bacon's work
as an interrogator of suspects in criminal examinations was the
source of his conception of inquisition into nature, or that he
adapted the procedures he prescribed in natural philosophy from
the procedures of English law.[70]

These views not only are based largely on specious verbal analogies
but spring from a superficial knowledge of Bacon's natural philosophy and its intellectual genealogy. The fact, for example, that he proposed to define the use as a legal device by first specifying what it was
not does not mean that he was employing induction with negative
instances. As should be obvious, the definition of a thing is in no way
equivalent to an inductively derived generalization. The maxims or
rules he collected out of the law were not middle axioms and empirical propositions achieved from inductive premises but rational principles discernible in the law as intuitively true and needing no justification.[71] It is noteworthy that while Bacon was in general very explicit
about his methodological precepts and their application, he never
spoke of using induction in connection with the law. The main and
supreme aim of his inductive logic was to aid in the discovery of forms
in order to make possible a science productive of works. In classifying
law as part of civil knowledge in *The Advancement of Learning* and *De
Augmentis*, he separated it from natural philosophy and its principles. His concept of the true method of advancing the knowledge of
nature originated not in his study or practice of law but in his critical
reflections on dialectics, on the failings of syllogistic logic as an instrument of discovery, and on the limitations of the traditional kind of
induction. His empiricism probably owed a considerable amount to
his interest in natural magic and the operations of the various crafts.
He had no need to draw on his legal experience of examining suspects to form his idea of the interrogation of or inquisition into nature. The devising of questions and articles of inquiry was a part of the

subject called Topics, a traditional subdivision of both logic and rhetoric, which Bacon's surveys of learning included among the logical
arts as an aspect of invention in the sense of the discovery of arguments.[72] When he remarked in *De Augmentis* that "a faculty of wise
interrogating is half a knowledge," he was referring to Topics, which
he termed "of prime use" to "particular subjects and sciences." The
example he gave in that work of "A Particular Topic, or Articles of
Inquiry Concerning Heavy and Light," was an illustration of the process of questioning to show how the effective employment of topics
could contribute to the progress of knowledge.[73]

Bacon's characteristic way of approaching every science or field of
knowledge was always to try to improve it if possible, and this was no
less manifest in his work on the law. A reformer to his very bones, he
strove persistently over many years for the reform of English law so
that it would be more certain and thus more predictable in its operation, and also more rational, coherent, and efficient and hence more
just. Although advocating some substantial innovations, he was not a
radical reformer, all his proposals being designed to make the existing legal order better. Well aware of the perils of introducing sweeping changes, he warned in his essay "Of Innovations" against trying
"experiments in states, except the necessity be urgent or the utility
evident." His comment in the same essay on the periodic need of
innovations might well sum up his attitude toward legal reform:
"Surely every medicine is an innovation; and he that will not apply
new remedies must expect new evils; for time is the greatest innovator; and if time of course alter things for the worse, and wisdom and
counsel shall not alter them for the better, what shall be the end?"[74]

Bacon was not the only lawyer who took an interest in law reform.
Among others who did so was one of his most eminent colleagues,
Lord Ellesmere, his predecessor as lord chancellor, who was troubled
about such faults in the law as excessive litigation, defects in procedure, and the common law courts' invasion of other jurisdictions.[75]
Bacon was worried not only about these shortcomings but about the
confusion and uncertainty of the common law, the many superfluous
and obsolete statutes that were a snare to entrap subjects, and other
problems of which his legal experience gave him an intimate knowledge.[76] The masque he wrote in 1594 for the Christmas revels at

Gray's Inn depicted a counselor advising a prince to undertake a large-scale reform to correct the many failings in the law and its administration.[77] In the parliaments of 1593 and 1601 he urged the abridgment and purgation of the laws and statutes and proposed the appointment of a committee in every parliament to bring in recommendations for the repeal of superfluous statutes and parts of statutes.[78] When writing to James I on the question of the union of England and Scotland, he noted the physical distance of many people from courts of justice and broached the possibility of a separate court attending on the king's person and available to both nations, which would evoke causes from the ordinary judges.[79] His private memoranda of 1608 touched on various aspects of the law he hoped to see reformed. Among the services he planned to undertake to this end, he mentioned a writing dealing with conflicts of jurisdiction between the common law and ecclesiastical courts and a project for "The Recompyling of the Lawes of England."[80]

Upon his appointment in 1616 as attorney general and member of the Privy Council, he sent the king "A Proposition . . . Touching the Compiling and Amendment of the Laws of England," which was one of his major efforts toward law reform. Although his proposals were far-reaching, he considered them neither "vast nor speculative, but real and feasible." We need not doubt his sincerity, moreover, when he praised English laws as wise, just, and moderate, nor his statement that his aim was to perfect, not attack, them, and to give them light rather than recast them anew. Anticipating several objections to his project, he pointed to the necessity of legal reform to rectify the present uncertainty in the law, which bred multitudinous, lengthy suits, left subjects vulnerable to oppressive litigation, and permitted great discretion to the judges. And because remedies by common law were often obscure and doubtful, litigants sought recourse to chancery suits, and men's sureties in their lands and estates were made liable to question and other inconveniences. The statute law was in an even worse condition than the common law, according to Bacon, owing to the large number of "ensnaring penal laws" that, if enforced, would "grind [subjects] to powder." Many of these laws were obsolete, others imposed excessive penalties, and in addition there was such an accumulation of statutes on a single matter that "the certainty of law is lost in the heap."

To the opinion that legal changes would bring unforeseen dangers, he replied that such an argument would prevent all "medicinal treatment" and "noble reformations." In any case, he averred that what he proposed was not an alteration but a reordering and explanation, for which there were many precedents, like the Roman Law of the Twelve Tables, the code of Justinian, and King Henry VIII's initiation of a review and reform of the canon laws. One of his most interesting comments was his response to the objection that the labor needed for his project would be better spent on reducing the common law "to a text law, as the statutes are, and setting them both down in a method and titles." Regarding the latter possibility, he declined to say whether a written code of law or a law based on custom well recorded and registered was better, but added that he would not advise putting English law into a new form and wanted only to prune and graft it, not to plow and replant it. Bacon thus made clear his commitment to the homegrown system of the common law, however widely his jurisprudential vision ranged and whatever he may have wished to borrow from Roman law.

What his project called for was a reduction, digest, and recompilation of the common law and statutes. To help attain this end for the common law, he made three recommendations. The first was the preparation of a book on the antiquities of the law based on a search of legal records like acts of Parliament, royal letters patent, and judgments; from these would be extracted and set down chronologically the ancient forms of most weight to be used as "reverend precedents," though not as "binding authorities." The second recommendation was the production of a complete body of the common law in the chronological form of yearbooks extending from Edward I's reign to the present. Here Bacon took as his model for digesting and updating the common law the old medieval yearbooks, which contained earlier records of cases and had been supplanted in the sixteenth century by the so-called modern law reports. The standards he prescribed for this compilation specified that it would include only the most important cases adjudged as law, plus well settled cases that would be entered solely as judgments without the arguments. Obsolete cases would be omitted but preserved as evidence of previous law and how it had changed. In repetitive cases only the best reported and argued were to be retained. Cases involving contrary judgments would be noted, collected, and referred to the judges or Parliament to be rendered certain. To continue the process into the future, Bacon asked the king to appoint some competent lawyers with an adequate stipend who would report cases "for time to come; and then this is settled for all times."

His third recommendation was the provision of certain auxiliary books for the study of "the science of law." One would be *Institutions*, a perspicuous and comprehensive textbook to serve students as an introduction to the law. Another would be a treatise *De Regulis Iuris* on the rules of the law, which he termed vital to the health, stability, and teaching of the law. Noting that neither English nor any other law possessed a treatise of this kind, he explained that the naked rule or maxim did not suffice and needed to be supplemented "by good differences, ampliations, and limitations, warranted by good authorities." He himself, he told the king, was engaged on such a book; and in a striking personal allusion to his keen rivalry with Sir Edward Coke, he added, "And I do assure your Majesty, I am in good hope, that when Sir Edward Coke's Reports and my Rules and Decisions shall come to posterity, there will be (whatsoever is now thought) question who was the greater lawyer." A third book he proposed was a dictionary or treatise *De Verborum Significationibus*, which would explicate the terms of the law and words in ancient records and precedents.

These suggestions pertained to the common law. For the amendment of the statute law he called for the removal and repeal of obsolete statutes; the repeal of unenforced and needless penal statutes that could ensnare subjects; the mitigation of the penalties in statutes that were to remain in force; and "the reducing of concurrent statutes, heaped one upon another, to one clear and uniform law." All of the work pertaining to the statutes, he pointed out, would "of necessity" come to Parliament. He therefore suggested that the two houses should appoint commissioners to prepare the necessary changes for Parliament's approval.[81]

Nothing comparable in scope and substance to Bacon's projected legal reforms had ever been proposed before by an English lawyer. In brief and comprehensive outline he described a list of changes calculated to improve the reasonableness, predictability, and equity of England's laws. The inspiration of Roman law was evident in the envisaged goal of a systematic digesting, reducing, and expurgating of the law, though there was no suggestion of a need for a codification. For the common law the chronological record and reports of cases going back to the thirteenth century were to be sifted, clarified, and rendered serviceable, while future judgments were to be reported by a corps of professional experts paid to do the job. Roman law inspiration was also visible in the books Bacon prescribed: *Institutions* for teaching the law, which was analogous to the *Institutes* included in the code of Justinian, accompanied by works on the rules of the law and terms of the law, both of which also had their counterparts in Justinian's codification. With respect to the common law, Bacon's goal was to obtain a dependable, accurate, and authoritative record of cases and judgments to guide lawyers and judges in making the law more certain, as well as to rationalize the law with the help of the collection of rules drawn from the laws and properly annotated. As for the statute law, he sought to rid it of out-of-date and inequitable statutes and to proportion penalties to the character of offenses, taking into account the changes time had wrought. It is important to notice, finally, that in all the improvements he hoped to see introduced in the statutes, as well as in resolving conflicting and differing judgments in the case record of the common law, he took it for granted that Parliament was the proper authority to which these matters should be referred.

At the end of this paper Bacon mentioned that as a result of his motion and by the king's direction, he and several other lawyers had already started work to reduce the multiplicity of concurrent statutes.[82] Later, the king likewise ordered two salaried lawyers to be appointed to serve as law reporters in the courts at Westminster.[83] Neither of these actions was ever followed up, however, so that Bacon's proposals remained without effect.

But aside from his program for law reform, he also exerted himself as a royal law officer to have the law better administered. When Sir

George Villiers, later duke of Buckingham, became James I's favorite with a major role in government, Bacon sent him detailed advice on a number of subjects, including suggestions for the promotion of justice and better use of the judges and other crown lawyers.[84] In this letter he called the common law "our Birthright and our Inheritance," declaring that if rightly administered, it was "the best" and "equallest in the world between the Prince and the People," giving to the king "the justest prerogative" and to the people "the best liberty."[85] The Court of Chancery, of which Bacon was judge after becoming lord keeper in 1617, was a court of equity to provide suitors with relief against the rigidity and defects of the common law. On assuming his position, he delivered a statement announcing the rules he would follow, which stressed among other things his intention to restrain the jurisdiction of his court in order to avoid conflicts with other courts, to grant speedy justice, and to reduce the charges of parties appealing to his court. The ordinances he drew up for the court's guidance introduced a number of reforms; they have been described by a legal historian as an impressive achievement that enhanced the Chancery's efficiency and equitable function.[86] As lord keeper and lord chancellor, he was the highest judge in the kingdom. In the speeches he made to newly appointed judges of other courts, he repeatedly reminded them of the standards they were to observe.[87] It is a heavy irony that he himself, a man who expressed the strongest allegiance to the principle of judicial integrity and tried in numerous ways to improve the administration of justice, should have been lax enough to accept gifts from suitors and to suffer the misfortune of removal from his high office for bribery.

Bacon's final and crowning work on jurisprudence was a portion of a treatise on universal justice and the fountains of equity, which he inserted in *De Augmentis*. Containing ninety-seven aphorisms, this composition was intended to constitute only the first title of such a treatise, the part that dealt with the certainty of the law. At an earlier date he had written some twenty aphorisms in a work called *Aphorismi de Iure Gentium Maiore, sive de Fontibus Justitiae et Juris* (*Aphorisms on the Greater Law of Nations, or The Fountains of Justice and Law*), which I have touched upon in the preceding chapter in connection with Bacon's political philosophy.[88] Although there is a little overlap between

these aphorisms and the later treatise, the former were chiefly concerned with the nature and limits of legal authority and obligation,
and also posited the necessity of a sovereign power. The lengthier
treatise, on the other hand, focused on the problem of certainty in
the law, and in addition to its general reflections, it reiterated and
elaborated some of Bacon's previous proposals for the reform of
the law.

The preface that opens the treatise traces the origin of the rule of
law to the agreement of the people to protect themselves against in-
jury. It also explains that private right requires the protection of public right and the authority of the magistrates, which in turn depend
on the sovereign power ("majestate imperii"), the political constitution ("fabrica politiae"), and the fundamental laws. Public right pro-
tects not only private right but religion, arms, discipline, wealth, and
everything pertaining to the state's well-being. The end and scope of
the law, the purpose of its decrees and sanctions, is the happiness of
the citizens. While the best laws attain this end, many laws fail to do
so, and Bacon states the aim of expounding "the law of laws" by which
the good or ill of particular laws can be determined. As he then defines it, the marks of a good law are that it should be certain in meaning, just in precept, convenient in execution, consistent with the form
of government, and productive of virtue in those subject to it.[89]

With these preliminaries out of the way, he comes to the certainty
of the laws, which he terms their primary dignity and an essential of
justice. Surveying the different kinds of uncertainty that can afflict
the law, he offers numerous prescriptions for dealing with them.
Here we find him observing, characteristically, that "reason," not custom, must direct the process of adapting law to similar cases: "custom
must not make cases."[90] Apropos of extending laws by example to
situations where they are lacking, he advises that examples should be
sought "in good and moderate times, not from such as are tyrannical,
factious, or dissolute," and that "the latest examples are the safest."
He also notes that "ancient examples are to be received cautiously"
because time makes so many changes that what is ancient may create
confusion by "its inconformity to the present state of things. . . ."[91]

One of the most important sections of the treatise proposes the
creation of "Praetorian" and "Censorian" courts possessing juris-

diction over cases in which the rule of law was deficient. Since the law cannot provide for all cases, and time daily creates new ones, such courts were a necessity, Bacon believed. The censorian courts would have the power to punish new offenses and increase the penalty required by law for existing ones in cases where the crimes were heinous and enormous. The praetorian courts would be empowered to abate the rigor and supply the defects of the law in order to grant equitable relief to those the law had injured. Both kinds of courts were to limit themselves to extraordinary cases, taking care not to encroach on the ordinary courts. Their jurisdictions would be exercised by supreme courts only, since "the power of supplying, extending, and moderating laws, differs little from that of making them." Bacon desired that these courts should have more than one judge on them, and summarized several aspects of their procedure. He denied them the right to inflict capital punishment, which should be decreed only, he said, "according to a known and certain law." For the censorian courts he advised the availability of three alternative verdicts: condemnation, acquittal, or not proven. Regarding the praetorian courts, he admonished that they must restrain their discretionary jurisdiction, and prohibited them from ordering, under the pretense of equity, anything contrary to an express statute. Following the example of the praetorian edicts of the Roman law, he also recommended that the judges of the praetorian courts should lay down rules for themselves that they should make public.[92]

These two courts that he proposed as part of a system of universal justice were discretionary tribunals armed with authority to deal with cases where the law was uncertain or wanting or inequitable. They were designed not to restrict or weaken the rule of law but to reinforce it. Both, however, especially the censorian courts, could have had dangerous potentialities under an unscrupulous authoritarian regime; but of this he took no notice. Although their names were borrowed from Roman law, their resemblance to the two great English tribunals, the Court of Star Chamber and the Court of Chancery, is obvious, and Bacon must have modeled them on the latter. The Star Chamber was a court of exceptionally impressive presence, its judges being the members of the king's Privy Council together with the two chief justices of the common law courts. Concerned in part with criminal offenses like riots, assaults, libel, slander, and other actions tending to provoke violence, it supplemented the common law jurisdiction and meted out a speedy justice to offenders, including powerful individuals, whom it called before it.[93] Like the censorian courts of Bacon's treatise, it had no power of capital punishment. Although in Bacon's day the Star Chamber was a highly respected, popular court, it later acquired a reputation for abetting arbitrary government and was abolished by the Long Parliament in 1641 as an illegal tribunal. The praetorian courts were civil courts of equity analogous to Bacon's own Court of Chancery and would have followed rules similar to the ones by which he sought to administer the latter.

From the subject of uncertainty owing to the absence of laws, he next turned to the problem of obscurity in the law arising from excessive accumulation of statutes, ambiguous language, poor methods of interpretation, and conflicting, inconsistent judgments. On all of these matters his proposals frequently repeated his earlier prescriptions for law reform. Excessive laws on a particular subject should be reduced to a single, uniform statute. To get rid of obsolete and contradictory statutes, he desired the legislature in every state to review the laws periodically, appointing commissioners to do the preparatory work. Praetorian courts should grant relief from old obsolete laws, while in the case of more recent laws found to be injurious, kings and the supreme authorities of the state should be empowered to suspend their execution until legislatures could repeal them. One of his major proposals was a new digest of the laws encompassing both the common law and the statutes. Echoing the title of his project for the reconstruction of philosophy, he called this new digest an "instauration of the laws" and outlined some of the principles for its compilation.[94] A further discussion dealt with remedies for bad draftsmanship of laws and with methods of expounding law to remove its ambiguities. Once again he urged the need for scrupulously careful law reports in chronological order, to be produced by learned lawyers paid by the state.[95]

The body of the law was to consist only of the common law, constitutional laws or statutes ("constitutionibus sive statutis"), and reported judgments. Alongside these, however, he desired several kinds of books that were necessary for the science and practice of law.

Institutes provided a survey of private law for the training of novices and students. *Terms of the Law* contained explanations of the technical language of the law books. *Rules of the Law*, to be taken from the laws themselves, were a great contribution to certainty; calling such rules "inherent in the very form of justice," Bacon pointed out that they were nearly the same in the civil laws of all states, barring some variations due to different forms of government. Books of antiquities preserved the earlier laws and judgments prior to the existing laws. Summaries of the law arranged under titles and heads were a great help to practice but needed to be done with great care, accuracy, and judgment. *Forms of Pleading* not only assisted practice but disclosed many things concealed in the laws. Bacon did not encourage reliance on the responses of jurisconsults to resolve doubts in the law and mandated that answers, opinions, and judgments should proceed solely from the judges. In conclusion, to avoid inconsistency of judgments, he urged mutual respect among the courts and the faithful reporting of judgments, and he stressed that appeals for repeal of judgment should be made difficult. The practice of courts' rescinding each other's judgments because of jurisdictional rivalries he pronounced an intolerable evil that should be repressed by kings and governments.[96]

Despite its being limited to the subject of certainty in the law, the knowledge, breadth, and insights of Bacon's treatise justified the word "universal" in its title. Although containing references to the example of Roman law and implicitly keeping English laws and institutions in view in some of its parts, it nevertheless sought to formulate principles and precepts applicable to any system of law. The allusion in it to "an instauration of law" may be said to show that the whole purpose of his jurisprudence was to advance the character of legal science and to render the law rational, modern, and as fair as possible in its operation. In this sense his work as a legal thinker paralleled his aims in natural philosophy. Nothing in the treatise implies any leaning toward autocratic government or the concession of a lawmaking power to kings. On the contrary, Bacon usually assumes that the authority to create law and to supervise and approve changes in the law rests with public assemblies or legislatures. His was an erudite age in which a few other English lawyers—like the great legal scholar and historian John Selden, or Sir Edward Coke, whose writings on the law exercised an unrivaled influence—may have exceeded him in legal learning. None of his contemporaries, though, equaled his comprehensive vision of the law or his systematic understanding of the improvements needed to make law and the English common law serve society with greater efficiency and justice.

HISTORY: THE IDEA OF PROGRESS, *ARS HISTORICA*, BACON THE HISTORIAN

Bacon was both a theorist and a writer of history. His philosophy included an exploration of the nature, kinds, and use of history as a form of human knowledge, and he was also the author of a major historical work, *The History of the Reign of King Henry the Seventh*. Besides these two domains, another aspect of his involvement with history was his overarching conception of the human past and the order of time, a matter generally disregarded by the numerous scholars who have discussed his ideas on history.

Nearly all the writers of Bacon's era who considered the order of time as it encompassed the history of mankind and the world commonly saw it either as a process of steady decay or as bound to a course of cyclical change that repeated the same stages in its revolutions. Only in the case of a few thinkers like the philosopher-jurist Jean Bodin were these notions of time slightly modified by an embryonic recognition of the possibility of change as progress.[97] Bacon's thought was imbued with historical perspective upon both the past and the present, and on this he founded a full-blown conception of progress. Intent on the renewal of philosophy and advancement of knowledge as the principal goal of his intellectual labors, he surveyed the past for its lessons and parallels. At various times, he observed that of the twenty-five hundred years of recorded history, little more than five centuries or so were propitious for the progress of knowledge. These comprised the period of the Greeks, that of the Romans, and the most recent past of the nations of Western Europe. The remaining ages were given over to war and other pursuits, while the intellectual activity of the Arabs and the medieval Schoolmen produced merely a multitude of sterile treatises that crushed rather than improved the sciences. He also noted that even in Greece itself natural philosophy had flourished only briefly, and that both Greeks and Romans devoted most of their attention to moral philosophy and politics. As for the Christian West, it had been occupied for the longer part of its history with theology, which had engaged the majority of the best minds.[98] Various further reflections filled out this perspective on the past. For instance, Bacon remarked upon the adverse effects that religious superstition and the triumph of Christianity had had upon the investigation of nature, and likewise, how the depreciation by both ancients and moderns of manual labor and the crafts as illiberal and ignoble had discouraged the pursuit of experimentally based knowledge.[99]

His historical perspective, however, also provided him with strong grounds for hope. Everyone agreed, he pointed out, that truth is the daughter of time. It was therefore absurd to grovel before old authors and so-called antiquity without giving time its due. For in its accurate meaning, the modern and present time, which was the riper, more advanced age of the world, was the true antiquity, enjoying a much greater store of experience, knowledge, and observations than the ancients had ever possessed.[100] He also recognized, of course, that time could perpetuate prejudice and error, and hence compared it to a river "which has brought down to us things light and puffed up, while those which are weighty and solid have sunk."[101] But though error may have flourished and learning stagnated for lengthy periods, Bacon nevertheless saw in the historical-temporal process itself a potentiality for growth, renewal, and the expansion of knowledge that fortified his belief in the future kingdom of man. It was this that allowed him to entertain the prospect of a great instauration of the sciences which would restore humanity in some measure to its pristine condition before its fall into sin. Writing prior to the outbreak of the Thirty Years War, he perceived political conditions in Europe as favorable to intellectual progress. England was stronger than it had been in the past, France was reunited after its long civil war, Spain was exhausted by its worldwide burdens, and Italy and Germany were undisturbed. "The balance of power" was thus restored, and "in this tranquil state of the most famous nations, there is a turning towards peace; and peace is fair weather for the sciences to flourish." He also took heart from the emergence of the art of printing, unknown in antiquity, which spread the thoughts of individuals abroad at lightning speed, and from the many recent distant voyages and travels, which had laid open the material globe and revealed many new things in nature. The steady improvement of the mechanical arts to ever greater perfection was another hopeful sign for the future. Moreover, the fact that many past discoveries could never have been anticipated proved that nature still held many secrets in its bosom which had eluded the thought and imagination of men and gave promise of fresh discoveries.[102]

The problem Bacon identified as the greatest obstacle to the progress of science lay in the fact that "men despair and think things impossible." Everything he wrote pertaining to natural philosophy and the history of learning was designed to overcome this despairing conviction of impossibility. Historical and philosophical reflection convinced him that continual and indefinite progress was achievable, and he regarded *The New Organon* as a contribution and first step toward this end. Aiming, as he said, to inspire hope, he recognized that the strongest means of doing so would be through a demonstration of particulars. Meanwhile, however, he sought to prepare men's minds for hope and published his findings "which make hope . . . reasonable." In this effort he felt himself to be similar to Columbus, whose reasons for believing that new continents and lands could be discovered were at first rejected but afterward confirmed by his wonderful voyage across the Atlantic and were thus "the causes and beginnings of great events."[103]

At the highest level of his historical reflection, therefore, Bacon evolved a philosophy of time and change that was a doctrine of progress foreseeing mankind's future conquest of nature.[104] But he also dealt with history as an intellectual discipline with its own distinctive place in the world of knowledge. He was by no means unusual in treating this subject, for the early modern period was rich in both original and important works of history and in discussions of the theory or art of history.

The educational program associated with Renaissance humanism placed history among the *studia humanitatis* or humanities together with grammar, rhetoric, poetry, and moral philosophy. Traditionally, rhetoric and history were interrelated, rhetoricians being advised to study history and historians being expected to exhibit certain qualities of style and language.[105] Writers on history took their conception of historiography from classical models and usually assigned it the joint task of giving a truthful relation of past events and of providing moral instruction. Among Italian thinkers in the first half of the sixteenth century, however, there were those like Machiavelli and Guicciardini who departed from the moral point of view by considering history primarily as indispensable to the understanding of politics. In addition to their political writings, both were also authors of pragmatic histories that regarded the historical narrative as a chronicle of experience capable of yielding political lessons and insights.[106] During the sixteenth century a type of reflection on history appeared that was sometimes entitled *ars historica* and addressed itself to such problems as the methods, credibility, truth, and uses of history. Numerous treatises on the art of history were written before and after 1600, of which one of the best known, published in 1566, was Jean Bodin's *Method for the Easy Comprehension of History*. Bacon quite possibly knew Bodin's work, and his own thoughts on history may be said to belong to the same genre of *ars historica*. In 1579 a Swiss scholar brought out a collection of eighteen of these *artes historicae*, which included Bodin's and two by classical authors.[107]

In England the sixteenth and seventeenth centuries witnessed the production of many chronicles and histories of parts of the English past, the growth of a prolific antiquarian scholarship concerned with the monuments, records, and other remains of early English history, and the appearance of a variety of observations on the nature and function of history as an area of study.[108] Arts of history were published like Thomas Blundeville's *The True Order and Methode of Wryting and Reading Hystories* (1574), which was based on the precepts of Italian theorists. Sir Philip Sidney's *An Apology for Poetry* (1595) compared history unfavorably with poetry not only because it fell short of truth in its dependence on hearsay and conjecture but because of its inferiority in teaching virtue. Because history was tied, according to Sidney, "not to what shoulde bee but to what is, to the particuler truth of things and not to the general reason of things," it often discouraged well-doing and encouraged wickedness.[109]

During the 1590s, the circle of the earl of Essex's friends and supporters, of whom Bacon was one until his breach with the earl, were keenly interested in the work of Tacitus. The latter had said in his *Annals* that history's highest function was "to let no unworthy action be uncommemorated and to hold out the reprobation of posterity as a terror to evil words and deeds."[110] Essex and his friends, however, probably read Tacitus more for his political realism and insights than for his commemoration of virtue and vice.[111] In 1591, Henry Savile, one of these friends and a friend of Bacon's as well, published the first English translation of Tacitus, consisting of four books of his *History* and the *Life of Agricola*.[112] Another student of Tacitus, as well as of the Greek historian Polybius, was the classical scholar and historian William Camden. In 1622 Camden endowed the earliest history lectureship at Oxford University, appointing a classicist, Degory Whear, as its first incumbent. As the fruit of his teaching Whear published an *ars historica* on the method and order of reading histories, which classified the several kinds of history, gave a sketch of universal history and a survey of historiography ancient and modern, and looked at events mainly from a moral and providential standpoint.[113]

Camden himself, who wrote mostly in Latin, was the author not only of *Britannia*, the greatest work of his generation on the topography and early history of Britain, but of annals of the reign of Queen Elizabeth published in 1615, the sole example in its time of an English national history that could rival Bacon's later *History of the Reign of Henry the Seventh*. A better, more thorough scholar than Bacon, he related the story of Elizabeth's rule down to 1588, producing an illuminating, lastingly valuable narrative of a momentous period. The brief preface to his annals was a small *ars historica* in itself. After referring to his extensive researches in a variety of sources, he professed the love of truth as his highest loyalty, declaring that to take truth from history was to pluck out its eyes. While all writers of histories were likely to avow their allegiance to truth, Camden held a strict conception of what this entailed. He explained that he had shunned prejudice yet had used "that ingenuous Freedom of speech joyned with Modesty which becometh an Historian," but without indulging in the licentiousness, malignity, and backbiting that often passed for freedom. At the same time, he had avoided prying into the secret designs of princes as both doubtful and dangerous. Like most contemporary historians, he believed that history's proper subjects were affairs of policy and war; he noted, though, that he had also included ecclesiastical matters, since religion and the commonwealth could not be separated. In his view, the task of history was not merely to describe events but to give their reasons and causes, a point on which he quoted Polybius to the effect that history was devoid of profit if it failed to show the "Why, How, and To what end things have been done." Expounding his method further, he explained that he had refrained from intruding his own opinions as a practice inappropriate for the historian. Neither had he invented any speeches or statements but rather had given the words of his subjects either verbatim or in paraphrase. In his choice of annals as the form of his history, he acknowledged following the example of Tacitus, from whom he had learned that "Weighty and remarkable Occurrences are to be digested by way of Annals." From Tacitus, too, he adopted the view that "the principall Business of Annals is, to preserve Vertuous Actions" from burial in oblivion and to "deterr men" from evil actions "for fear of after Infamy with Posterity." About style and language he said little other than to mention that he had avoided digressions and the adornment of his discourse with observations, had used common language, and had chosen a coarser, more curt style such as was proper to annals. In this last, of course, he also followed Tacitus, whose prose was noted for its terseness and compression. Predominant in Camden's conception was his belief in the dignity of history, which dealt with the weightiest matters, his sense of the historian's obligation to state the truth without passion or prejudice, and his conviction that one of history's main functions was to yield profit and instruction by providing both a narrative of events and an account of their causes.[114]

Bacon's reflections on history were thus part of an intellectual setting of considerable discussion of history by contemporary and preceding authors who endeavored to define its properties and rules. His own intention to undertake a history went back many years in his career. Before the death of Queen Elizabeth he conceived the plan, unfortunately never fulfilled, of writing the history of the period from Henry VIII's reign to sometime in that of Elizabeth's. In the draft of this project he stated that in no kind of writing was there a bigger distance between the good and the bad than in histories.[115] He, too, held Tacitus in high esteem, terming him a better moralist than Plato and Aristotle and the best of all historians.[116] He always assigned historical knowledge a central place in education. "Histories make men wise," he declared in his essay on studies, and in 1595, when advising the young earl of Rutland on his choice of reading, he recommended histories above all other books because they contained the best instruction "in matter moral, military, and politic. . . ."[117] In the case of moral philosophy and the culture of the mind, he maintained that reading works of history was the best way to understand the different characters and dispositions of human beings as an essential part of moral knowledge. By studying a man's character within a historical narrative, one could gain a much better idea of him than from a formal description. This was the kind of understanding that he believed Livy gave of Scipio Africanus and Cato the Elder, Tacitus of Tiberius and Nero, and Guicciardini of Popes Leo X and Clement VII.[118]

For Bacon's own *ars historica*, his most general and systematic analysis of history as a division of knowledge, it is necessary to turn to *De Augmentis*, which expanded his previous discussion of the subject in *The Advancement of Learning*.[119] After first explaining that history was exclusively concerned with individuals circumscribed by time and place, he then associated it with the faculty of memory in the same manner that philosophy was associated with reason and poetry with imagination. In joining history to memory because its province was the past, he did not mean to deny that it was also a species of thought.[120] As his interpretation of the myth of Pan pointed out, the human mind "dances to the tune of the thoughts," and memory, imagination, and reason were all expressions of thinking.[121] He marked out as the two main divisions of history natural and civil, thus making no fundamental separation at this stage of his discussion between the history of nature and that of mankind.[122] If we ask why he put them together, the reason he gives is that both kinds of history have to do with individuals or particular facts. In the case of natural history, this entailed that its objects were either species, whose members were so alike that they could all be known from the study of a single individual, or unique individual things like the sun and moon, or individual deviations from species such as monsters.[123] The three-fold task of natural history, as he had likewise earlier said in *The New Organon*, was to give an account of nature in its ordinary course, in its errors and divagations, and in its confinement by art and as made new by the hand of man. He also proposed a further division of natural history into narrative and inductive, the purpose of the latter being to serve as a foundation for natural philosophy. We have previously seen the great importance he attached to this sort of history, of which he found no existing examples. Equally lacking were histories of nature in its deflections from its regular course and of the mechanical arts. In his estimate, although there were many extant natural histories, they amounted to little if shorn of their extraneous matter and were quite unfit to advance the ends of natural philosophy.[124]

The greater part of his discussion, however, was given over to civil history, whose three divisions were ecclesiastical history, civil history proper, and the history of literature or learning. Although students of Bacon's concept of history have taken slight notice of the fact, he was among the earliest of modern thinkers to envisage the need for a history of learning, without which, he said, the history of the world would be like the statue of Polyphemus without the eye.[125] As he sketched its contents, it would comprise a treatment of the evolution, vicissitudes, flourishings, and decays of the arts, together with accounts of intellectual controversies, authors, books, academies, schools, and colleges; in essence, a history of all that related to the state of learning. Since the soul of civil histories, he observed, was the coupling of events with their causes, he required the history of learning to describe the effects produced on learning by the character of regions and people, the accidents of times, the operation of the laws, the contributions of individuals, and other relevant conditions. The material should be handled "entirely historically" ("plane historice"), unaccompanied by either praise or blame and with a minimum of personal opinion. Such a history would have the effect of "charming the literary spirit of each age from the dead" ("genius illius temporis literarius veluti incantatione . . . a mortuis") and would greatly help to advise learned men on the use and administration of learning.[126] The significance of this scheme lies in the originality of its conception of an intellectual history in the broadest sense, with due attention given to both the works and contributions of individuals and to the social and institutional context shaping the development of learning.

Turning next to civil history proper, Bacon began by stressing its special dignity and difficulty. Its subjects included the examples of ancestors, changes in things, and the reputations of men; yet to carry the mind back in sympathy with antiquity and to make the past visible to the eye were extremely difficult.[127] Civil history was obliged to examine freely and report faithfully the movements of times, characters of individuals, fluctuations of counsels, and secrets of government—a task of great labor and judgment, because in ancient transactions the truth was hard to ascertain, while in modern ones it was also dangerous to tell. By his standard, good civil histories were few, indeed more rare than any other kind of writing.[128] He distinguished three species of civil history. The first two, memorials and antiquities, were imperfect or incomplete histories that might be better considered as sources or materials of history. Memorials consisted either of commentaries on events lacking an account of their causes or pretexts, or of annals, chronicles, and chronologies that set out things, persons, and public acts in order of time but without a narrative thread or historical context. Antiquities were the remains recovered from the ruins of time—genealogies, monuments, coins, names, etymologies, proverbs, styles, traditions, archives, and fragments of histories.[129]

The third kind of history, to which he gave the most attention, was perfect history ("historia justa"), by which he did not mean the attainment of perfection but a writing that completely fulfilled the requirements of a history. Perfect civil histories could be classified into chronicles or histories of times, lives, and narrations. Chronicles, which dealt with great public events, enjoyed the greatest glory but ignored the true inner causes of things and exaggerated the gravity and prudence of human actions, thus failing to give a true picture of human life. Lives, on the other hand, whose subject was a single person, were more profitable in furnishing examples, because in depicting both the public and private sides of an individual, and small things as well as great, they provided a more faithful, lifelike representation. Narrations, which were special relations centering upon a single major event or action, like the Peloponnesian War or the conspiracy of Catiline, were preferable to large-scale histories of times

because they had a more manageable subject on which full information could be obtained. Bacon recognized that narrations, if concerned with a time close to the present, would be suspected of partiality, while if they dealt with an early period, they would meet with
gaps in the record. Despite these limitations, however, he judged that
a history of this kind was likely to exceed the others in truth and
sincerity.[130]

His subsequent remarks propounded several further distinctions
among civil histories. In the histories of times, for instance, there was
a difference between universal histories of worldwide scope and particular histories of a single state or people. Of the former he considered that its field was too broad to allow it to comply with the strict
rules of a perfect history, and that it was liable in consequence to
many errors and significant omissions. A difference likewise existed
between annals and journals, the one concerned with important matters of state, the other with lesser actions. Civil histories could also be
pure or mixed. Among the mixed kind was a "ruminated history"
related to civil science, in which the author used the narrative as an
occasion for political observations. Bacon approved this method as
suitable to a civil history, provided it was kept within limits and did
not repeatedly interrupt the narrative. History of cosmography was
another form of mixed history, which blended natural and civil history in a description of the regions of the world and the manners,
governments, and habitations of the people who lived in them. Bacon
believed that the modern age's navigations and discoveries, encir-
cling the whole earth, had made it rich in histories of cosmographies,
which he described as both "historia" and "scientia."[131]

The last topic he addressed was ecclesiastical history, the remaining division of civil history, which embraced church history proper,
the history of prophecy, and the history of providence or divine judgments. To these he gave only the briefest consideration. Of ecclesiastical history he noted that there was a superfluity of examples more
notable for their mass of matter than for their sincerity and truth. Of
the other two, concerned with events fulfilling the prophecies in the
Bible and with the visible confirmation of God's judgments, he spoke
respectfully, but in a manner to imply doubts that such histories were
possible. It seems obvious, at any rate, that he took little interest in

this branch of history.[132] Finally, as a pendant to his discussion, he added a few comments on what he termed "appendices to history." These were the records statesmen left in their speeches, letters, and apophthegms, which, if they existed in a continuous series, could provide most valuable materials for history as well as for instruction in civil prudence.[133]

Bacon's treatment of history, its theory, varieties, and practice, was one of the most significant analyses of the subject by any philosopher or historian of his time and surpassed all previous discussions of history by English writers in its thoroughness and breadth. His understanding of its nature left room for many kinds of history, not least the history of learning to which he accorded a high value. Among the most striking aspects of his discussion was his insistence that history needed to be true to life and that the historian must be able to bring his mind into sympathy with the past.[134] It was this thought alone that made it possible for him to conceive of a history of learning that would recall "the literary spirit of each age . . . from the dead" through the study of the argument, style, and method of its principal books. Although much broader than Camden's, his view of history was not far different in allotting a central importance to politics and state affairs and in conceiving the imparting of civil knowledge and political prudence as history's foremost function. This was equally the most common opinion of history's office in Bacon's time, although it was usually also coupled with a moral purpose. For Bacon, moreover, the performance of this function involved a psychological penetration into the character, passions, and dispositions of historical persons. Finally, it is apparent that of the different kinds of civil history, he deemed lives and narratives of a particular period or event as the most useful because they gave the truest representation of life and the largest political instruction. His own work on the reign of Henry VII may be regarded as a combination of these two kinds in a civil history.

Bacon had long spoken of the need for an English history covering the rule of the Tudor dynasty. At one time, as has been seen, he sketched the plan for a history of the reign of Henry VIII and his successors down into the period following Queen Elizabeth's accession. Later, when discussing history in *The Advancement of Learning*, he

deplored the unworthiness of existing English histories and proposed a history of England from the union of the houses of York and
Lancaster in 1485 to the union of the crowns of England and Scotland under James I in 1603.[135] Among his early experiments in historiography were a brief Latin commemoration of Queen Elizabeth,
the beginning of a history of Great Britain, and a brief Latin character portrait of Julius Caesar.[136] Not until 1622, however, following his
fall from office, was he able to produce a complete historical work
along the lines he had previously envisaged, *The History of the Reign of
King Henry the Seventh*, which sufficed to gain him a permanent place
of distinction in English historiography.[137]

Bacon cast his history in the form of annals, but this arrangement
was not obtrusive nor an impediment to the coherence of the narrative. In the dedication to James I's heir Prince Charles, the direct
descendant of Henry VII, he did not misrepresent in stating that he
had not flattered the king "but took him to the life as well as I could,
sitting so far off and having no better light."[138] A prime specimen of
Baconian civil history, his work stands out as a dispassionate study
which exposed the monarch's faults and failures as well as the qualities that preserved his throne and made him a successful ruler. So
compelling was its portrayal of Henry and his government as a piece
of political analysis that despite its shortcomings and errors, it continued to shape the historical conception of him almost until the
present.[139]

Bacon certainly aimed at historical truth, and his notion of history
included a strong realization of the constraints of fact under which
the historian operated. In one of his early projects for a history he
stated that of all the various kinds of writing, "history . . . holdeth least
of the author, and most of the things themselves."[140] The same idea
underlay his comparison of history with poetry, in which he observed
that whereas in poetry the mind was free to invent ideal possibilities,
in history it was tied to reality and obliged to bow down to the nature
of things.[141] Nevertheless, his conception of historical truth was limited in a number of respects and much less rigorous, sophisticated,
and rich than that of modern historians.

His *History* was not a work of research. He made no attempt to base
it on a thorough foundation of the evidence derived from contempo-

rary sources, nor did he undertake a critical examination of the writings on which he drew. He was sometimes careless of facts and chronology, and he invented speeches, although it must be remembered that this practice had respectable precedents in classical historians and was still an acceptable convention in his time. While he used a few original sources and cited such easily accessible documents as the statutes of Henry VII's reign, he constructed his account largely out of the chronicles of the period composed by previous writers of the sixteenth century, from which he took most of the information he presented.[142] A clue to his procedure was a remark in one of his unrealized plans for a history, which spoke of the need for digested chronicles containing narrations of events as a help to ease the historian's labor.[143] His history was thus to a large extent a "second-order history," not organically rooted in original research, but a synthesis, selection, reconsideration, and interpretation of facts made available to him by preceding authors. He undoubtedly believed that his political insight and great experience as a statesman equipped him to understand and explain Henry VII's character and methods of rule far better than any of his predecessors ever could.

While philosophy and civil history were quite distinct disciplines for Bacon, they nevertheless shared a common interest in causal explanation. The kind of history he desiderated had to relate events to their causes. In *Henry the Seventh*, the principal cause is the king himself, whose character, political intelligence, and decisions in both their positive aspects and limitations are the main shaper of events. Of course, the king was often forced to react to situations not of his own making, but it was his manner of dealing with them that constitutes the main causal agency in Bacon's treatment.

The history's master theme is how Henry Tudor—a monarch who came to the throne as the victor in a dynastic civil war, whose position was weak and whose title to the crown as the representative of the house of Lancaster was questionable and disputed, and who had to contend repeatedly with rival claimants, pretenders, and rebellions—nevertheless succeeded in overcoming all his enemies, building up his power, and mastering his kingdom. By the end of his reign, the "temporal felicity" of his rule had brought him a huge accumulation of treasure, the high marriages of his children with the monarchies of

Spain, France, and Scotland, European renown, and the prospect of a secure succession for his heir.[144] In the course of the history, Bacon adverts frequently to Henry VII's prudence and wisdom, although from early on he likewise notes flaws. Discussing the beginning of the reign, he comments that Henry was "in his nature and constitution of mind not very apprehensive or forecasting of future events, but an entertainer of fortune by the day. . . ." After describing Henry's fixed determination to depress all the eminent members of the rival dynasty of York, he observes that in this policy the king, out of either "strength of will or weakness of judgment, did use to shew a little more of the party than of the king." In noticing Henry's first exactions to bring "profit to his coffers, whereof from the very beginning he was not forgetful," Bacon also gives an early foreshadowing of his avarice as a motif that recurs through the history.[145]

To explain Henry VII's actions, Bacon depicts his thinking. He does so not from the outside but as if he had the ability to enter his mind and relate his true reasons and intentions. Since he possessed no evidence from which to ascertain the king's thoughts, he could have achieved this kind of interior perspective only by an imaginative and conjectural reconstruction.[146] Although he mixes it with comments of his own, the effect is to suggest a privileged access to the king's inmost reflections. An instance of this interior perspective, on which Bacon relies at various points in his narrative, is Henry VII's reasonings on the question of a war with France over the French king's annexation of the duchy of Brittany. In Bacon's account, Henry first informs his parliament of his decision to wage war. The narrative then proceeds with an exposition of his real thoughts as seen from within. Although showing to almost everybody his

> great forwardness for a war . . . nevertheless in his secret intentions he had no purpose to go through with any war upon France. . . . He knew full well that France was now entire and at unity with itself, and never so mighty many years before. He saw by the taste he had of his forces [previously] sent into Brittaine that the French knew well enough how to make war with the English . . . by wearying them by long sieges of towns. . . . James the Third of Scotland, his true friend and confederate gone; and James the Fourth . . . wholly at the devotion of France. . . .

Neither was he out of fear of the discontents and ill blood within the realm. . . . Finding therefore the inconvenience and difficulties in the prosecution of a war, he cast with himself how to encompass two things. The one, how by the declaration and inchoation of a war to make his profit. The other, how to come off from the war with the saving of his honour.

Then, after describing the way the king proposed to achieve these two objects, the account ends: "These things [Henry] did wisely foresee, and did as artificially conduct, whereby all things fell into his lap as he desired."[147]

Besides the device of interior perspective to shed light on actions, Bacon also makes effective use of pointed characterizations. Explaining the hostility to Henry VII of Margaret duchess of Burgundy, who belonged to the house of York, he writes, "This Princess (having the spirit of a man and the malice of a woman) abounding in treasure by the greatness of her dower and her provident government, and being childless and without any nearer care, made it her design and enterprise to see the Majesty Royal of England once again replaced in her house; and had set up King Henry as a mark at whose overthrow all her actions should aim and shoot; insomuch as all the counsels of his succeeding troubles came from that quiver."[148] Bacon gives short characterizations of a number of individuals who figure in the history, and employs this method most impressively at the conclusion in a detailed character portrait of the king himself.[149]

Bacon's work is both a political biography and a politic or pragmatic history, a study not only of actions but of policy and statecraft. For this purpose he does not hesitate to draw attention to flaws and errors by observations that are themselves nuggets of political wisdom. Thus, following a description of the king's thoughts in his dealings with France in which "he promised himself money, honour, friends, and peace in the end," Bacon adds the comment "But those things were too fine to be fortunate and succeed in all parts; for that great affairs are commonly too rough and stubborn to be wrought upon by the finer edges of or points of wit." He then goes on to show how the king "was . . . deceived in his two main grounds."[150] Of the king's defects, he refers frequently to his avarice, underscoring the first appearance (in the 1490s) of this disposition "which afterwards nourished and whet on by bad counsellors and ministers proved the blot of his times."[151] Polydore Vergil, one of the chroniclers he relied on, had also dwelt on Henry VII's avariciousness as his chief vice, and Bacon alludes to it again at the end of the history as a cause "of the great hatred of his people" toward him.[152]

The history also devotes considerable attention to the laws and statutes passed in Henry VII's time, to which Bacon accorded high praise. In his judgment, the monarch could "justly be celebrated for the best lawgiver to this nation after King Edward the First. For his laws . . . are deep and not vulgar; not made upon the spur of a particular occasion for the present, but out of providence of the future; to make the estate of his people still more and more happy, after the manner of the legislators in ancient and heroical times." In this connection Bacon insisted that histories must include an account of memorable laws as "the principal acts of peace" which would inform the judgments of kings, counselors, and statesmen, and he recorded it as a defect that some of the best writers of histories omitted this vital subject.[153]

The annalistic form obliged the history to find room for memorable events unrelated to the main line of the narrative. Bacon mentions, for example, the outbreak of the "sweating sickness" at the beginning of the reign, a new disease of which he carefully describes the symptoms. He takes notice of the Italian John Cabot's voyage of discovery in North America, which the king had sponsored. Also noted are matters like the fire that destroyed the king's palace at Sheen, the births and deaths of royal children and royal counselors, and the prosecution of heretics, which "was rare," he says, in this king's reign.[154] In discussing legislation, he points to the beneficial effects of the law passed in 1489 against depopulating enclosures in contributing to the kingdom's military power. This subject affords him the opportunity for a brief significant digression on the social foundations of military power, in which he expounds his long-standing view that a servile peasantry like that in France and elsewhere can never constitute the good infantry on which the strength of an army chiefly depends; and that only in countries like England, where there exists a numerous "middle people" of free, prosperous agriculturalists, is it possible to have an effective infantry.[155]

To Bacon's understanding, Henry VII appeared as "this Salomon of England," and the portrait that concludes the work is a balanced appraisal of his abilities as a ruler. His manner of government and personal traits are incisively reviewed with impartial judgment. His efficient administration of justice, inclinations to peace, subjugation of the nobility, and choice of the ablest men to serve him are noted; so likewise are his extreme covetousness of riches, his secretive and suspicious ways, and the lack of foresight that made him more skillful in dealing with present dangers than in preventing those that lay far off. Of his subjects' feeling toward him, Bacon declares that he was regarded with fear and reverence but not with love. Toward the end, when pointing out how troubled the king's times and fortunes were, he remarks that "this could not have been without some great defects and main errors in his nature, customs, and proceedings. . . ." In spite of these criticisms, however, he places him "with all his defects" in the company of Louis XI of France and Ferdinand of Aragon as "the *tres magi* of kings of those ages." Henry's achievement itself is summed up in the lapidary verdict, "if this King did no great matters, it was long of himself, for what he minded he compassed."[156]

The History of the Reign of King Henry the Seventh was not a product of inquiry to which Bacon brought the kind of scrupulous care for factual accuracy that he considered necessary in a natural history. It was a rethinking and redesign of the work of other historians, which nevertheless bore the stamp of his personal genius. Its originality lay in the consistency of its political realism, the distinction of its literary style, which conveys an unmistakable impression of authority and fitness to deal with his subject, and the statesmanlike sagacity it brought to bear in the depiction and explanation of events, persons, and policies. It contains little trace of moral appraisal. Even the king's avarice is treated as a political failing rather than a moral evil, and throughout the work Bacon estimates policies by their effectiveness and success and not their moral character. He did not write his history for everyone. He had dedicated it to the Prince of Wales, and the readers he especially intended were those like himself who belonged to the

English governing class and could gain political knowledge from its descriptions and analyses. For them he produced a distinguished contribution to English historical writing, a work that met his specifications for a perfect civil history of a limited tract of time, and which, by his own lights, gave a true representation of life.

6

Conclusion

IN ONE of his courtly entertainments Bacon wrote that "the monuments of wit survive the monuments of power." Ten years later he enlarged upon this thought in the following passage of *The Advancement of Learning*:

> We see then how far the monuments of wit and learning are more durable than the monuments of power or of the hands. . . . The images of men's wits and knowledge remain in books, exempted from the wrongs of time and capable of perpetual renovation. Neither are they fitly to be called images, because they generate still, and cast their seeds in the minds of others, provoking and causing infinite actions and opinions in succeeding ages.[1]

This comment can be applied to his own writings, principally to the ones connected with his natural philosophy, but also to his surveys of learning, his contributions to law and historiography, and to works like his essays with their incisive observations on human problems, conduct, and policy. These products of his mind have had the generative effect of which he spoke in inciting others to fresh thought and to extend further and in unexpected directions the inquiries that he himself pursued. Modern scientists are apt with the passing of time to forget or ignore their predecessors as the latter's works are convicted of error or inadequacy and superseded. Historians, however, have as one of their foremost duties the task of studying these predecessors in order to understand the meaning and importance of their ideas in their historical context. Bacon's reputation has had its vicissitudes

and no longer stands as high as it once did. Nevertheless, the phi-
losopher A. N. Whitehead was not mistaken or out-of-date when, in
terming the seventeenth century "the century of genius," he named
Bacon as an example in a list that included Harvey, Kepler, Galileo,
Descartes, Pascal, Huyghens, Boyle, Newton, Locke, Spinoza, and
Leibniz.[2]

Bacon, born in 1561, was the oldest in this galaxy, three years older
than Galileo and ten years older than Kepler. More than any of the
others he remains a forerunner and threshold figure in the evolution
of seventeenth-century science. He has no scientific discoveries to his
credit, he failed to realize the vital necessity of mathematics in the
great strides made during his time and after in such branches of natural philosophy as physics and mechanics, and his belief that he had
pointed the way to penetrate the secrets of nature through the discovery of forms by means of induction was unfounded. On the other
hand, he gave science an ethos and social function, the investigation
of nature for human betterment, which, if never universally accepted,
continues to be very widely regarded up to the present day as its ultimate rationale. He had shown that this investigation needed to be a
collective enterprise based on mutual communication among its
members, who were all engaged in a common and progressive endeavor from one generation to the next. He had foreseen the emergence of science as a social institution supported by society, and of
the scientist as a distinct cultural type who, as Antonio Pérez-Ramos
has remarked, would be neither academic philosopher, ancient sage,
nor Renaissance magician.[3]

The words "experiment" and "experience" appear prominently in
Bacon's philosophical discourse as an expression of the systematic
critical empiricism that was an essential part of his conception of the
practice of science. No one had ever been so clear in distinguishing
the naive empiricism of "simple experience" from what he called "the
true method of experience" which, like a candle that lights the way,
relies on experience "ordered and digested" in the form of careful
experiments from which axioms could be educed that led in turn to
new experiments.[4] In a well-known letter of 1953 on the question of
why modern science developed only in the West, Albert Einstein
wrote that this was due to "two great achievements, the invention of

the formal logical system (in Euclidean geometry) by the Greek philosophers, and the discovery of the possibility of finding out causal relationships by systematic experiment (at the Renaissance)."[5] Bacon was closely associated with the second of these developments. He spoke repeatedly of the necessity of experiment and framed rules for its conduct, geared his concept of induction to the performance of experiments, and assigned to this topic a priority in the discovery of causal laws that formed an important ingredient of his intellectual legacy.

Owing to the possibilities it attributed to experiment in the service of an operative science, Bacon's philosophy went far toward the very unorthodox conclusion of abolishing the distinction between art and nature, the natural and the artificial. For Aristotle this distinction was absolute: although art might assist or imitate nature, nature and its actions were one thing, art was another. Bacon came to believe, however, that "the opinion . . . long . . . prevalent, that art is something different from nature, and things artificial different from things natural," was mistaken. Just as Proteus had to be bound fast before he would change his shapes, so nature "exhibits herself more clearly under the trials and vexations of art than when left to herself." Art was thus not merely an assistant to nature but possessed the power "to change, transmute, [and] fundamentally alter nature." The artificial accordingly did not differ from the natural in its form and essence but only in being the effect of human knowledge and intervention.[6]

Besides his reflections on experiment and method, Bacon devoted considerable attention to justifying the hope he placed in the unlimited prospects of a revitalized natural philosophy. So far as the sciences are concerned, he may even be fairly described as uniquely the philosopher of hope. Of all the obstacles to the progress of science and the undertaking of the new tasks needed for its advance, he was convinced that the greatest lay in the fact "that men despair and think things impossible." To eliminate this despair was one of the foremost objectives of his work and of some of the most striking passages in *The New Organon*. He mustered a large array of arguments to demonstrate the rational grounds of hope for the progress of the sciences far beyond anything yet attained. From these arguments he concluded that "there is hope and enough to spare, not only to make a bold man try, but also to make a sober-minded and wise man believe." To try a new path was accordingly both wise and necessary, for by not trying mankind might throw away an immense good, whereas lack of success would mean only the loss of a little human effort.[7]

Bacon's main and permanent significance, therefore, is as a thinker about science: the conditions favorable to its growth; the changes and procedures required to insure its progress; its contribution to the inauguration of a new regime of knowledge; and its technological and moral realization in works to improve the human condition. He regarded the development of the sciences and their growing comprehension of the laws of nature as a vital and transformative part of the civilization of the future that would usher in the kingdom of man. He would not have been moved by Max Weber's disenchanted comment that science as a value-free activity can say nothing about the meaning of the world or give any answer to Tolstoy's anguished question, "What shall we do and how shall we live?"[8] For the meaning of the world Bacon looked not to science but to the teachings of the Christian religion, in which he was a believer. Nor could he have considered science to be a value-free activity, since for him the investigation of nature, the book of God's works, for the purpose of increasing knowledge and human welfare, could itself be seen as a religious activity, a form of service to God.[9]

There are nonetheless some major paradoxes in Bacon's thought on the character and goals of science. He fully understood that discovery could have momentous consequences for society. *The New Organon* claimed that the introduction of famous discoveries deserved the highest rank among human actions. To the authors of inventions, Bacon said, former ages had awarded divine honors, while those who served the state as founders of cities or empires, legislators, and saviors of their country had received honors no higher than heroic. In the case of the inventions of printing, gunpowder, and the magnetic compass, he pointed out that they had changed the whole face of the world—so much so "that no empire, no sect, no star seems to have exerted greater influence in human affairs than these mechanical discoveries."[10] In the enumeration of *magnalia naturae*, or great works of nature for human use, which he put at the end of *New Atlantis*, in addition to the prolongation of life, restitution of youth and retarding of age, the cure of incurable diseases, and the mitigation of pain, he mentioned such other things as the following: increasing human strength and activity; altering statures and features; enhancing the intellectual parts; creating new species; new instruments of destruction for war and new poisons; acceleration of natural processes; extracting foods from substances not in use; making new textiles and materials; producing artificial minerals and cements.[11] He imagined all these discoveries among the future possibilities of science; and he would have realized that, if they should ever come to pass, their repercussions on human life were bound to be far-reaching.

Yet when he turned to the social and political domains, he remained largely fixed within the assumptions of his own time. In politics, where service to the state and public good was his ideal, his chief objectives, even as a reformer, were the maintenance of political stability by more efficient government and equitable administration of the law, and the expansion of English and British dominion into a world empire. In his social perspective and conceptions of political economy, he took for granted the durability of the hierarchic social order, dominated by landed nobilities and civic oligarchies, which then existed almost everywhere in Europe, in both monarchies and urban republics. The society pictured in *New Atlantis* appears to be such a hierarchy, though one in which an aristocracy of intellect rather than of birth and ascriptive status, played a major role, based at the bottom on a tranquil population subject to strong paternal and familial authority, and rising up to the Fathers of Salomon's House and a remote king. Bacon's vision thus paradoxically combined a perception of the dynamic possibilities inherent in a renovated natural science and the supposition of the continuance of Europe's hierarchic society. He expected science to be prolific in creating new inventions for human benefit yet took no account of the disruptive consequences and social changes that might ensue from them. It did not occur to him to wonder whether a dynamic science such as he desired could coexist indefinitely with the traditional society and polity or the values that sustained them.

This paradox is sharpened when we recollect that Bacon's science originated in a revolt against antiquity, Aristotle, and traditional philosophy, all of whose authority he rejected. Throughout his writings on natural philosophy he championed habits of inquiry that questioned intellectual authority. Truth, he said in *The New Organon*, is "rightly . . . called the daughter of time, not of authority," and he therefore condemned "those enchantments of antiquity and authority" that had rendered men impotent to advance the understanding of nature.[12] He failed to consider, though, that the antiauthoritarian attitude he associated with the practice of science might migrate into the political and social realms and put traditional political and social institutions into question. This possibility, implicit in Bacon's challenge to intellectual authority and the ascendancy of the past, was actualized for the first time during the English revolution in the middle decades of the seventeenth century, when many of the disciples of his philosophy became supporters of the civil war against Charles I and critics and reformers of various existing institutions.[13]

Paradoxes are present, too, in Bacon's program for the growth of knowledge and his faith in technological progress. Although he always insisted that the investigation of the secrets of nature was in conformity with God's will and plan, the ultimate aim of his science in the restitution of mankind to its original estate before the Fall was not devoid of hubris. In anticipating that science would remove so many of the ills of human life, was he not aspiring to make man godlike? He would have denied it, of course. Nevertheless, the Faustian quest for knowledge that he endorsed could not fail in due time to react detrimentally upon the older forms of Christianity and the place they assigned to man. The poet Rainer Maria Rilke reflected this fact when, writing in the dark years of the First World War, he once observed that by dint of its belief in humanity and "so-called progress," the modern world had forgotten the ultimate limitations in human life and "that it has once and for all been surpassed by death and by God."[14] In the ambitions and expectations of Baconian science this forgetfulness remarked by Rilke was already foreshadowed.

When imagining the unlimited technological progress to come from a renovated science, Bacon usually assumed that its results would be benign—a realization of the *philanthropia* that was one of the inspirations of his project. Now and then, it is true, he did recognize the destructive effects that might accompany such progress.

Thus though in *De Augmentis* he hailed the mariner's compass as a great invention without which the West Indies would never have been discovered, he deplored elsewhere that the Spanish conquest and Christianization of the Indies had reduced the natives "from freemen to slaves, and slaves of most miserable condition."[15] He praised the invention of gunpowder, despite the fact that gunpowder killed. His interpretation of the fable of Daedalus described how the mythical craftsman, besides creating great works for the ennoblement of cities and public places, had also used his mechanical skills to devise "unlawful artifices and depraved applications" such as the Minotaur's labyrinth. This led him to take note of the dual character of the mechanical arts. While they had brought many benefits to human life, out of them had also come instruments of death like guns and poisons, which exceeded the Minotaur in their cruelty and destructiveness.[16] This conclusion, though, did not cause him to be more cautious in estimating the effects of scientific progress. He saw progress essentially as a linear movement forward, one that would bring mankind into a bright future, without reckoning its possible dangers and harmful consequences, even though he did not entirely ignore them.

Bacon called the establishment of human dominion over the universe the noblest work of man, and his aim of mastering nature remains one of the foremost objects of scientific knowledge.[17] A herald of the era of modern progress that lay in the future, he lived too soon to witness or understand the many ironies and paradoxes inherent in the march of progress that have given rise in our time to skepticism or disillusionment over the effects of technology and science. All that he could envisage were their benefits.

In summing up Bacon's scientific program, Pérez-Ramos has seen its best analogy in Kant's forensic image "of the stern judge who dictates his questions [to nature] in order to extract manipulative directions with regard to his sole practical interests"; and he has spoken in this connection of "the ethos of domination which pervades such inquisitorial dreams."[18] In fact, what Kant actually said is much milder and less intimidating than Pérez-Ramos's paraphrase.[19] In any case, however, rather than such cruel inquisitorial metaphors, we ought to select a different and kinder analogy, one also supplied by Bacon himself, that not only fits the animating spirit of his science far better

but does him more justice. It is an image he often invoked, which
likens science to the marriage of man's mind with the universe or
nature. A particularly striking expression of it occurs in the plan of
The Great Instauration in a passage comparing the understanding
of the true relationship between the nature of things and the nature
of the mind to the preparation "of the bridal chamber of the Mind
and the Universe, the Divine Goodness assisting"; and out of this marriage, Bacon continued, "let us hope (and be this the prayer of the
bridal song) there may spring helps to man, and a line and race of
inventions that may in some degree subdue and overcome the necessities and miseries of humanity."[20]

NOTES

CHAPTER 1
INTRODUCTION: BACON'S TWO LIVES

1. *LL*, 7:230. In the Authorized Version this psalm is numbered 120. Bacon often quoted the line from the Vulgate version. He did so to a friend in 1605, to whom he wrote that his mind had been absent from many things he had done and that "I have led my life in civil causes; for which I was not very fit by nature, and more unfit by the preoccupation of my mind"; ibid., 3:253. In the essay "Of Nature in Men," he observed that "They are happy men whose natures sort with their vocations; otherwise they may say, *Multum incola fuit anima mea,* when they converse in those things they do not affect"; *Essays, Works,* 12:213.

2. Lytton Strachey, *Elizabeth and Essex* (New York: Harcourt Brace, 1928), p. 9.

3. Charles W. Lemmi, *The Classical Deities in Bacon: A Study in Mythological Symbolism* (Baltimore: Johns Hopkins University Press, 1933), p. 151.

4. Thomas B. Macaulay, "Lord Bacon" (1837), in *Works,* 8 vols. (New York: Longmans, Green, 1900), vol. 6.

5. Numerous biographies of Bacon exist, nearly all of which are heavily dependent on Spedding's *The Letters and Life of Francis Bacon,* on whose scrupulous and devoted scholarship I have drawn extensively for almost all of the biographical material in this chapter. Owing to Spedding's diligence in publishing Bacon's correspondence, private papers, and related sources together with an extended historical elucidation, his personal history and political career are better documented than that of any other prominent Englishman of his time. An excellent survey and estimate of Bacon's life is given by S. R. Gardiner in *DNB,* s.v. Recent biographical studies include Catherine Drinker Bowen, *Francis Bacon: The Temper of a Man* (Boston: Little Brown, 1963), and Joel J. Epstein, *Francis Bacon: A Political Biography* (Athens: Ohio University Press, 1977). Jonathan Marwill, *The Trials of Counsel: Francis Bacon in 1621* (Detroit: Wayne State University Press, 1976), deals with Bacon's political ambitions and beliefs. Julian Martin, *Francis Bacon, the State, and the Reform of Natural Philosophy* (Cambridge: Cambridge University Press, 1992), includes some useful material on his career as a lawyer and statesman. Nieves Mathews, *Francis Bacon: The History of a Character Assassination* (New Haven: Yale University Press, 1996), is a very long defense of almost every facet of Bacon's actions and career and is directed against both Macaulay's highly prejudiced essay of 1837 and many other of Bacon's critics past and present. The work by Bacon's editor and biographer James Spedding, *Evenings with a Reviewer or Macaulay and Bacon,* 2 vols. (London, 1881), which was

written in 1846 and posthumously published, was an earlier refutation of Macaulay's essay on Bacon.

6. For Sir Nicholas Bacon's life and career, see the notice in *DNB*, s.v., and Robert Tittler, *Nicholas Bacon: The Making of a Tudor Statesman* (Athens: Ohio University Press, 1976).

7. Willam Rawley, *The Life of the Right Honourable Francis Bacon, Baron of Verulam, Viscount St. Alban* (1657), in *Works*, 1:39–40.

8. See his two letters to Burghley, *LL*, 1:12–15.

9. Although Spedding stated, ibid., pp. 36–37, that Bacon was first elected in 1584, this is a mistake; see *The History of Parliament: The House of Commons 1558–1603*, ed. P. W. Hasler, 3 vols. (London: HMSO, 1981), 1:375.

10. Besides the material contained in *LL*, passim, see the references to Bacon's activity in Elizabethan parliaments in J. E. Neale, *Elizabeth I and Her Parliaments 1584–1601* (London: Jonathan Cape, 1957), passim.

11. *LL*, 1:57.

12. Ibid., pp. 47–56. Although this *Letter of Advice to Queen Elizabeth* is of uncertain authorship, Spedding plausibly attributed it to Bacon; for the reference to "reason of state," see pp. 45–46.

13. *An Advertisement Touching the Controversies of the Church of England*, in ibid., pp. 74–95. The quotation from Machiavelli is on p. 60.

14. Ibid., pp. 102–3.

15. See, for example, his treatise *Maxims of the Law*, which dates from 1596 and was printed after his death, *Works*, vol. 14. This work is discussed below, chap. 5.

16. Ibid., pp. 108–9.

17. *Of the Interpretation of Nature Proem, LL*, 3:84–87. This autobiographical statement was written around 1603; the Latin original, *De Interpretatione Naturae Prooemium*, is printed in *Works*, 6:446–50.

18. All the biographies of Queen Elizabeth and histories of her reign discuss her relationship with the earl of Essex and its consequences. For a recent account of Essex's rise and his factional rivalry with the Cecils, see Wallace T. MacCaffrey, *Elizabeth I: War and Politics 1588–1603* (Princeton: Princeton University Press, 1992), pt. 6. There is no adequate political biography of Essex. G. B. Harrison, *The Life and Death of Robert Devereux Earl of Essex* (New York: Henry Holt, 1937), describes his career and relationship with Bacon.

19. *Essays, Works*, 12:254. This essay appeared in the first edition of the *Essays* in 1597, as well as in a larger version in the subsequent editions of 1612 and 1625.

20. Spedding describes Bacon's actions in the 1593 parliament and their consequences in *LL*, 1:209–35; for Bacon's letter to Burghley, see ibid., pp. 233–34. J. E. Neale, *Elizabeth I and Her Parliaments*, pp. 303, 309–10, summarizes the episode of Bacon's opposition.

21. This work, which was circulated in numerous manuscript copies and not published until after Bacon's death, is printed in *LL*, 1:146–208.

22. Ibid., pp. 309, 313–14, 316–20; 2:108–9; on Bacon's involvement in the torture of prisoners, see Daniel Coquillette, *Francis Bacon* (Edinburgh: Edinburgh University Press, 1992), p. 325, and Mathews, *Francis Bacon*, pp. 286–91.

23. See his letter to Sir Robert Cecil, *LL*, 2:355–56, which is undated but evidently pertains to the matter of the solicitorship.

24. Ibid., pp. 356, 359.

25. Ibid., pp. 370–71, 373. Spedding prints the relevant documents and relates the entire story of Essex's efforts to secure the offices of attorney general and solicitor general for Bacon, ibid., pp. 231–70. With regard to his work as a lawyer, Bacon informed Burghley during his futile pursuit of the solicitorship, ". . . I do not think that the ordinary practice of the law, not serving the Queen in place, will be admitted for a good account of the poor talent which God hath given me"; ibid., p. 358.

26. ibid., 3:40–45.

27. *Works*, 1:38.

28. Bacon addressed Anthony in this dedication as "Loving and beloved Brother"; see ibid., 12:289. In the essay "Of Followers and Friends" in the 1597 edition of his *Essays*, Bacon expressed a disenchanted view of friendship, observing that "There is little friendshipe, and least of all betweene equals" and that what exists "is betweene superiour and inferiour, whose fortunes may comprehend the one the other"; ibid., pp. 295–96.

29. See Paul H. Kocher, "Francis Bacon and His Father," *Huntington Library Quarterly* 20, no. 2 (1958): 133–58.

30. *DNB.*, s.v., contains an account of Lady Bacon's life. Spedding discusses her Puritanism, *LL*, 1:2–3. Her letter to Lord Burghley in December 1584 in behalf of Puritan Nonconformists contains revealing expressions of the intensity of her religious convictions; ibid., pp. 420–22. Her letters to her son Anthony, which Spedding cites, throw light on her beliefs and relationship with her children.

31. Ibid., p. 326. In the 1590s Bacon wrote speeches for pageants that Essex presented at court in honor of the queen, and he contributed to the Christmas revels at Gray's Inn in 1594 with his masque *Gesta Grayorum*; see ibid., pp. 119–21, 325–26, 374–75.

32. Ibid., pp. 110–11.

33. Ibid., pp. 113, 244.

34. This letter from Anthony Bacon's correspondence, which Spedding apparently missed, is printed in Thomas Birch, *Memoirs of the Reign of Queen Elizabeth*, 2 vols. (London, 1754), 1:173.

35. John Aubrey, *Brief Lives*, ed. Andrew Clark, 2 vols. (Oxford, 1898), 1:71.

36. *The Autobiography and Correspondence of Sir Simonds D'Ewes*, ed. J. O. Halliwell, 2 vols. (London, 1845), 1:191–92, and editor's note, which states that "D'Ewes here specifically charges Bacon with an abominable offence, in language too gross for publication."

37. *LL*, 1:245.

38. Pérez's letter, dated January 1595 and written in Latin like all his correspondence with Anthony Bacon and Essex, is printed in Gustave Ungerer, *A Spaniard in Elizabethan England: The Correspondence of Antonio Pérez's Exile*, 2 vols. (London: Tamesis Books, 1974), 1:490–91. Ungerer describes his character and his career in England; see also the biography by Gregorio Marañon, *Antonio Pérez* (London: Hollis and Carter, 1954), which discusses Pérez's homosexuality, pp. 154–55, and the introduction by Alfredo Alvar Ezquerra to *Antonio Pérez: Relaciones y cartas*, 2 vols. (Madrid: Ediciones Turner, 1987), vol. 1. Alan Smith speaks

of the relationship between the Bacon brothers and Pérez in "Homosexuality and the Signs of Male Friendship," in *Queering the Renaissance,* ed. Jonathan Goldberg (Durham, N.C.: Duke University Press, 1994).

39. This episode was made known by Daphne Du Maurier, *Golden Lads* (Garden City, N.Y.: Doubleday, 1975), pp. 49–53, an account of the Bacon brothers. The author states that she located the documents attesting the accusation of sodomy against Anthony Bacon in the Archives Départementales of Tarn et Garonne in Montauban.

40. On Bacon's friendship with Mathew, see *DNB,* s.v. "Sir Tobie Mathew"; *LL,* 3:61; David Mathew, *Sir Tobie Mathew* (London: Max Parrish, 1950), pp. 23–35.

41. "Of Marriage and Single Life" and "Of Love," *Essays, Works,* vol. 12.

42. *LL,* 2:53–56, 3:291.

43. Ibid., 3:290–91; 7:538–39, 545. According to Daphne Du Maurier, *The Winding Stair: Sir Francis Bacon, His Rise and Fall* (Garden City, N.Y.: Doubleday, 1977), p. 33, Bacon's wife was only fourteen when he married her; she bases this statement on the reckoning by Rev. C. Moor in "Bacon Deeds at Gorhambury," *Genealogist's Magazine,* 1937. It is hard to believe that Alice Barnham was as young as this; if she had been, it would probably have provoked some contemporary comment. The letter writer John Chamberlain, who reported Bacon's marriage, referred to the bride as "his young wench"; *LL,* 3:291.

44. Some scholars argue that homosexuality is wholly a social or cultural construction and that the category or concept of homosexuality did not exist in Elizabethan or Stuart England; see Alan Bray, *Homosexuality in Renaissance England* (London: Gay Men's Press, 1982), and the discussion in Bruce R. Smith, *Homosexual Desire in Shakespeare's England* (Chicago: University of Chicago Press, 1991), chap. 1. I am inclined to be skeptical of this view, but it is clear in any case that people of this era could and did distinguish between those whose sexual desires were directed toward persons of their own sex and those whose sexual object-choice belonged to the opposite sex; and further, that homosexuality was treated as a sin and a crime and was subject to social stigma. See also in connection with the attitude toward homosexuality, John M. Archer, *Sovereignty and Intelligence: Spying and Court Culture in the English Renaissance* (Stanford: Stanford University Press, 1993), pp. 75–78.

45. *Promus of Formularies and Elegancies, Works,* 14:13.

46. These essays, "Of Simulation and Dissimulation" and "Of Cunning," were first included in the 1625 edition of his *Essays, Works,* vol. 12; see the discussion of them below, chap. 4.

47. See MacCaffrey, *Elizabeth I,* chap. 26, for an account of Essex's fall.

48. See his letters to Essex, *LL,* 2:94–96, 98–100, 129–33.

49. Ibid., pp. 190–91.

50. Ibid., pp. 225–26, 227, 229–30.

51. Ibid., 3:14.

52. *A Declaration of the Practices and Treasons Attempted and Committed by the Late Earl of Essex* (1601), printed in ibid., 2:245–321. This document was considerably edited by the queen and others before it was published.

53. *Sir Francis Bacon His Apologie in Certain Imputations Concerning the Late Earle*

of Essex, printed in ibid., 3:141–60. This statement takes the form of a letter to the earl of Devonshire, one of Essex's friends.

54. In his careful examination E. A. Abbott pointed out the misstatements and unreliability of portions of Bacon's apology; see *Bacon and Essex* (London, 1877), pp. 112–15, 129–30, 151, 159–60, 164–65, 181, 183–84, and the same author's *Francis Bacon: An Account of His Life and Works* (London, 1885), pp. 61, 81–82. Abbott was also highly critical of the part Bacon took in Essex's trial and condemnation. On the other hand, Harrison in his life of Essex found nothing to except against in Bacon's actions. Mathews, *Francis Bacon*, chaps. 4–7 and pp. 343–45, defends Bacon's conduct toward Essex and denies the charge that he was guilty of misrepresenting various facts in his account of his relationship with Essex. I have not found her discussion persuasive and do not think she has given sufficiently careful consideration to some of Abbott's charges against Bacon that she attempts to refute.

55. *LL*, 3:2.

56. Ibid., pp. 57, 58–66.

57. Ibid., pp. 80, 82, 217.

58. Ibid., pp. 247, 296.

59. Ibid., pp. 293–97, 362. Even allowing for the deferential manner customary at the time, the humility with which Bacon asked Salisbury's assistance in obtaining the solicitor's place is uncomfortable to read.

60. Ibid., 4:19. Although Mathews briefly mentions these memoranda, *Francis Bacon*, p. 439, she fails to discuss them for their relevance to the understanding of Bacon's character and prescriptions for self-advancement. Gardiner observed in his biography of Bacon in *DNB* that nowhere is Bacon's character exhibited so completely as in these loose jottings.

61. *LL*, p. 53; cf. also his mention of a "disposition to melancholy and distast" when he had neither company nor business; ibid., p. 79.

62. Ibid., pp. 40–42, 50–52.

63. Ibid., p. 93.

64. Ibid., p. 63.

65. Ibid., p. 93.

66. Ibid., pp. 52, 93.

67. ibid., pp. 73–74; for a discussion of Bacon's proposals for the expansion of England's power, see below, chap. 4.

68. In 1609 Bacon dedicated his *De Sapientia Veterum* (*The Wisdom of the Ancients*) to Cambridge University and to Salisbury, who was the university's chancellor. His dedicatory statement to the latter includes strong expressions of his devotion and affection; see the English translation, *Works*, 13:75–76.

69. *LL*, 4:279–80, 282; see also Bacon's indictment of Salisbury's financial management and his suggestion that the latter's death was a sign of God's favor to the king; ibid., p. 313 and n.

70. Ibid., pp. 379, 382.

71. Ibid., 5:245.

72. Ibid., pp. 255, 260, 347–49.

73. Ibid., 6:6–7, 13–56.

74. Ibid., pp. 151–52.

75. For the correspondence and circumstances relating to Bacon's falling out with Buckingham, see ibid., pp. 220–53.

76. Ibid., p. 287, 7:166.

77. Ibid., pp. 220–21.

78. Ibid., p. 270; see the accounts of the developments in Parliament connected with Bacon's fall in Robert Zaller, *The Parliament of 1621* (Berkeley and Los Angeles: University of California Press, 1971), chap. 2, and Conrad Russell, *Parliaments and English Politics 1621–1629* (Oxford: Clarendon Press, 1979), pp. 104, 111–13. Coke's enmity to Bacon and role in his impeachment are discussed in Stephen D. White, *Sir Edward Coke and "the Grievances of the Commonwealth," 1621–1628* (Chapel Hill: University of North Carolina Press, 1979), passim. Reviewing Bacon's record as a judge and the transactions resulting in his condemnation, Mathews, *Francis Bacon*, pt. 2, presents a convincing defense of his judicial probity and actions.

79. *LL*, 7:280–81, 294–99, 301, 304–16, 328–29, 334, 340–41, 346–47, 354–55.

80. See his statement in the dedication to Bishop Lancelot Andrewes of his *Advertisement Touching an Holy Warre*, posthumously published in 1629, *Works*, 13:184.

81. *LL*, 7:364–65; this passage comes from a letter of April 1622 written to James I's daughter Queen Elizabeth of Bohemia.

82. Ibid., pp. 407–9, 423–24, 442–51.

83. Ibid., pp. 453–55.

84. Ibid., p. 539.

85. *Essays, Works*, 12:111–12.

CHAPTER 2
PHILOSOPHY AND THE RECONSTRUCTION OF KNOWLEDGE:
THE GENESIS OF BACON'S PROJECT

1. *LL*, 1:108.

2. In *Francis Bacon, the State, and the Reform of Natural Philosophy* (Cambridge: Cambridge University Press, 1992), Julian Martin has endeavored to show that Bacon's project for the reform of natural philosophy was political in its inspiration and sprang from his ideas and experience as a lawyer and statesman intent on making his country great and powerful. This view seems to me to misrepresent Bacon's thought and is at odds with all that he says in his works about the reasons for his dissatisfaction with traditional philosophy and his aims in seeking a new method to promote the progress of knowledge. Bacon never connected his hope that mankind would gain dominion over nature with politics or the interests of the state, and in projecting this goal he looked to the welfare of human beings in general. See also Brian Vickers's critical notice of Martin's book in *Renaissance Quarterly* 47, no. 3 (1994): 704–7.

3. B.H.G. Wormald, *Francis Bacon, History, Politics, and Science 1561–1626* (Cambridge: Cambridge University Press, 1993), chap. 2 and passim. Despite my disagreement with the main argument of this book and several of its other

claims, I am glad to acknowledge its usefulness as a well-documented survey of some of Bacon's ideas in the areas on which it focuses.

4. Preface to *NO*, *Works*, 8:60, 62, 63–64.

5. In the dedication to Bishop Lancelot Andrewes of his late composition *An Advertisement Touching an Holy Warre*, written in 1622 and posthumously published in 1629, Bacon stated that of all his works he held *The Great Instauration* in highest esteem because it conveyed new thoughts unmixed with the old; he also said that what he contemplated in it was "the general good of men in their very being. . . ."; *Works*, 13:186–87, 188.

6. *The Wisdom of the Ancients* (*De Sapientia Veterum*) (1609), *Works*, 13:69; this statement occurs in the dedication to the earl of Salisbury.

7. See Emil Wolff, *Francis Bacon und seine Quellen*, 2 vols. (Berlin: Emil Felber, 1913; reprint, Nendeln/Liechtenstein: Kraus, 1977), which provides a useful and interesting survey of Bacon's citations from and knowledge of Greek and Roman philosophers and authors, with the longest treatment being given to Plato and Aristotle. Wolff's study remained incomplete, as his preface states that it was to include two more volumes, which were apparently never published; ibid., 1:vii. This would explain his omission of a number of authors, including Cicero, Tacitus, Ptolemy, and Galen, whom Bacon quotes or mentions in his writings.

8. Antoinette M. Paterson, *Francis Bacon and Socialized Science* (Springfield, Ill.: Charles C. Thomas, 1973), has attempted unconvincingly to show that Bacon was heavily indebted to Bruno. Although Bruno lived in London in the French embassy in 1583–85 and debated his ideas on a well-known visit to Oxford University, we have no indication that Bacon ever met him or studied any of his works.

9. This is what Bacon told his chaplain, secretary, and biographer William Rawley; *Works*, 1:37.

10. "In Praise of Knowledge," printed in *LL*, 1:123–26. This discourse is part of a larger work entitled *Of Tribute*, also containing speeches in praise of fortitude, love, and Queen Elizabeth, which is printed from a newly discovered manuscript in *Francis Bacon: A Critical Edition of the Major Works*, ed. Brian Vickers (Oxford: Oxford University Press, 1996). Although Spedding believed that the discourse was part of a performance presented at court before Queen Elizabeth, Vickers points out in his editorial note, pp. 514–15, that this is unlikely.

11. This autobiographical fragment is contained in *De Interpretatione Naturae Proemium*, *Works*, 6:446–50; an English translation is in *LL*, 3:84–87. The entire statement is of very great interest as a revelation of Bacon's self-confidence and vast intellectual ambition. Among other things he declares that the man who succeeds in the aim he has set forth would be the benefactor of the human race and "the propagator of man's empire over the universe, the champion of liberty, the conqueror and subduer of necessity."

12. *NO*, *Works*, 8:67.

13. The chapters in *The Cambridge History of Renaissance Philosophy*, ed. Charles B. Schmitt, Quentin Skinner, and Eckhard Kessler (Cambridge: Cambridge University Press, 1988), and the survey by Brian Copenhaver and Charles B. Schmitt, *Renaissance Philosophy* (Oxford: Oxford University Press,

1992), present an account of European philosophy in the fifteenth and sixteenth centuries. For the Aristotelianism of this period, which was highly eclectic in absorbing other diverse currents into itself, see the essential studies by Charles B. Schmitt, *Aristotle and the Renaissance* (Cambridge: Harvard University Press, 1983), and *John Case and Aristotelianism in Renaissance England* (Montreal: McGill University Press, 1983).

14. Wolff pointed out, *Francis Bacon*, 1:161, that Bacon's statements about Aristotle's logic, for example, were general rather than specific and do not show a direct acquaintance with the *Organon*.

15. Schmitt suggests that most people of this period learned their Aristotle through Latin translations; *Aristotle and the Renaissance*, pp. 44–45. I suspect that this was probably the case with Bacon as well. Wolff likewise believed, *Francis Bacon*, 1:237, that in his treatment of Aristotle Bacon did not go back to the Greek text. Vickers comments that like many Renaissance humanists, Bacon got to know Greek authors in a Latin version; *Francis Bacon: A Critical Edition*, introduction, p. xxxix. In Bacon's day, it should be recalled, Latin was taught and learned as a living language that was spoken as well as written, while Greek was taught as a foreign tongue.

16. For the displacement of Scholastic logic in the curriculum of the sixteenth-century universities by the new dialectics, see E. J. Ashworth, "Traditional Logic," and Lisa Jardine, "Humanistic Logic," in *The Cambridge History of Renaissance Philosophy*, chaps. 6–7. The dialectics Bacon learned was pioneered by humanists and reformers like Lorenzo Valla, Rudolph Agricola, and Philipp Melanchthon, and was expounded in numerous textbooks. Lisa Jardine, *Francis Bacon: Discovery and the Art of Discourse* (Cambridge: Cambridge University Press, 1974), contains a valuable discussion of the importance of dialectics in Bacon's intellectual history. Agricola's *De Inventione Dialectica Libri Tres*, completed ca. 1480 and first printed in 1515, played a major role in the teaching and spread of the new dialectics. Dialectical manuals based on Agricola were part of the syllabus at Cambridge and were required at Trinity College when Bacon was a student there. Agricola defined dialectics as "the art of discoursing with probability on every proposed subject insofar as its nature is capable of creating conviction"; see Jardine, *Francis Bacon*, p. 30. For the importance of dialectics and the centrality of Agricola's work in what the author terms the "dialectical revolution," see also Walter J. Ong, *Ramus, Method, and the Decay of Dialogue*, 2d ed. (Cambridge: Harvard University Press, 1983), chap. 5, and E. J. Ashworth, *Language and Logic in the Post-Medieval Period* (Dordrecht: D. Reidel, 1974), chap. 1, esp. pp. 8–15. Mordechai Feingold's chapter on the place of the humanities at Oxford University in the late sixteenth and the seventeenth centuries, which is part of the forthcoming volume of the history of Oxford during this period, includes an interesting account of the teaching and status of logic in the university curriculum. As he points out, Oxford had dispensed with the older technical formal logic and put in its place a consolidation of language, eloquence, and logic under the banner of the art of discourse. He also notes that the curriculum at Cambridge was very similar to Oxford's. I am grateful to Professor Feingold for sending me a copy of this chapter in advance of publication.

17. *Coleridge on the Seventeenth Century,* ed. Roberta F. Brinkley (Durham, N.C.: Duke University Press, 1955), pp. 45, 47.

18. Rawley reported that he had seen at least twelve revisions of *NO,* "every year altered and amended in the frame thereof," before a final version was sent to the press; *Works,* 1:47.

19. The Latin text of *The Masculine Birth of Time* is printed in ibid., vol. 7. I have used the English translation in Farrington. Farrington translates the subtitle, *Instauratio Magna Imperii Humani in Universam,* as *The Great Instauration of the Dominion of Man,* but I believe that "Human Dominion" is correct in its consonance with Bacon's hope of relieving the miseries of the human race ("humani generis") of which he speaks in the prayer to God that opens the work; *Works,* vol. 7:15; Farrington, p. 59.

20. Printed in *Works,* vol. 12.

21. For some of the earlier references to this doctrine, see *The Masculine Birth of Time,* Farrington, p. 62; *Valerius Terminus of the Interpretation of Nature, with the Annotations of Hermes Stella* (probably dating from 1603), *Works,* 6:61–62; *AL,* ibid., pp. 276–80.

22. F. H. Anderson, *The Philosophy of Francis Bacon* (Chicago: University of Chicago Press, 1948), contains a detailed treatment of Bacon's critique of the philosophical tradition and of particular thinkers. In his painstaking survey Anderson was unaware of the part played in the formation of Bacon's philosophy by his exposure to dialectics as a university subject and his interest in the occult sciences; for the importance of these subjects, see below in the present chapter.

23. The Latin text of *The Refutation of Philosophies* is in *Works,* vol. 7. I have used the English translation in Farrington; for the passages referred to, see pp. 110, 112, 114–15, 116, 121–24, 127, 130. The Latin passage quoted is in *Works,* 7:82.

24. For the Latin text of *Cogitata et Visa,* see *Works,* vol. 7. I have used the English translation in Farrington; for the passages referred to, see pp. 75, 83, 89–90, 93–95, 97–100.

25. On the sixteenth-century revival of ancient skepticism, especially its Pyrrhonian variety, see Richard H. Popkin, *The History of Scepticism from Erasmus to Descartes,* rev. ed. (Berkeley and Los Angeles: University of California Press, 1979); Copenhaver and Schmitt, *Renaissance Philosophy,* pp. 239–60; Luciano Floridi, "The Diffusion of Sextus Empiricus's Works in the Renaissance," *Journal of the History of Ideas* 56, no. 1 (1995): 63–85.

26. *The Refutation of Philosophies,* Farrington, p. 127.

27. See, e.g., his remarks in *Thoughts and Conclusions,* Farrington, pp. 88–89.

28. *Thoughts on the Nature of Things, Works,* 10:287, 293–94; the Latin version is printed in ibid., vol. 5. Bacon's relation to atomism is discussed by Robert Kargon, *Atomism in England from Hariot to Newton* (Oxford: Clarendon Press, 1966), chap. 5; Graham Rees, "Atomism and 'Subtlety' in Francis Bacon's Philosophy," *Annals of Science* 37, no. 4 (1980): 549–71; Ferdinando Abbri, "Bacon, Boyle e le forme delle materia," in *Francis Bacon: Terminologia e fortuna nel XVII secolo,* ed. Marta Fattori (Rome: Edizioni dell'Ateneo, 1984). Bacon modified his atomic doctrine in his later writings in favor of a somewhat different theory of matter, which nevertheless remained corpuscularian. Regarding his view of motion, see

also the illuminating passage in another unfinished work in which he stated that the only power man has over nature is that of motion or the power of putting natural bodies together or separating them. Whenever it is possible to move natural bodies toward or away from one another, "man and art can do everything; where there is no such possibility, they can do nothing"; *A Description of the Intellectual Globe* (1612), *Works*, 10:408; the Latin original, *Descriptio Globi Intellectualis*, is in ibid., vol. 7.

29. *A Description of the Intellectual Globe*, ibid., 10:413–16, 434; for the Latin phrase in the original, see ibid., 7:296; cf. also the rejection of the dissimilarity of celestial and sublunary bodies with regard to eternity and mutability in *Thoughts on the Nature of Things*, ibid., 10:312–15.

30. *A Description of the Intellectual Globe*, ibid., 10:421–23; see the discussion of Bacon's attitude toward Copernicanism in Peter Urbach, *Francis Bacon's Philosophy of Science* (La Salle, Ill.: Open Court, 1987), pp. 125–34, and below, chap. 3, for his later view of Copernicus and his estimate of mathematical astronomy.

31. Antonio Pérez-Ramos, *Francis Bacon's Idea of Science and the Maker's Knowledge Tradition* (Oxford: Clarendon Press, 1988).

32. The French philosopher and scientist Marin Mersenne was another eminent seventeenth-century thinker who held that one could know the reason or principles only of something one had made or could reconstruct oneself; see A. C. Crombie, "M. Mersenne (1588–1648) and the Problem of Scientific Acceptability," in *Grotius to Gassendi*, ed. Vere Chappell (New York: Garland, 1992), pp. 196–97. Vico's equation of *verum* and *factum* is one of the fundamental concepts of his most important philosophical treatise, *Principi di scienza nuova*; see the translation from the third, 1744 edition, *The New Science*, ed. Thomas Bergin and Max H. Fisch (Ithaca: Cornell University Press, 1984), "Principles," pp. 96–97. Isaiah Berlin, *Vico and Herder* (New York: Vintage Books, 1977), pt. 2, and Perez Zagorin, "Vico's Theory of Knowledge," *Philosophical Quarterly* 34, no. 134 (1984): 15–30, and "Berlin on Vico," ibid. 35, no. 140 (1985): 290–95, discuss the theory of maker's knowledge in Vico, Hobbes, and Locke and include references to the relevant literature.

33. Pérez-Ramos, *Francis Bacon's Idea of Science*, chaps. 5, 10, and passim. In his valuable study, "The Aristotelian Backgrounds of Bacon's *Novum Organum*" (Ph.D. diss., Harvard University, 1964), Louis A. Kosman comes close to Pérez-Ramos's view in stressing the artificial production of natural phenomena as the aim of Baconian induction; see pt. 3, chap. 7 and pp. 338–39, which refer to Vico.

34. Giambattista Vico, *Autobiography*, ed. Max. H. Fisch and Thomas G. Bergin (Ithaca: Cornell University Press, 1963), p. 139. Vico made numerous references to Bacon in *The New Science*; for his view of Bacon and the latter's influence upon him, see Enrico De Mas, "Vico's Four Authors," in *Giambattista Vico: An International Symposium*, ed. Giorgio Tagliacozzo and Hayden White (Baltimore: Johns Hopkins University Press, 1969).

35. Pérez-Ramos, *Francis Bacon's Idea of Science*, p. 92 and conclusion.

36. *Valerius Terminus of the Interpretation of Nature: with the Annotations of Hermes Stella*, *Works*, 6:62–63.

37. *A Description of the Intellectual Globe*, ibid., 10:407; cf. the statement that "we should try to enchain nature, like Proteus; for the right discovery and distinction

of the kinds of motion are the true bonds of Proteus"; *Thoughts on the Nature of Things*, ibid., 10:295.

38. See Paolo Rossi, *Francis Bacon: From Magic to Science* (London: Routledge & Kegan Paul, 1968), chap. 1, an essential discussion of the role of magical ideas in the evolution of Baconian science. The pioneer writings of Frances Yates have exerted a seminal influence in both revealing and overestimating the significance of the occult sciences and philosophy in the emergence of the scientific revolution of the seventeenth century; see in particular her *Giordano Bruno and the Hermetic Tradition* (London: Routledge & Kegan Paul, 1964). In *The Rosicrucian Enlightenment* (London: Routledge & Kegan Paul, 1972), chap. 9, she seems to me to exaggerate Bacon's immersion in magical beliefs and to make unsubstantiated claims for the affiliation between some of his ideas and those of the mysterious Rosicrucian brotherhood that made its sudden appearance in the early seventeenth century. For a number of criticisms of the speculative and unfounded character of some of Yates's views, see Robert Westman, "Magical Reform and Astronomical Reform: The Yates Thesis Reconsidered," in *Hermeticism and the Scientific Revolution* (Los Angeles: Clark Library, 1984), and the introduction by Brian Vickers to *Occult and Scientific Mentalities in the Renaissance*, ed. Brian Vickers (Cambridge: Cambridge University Press, 1984), together with the same author's "Frances Yates and the Writing of History," *Journal of Modern History* 51, no. 2 (1979): 287–316. In his essay "Hermeticism, Rationality, and the Scientific Revolution," in *Reason, Experiment, and Mysticism in the Scientific Revolution*, ed. M. L. Righini Bonelli and William R. Shea (London: Macmillan, 1975), Paolo Rossi strove to reduce to its proper proportions the excessive importance some recent scholars have assigned to magical and occult beliefs in explaining the development of the scientific revolution.

39. For the history of the idea of the secrets of nature and its relationship to natural magic, see William Eamon, *Science and the Secrets of Nature: Books of Secrets in Medieval and Early Modern Culture* (Princeton: Princeton University Press, 1994). Alphonso Ingegno, "The New Philosophy of Nature," in *The Cambridge History of Renaissance Philosophy*, chap. 9, also touches upon the ideas of the secrets of nature and the use of nature for human benefit in sixteenth-century philosophy. On the theory and history of natural magic and the writings associated with it, see D. P. Walker, *Spiritual and Demonic Magic from Ficino to Campanella* (London: Warburg Institute, 1958); Wayne Shumaker, *Natural Magic and Modern Science: Four Treatises 1590–1657* (Binghamton: State University of New York Press, 1989); Brian P. Copenhaver, "Hermes Trismegistus, Proclus, and the Question of a Philosophy of Magic in the Renaissance," in *Hermeticism and the Renaissance*, ed. Ingrid Merkel and Allen G. Debus (Washington: Associated University Presses, 1988), and "Natural Magic, Hermetism, and Occultism in Early Modern Science," in *Reappraisals of the Scientific Revolution*, ed. David C. Lindberg and Robert S. Westman (Cambridge: Cambridge University Press, 1990). On Ficino's treatise *De Vita* and its relationship to natural magic, see the Latin text with English translation and introduction, *Three Books on Life*, ed. Carol V. Kaske and John R. Clark (Binghamton: State University of New York Press, 1989), and the section on magic in the introduction, pp. 45–55. The essay by Brian Vickers, "On the Function of Analogy in the Occult," in *Hermeticism and the Renaissance*,

presents an illuminating analysis of the patterns of thought characteristic of the occult sciences in their embrace of magic, including features such as the reification of analogies, the valuational grading of the parts of the physical world, animism and anthropomorphism, and the assignment of causal agency to symbols.

40. See Eamon, *Science and the Secrets of Nature*, for a discussion of the writings and philosophy of Della Porta relating to natural magic.

41. *AL, Works*, 6:127, 229–30, 256.

42. See below, chap. 3.

43. Brian Copenhaver's discussion of Bacon in his chapter, "Astrology and Magic," in *The Cambridge History of Renaissance Philosophy*, chap. 10, seems to me to exaggerate considerably the persistence of magical beliefs in Bacon's natural philosophy and to fail to realize the fundamental naturalism that pervades his thought.

44. Rossi, *Francis Bacon*, p. 16.

45. *AL, Works*, 6:127, 229–30.

46. Ibid., p. 127.

47. *Thoughts and Conclusions*, Farrington, p. 87; see also his critical remarks in *The Refutation of Philosophies*, Farrington, pp. 122–23, which disparage the philosophy of the alchemists fabricated out of a few experiments.

48. On Paracelsus and his teachings, see Walter Pagel, *Paracelsus: An Introduction to Philosophical Medicine in the Era of the Renaissance*, 2d rev. ed. (Basel: Karger, 1982), and Allen G. Debus, *The English Paracelsians* (New York: Franklin Watts, 1965), chap. 1.

49. *AL, Works*, 6:241, 256; Earlier, Bacon speaks very disparagingly of Paracelsus in *The Masculine Birth of Time*, Farrington, pp. 65–67. Bacon's relationship to alchemy is discussed by Joshua C. Gregory, "Chemistry and Alchemy in the Natural Philosophy of Francis Bacon," *Ambix* 2, no. 1 (1938): 94–111. Stanton J. Linden, "Francis Bacon and Alchemy: The Reformation of Vulcan," *Journal of the History of Ideas* 35, no. 4 (1974): 547–60, points to several beliefs that Bacon shared with the alchemists, but does not sufficiently note his differences from them.

50. *AL, Works*, 6:127–28; *The Masculine Birth of Time*, Farrington, p. 66. Bacon drew on the Paracelsian triad in his own speculative philosophy, for which see below, chap. 3.

51. On the subject of esotericism and its connection with the occult sciences, see the present writer's *Ways of Lying: Dissimulation, Persecution, and Conformity in Early Modern Europe* (Cambridge: Harvard University Press, 1990), chap. 11. Esotericism remained a characteristic of alchemy in the later seventeenth century and was still a feature of the alchemical experiments of both Boyle and Newton, who sought to clothe them in secrecy; see L. M. Principe, "Robert Boyle's Alchemical Secrecy: Codes, Ciphers and Concealments," *Ambix* 39, no. 2 (1992): 63–74.

52. Anderson, *The Philosophy of Francis Bacon*, p. 16, suggested that the name Hermes Stella was an allusion to James I, but it seems more likely to be connected with the mythical Hermes Trismegistus.

53. *Valerius Terminus, Works*, 6:71; *AL*, ibid., pp. 290–91; *Of the Interpretation of Nature Proem, LL*, 3:84–87; ibid., 4:66.

54. *The Refutation of Philosophies*, Farrington, p. 108.

55. See below, chap. 4.

56. See Spedding's discussion of this question in *Works*, vol. 1, n. B, pp. 182–89. Despite Rossi's interest in the problem of Bacon's relationship to the occult sciences, his treatment of the subject in his earlier work neglected to deal with the important question of Bacon's attraction to esotericism. In his most recent discussion of Baconian science he claims incorrectly that Bacon was completely opposed to withholding some kinds of knowledge from the profane, but reiterates his convincing rejection of attempts to assimilate Bacon's natural philosophy to magic and his critique of Francis Yates's affiliation of Bacon with the Hermetic tradition; see Paolo Rossi, "Bacon's Idea of Science," in *The Cambridge Companion to Bacon*, ed. Markku Peltonen (Cambridge: Cambridge University Press, 1996), pp. 30–32.

57. *The Masculine Birth of Time*, Farrington, p. 72.

58. *Valerius Terminus of the Interpretation of Nature*, *Works*, 6:32, 34, 35. He quoted this prophecy again in *The Refutation of Philosophies*, Farrington, pp. 131–32, when he speaks of the coming expansion of the intellectual globe. Most famously, it appears as the Latin motto "Multi pertransibunt & augebitur scientia" in the frontispiece of the volume of 1620 containing *The Great Instauration* and *The New Organon* (see pl. 5), which depicts a ship returning through the pillars of Hercules from its exploratory voyage in the vast open sea of undiscovered knowledge. It is also quoted in *NO*, *Works*, 8:130 = bk. 1, xciii. Charles Webster discusses Bacon's use of this passage from Daniel in *The Great Instauration: Science, Medicine and Reform 1626–1660* (London: Duckworth, 1975), pp. 23–25.

59. I describe this doctrine as inherently pessimistic in spite of the fact that there also existed in the Christian tradition the idea of what Arthur O. Lovejoy called "the paradox of the fortunate fall," which stressed that if not for the Fall, the infinite benefits of the Incarnation and Redemption could not have occurred. Lovejoy has traced the history of this conception in Christian literature back to the fourth century and noted its most famous expression in Milton's *Paradise Lost* in Adam's words in bk. 12, lines 469–79, expressing wonder at the infinite good that sprang from the evil of the Fall. Needless to say, however, this was not the dominant conception. The latter held that the Fall, as an act of disobedience that contained in itself all other sins, could never be sufficiently condemned or lamented; see Arthur O. Lovejoy, "Milton and the Paradox of the Fortunate Fall," in *Essays in the History of Ideas* (New York: George Braziller, 1955).

60. See Norman P. Williams, *Ideas of the Fall and of Original Sin* (London: Longmans, Green, 1929), which gives an erudite account of the doctrine of mankind's fall from its Jewish and Christian origins to the period of the Reformation. Williams describes the church father Augustine's authoritative formulation of the Fall doctrine for the Latin church in his anti-Pelagian writings, which presumed humanity's inheritance of and participation in Adam's guilt, with the result that human nature became totally corrupted, depraved, and in bondage to sin without freedom of the will. Some of the medieval Scholastics like Aquinas presented a milder understanding of the effects of the Fall, but the Augustinian conception was revived in the theology of Luther and Calvin. Even in its somewhat softened interpretation, the Christian view of the Fall was inconsistent with Bacon's belief

in the limitless possibilities opened to mankind by science, which lay at the heart of his philosophy.

61. Graham Rees has published this hitherto unknown treatise with an English translation and informative introduction and commentary in *Francis Bacon's Natural Philosophy: A New Source* (Kendal: British Society for the History of Science, 1984). He describes it as the longest and most important text on natural philosophy by Bacon that has been discovered since the seventeenth century. For further discussion of this work, see below, chap. 3.

62. *The History of Life and Death, Works,* vol. 10; the Latin original, *Historia Vitae et Mortis,* is printed in ibid., vol. 3.

63. Ibid., 10:9. The statement from which this passage is quoted is addressed to "the present and future ages." Robert L. Ellis's preface to this treatise, *Works,* 3:315–26, contains an account of Bacon's ideas on longevity and some of their sources; see also Webster, *The Great Instauration,* chap. 4, which discusses medical views on the prolongation of life by some of Bacon's successors. For the background to Bacon's deep interest in this subject, see Gerald G. Gruman, *A History of Ideas about the Prolongation of Life: The Evolution of Prolongevity Hypotheses to 1800, Transactions of the American Philosophical Society,* n.s., 56, pt. 9 (1966).

64. *DA, Works,* vols. 2–3; the English translation of this later Latin version is printed in ibid., vols. 8–9; for the discussion of the prolongation of life, see ibid., 9:39–44.

65. *New Atlantis* (1627), ibid., 5:415.

66. Writers on Bacon have devoted much more attention to his concepts of philosophy and science than to his view of the relationship between philosophy and religion and theology. On the latter subject, see Anderson, *The Philosophy of Francis Bacon,* pp. 151–53, 171–72, 212–14, and Urbach, *Francis Bacon's Philosophy of Science,* pp. 98–100, 102–5. The most recent discussion, by John C. Briggs, "Bacon's Science and Religion," in *The Cambridge Companion to Bacon,* is somewhat incomplete and also makes the questionable argument that Bacon actually mixes religion with his natural philosophy in various ways.

67. *Filum Labyrinthi, sive Formula Inquisitionis* (ca. 1607), *Works,* 6:420; *Thoughts and Conclusions,* Farrington, p. 77. The first of these works, an unpublished fragment written in English despite its Latin title, is closely related to the second, which was written in Latin, and is perhaps a draft or free translation of the latter.

68. *Valerius Terminus, Works,* 6:27–37.

69. *AL,* ibid., pp. 91–92.

70. William Perkins, *A Discourse of the Damned Art of Witchcraft* (1631), printed in *The Workes of . . . William Perkins,* 3 vols. (London, 1626–31), 3:609. This is a posthumous edition of the writings of Perkins, who died in 1602.

71. *AL, Works,* 6:92–93, 94, 96–97.

72. "Of Atheism," *Essays,* ibid., 12:131–32.

73. Ibid., 6:207, 211–13. In a further discussion of divinity or theology near the conclusion of this work, Bacon again sought to define the limits of faith and reason in religion and the subordinate position of reason in regard to truths grounded on the word of God; ibid., pp. 393–99.

74. *Thoughts and Conclusions,* Farrington, pp. 77–79.

75. For some examples of this opinion, see Howard White, *Peace among the*

Willows: The Political Philosophy of Francis Bacon (The Hague: Martinus Nijhoff, 1968), pp. 60, 75, 110–11, 153; Jerry Weinberger, *Science, Faith, and Politics: Francis Bacon and the Utopian Roots of the Modern Age* (Ithaca: Cornell University Press, 1985), pp. 34–35; Lawrence Lampert, *Nietzsche and Modern Times: A Study of Bacon, Descartes, and Nietzsche* (New Haven: Yale University Press, 1993), chaps. 3–4; Robert K. Faulkner, *Francis Bacon and the Project of Progress* (Lanham, Md.: Rowman and Littlefield, 1993), passim. None of these authors is able to produce any evidence or proof to support the claim of Bacon's irreligion.

76. Paul H. Kocher, *Science and Religion in Elizabethan England* (San Marino, Calif.: The Huntington Library, 1953), pp. 26–28, 75–76, and see also the summary in chap. 16. According to Kocher, p. 28, the view Bacon expressed in *The Advancement of Learning* "represented the essence of the Elizabethan apologia for science."

77. *Thoughts and Conclusions*, Farrington, p. 77.

78. *AL, Works*, 6:94–96.

79. *The Great Instauration*, ibid., 8:35, 53–54.

80. These translations are printed in ibid., 14:119–35.

81. *Religious Meditations*, ibid., pp. 81–96; the Latin original is printed in the same volume.

82. *A Confession of Faith*, ibid., pp. 47, 48, 49–51; Spedding's statement is quoted from his preface to this work, pp. 41–42. Vickers, who reprints this confession in *Francis Bacon: A Critical Edition*, provides a valuable editorial note on it, pp. 560–65, which suggests among other things several of its affinities with Calvinism. Benjamin Milner, "Francis Bacon: The Theological Foundations of *Valerius Terminus*," *Journal of the History of Ideas* 58, no. 2 (1997): 245–64, discusses both the *Religious Meditations* and *A Confession of Faith*, in which he discerns both Calvin's influence, including the belief in double predestination, and departures from Calvin.

83. Rule IV in particular of Descartes's *Rules for the Direction of The Mind* (*Regulae ad Directionem Ingenii*) discusses the necessity of a method, which the following rules elaborate; both this and *Discourse on Method* (*Discours de la méthode*) are printed in English translation in *The Philosophical Writings of Descartes*, 2 vols. (Cambridge: Cambridge University Press, 1985). For Descartes's search for a method, which came to involve such precepts as the necessity of clear and distinct ideas, see the recent work by Stephen Gaukroger, *Descartes: An Intellectual Biography* (Oxford: Clarendon Press, 1994), chap. 4. The author, p. 112, cites a remark made in 1565 by the great French classical scholar Adrian Turnebus that the problem of method is the most discussed philosophical problem of the day.

84. Aristotle *Nichomachean Ethics* 1094a = bk. 1, chap. 1.

85. Cicero *Orator* 116: "Et quoniam in omnibus quae ratione docentur et via. . . ."

86. Henricus Stephanus, *Thesaurus Graecae Linguae*, ed. C. B. Hase, W. Dindorf, and L. Dindorf, 8 vols. in 9 (Paris, 1842–46), s.v. "méthodos."

87. See Brian Copenhaver, "Translation, Terminology, and Style in Philosophical Discourse,"in *The Cambridge History of Renaissance Philosophy*, pp. 108–9, for an account of the Greek *méthodos* and its rendering in Renaissance Latin translations of Plato and Aristotle. See also the linguistic and philosophical

etymology of the term "method" in Neal Gilbert, *Renaissance Concepts of Method* (New York: Columbia University Press, 1960), chap. 2, and the remarks by Ong, *Ramus*, pp. 225–26.

88. *The Oxford English Dictionary*, s.v. "method," gives a number of sixteenth-century illustrations of this meaning of the word. The earliest use it records is 1541.

89. For the relationship of method to dialectics, its meaning in sixteenth-century philosophy, and the matters it encompassed, see Cesare Vasoli, *La dialettica e la retorica dell' umanesimo: Invenzione e metodo nella cultura del XV e XVI secolo* (Milan: Feltrinelli, 1968), and the same author's discussion in "The Renaissance Concept of Philosophy," in *The Cambridge History of Renaissance Philosophy*, pp. 71–72, and his introduction to Jacopo Zabarella, *De Methodis Libri Quattuor: Liber de Regressu*, ed. Cesare Vasoli (Bologna: Cooperative Libraria Universitaria Editrice Bologna, 1985), pp. xiv–xvi; Jardine, *Francis Bacon*, chap. 1; Gilbert, *Renaissance Concepts of Method*, pp. 65–66. Historians of Renaissance humanism and the development of the humanities as a curricular subject have pointed out how "method" in this context came to mean the distinctive educational practice pertaining to a classical education and the manner of transmitting information in the teaching of the liberal arts. They note that "method" was "the catchword of promoters of humanist education from the 1510s onwards"; Anthony Grafton and Lisa Jardine, *From Humanism to the Humanities: Education and the Liberal Arts in Fifteenth- and Sixteenth-Century Europe* (Cambridge: Harvard University Press, 1986), pp. 124–25 and chap. 6.

90. "Sic Graeci definiunt. . . . Methodus est habitus, videlicet, scientia seu ars, viam faciens certa ratione, id est, quae quasi per loca invia et obsita sentibus, per rerum confusionem, viam invenit et aperit, ac res ad propositum pertinentes, eruit ac ordine promit"; quoted from Melanchthon's *Erotemata Dialectices* (Wittenberg, 1555), in Jardine, *Francis Bacon*, p. 28n.

91. Quoted from the definitions of method in Wilson's *Logike* (1551) and Fraunce's *Lawiers Logike* (1588), in *Oxford English Dictionary*, s.v. "method."

92. "Omnis docendi ratio . . . sive ordo totius artis . . . quo partes artis explicantur"; Rudolf Goclenius, *Lexicon Philosophicum* (Frankfurt, 1613; reprint, Hildesheim: Georg Olms, 1980), p. 683. Goclenius attributes this conception to Theodor Zwinger, a Swiss physician and philosopher, in the latter's commentary on Aristotle's *Nichomachean Ethics*.

93. The following two syllogisms may serve as an illustration: 1. Animals that suckle their young are mammals; whales suckle their young; therefore whales are mammals. 2. Whales are mammals; mammals suckle their young; therefore whales suckle their young. In these syllogisms the rearrangement of the terms yields two different conclusions. The first, demonstration of the fact or *demonstratio quia*, infers a cause, that whales are mammals, from the effect that mammals suckle their young. The second, demonstration of the reasoned fact or *demonstratio propter quid*, infers an effect, that whales suckle their young, from the cause that they are mammals. In advocating this double method of demonstration, which was also called the regress method, as the basis of science, Zabarella also defended it against the argument that the two types of syllogism depended on circular reasoning; see the discussion in Heikki Mikkeli, *An Aristotelian Response*

to Renaissance Humanism: Jacopo Zabarella on the Nature of the Arts and Sciences
(Helsinki: Societas Historica Finlandiae, 1992), pp. 96–98, and Jardine, *Francis
Bacon*, p. 56 and n.

94. Zabarella's *De Methodis* was included in his *Opera Logica* (Venice, 1578) and
is reprinted in Vasoli's edition, cited above, n. 89. The common point of departure for the discussion of these two kinds of demonstrations was Aristotle's brief
treatment of the distinction between knowledge of the fact and knowledge of the
reasoned fact in *Posterior Analytics* 78a23–39 = bk. 1, chap. 13. Kosman's disserta-
tion, "The Aristolelian Backgrounds," pt. 2, chap. 1, deals with this distinction as
part of his useful account of Aristotle's theory of scientific knowledge. For Zabarella's conception of science and method, see the clear and helpful exposition
in Mikkeli, *An Aristotelian Response*, chaps. 1–4. Both Jardine, *Francis Bacon*, pp.
54–58, and Pérez-Ramos, *Francis Bacon's Idea of Science*, pp. 225–29, discuss Zabarella's work. See also on both Zabarella and the Paduan Aristotelians' conception of method, Vasoli's introduction to *De Methodis*, pp. 167–73; Kosman,
pt. 2, chap. 5; Nicholas Jardine, "Epistemology of the Sciences," in *The Cambridge
History of Renaissance Philosophy*, pp. 689–93; Wilhelm Risse, *Die Logik der Neuzeit*,
2 vols. (Stuttgart: Frommann Verlag, 1964), 1:278–90; and the essays by William
F. Edwards, "Paduan Aristotelianism and the Origins of Modern Theories of
Method," Wilhelm Risse, "Zabarella's Methodenlehre," and Giovanni Papuli, "La
teoria de 'regressus' come metodo scientifico negli autori della scuola di Pa-
dova," in *Aristotelismo Veneto e scienza moderna*, ed. Luigi Olivieri, 2 vols. (Padua:
Editrice Antenore, 1983), vol. 1.

95. Kosman, "The Aristotelian Backgrounds," pt. 3, chap. 1, points out that
Zabarella's writings were read by a number of English Aristotelians such as the
Oxford teacher John Case, and argues for the likelihood that Bacon was acquainted with his and the work of other Paduan philosophers on the logic and
theory of science.

96. Quoted from Peter Ramus, *Dialectique* (1555), and *Dialectica* (1569), in
Ong, *Ramus*, pp. 248–49.

97. Ong, *Ramus*, chaps. 8 and 9, gives an interesting account of Ramus's ideas
and his concept of method. On Ramus and Ramism, see also Wilbur S. Howell,
Logic and Rhetoric in England 1500–1700 (Princeton: Princeton University Press,
1956): Nelly Bruyère, *Méthode et dialectique dans l'oeuvre de La Ramée* (Paris: Vrin,
1984); Jardine, "Humanistic Logic," pp. 184–86; Copenhaver and Schmitt, *Renaissance Philosophy*, pp. 227–39. The source of Ramus's three axioms, which
Ramists called the laws of truth, justice, and wisdom or prudence, was Aristotle's
Posterior Analytics 73a21–74a5 = bk. 1, chap. 4.

98. *The Masculine Birth of Time*, Farrington, pp. 63–64.

99. *AL, Works*, 6:294. Bacon also touched favorably on these rules or axioms in
Valerius Terminus, ibid., p. 53, where he attributed them to Aristotle and referred
indirectly to Ramus in this connection. In the same work, pp. 59–60, I believe he
had Ramus's rules in mind when he spoke of the requirements of directions for
operations and the discovery of simple natures. In his editorial preface to *Valerius
Terminus*, ibid., pp. 12–14, Robert L. Ellis discussed Ramus's rules and Bacon's
commendation of them and concluded that he was influenced by Ramus's notions of logic; see also Rossi, *Francis Bacon*, pp. 193–98, who finds an affinity

between Bacon and Ramist doctrine on the basis of these rules. Craig Walton, "Ramus and Bacon on Method," *Journal of the History of Philosophy* 10, no. 3 (1971): 289–302, also perceives some similarities between the two.

100. *AL, Works*, 6:288–96.

101. *DA*, ibid., 2:427–36.

102. *AL*, ibid., 6:261, 268–69.

103. See also the severe criticism of dialectics in *Thoughts and Conclusions*. In this Latin work dating from about 1607 he uses the term "modus" for the English "method" and points out that dialectics has no genuine method of "inventio" or discovery, of which it possesses only the name. It does not look for the principles and axioms on which the arts depend, but cares only for logical consistency; Farrington, p. 90. The Latin text is in *Works*, 7:126.

104. *NO*, ibid., 1:295, 299, 309 = bk. 1, 86, 89, 100; for the English version, see *NO*, ibid., 8:120, 124, 135.

105. *NO*, praefatio, ibid., 1:234, 237; the English is in ibid., 8:60, 63. Marta Fattori, *Lessico del Novum Organum di Francesco Bacone*, 2 vols. (Rome: Edizione dell'Ateneo & Bizzari, 1980), lists five occurrences of "methodus" in *NO*, while the uses of "ratio" in several senses are too numerous to count; see 1:419–22 and 2:185, 261–62. For Bacon's understanding of "methodus" and "ratio," see also Jean-Marie Pousseur, "La distinction de la ratio et de la methodus dans le *Novum Organum* et ses prolongements dans le rationalisme cartesien," in *Francis Bacon: Terminologia e fortuna*. Wormald is another recent scholar who has pointed out, *Francis Bacon*, pp. 173–75, that Bacon reserved the word "method" for the delivery of knowledge and would not apply it to the discovery of knowledge.

106. Brian Vickers, *Francis Bacon and Renaissance Prose* (Cambridge: Cambridge University Press, 1968), p. 3.

107. *Of The Interpretation of Nature Proemium, LL*, 3:84. The Latin original is in *Works*, 6:447.

108. *LL*, 4:66, 67.

109. Besides the dedication at the beginning of *The Advancement of Learning*, Bacon frequently addressed the king in the course of the work and included a further statement to him at the beginning of book 2 appealing for material support for the various facilities needed to promote the progress of knowledge.

110. Bacon did not identify against whom he felt it necessary to defend learning. Geoffrey Bullough has attempted to place this defense in its contemporary context of other writings with a similar purpose in "Bacon and the Defense of Learning," reprinted in *Essential Articles for the Study of Francis Bacon*, ed. Brian Vickers (Hamden, Conn.: Archon Books, 1968).

111. See Sachiko Kusukawa, "Bacon's Classification of Knowledge," in *The Cambridge Companion to Bacon*, which brings out some of the distinctive features in Bacon's treatment.

112. *AL, Works*, 6:412.

113. Ibid., pp. 117–27.

114. Ibid., p. 128.

115. Ibid., pp. 129–30, 132, 134–35.

116. Ibid., pp. 173–80.

117. Although Bacon may have been the first author to base the divisions of

knowledge on the three faculties of the mind, the classification of these faculties derives from Aristotle and more directly from Galen; see Grazia Tonelli Olivieri, "Galen and Francis Bacon: Faculties of the Soul and the Classification of Knowledge," in *The Shapes of Knowledge from the Renaissance to the Enlightenment*, ed. Donald R. Kelley and Richard H. Popkin (Dordrecht: Kluwer Academic Publishers, 1991).

118. *AL, Works*, 6:183–85.

119. Ibid., pp. 186–88.

120. Ibid., pp. 207, 211–13.

121. ibid., pp. 214–15.

122. Ibid., pp. 207–11, 217–19.

123. Aristotle *Physics* 194b17–195b30, 198b14–24 = bk. 2, chaps. 3, 7; *Metaphysics* 983a24–33, 1013a25–b3 = bk. 1, chap. 3; bk. 4, chap. 2.

124. Wolff, *Francis Bacon*, 1:12–20, has traced the ancient sources and parallels in Plato, Aristotle, and Lucretius of Bacon's analogy between the limited repertoire of forms and the letters of the alphabet.

125. *AL, Works*, 6:207–10, 215–23.

126. Ibid., pp. 223–25.

127. Ibid., pp. 225–27; Galileo's statement comes from his *Il saggiatore* (1623), question 6, which is quoted and discussed by E. A. Burtt, *The Metaphysical Foundations of Modern Physical Science*, rev. ed. (New York: Harcourt, Brace, 1932), pp. 65–66.

128. *AL, Works*, 6:228–30.

129. Ibid., pp. 261, 264–68.

130. *Valerius Terminus*, ibid., pp. 61, 62.

131. *AL*, ibid., pp. 276–80.

132. Ibid., p. 280.

133. Ibid., pp. 391–92.

134. Ibid., pp. 204–5.

135. *De Sapientia Veterum* is printed in *Works*, vols. 12–13; its English translation is in ibid., vol. 13. On its popularity in the earlier seventeenth century, see the editor's preface, ibid., 12:406.

136. Ibid., 13:69–71.

137. In *Reflections on Human Knowledge* (*Cogitationes de Scientia Humana*), the fragments of an unfinished composition probably written before 1605, Bacon included an interpretation of four of the myths he later incorporated in *The Wisdom of the Ancients*; see the preface to this work, ibid., 5:430–32.

138. See Jean Seznec, *The Survival of the Pagan Gods: The Mythological Tradition and Its Place in Renaissance Humanism* (New York: Harper Torchbooks, 1961); Douglas Bush, *Mythology and the Renaissance Tradition in English Poetry* (New York: Pageant Book Company, 1957); Edgar Wind, *Pagan Mysteries in the Renaissance*, rev. ed. (New York: Norton, 1968), introduction and chap. 1. Charles Lemmi's valuable monograph, *The Classic Deities in Bacon: A Study in Mythological Symbolism* (Baltimore: Johns Hopkins University Press, 1937), remains the fullest study of *De Sapientia Veterum* and the sources such as Comes's *Mythologiae* on which it drew. See also the discussion of Bacon's treatment of myth in Rossi, *Francis Bacon*, chap. 3; Jardine, *Francis Bacon*, chap. 10; Barbara C. Garner, "Francis Bacon,

Natalis Comes and the Mythological Tradition," *Journal of the Warburg and Courtauld Institutes* 33 (1970): 264–90. Rossi, p. 256 n. 30, is critical of some of Lemmi's findings, and I must say that I share his disagreement with the latter's judgment that Bacon's interest in myth and allegory indicates that in many ways he had a "distinctively medieval turn of mind" and was "a medieval philosopher haunted by a modern dream"; see Lemmi, pp. 45, 211.

139. *AL, Works,* 6:206; *The Wisdom of the Ancients,* ibid., 13:75–76.

140. Rossi, *Francis Bacon,* pp. 84–88. Garner also expresses the questionable view that Bacon believed the highest wisdom was enshrined in the myths of the ancients.

141. *The Wisdom of the Ancients, Works,* 12:428.

142. *The Refutation of Philosophies,* Farrington, pp. 120–21.

143. *The Wisdom of the Ancients, Works,* 13:79–80.

144. Ibid., pp. 92–101.

145. Ibid., pp. 110–12.

146. Ibid., pp. 122–25.

147. Ibid., pp. 116–18.

148. Ibid., pp. 144–56.

149. Ibid., pp. 142–44.

150. Ibid., pp. 129–31.

151. Ibid., pp. 159–62.

152. *De Dignitate et Augmentis Scientiarum,* ibid., 2:226–50; the English translation is in ibid., 8:444–69. *De Principiis atque Originibus, secundum Fabulas Cupidinis et Coeli,* ibid., vol. 5; the English translation of this unfinished treatise, *On Principles and Origins according to the Fables of Cupid and Coelum,* is in ibid., vol. 10.

CHAPTER 3
THE GREAT INSTAURATION

1. *The Great Instauration, Works,* 8:39–64, describes the plan of the work.

2. See Robert L. Ellis's preface to *NO,* ibid., 1:132–40, which discusses the unfinished character of *The Great Instauration* and surveys the surviving writings related to the latter.

3. See the proemium and preface, ibid., 8:17–19, 25–37.

4. See Lynn Thorndike's essay, "Newness and Craving for Novelty in Seventeenth-Century Science and Medicine," *Journal of the History of Ideas* 12, no. 4 (1952): 584–98.

5. See 4 Kings 12:5–12, 22:5–6, in the Vulgate version, and Charles Whitney, *Francis Bacon and Modernity* (New Haven: Yale University Press, 1986), pp. 24–25.

6. *The Great Instauration, Works,* 8:18, 25.

7. Marta Fattori, "La terminologie du *Novum Organum,*" in *Science et méthode,* ed. Michel Malherbe and Jean-Marie Pousseur (Paris: Vrin, 1985). This essay is based on the author's computerized *Lessico del Novum Organum,* 2 vols. (Rome: Edizione dell'Ateneo e Bizzari, 1980).

8. *NO, Works,* 8:116–17 = bk. 1, lxxiv.

9. *The Great Instauration,* ibid., pp. 40–41, 53.

10. Ibid., p. 55.

11. *NO*, ibid., p. 159 = bk. 1, cxxvii.

12. *AL*, ibid., 6:289–90.

13. A foreshadowing of this phrase occurs in the discourse "Of Tribute," written for some unknown occasion in 1592, which includes a speech in praise of knowledge. Here Bacon declared that "the sovereignty of man lieth hid in knowledge"; *LL*, 1:125. For the background to this discourse, see above, chap. 2, n. 10.

14. *NO, Works*, 8:99 = bk. 1, lxviii.

15. Ibid., p. 67 = bk. 1, i.

16. Ibid., pp. 67–68 = bk. 1, iii.

17. Ibid., pp. 99–100, 146–47 = bk. 1, lxvii–lxix, cxv.

18. Ibid., pp. 63, 159–60 = preface and bk. 1, cxxviii.

19. *The Great Instauration*, ibid., pp. 31–32, 41–42.

20. See on this point the discussion in Michel Malherbe, "Bacon's Method of Science," in *The Cambridge Companion to Bacon*, ed. Markku Peltonen (Cambridge: Cambridge University Press, 1996), pp. 78–82.

21. *NO, Works*, 8:69–71 = bk. 1, xi–xv.

22. Ibid., p. 71 = bk. 1, xix.

23. See also the note on "axiomata" in *Bacon's Novum Organum*, ed. Thomas Fowler, 2d ed. (Oxford, 1889), pp. 194–95.

24. *NO, Works*, 8:99–100 = bk. 1, lxix.

25. Ibid., p. 73 = bk. 1, xxv.

26. Ibid., pp. 73–74 = bk. 1, xxvi–xxx.

27. Ibid., p. 103 = bk. 1, lxxi.

28. Bacon speaks of the skeptics in connection with their doctrine of *acatalepsia*, the denial of the mind's ability to attain truth; for his criticisms, see ibid., pp. 75–76, 98, 158 = bk. 1, xxxvii, lxvii, cxxvi.

29. Ibid., pp. 91–92, 93–94, 98, 102, 104 = bk. 1, lxiii, lxv, lxvii, lxxi, lxxii.

30. Ibid., p. 76 = bk. 1, xxxviii.

31. Ibid., p. 76 = bk. 1, xl.

32. Ibid., pp. 76–78 = bk. 1, xli–xliv.

33. Ibid., pp. 79–81 = bk. 1, xlv–xlviii.

34. Ibid., p. 82 = bk. 1, xlix.

35. Ibid., p. 83 = bk. 1, li.

36. Ibid., pp. 82–83 = bk. 1, l.

37. Ibid., pp. 84–86 = bk. 1, liii–lvi, lviii.

38. Ibid., pp. 86–89 = bk. 1, lix–lx.

39. Ibid., pp. 89–94 = bk. 1, lxi–lxv.

40. By exclusions and solutions and separations of nature, Bacon meant the analysis of complex into more simple phenomena and the use of an eliminative type of induction; see the note on this passage in Fowler's edition of *NO*, pp. 257–58, and the discussion of eliminative induction later in this chapter.

41. *NO, Works*, 8:99–102 = bk. 1, lxix–lxx.

42. Ibid., p. 89 = bk. 1, lxi. Later in bk. 1 Bacon repeated this view, maintaining that his method depended little on individual excellence because it performs everything by the surest rules and demonstrations; ibid., p. 155 = bk. 1, cxxii.

43. Ibid., p. 99 = bk. 1, lxviii.

44. Goya's commentary on this etching, which is no. 43 in the series, is quite Baconian: "Imagination, deserted by reason, begets impossible monsters. United with reason, she is the mother of all arts, and the source of their wonders"; see José López-Rey, *Goya's Caprichos*, 2 vols. (Princeton: Princeton University Press, 1953), 1:200.

45. *NO, Works*, 8:104–7 = bk. 1, lxxiii–lxxv.

46. Ibid., pp. 109–11, 113–18, 124–28 = bk. 1, lxxviii–lxxix, lxxxi–lxxxv, lxxxix–xc, xcii.

47. Ibid., pp. 129, 133 = bk. 1, xcii, xcvii.

48. Ibid., pp. 130–37 = bk. 1, xciv–xcv, xcviii—xcix, ci–ciii.

49. Ibid., pp. 138–39 = bk. 1, cv–cvi.

50. Ibid., pp. 148–59 = bk. 1, cxvii–cxviii.

51. Ibid., pp. 150, 152 = bk. 1, cxix, cxxi.

52. Ibid., pp. 156–57 = bk. 1, cxxiv.

53. Ibid., p. 163 = bk. 1, cxxix. On Bacon's conception of the relationship between truth and utility, see also Paolo Rossi, "Truth and Utility in Francis Bacon," in his *Philosophy, Technology, and the Arts in the Early Modern Era* (New York: Harper and Row, 1970), and Antonio Pérez-Ramos, *Francis Bacon's Idea of Science and the Maker's Knowledge Tradition* (Oxford: Clarendon Press, 1988), chap. 2. Brian Vickers, "Bacon's So-Called 'Utilitarianism': Sources and Influence," in *Francis Bacon: Terminologia e fortuna nel XVII secolo*, ed. Marta Fattori (Rome: Edizioni dell'Ateneo, 1984), contains a critique of modern scholars who have seen Bacon as a utilitarian. On the statement in bk. 1, cxxiv, that "ipsissimae res sunt . . . veritas et utilitas," see the comments in Fowler's edition of *NO*, pp. 329–30.

54. *NO, Works*, 8:156, 161–62 = bk. 1, cxxiv, cxxix.

55. Ibid., pp. 163–64 = bk. 1, cxxx.

56. Ibid., p. 347 = bk. 2, lii.

57. Ibid., pp. 218–19 = bk. 2, xxi.

58. No detailed study exists of the history of Bacon's reputation and influence as a philosopher of science. Fowler's introduction to his edition of *NO*, pp. 98–145, contains an account of the opinions of writers on Bacon from the seventeenth into the nineteenth centuries. Pérez-Ramos, *Francis Bacon's Idea of Science*, chap. 2, surveys Bacon's reputation and the criticism of him by contemporary philosophers, with references to the relevant literature; in chap. 18, he defends Bacon against the strictures of Popper and his followers. Peter Urbach, *Francis Bacon's Philosophy of Science* (La Salle, Ill.: Open Court, 1987), chap. 1, also reviews some of the criticisms by philosophers in what he calls "the standard interpretation" of Bacon, as part of his discussion vindicating the latter from their negative evaluation; he even tries to show how much Bacon and Popper have in common. For Popper's critique of the limitations of Bacon's understanding of science, see his *Conjectures and Refutations* (New York: Basic Books, 1962), pp. 212–17, 255–56. Mary Hesse discusses Bacon in her helpful essay "Francis Bacon's Philosophy of Science," in *Essential Articles for the Study of Francis Bacon*, ed. Brian Vickers (Hamden, Conn.: Archon Books, 1968). While she perceives a number of positive features in his conception of science, she criticizes his failure to realize the

importance of hypotheses and other aspects of his inductive method. Adolf Grunbaum, "Is Falsifiability the Touchstone of Scientific Rationality?" in *Essays in Memory of Imre Lakatos*, ed. R. S. Cohen, P. K. Feyerabend, and M. M. Wartofsky (Dordrecht: D. Reidel, 1976), an acute criticism of Popper's opposition to inductivism, shows, pp. 216–18, that he is mistaken in his characterization of Bacon's treatment of induction. For what is to my mind a convincing exposure of the fallacies and errors of Popper's exclusively deductivist conception of science, see David C. Stove, *Popper and After: Four Modern Irrationalists* (Oxford: Pergamon Press, 1982).

59. Karl Popper, *The Logic of Scientific Discovery* (London: Hutchinson, 1975), p. 420; on this subject see the critical comments of Grunbaum, "Is Falsifiability the Touchstone?" pp. 216–20, and Pérez-Ramos, *Francis Bacon's Idea of Science*, pp. 272–77. In his plan of *The Great Instauration*, for example, Bacon repeated the view expressed in a number of his previous writings that "the induction of which the logicians speak, which proceeds by simple enumeration, is a puerile thing . . . and leads to no result"; *Works*, 8:42. He makes the same point in *NO*, ibid., pp. 138–39 = bk. 1, cv.

60. Popper was in error when he said that the "anticipations" Bacon warned against in his discussion of method were similar to hypotheses; *Conjectures and Refutations*, p. 255; *The Logic of Scientific Discovery*, p. 279 n. Hesse, "Francis Bacon's Philosophy of Science," pp. 121–22, makes the same mistake. By "anticipations of nature" Bacon nearly always meant preconceptions and hasty conclusions from a few bits of evidence that foreclose further inquiry; see *NO*, *Works*, 8:73–74 = bk. 1, xxvi–xxvii. By ascribing to him "the myth that all science starts from observations and then slowly and cautiously proceeds to theories" (*Conjectures and Refutations*, p. 137), Popper himself contributed to the perpetuation of a myth about Bacon's theory of science.

61. The Continental academies and societies founded in Bacon's time, like the Accademia dei Lincei in Italy, were remote from him and were in any case associations of individuals whose interests included natural inquiry, not communities of scientists engaged in investigations based on a shared understanding of scientific principles and the practice of science.

62. Bacon might well have profited from Galileo's brilliant discussions of the method of science and the logic of scientific inquiry, but these were not accessible to him; see the extended treatment of Galileo's conceptions on this subject, with substantial excerpts from his writings and letters, by A. C. Crombie, *Styles of Scientific Thinking in the European Tradition*, 3 vols. (London: Duckworth, 1994), 1:543–626, in a chapter entitled "The Rational Experimenter." Bacon commented on Gilbert in a number of writings, and almost always critically. Although noting his use of the "experimental method" ("viam experimentalem") and praising his experiments, he classified Gilbert in the empirical school as having extrapolated from them a fictional magnetic philosophy of nature; see *DA*, *Works*, 8:451 = bk. 2, chap. 13; *NO*, ibid., pp. 84, 93 = bk. 1, liv, lxiv. Gilbert's *De Magnete* was published in 1600; Bacon based his view of Gilbert's ideas principally on the latter's *De Mundo Nostro Sublunari Philosophia Nova*, not published until 1651, of which he had a manuscript copy; see Marie Boas, "Bacon and Gilbert," *Journal*

of the History of Ideas 12, no. 3 (1951): 466–67, and the discussion of his attitude toward Gilbert's work in Urbach, *Francis Bacon's Philosophy of Science*, pp. 109–21.

63. Aristotle discusses induction in several senses and in various writings and devotes a section to the subject in *Prior Analytics* 68b8–37 = bk. 2, chap. 23. For his understanding of induction and the different meanings of *epagogé*, see W. D. Ross, *Aristotle's Prior and Posterior Analytics* (Oxford: Clarendon Press, 1949), pp. 47–51, 481–87, the latter pages a commentary on the treatment in *Prior Analytics.* Pérez-Ramos, *Francis Bacon's Idea of Science*, chap. 15, presents a very useful account of the Aristotelian concept of induction as a background to his discussion of Bacon, which quotes the relevant texts and includes extensive references to the secondary literature.

64. See Pérez-Ramos, *Francis Bacon's Idea of Science*, chap. 16, who surveys the medieval and Renaissance understanding of induction and its treatment in dialectics and by Paduan philosophers like Zabarella. For the latter's account of induction, see Heikki Mikkeli, *An Aristotelian Response to Renaissance Humanism: Jacopo Zabarella on the Nature of the Arts and Sciences* (Helsinki: Societas Historica Finlandiae, 1992), chap. 4.

65. On inductive logic and the problem of induction arising from Hume's view of causation, see Max Black's convenient survey, "Induction," in *The Encyclopedia of Philosophy*, 8 vols. (New York: Macmillan, 1967), vol. 4. For Hume's discussion, see his *An Enquiry concerning Human Understanding*, ed. L. A. Selby-Bigge, 2d ed. (Oxford: Clarendon Press, 1951), pts. 4–5. While Hume did not speak of induction, there is no doubt of his inductive skepticism based on his argument against the possibility of proving causal necessity. It needs to be borne in mind, however, as various writers have pointed out, that Hume's skepticism about causality does not appear to have shaken the faith of most nineteenth-century philosophers and scientists in induction as a major part of science. The anti-inductivist view became influential only later; see J. R. Milton, "Induction before Hume," *British Journal for the Philosophy of Science* 38, no. 1 (1987): 49–74. For a careful discussion of Hume's argument, its influence on Popper, and the deductivism to which it has led in twentieth-century philosophy of science, see Stove, *Popper and After*, chaps. 3–5, as well as the same author's *The Rationality of Induction* (Oxford: Clarendon Press, 1986).

66. The writers who have dealt with Bacon's natural philosophy have generally discussed his concept of form, though owing to its obscurity, their interpretations have not always agreed. The best account now is by Pérez-Ramos, *Francis Bacon's Idea of Science*, chaps. 6–11, which surpasses all previous studies in its treatment of the Aristotelian and Scholastic background to Bacon's discussion in *NO.* His own exposition of Baconian form, however, is not entirely clear and is dominated by his somewhat misguided effort to assimilate it to the theory of maker's knowledge. In chap. 6 and elsewhere he takes note of the different interpretations of Bacon's understanding of form. His essay, "Bacon's Forms and the Maker's Knowledge Tradition," in *The Cambridge Companion to Bacon*, again explains Bacon's idea of form in terms of maker's knowledge and an operative science. Urbach, *Francis Bacon's Philosophy of Science*, in dealing with the subject in chap. 3 and passim, is typical of many scholars in trying to determine how closely

Bacon's concept accords with the present theory and practice of science. He argues for a favorable judgment on this score, as on other aspects of Bacon's natural philosophy.

67. *NO, Works,* 8:168 = bk. 2, ii.

68. Norma E. Emerton, *The Scientific Reinterpretation of Form* (Ithaca: Cornell University Press, 1984), chap. 2, contains a useful survey of the concept of form in Plato, Aristotle, and later thinkers down to the nineteenth century. She discusses Bacon's view on pp. 66–69. For Aristotle's understanding of form and its place in the structure of knowledge and the particular sciences, see J. L. Stocks, *Aristotelianism* (New York: Longmans, Green, 1927), pp. 34–50; W. D. Ross, *Aristotle* (London: Methuen, 1964), pp. 63–65, 74–75, 167–76; G.E.R. Lloyd, *Aristotle: The Growth and Structure of His Thought* (Cambridge: Cambridge University Press, 1968), chap. 3 and passim.

69. On Bacon's relationship to Aristotle with regard to both form and induction, see the instructive discussion by William M. Dickie, "A Comparison of the Scientific Method and Achievement of Aristotle and Bacon," *Philosophical Review* 31, no. 5 (1922): 471–94.

70. *NO, Works,* 8:167 = bk. 2, i.

71. Ibid., pp. 168–69 = bk. 2, ii–iii.

72. Ibid., pp. 169–70 = bk. 2, iv.

73. Both Mary Horton, "In Defence of Francis Bacon: A Criticism of the Critics of the inductive Method," *Studies in the History and Philosophy of Science* 4, no. 3 (1973): 241–78, and G. H. von Wright, *The Logical Problem of Induction,* 2d rev. ed. (Oxford: Blackwell, 1957), pp. 62, 200 n. 8, also explain Bacon's concept of form as equivalent to a necessary and sufficient cause.

74. *NO, Works,* 8:173, 177–78, 206 = bk. 2, v, ix, xvii.

75. Ibid., pp. 169–71 = bk. 2, iii–iv.

76. *AL, Works,* 6:222.

77. Bacon's contribution to the formation of the concept of laws of nature in the sciences seems not to have been generally recognized. For some discussions of the historical origins of this concept, see A. R. Hall, *The Scientific Revolution 1500–1800* (Boston: Beacon Press, 1956), pp. 171–73; Joseph Needham, "Human Law and the Laws of Nature," *The Grand Titration* (Toronto: University of Toronto Press, 1969); Jane E. Ruby, "The Origins of Scientific Law," *Journal of the History of Ideas* 47, no. 3 (1986): 341–59; William L. Hine, "Inertia and Scientific Law in Sixteenth-Century Commentaries on Lucretius," *Renaissance Quarterly* 48, no. 4 (1995): 728–41. Several of these authors omit any mention of Bacon and refer to the development of ideas of particular laws in different sciences rather than to laws of nature as such. Pérez-Ramos, *Francis Bacon's Idea of Science,* chap. 11, discusses the Baconian concept of the law of nature partly to show, in opposition to R. E. Larsen, "The Aristotelianism of Bacon's *Novum Organum,*" *Journal of the History of Ideas* 23, no. 4 (1962): 435–50, its difference, based on Bacon's understanding of form, from any such idea in Aristotle. Like the present author, Pérez-Ramos, p. 127, perceives a "development of the concept of natural/physical law" in Bacon's thought and "its final expression in terms of matter and motion. . . ."

78. *Valerius Terminus, Works,* 6:60, 61.

79. *NO*, ibid., 8:171 = bk. 2, v.

80. Ibid., pp. 171–76 = bk. 2, v–vii; the quotation is on p. 174.

81. Ibid., p. 177 = bk. 2, viii.

82. Ibid., pp. 177–78 = bk. 2, ix.

83. Ibid., p. 178 = bk. 2, x.

84. Ibid., p. 179 = bk. 2, x. Baconian induction is discussed by many writers. Useful descriptions and observations may be found in Lisa Jardine, *Francis Bacon: Discovery and the Art of Discourse* (Cambridge: Cambridge University Press, 1974), chap. 6, and in Hesse, "Francis Bacon's Philosophy of Science"; Horton, "In Defence of Francis Bacon"; von Wright, *The Logical Problem of Induction*; and Urbach, *Francis Bacon's Philosophy of Science*. The closest, most detailed examination is in Pérez-Ramos, *Francis Bacon's Idea of Science*, chap. 17, a difficult and not always clear account that identifies some of the central features of Bacon's treatment of induction and also the elements of deductive and hypothetical inference that come into play in the Baconian method of discovery.

85. *NO*, *Works*, 8:138 = bk. 1, cv.

86. Urbach, *Francis Bacon's Philosophy of Science*, pp. 38–46, argues that Bacon's method did not aim at infallible and certain knowledge, and that the most he meant by certainty was an extreme degree of confidence such as may be felt about a strongly supported theory. I find no evidence for this qualification in Bacon's writings. L. Jonathan Cohen, *The Philosophy of Induction and Probability* (Oxford: Clarendon Press, 1989), pp. 4–5, claims that Bacon sought not certainty but degrees of certainty. Of course, Bacon did not think certain knowledge could be attained at once, but he also made clear that this was his aim. In the preface to *NO*, he contrasted "probable conjectures" with the "certain and demonstrable knowledge" to which he aspired; *Works*, 8:64. He also speaks in this preface, ibid., p. 60, of establishing "progressive stages of certainty," which can mean only at its furthest stage a knowledge not subject to error. He distinguished his own view from those who have denied that certainty can be attained, ibid., p. 75 = bk. 1, xxxvii. I believe that Bacon understood the term in its literal sense and that certainty was an integral part of his project for the reconstruction of natural philosophy.

87. This is how von Wright describes Baconian induction; *The Logical Problem of Induction*, pp. 62–64. John Stuart Mill was apparently the first to use the name "eliminative induction" for the methods of experimental inquiry he discussed in his *A System of Logic*; see J. L. Mackie's article, "Mill's Methods of Induction," in *The Encyclopedia of Philosophy*, 5:324. One of Mill's predecessors was, of course, Bacon, whom he called the founder of inductive philosophy and praised for developing a logic that went beyond the simple enumeration of instances; *A System of Logic*, 8th ed. (New York, 1884), p. 227.

88. *NO*, *Works*, 8:179–81 = bk. 2, xi.

89. Ibid., pp. 181–93 = bk. 2, xii.

90. Ibid., pp. 178, 184 = bk. 2, x, xii. Further on, he laments that the lack of a natural history has forced him to insert "mere traditions and reports" in his tables as well as to suggest the need for further inquiry on various topics; ibid., pp. 203–4 = bk. 2, xiv.

91. Ibid., pp. 193–203 = bk. 1, xiii.

92. Ibid., pp. 207–9, 210–18 = bk. 2, xviii, xx.

93. Ibid., p. 209 = bk. 2, xix.

94. Ibid., pp. 210, 217 = bk. 2, xx.

95. Fowler's edition of *NO*, p. 403, interpreted the phrase "permissio intellectui" in this passage to mean that Bacon was advocating the employment of hypotheses. I believe this is a mistake and that he was claiming permission to include speculation in the course of a first vintage or preliminary interpretation.

96. *NO, Works*, 8:218–19 = bk. 2, xxi. The treatment of prerogative instances runs from aphorisms xxi to li, with which the work ends. For the description of them as having a special evidential value and therefore constituting not merely positive but supportive instances in induction, see the comments by Grunbaum, "Is Falsifiability the Touchstone?" p. 217.

97. *NO, Works*, 8:253–68 = bk. 2, xxxvi.

98. Ibid., p. 243 = bk. 2, xxxi. Bacon also discusses magic in the last of the prerogative instances, with a view to its use in transforming bodies much more quickly than nature alone can do, and again deals with it from a completely naturalistic standpoint; ibid., pp. 346–47 = bk. 2, li.

99. Ibid., p. 131 = bk. 1, xcv.

100. Ibid., p. 75 = bk. 1, xxxv.

101. Ibid., p. 80 = bk. 1, xlvi.

102. See Ellis's preface to *NO* in ibid., 1:151, and his earlier remarks, pp. 117–18, which observe that Bacon failed to appreciate the infinite variety of nature and hence believed that it was possible to analyze all phenomena into their real elements; cf. also von Wright, *The Logical Problem of Induction*, pp. 76–77. In his explanation of the investigation of forms, Bacon said that "a nature being given, we must first of all have a muster or presentation . . . of all known instances which agree in the same nature, though in substances the most unlike"; *NO, Works*, 8:179 = bk. 2, xi. He did not consider the possible relevance of instances not known.

103. On Bacon's mistaken belief that his eliminative induction made it possible to know and exclude all negative instances, see also von Wright, *The Logical Problem of Induction*, pp. 76–80, 84.

104. *NO, Works*, 8:148 = bk. 1, cxvii.

105. Urbach, *Francis Bacon's Philosophy of Science*, pp. 15, 108, 192. For other discussions of the place of theory and hypotheses in Bacon's conception of science, see Paolo Rossi, "Ants, Spiders, Epistemologists," in *Francis Bacon: Terminologia e fortuna*, and Curt J. Ducasse, "Francis Bacon's Philosophy of Science: Structure, Method, and Meaning," in *Theories of Scientific Method: The Renaissance through the Nineteenth Century*, ed. E. H. Madden (Seattle: University of Washington Press, 1960).

106. The English version is printed in *Works*, vol. 8; the Latin original is in ibid., vol. 2.

107. In *NO*, Bacon listed seven subjects relating to induction and the investigation of nature that he promised to treat in the work but never did; ibid., 8:218–19 = bk. 2, xxi.

108. *Natural and Experimental History for the Foundation of Philosophy*, ibid., 9:373. The Latin original of this work is in ibid., vol. 3.

109. For a survey of the various writings on natural history pertaining to the third part of *The Great Instauration*, see the editor's preface to *NO, Works*, 1: 135–39.

110. For Bacon's extensive use of Pliny's *Natural History*, Aristotle's *Problemata* (actually a spurious work falsely attributed to Aristotle), Della Porta's *Natural Magic*, the Spanish Jesuit José de Acosta's writings on the New World, and other authors as sources for some of his natural histories, see the editor's preface to *Historia Ventorum*, ibid., 3:94–95, *Historia Vitae et Mortis*, ibid., pp. 320–23, 326, and *Sylva Sylvarum*, ibid., 4:146–48.

111. *A Preparative towards a Natural and Experimental History*, ibid., 8:357–58. The Latin original of this treatise is in ibid., vol. 2.

112. Ibid., 8:359–60. Ceremonial magic involved the manipulation of occult and celestial forces by such means as talismans, incantations, and images.

113. Ibid., pp. 361–63.

114. Ibid., pp. 365–66.

115. Ibid., p. 368; *Natural and Experimental History for the Foundation of Philosophy*, ibid., 9:376.

116. *A Preparative*, ibid., 8:368–69. For further information on Bacon's idea of a natural history, see also his letter of July 1622 to the Italian philosopher Father Baranzano, which touched on the subject of a history of the heavens; *LL*, 7:377.

117. *A Preparative, Works*, 8:354–55.

118. *NO*, ibid., p. 219 = bk. 2, xxi.

119. The fragment of *Abecedarium Naturae* is in ibid., 3:306–11, and an English translation in ibid., 9:475–79. The character of this work is clarified by the discovery of a longer manuscript version of it that is discussed by Graham Rees, "Bacon's Philosophy: Some New Sources with Special Reference to the *Abecedarium Novum Naturae*," in *Francis Bacon: Terminologia e fortuna*. Bacon had spoken of an alphabet of forms in *AL*, ibid., 6:220. He referred to it again in his rules for a natural history in *Natural and Experimental History for the Foundation of Philosophy*, ibid., 9:375, which indicates that *Abecedarium Naturae* was intended to be an alphabet of the different configurations of matter.

120. *A Preparative*, ibid., 8:373–81.

121. In *De Dignitate et Augmentis Scientiarum*, the enlarged 1623 Latin edition of *AL*, Bacon devoted a brief discussion to natural history as one of the divisions of historiography, which repeated the points made in *A Preparative* and placed its main importance in supplying the material for induction. He also said that no natural history for the purpose of induction, which he called an inductive history, yet existed; see the English version, ibid., 8:409–18 = bk. 2, chaps. 2–3.

122. The first book of *DA* was a translation of the same material in *AL*. The remaining eight books modified, elaborated upon, and added to parts of the earlier treatment in *AL*. The Latin text of *DA* is in *Works*, vols. 2–3; the English translation is in ibid., vols. 8–9. Bacon's chaplain and secretary, Rawley, wrote a short introduction to *DA* explaining its relationship to the earlier *AL*; see *DA*, ibid., 2:83–84.

123. *DA, Works*, 8:486–89 = bk. 3, chap. 4. See also the discussion and historical

background of Bacon's view of astronomy in Ellis's preface to *Descriptio Globi Intellectualis*, ibid., 7:270–84; the account and references in Louis A. Kosman, "The Aristotelian Backgrounds of Bacon's *Novum Organum*" (Ph.D. diss., Harvard University, 1964), pt. 3, chap. 3; and Urbach, *Francis Bacon's Philosophy of Science,* pp. 125–34.

124. *DA, Works,* 8:489–98 = bk. 3, chap. 4. The celestial or astral magic that Bacon would have banned from astrology was one of the kinds of magic discussed by Marsilio Ficino in the third book of his treatise *De Vita.*

125. Ibid. p. 485 = bk. 3, chap. 4.

126. *LL,* 7:377,

127. In *DA, Works,* 8:513 = bk. 3, chap. 5, as previously in *NO,* he speaks of the investigation of forms by metaphysics as the only way to achieve fundamental alterations and innovations in nature, and therefore of much greater importance than the particular (efficient) causes sought by physics.

128. Ibid., pp. 508–12 = bk. 3, chaps. 4–5.

129. Ibid., pp. 513–16 = bk. 3, chap. 5.

130. Ibid., 9:51–54 = bk. 4, chap. 3.

131. *NO, Works,* 8:137, 143 = bk. 1, ciii, cx. In aphorisms lxx and c, ibid., 100–101, 135, Bacon pointed out some of the failures in the current fashion of doing experiments; see also the notes on Bacon's criticism of experiments and on "experientia literata," in Fowler's edition of *NO,* pp. 259, 306–7.

132. *DA, Works,* 9:71–83 = bk. 5, chap. 2; see also Lisa Jardine, "Experientia Literata or *Novum Organum?* The Dilemma of Bacon's Scientific Method," in *Francis Bacon's Legacy of Texts,* ed. William A. Sessions (New York: AMS Press, 1990).

133. *DA, Works,* 9:84–92 = bk. 5, chap. 3.

134. R. G. Collingwood, *The Idea of History* (Oxford: Clarendon Press, 1951), pp. 269, 273.

135. See Graham Rees, *Francis Bacon's Natural Philosophy: A New Source* (Kendal: The British Society for The History of Science, 1984), which prints this manuscript with a valuable introduction and notes. According to Rees, the original draft was written in 1611–12 and subsequently revised by Bacon over a period of time before being finally abandoned. Rees gives a brief account of several recently discovered manuscript works by Bacon in "Bacon's Philosophy: Some New Sources with Special Reference to *Abecedarium Novum Naturae.*"

136. Graham Rees, "Francis Bacon's Semi-Paracelsian Cosmology," *Ambix* 22, pt. 2 (1975): 81–101; "Francis Bacon's Semi-Paracelsian Cosmology and *The Great Instauration,*" ibid. 22, pt. 3 (1975): 161–73; "Francis Bacon's Biological Ideas: A New Source," in *Occult and Scientific Mentalities in the Renaissance,* ed. Brian Vickers (Cambridge: Cambridge University Press, 1984); "Bacon's Speculative Philosophy," in *The Cambridge Companion to Bacon.* Rees deals specifically with Bacon's understanding of spirit in "Francis Bacon and *Spiritus Vitalis,*" in *Spiritus,* ed. Marta Fattori and M. Bianchi (Rome: Edizione dell'Ateneo, 1984). The essays in this volume contain a historical survey of both the word and the concept, spirit, including an essay on Bacon by Marta Fattori, "Spiritus dans l'*Historia vitae et mortis de Francis Bacon.*" On Bacon's spirit theory, see also D. P. Walker, *Spiritual and Demonic Magic from Ficino to Campanella* (London: The Warburg Institute,

1958), pp. 199–202, and "Spirits in Francis Bacon," in *Francis Bacon: Terminologia e fortuna.*

137. *Sylva Sylvarum, Works,* 4:219–20.

138. Quoted from the general scholium to bk. 3 of Newton's *Principia* by Ernan McMullin, "The Significance of Newton's *Principia* for Empiricism," in *Religion, Science, and Worldview: Essays in Honor of Richard S. Westfall,* ed. Margaret J. Osler and Paul Lawrence Farber (Cambridge: Cambridge University Press, 1985), p. 49. Newton went on to say that there have not been enough experiments for an accurate determination and demonstration "of the laws by which this electric and elastic spirit operates."

139. *History of Life and Death, Works,* 10:14, 21. The Latin original of this treatise is in ibid., vol. 3.

140. Ibid., pp. 156–57; Bacon's remarks on spirit in *History of Life and Death* are paralleled in *The Ways of Death;* see Rees, *Francis Bacon's Natural Philosophy,* pp. 131, 151.

141. *DA, Works,* 9:48–50 = bk. 4, chap. 3.

142. Ibid., pp. 56–57 = bk. 4, chap. 3; see also Maxwell Primack, "Outline of a Reinterpretation of Francis Bacon's Philosophy," *Journal of the History of Philosophy* 5, no. 1 (1967): 123–33, which takes Bacon's attribution of spirits to bodies as evidence that he was not a mechanist. Primack makes the doubtful claim, however, that Bacon ascribed purpose to bodies, although he recognizes that Bacon did not believe that they are endowed with souls or that their purposiveness has anything to do with final causes.

143. *NO, Works,* 8:342–46 = bk. 2, l. This discussion of consents and aversions is part of the survey of prerogative instances.

144. Ibid., p. 342 = bk. 2, l; see the similar comment in the short introduction to *History of the Sympathy and Antipathy of Things,* one of Bacon's projected but unwritten natural histories, ibid., 9:470.

145. *Sylva Sylvarum,* ibid., 5:120–21. In a subsequent passage he noted that there were no clear proofs of witchcraft, but allowed for the possibility that it could be due to the tacit operation of malign spirits, ibid., p. 143.

146. Ibid., p. 143.

147. *Theory of The Heaven,* ibid., 10:463–67. The Latin original is printed in ibid., 7:344–59. Rees, "Bacon's Speculative Philosophy," includes an account of Bacon's explanation of celestial motions around a central earth.

148. See the statement of this chemical theory in the brief preface to one of Bacon's unwritten natural histories, *The History of Sulphur, Mercury, and Salt,* ibid., 9:472–73, and Rees's discussion in "Francis Bacon's Semi-Paracelsian Cosmology," "Francis Bacon's Semi-Paracelsian Cosmology and *The Great Instauration,*" *Francis Bacon's Natural Philosophy,* pp. 22–29, and most recently in the summary in "Bacon's Speculative Philosophy."

149. *NO, Works,* 8:342–43 = bk. 1, l.

150. *History of Life and Death,* ibid., 10:83, 159–69; Rees, *Francis Bacon's Natural Philosophy,* pp. 95, 97, 131, 133, 135, 137, and introduction, chap. 3. Ellis's introduction to Bacon's philosophical works, *Works,* 1:102–7, Walker, "Spirits in Francis Bacon," and Rees, *Francis Bacon's Natural Philosophy,* p. 68, all draw atten-

tion to Telesio as a source of Bacon's notion of spirit and vital spirit. In speaking of the spirit of life in *DA, Works,* 9:50–51 = bk. 4, chap. 3, Bacon cites Telesio's view on this subject. Although he described him as an inventor of fables who was better at pulling down than building up, he also rated him highly among recent philosophers and called him "the first of the moderns." In *On Principles and Origins according to the Fables of Cupid and Coelum,* he presented a lengthy summary and criticism of Telesio's theory of the universe based on the opposition between heat and cold; see ibid., 10:365–99. The Latin original, *De Principiis et Originibus secundum Fabulas Cupidinis et Coeli,* is in ibid., 5:289–346. Luigi De Franco, *Bernardino Telesio: La Vita e L'Opera,* 2d ed. (Cosenza: Edizioni Periferia, 1989), gives an account of Telesio's philosophy that includes a chapter on his conception of heat and cold as the active principle of all things. Valeria Giachetti Assenza has documented Bacon's references to Telesio in "B. Telesio, Il migliore dei moderni: I referimenti a Telesio negli scritti di Bacone," *Rivista critica di storia della filosofia* 35, no. 1 (1980): 41–78; see also Jean-Marie Pousseur, "Bacon, a Critic of Telesio," in *Francis Bacon's Legacy of Texts.*

151. See Ellis's preface to *Historia Vitae et Mortis, Works,* 3:319.

152. See Rees's discussion of Bacon's two philosophies in *Francis Bacon's Natural Philosophy,* pp. 72–73, his comments to the same effect in "Francis Bacon's Biological Ideas: A New Source," p. 308, and the remarks in "Bacon's Speculative Philosophy," p. 121.

153. *NO, Works,* 8:147 = bk. 1, cxvi; *The Great Instauration,* ibid., p. 38.

154. "Francis Bacon's Semi-Paracelsian Cosmology and *The Great Instauration,*" pp. 171–73.

155. *The Great Instauration, Works,* 8:51–52.

156. See also Pérez-Ramos's reservations and criticisms regarding Rees's suggestion that Bacon had two philosophies; "Bacon in the Right Spirit," a review of Rees's *Francis Bacon's Natural Philosophy,* in *Annals of Science* 42, no. 3 (1985): 610–11.

157. *LL,* 1:109. Regarding his aim of reforming knowledge, the whole passage reads: ". . . whether it be curiosity, or vain glory, or nature, or (if one take it favorably) *philanthropia,* [it] is so fixed in my mind as it cannot be removed."

158. "Of Goodness and Goodness in Nature," *Essays, Works,* 12:118. This essay appears in both the 1612 and 1625 editions.

159. Anne Righter, "Francis Bacon," in *Essential Articles for the Study of Francis Bacon,* pp. 301–2.

160. Lynn White, "The Historical Roots of Our Ecologic Crisis," in *Machina ex Deo: Essays in the Dynamism of Western Culture* (Cambridge: MIT Press, 1968); William Leiss, *The Domination of Nature* (New York: George Braziller, 1972), chap. 3. White notes in his essay that the implementation of the Baconian creed that scientific knowledge means technological power over nature did not really begin to take effect until after 1850.

161. Theodor W. Adorno and Max Horkheimer, *Dialektik der Aufklärung* (Frankfurt am Main: S. Fischer Verlag, 1969), pp. 9–15.

162. Whitney, *Francis Bacon and Modernity,* pp. 123, 199.

163. Carolyn Merchant, *The Death of Nature: Women, Ecology, and the Scientific*

Revolution (San Francisco: Harper & Row, 1983), chap. 7; Sandra Harding, *The Science Question in Feminism* (Ithaca: Cornell University Press, 1986), pp. 113, 115–16.

164. For a summary of the conditions of life in preindustrial, early modern England and Europe, see Keith Thomas, *Religion and the Decline of Magic* (London: Weidenfeld and Nicolson, 1971), chap. 1, and the account and data in Michael W. Flinn, *The European Demographic System 1500–1820* (Baltimore: Johns Hopkins University Press, 1981), chap. 2.

165. See Rosalie L. Colie, "Cornelis Drebbel and Salomon de Caus: Two Jacobean Models for Salomon's House," *Huntington Library Quarterly* 18, no. 3 (1955): 245–60, and Charles Webster, *The Great Instauration: Science, Medicine and Reform, 1626–1660* (London: Duckworth, 1975), pp. 345–47 and passim.

166. *New Atlantis, Works,* 5:398.

167. See below. chap. 5, on Bacon's idea of history and his practice as a historian.

168. *AL, Works,* 6:183–84.

169. Paolo Rossi has commented on this point in *Francis Bacon: From Magic to Science* (London: Routledge & Kegan Paul, 1968), pp. 69–70, as has A. L. Crombie more recently, *Styles of Scientific Thinking,* 3:1576–77, in what he calls Bacon's "genetic history of scientific knowledge."

170. Quoted in both I. Bernard Cohen, *Revolution in Science* (Cambridge: Harvard University Press, 1985), p. 529, and H. Floris Cohen, *The Scientific Revolution: A Historiographical Inquiry* (Chicago: University of Chicago Press, 1994), p. 32.

171. E. J. Dijksterhuis, *The Mechanization of the World Picture* (Oxford: Clarendon Press, 1961), pp. 396, 397, 400, 401, 402.

172. In his *Etudes Galiléennes* (1939), Koyré considered it a "bad joke" to suppose that Bacon had anything to do with the scientific revolution; see this and other quotations of his judgment in Pérez-Ramos, *Francis Bacon's Idea of Science,* p. 29 and n. For Koyré's conception of the scientific revolution, expressed in a number of his writings, see his *From the Closed World to the Infinite Universe* (New York: Harper Torchbooks, 1958), and the discussion of his view in H. Floris Cohen, *The Scientific Revolution,* pp. 73–88.

173. Thomas S. Kuhn, "Mathematical versus Experimental Traditions in the Development of Physical Science," in *The Essential Tension: Selected Studies in Scientific Tradition and Change* (Chicago: University of Chicago Press, 1977). Pérez-Ramos, *Francis Bacon's Idea of Science,* pp. 33–39, discusses Kuhn's account with reference to Bacon and enters several caveats; H. Floris Cohen, *The Scientific Revolution,* pp. 126–35, also notes some reservations in his discussion of Kuhn's historical schema.

174. See the comment of C. D. Broad in his estimate of Bacon's achievement, *The Philosophy of Francis Bacon* (Cambridge: Cambridge University Press, 1926), pp. 63–64.

175. Charles C. Gillespie, *The Edge of Objectivity: An Essay in the History of Scientific Ideas* (Princeton: Princeton University Press, 1960), p. 79.

176. See Koyré's preface to *From the Closed World to the Infinite Universe,* p. vi, and his statement in *Newtonian Studies* (1965) quoted in H. Floris Cohen, *The Scientific Revolution,* p. 80.

CHAPTER 4
HUMAN PHILOSOPHY: MORALS AND POLITICS

1. *NO, Works,* 8:159 = bk. 1, cxxvii.

2. *AL,* ibid., 6:236–37; *DA,* ibid., 9:14–5 = bk. 4, chap. 1.

3. In several of his earliest surviving works written as entertainments, namely, *Of Tribute* (1592), the device for the 1594 Christmas revels at Gray's Inn, and *Of Love and Self-Love* (1595), Bacon also touched lightly on moral topics such as fortitude and other virtues; see *LL,* 1:119–20, 325–43, 374–86, and the reprint of the complete texts of these three compositions in *Francis Bacon: A Critical Edition of the Major Works,* ed. Brian Vickers (Oxford: Oxford University Press, 1996), pp. 22–68, together with the editor's comments, pp. 514–16, 531–32, 535–37.

4. Ian Box includes an interesting discussion of Bacon's moral conceptions in *The Social Thought of Francis Bacon* (Lewiston, N.Y.: Edwin Mellen Press, 1989). My approach in the following pages is quite different from his, which places considerable emphasis on the contradictions and disparities between the character and aims of Bacon's science and his moral philosophy. The same author's "Bacon's Moral Philosophy," in *The Cambridge Companion to Bacon,* ed. Markku Peltonen (Cambridge: Cambridge University Press, 1996), is a perceptive account that nevertheless seems to me to underestimate the amoral aspects of Bacon's observations and precepts on human conduct in public life.

5. *DA, Works,* 9:191–96 = bk. 7, chap. 1.

6. Ibid., 8:472–74 = bk. 3, chap. 1.

7. Ibid., 9:196–97 = bk. 7, chap. 1.

8. Ibid., pp. 197–201 = bk. 7, chap. 1.

9. Ibid., pp. 201–11 = bk. 7, chap. 2.

10. On the intellectual background to Bacon's valuation of the active life, see Brian Vickers, "Bacon's So-Called Utilitarianism: Sources and Influence," in *Francis Bacon: Terminologia e fortuna nel XVII secolo,* ed. Marta Fattori (Rome: Edizione dell' Ateneo, 1984), pp. 296–307; Cicero's *De Officiis* is a locus classicus of the moral philosophy of the active life and of duties to others embracing men's social ties to family, friends, dependents, and country. On the *vita activa* in the thought of Renaissance humanism, see Denys Hay, *The Italian Renaissance and Its Historical Background* (Cambridge: Cambridge University Press, 1964), pp. 124–28; Hans Baron, *The Crisis of the Early Italian Renaissance,* rev. ed. (Princeton: Princeton University Press, 1966), passim; Fritz Caspari, *Humanism and the Social Order in Tudor England* (New York: Teachers College, 1954), passim. The subject is also discussed in the survey by Jill Kraye of fifteenth- and sixteenth-century moral philosophy and its classical sources, *The Cambridge History of Renaissance Philosophy,* ed. Charles B. Schmitt, Quentin Skinner, and Eckhard Kessler (Cambridge: Cambridge University Press, 1988), chap. 11, and in Quentin Skinner's survey of political philosophy in ibid., chap. 12.

11. On Stoic ethics, see Edward V. Arnold, *Roman Stoicism* (1911; New York: Arno Press; reprint, 1971), chap. 13. The Roman philosopher Seneca's *De Otio* is an exemplary expression of the Stoic preference for the private life. For the moral teaching of sixteenth-century neo-Stoicism in Lipsius's treatise *De Constantia* (1584) and other authors, see the discussion by Kraye, in *The Cambridge History*

of Renaissance Philosophy, pp. 370–74; Perez Zagorin, *Ways of Lying: Dissimulation, Persecution, and Conformity in Early Modern Europe* (Cambridge: Harvard University Press, 1990), pp. 122–24; Peter Burke in *The Cambridge History of Political Thought 1450–1700* (Cambridge: Cambridge University Press, 1991), pp. 491–92; Richard Tuck, *Philosophy and Government 1572–1651* (Cambridge: Cambridge University Press, 1993), chap. 2.

12. *DA, Works,* 9:214–18 = bk. 7, chap. 3.

13. Ibid., pp. 226–27 = bk. 7, chap. 3.

14. Ibid., pp. 232–33 = bk. 8, chap. 1.

15. Ibid., pp. 233–36 = bk. 8, chap. 1.

16. Ibid., pp. 236–37 = bk. 8, chap. 2.

17. Ibid., pp. 267–70 = bk. 8, chap. 2.

18. On the history of the idea of fortune and its place in Renaissance thought, see Antonino Poppi's account in *The Cambridge History of Renaissance Philosophy,* chap. 17; Quentin Skinner, *Machiavelli* (New York: Hill and Wang, 1981), pp. 25–28, and *The Foundations of Modern Political Thought,* 2 vols. (Cambridge: Cambridge University Press, 1978), 1:95–98, 119–22; Howard R. Patch, *The Goddess Fortuna in Medieval Literature* (Cambridge: Harvard University Press, 1927).

19. Niccolò Machiavelli, *The Prince,* chap. 25.

20. Sir Robert Naunton, *Fragmenta Regalia* (1641), in *Harleian Miscellany,* 10 vols. (London, 1810–13), 2:95.

21. "Of Fortune," *Essays, Works,* 12:214–18. These remarks also appear in the 1612 version, which is printed in ibid., pp. 358–59. For Bacon's treatment of fortune, see also Rexford C. Cochrane, "Francis Bacon and the Architect of Fortune," *Studies in the Renaissance* 5 (1958): 176–95.

22. *NO, Works,* 8:87 = bk. 1, lx.

23. *DA,* ibid., 9:270 = bk. 8, chap. 2.

24. Ibid., pp. 271–77 = bk. 8, chap. 2.

25. Ibid., pp. 278–80 = bk. 8, chap. 2.

26. Ibid., pp. 281–88 = bk. 8, chap. 2.

27. Machiavelli, *The Prince,* chap. 25.

28. *DA, Works,* 9:288–95 = bk. 8, chap. 2; see Machiavelli, *The Prince,* chaps. 17–18, and *Discourses on the First Ten Books of Livy,* bk. 2, chap. 10.

29. *DA, Works,* 9:295–97 = bk. 2, chap. 2.

30. All three editions of the *Essays* are printed in *Works,* vol. 12. My references are to the 1625 edition, whose preface gives an account of the work's history. For an essential discussion of the nature of the essays, their evolution, form, and style, see the introduction to the new edition by Michael Kiernan in Sir Francis Bacon, *The Essayes or Counsells, Civill and Morall* (Oxford: Clarendon Press, 1985). The text of the *Essays* in *Francis Bacon: A Critical Edition* is accompanied by a perceptive editorial note, pp. 711–17.

31. R. S. Crane, "The Relation of Bacon's *Essays* to His Program for the Advancement of Learning" (1923), reprinted in *Essential Articles for the Study of Francis Bacon,* ed. Brian Vickers (Hamden, Conn.: Archon Books, 1968).

32. Karl R. Wallace, *Francis Bacon on Communication and Rhetoric* (Chapel Hill: University of North Carolina Press, 1943), p. 118.

33. Stanley E. Fish, "Georgics of the Mind: The Experience of Bacon's Essays,"

in *Self-Consuming Artifacts* (Berkeley and Los Angeles: University of California Press, 1972). In applying this theory of the reader's experience to the particular essays he discusses, Fish does not always give an accurate description of them. His analysis of the way the essays operate seems to me not to accord with Bacon's intention, which aims to instruct and persuade, not unsettle, nor to correspond to the experience of other readers and critics. See also the critique by Jeffrey Barnouw, "The Experience of Bacon's *Essays*: Reading the Text vs. 'Affective Stylistics,'" in *Literature and the Other Arts*, Proceedings of the Ninth Annual Congress of the International Comparative Literature Association (Innsbruck, 1979), pp. 351–57, and the observations on Fish's critical method by Brian Vickers in a review of *Self-Consuming Artifacts* in *Renaissance Quarterly* 17, no. 1 (1974): 117–22.

34. Robert K. Faulkner, *Francis Bacon and the Project of Progress* (Lanham, Md.: Rowman and Littlefield, 1993), chap. 2.

35. See Brian Vickers, *Francis Bacon and Renaissance Prose* (Cambridge: Cambridge University Press, 1968), pp. 217–31 and passim, which contains an excellent literary analysis of the essays together with many useful observations on their substance.

36. *Works*, 12:72, 75, 77.

37. Ibid., pp. 89, 90. 109, 118.

38. Ibid., pp. 246–47.

39. Ibid., pp. 248, 249; "Of Friendship," ibid., pp. 165–74.

40. Ibid., pp. 249, 251.

41. Ibid., p. 254.

42. Ibid., p. 257.

43. Ibid., p. 215.

44. Ibid., pp. 153, 154, 155.

45. See Zagorin, *Ways of Lying*.

46. Ibid., pp. 7–8, and Perez Zagorin, "Sir Thomas Wyatt and the Court of Henry VIII: The Courtier's Ambivalence," *Journal of Medieval and Renaissance Studies* 23, no. 1 (1993): 113–41; and see Bacon's remark on the many examples of dissimulation and simulation in the courts of princes and "all politic traffic" in *A Letter and Discourse to Sir Henry Savill, Touching Helps for the Intellectual Powers, Works*, 13:301

47. Zagorin, *Ways of Lying*, pp. 6–8; Machiavelli, *The Prince*, chap. 18.

48. Zagorin, *Ways of Lying*, pp. 123–24, 257.

49. *Essays, Works*, 12:95–99.

50. See Bacon's short portrait of Julius Caesar as a man who had "greatness of mind," sought power as his highest good, and was "a consummate master of simulation and dissimulation, and made up entirely of arts, insomuch that nothing was left to his nature except what art had approved, nevertheless there appeared in him nothing of artifice, nothing of dissimulation. . . ."; *Character of Julius Caesar*, ibid., p. 35. This is an English translation of the original Latin work, *Imago Civilis Julii Caesaris*, printed in ibid. Caesar is a model of the kind of strong man Bacon had in mind in discussing dissimulation as a policy.

51. "Of Love," ibid., pp. 109–12.

52. Ibid., pp. 158–59.

53. Edwin A. Abbott, a close student of Bacon's life and work, expressed the opinion in his edition of the *Essays* that Machiavelli was Bacon's guide in questions of practical morality and that the morality in the essays "is the pure and simple morality of Machiavelli"; *Essays*, ed. Edwin A. Abbott, 2 vols. (London, 1876), 1:136–37. Thomas Fowler took issue with this view in his *Bacon* (New York, 1881), and Abbott replied to Fowler's criticism in his *Francis Bacon: An Account of His Life and Works* (London, 1885), app., pp. 457–60. Fowler referred to this controversy and again defended Bacon against Abbott's strictures in *Bacon's Novum Organum*, ed. Thomas Fowler, 2d rev. ed. (Oxford, 1889), pp. xiii–xviii. Despite Fowler's claim that Bacon placed benevolent principles of action above self-regarding ones, there can be no doubt that the affinity in morals between Bacon and Machiavelli is quite close in a number of respects, as has been shown in the study by Napoleone Orsini, *Bacone e Machiavelli* (Genoa: Emigliano degli Orfini, 1936). B.H.G. Wormald, *Francis Bacon: History, Politics and Science 1561–1626* (Cambridge: Cambridge University Press, 1993), pp. 200–209 and passim, also contains an interesting discussion of the relationship between Bacon and Machiavelli. Although taking note of various influences and points in common, he argues that Bacon refused to accept Machiavelli's belief that in matters of policy one should ignore morality. In expressing this judgment, Wormald mentions Bacon's rejection of Machiavelli's "evil arts" but fails to confront many of the passages in the *Essays* that reflect a rather amoral standpoint.

54. *DA*, *Works*, 9:116–20 = bk. 6, chap. 1. In a note on Bacon's discussion of ciphers, his editor, Ellis, has pointed out his use of the ciphers devised by Giambattista Della Porta, the well-known writer on natural magic, whose works included a treatise on secret writing, *De Occultis Literarum Notis*; see Ellis's remarks in the Latin ed. of *DA*, *Works*, 2:499–501.

55. *DA*, ibid., 9:297–99 = bk. 8, chap. 3. In his discussion of civil knowledge in *AL*, Bacon also spoke of parts of the knowledge of government as "secret" and "not fit to utter"; ibid., 6:388.

56. For several recent discussions of Bacon's political thought, see Wormald, *Francis Bacon*, passim; the occasional comments in Box, *The Social Thought of Francis Bacon*; and the informative account by Markku Peltonen, "Bacon's Political Ideas," in *The Cambridge Companion to Bacon*. Two other treatments of Bacon's politics are those by Howard White, *Peace among the Willows: The Political Philosophy of Francis Bacon* (The Hague: Martinus Nijhoff, 1968), and by Faulkner, *Francis Bacon and the Project of Progress*. White's work falls short of providing an adequate understanding of Bacon's political ideas and fails to place them in their historical context. It is based on the belief that Bacon harbored a secret teaching which he sought to convey by means of an esoteric or enigmatic method, but is unable to provide any evidence for this view. It also holds that Bacon had both a provisional and a definitive politics, the first relating to the actual problems of his country in his time, the second to the desirable political order men could attain, such as is sketched in *New Atlantis*, but again, it can offer no evidence to support this claim. I have referred to Faulkner's book above in connection with Bacon's *Essays*. While it contains some points of interest, it is seriously flawed by its misreadings of some of Bacon's writings and its unsubstantiated thesis that Bacon

was secretly irreligious and that he used an enigmatic method of communication to prepare the way for the introduction of a progressive new political and social order. Both of these works show definite signs of the influence of Leo Strauss's wearisome method of reading premodern texts of political philosophy, based on the often arbitrary assumption that they contain an esoteric meaning intended for select, initiated readers, which their authors concealed under the apparent or surface meaning; see Leo Strauss, *Persecution and the Art of Writing* (Glencoe, Ill.: Free Press, 1952), and the critical discussion in Zagorin, *Ways of Lying*, pp. 9–11, and Shadia Drury, *Political Ideas of Leo Strauss* (New York: St. Martin's Press, 1988).

57. This background is described and illustrated in works such as E.M.W. Till-yard, *The Elizabethan World Picture* (Harmondsworth: Penguin, 1963); James W. Winney, *The Frame of Order* (London: Allen and Unwin, 1957); and E. W. Talbert, *The Problem of Order* (Chapel Hill: University of North Carolina Press, 1962). W. H. Greenleaf, *Order, Empiricism and Politics: Two Traditions of English Political Thought 1500–1700* (London: Oxford University Press, 1964), chaps. 9 and 10, is the first historian to discuss Bacon's politics in the light of this background and to place him within what he has called the alternative tradition of an empirical science of politics in contrast to the "order" tradition.

58. Richard Hooker, *Of the Laws of Ecclesiastical Polity*, in *Works*, ed. John Keble, 2 vols. (New York, 1873). The first four of its eight books were published in 1593, the fifth in 1597, and the remainder in 1648 and 1662. Hooker died in 1600. Bacon never mentions or takes any notice of his work.

59. See Markku Peltonen, "Bacon's Political Philosophy"; "Politics and Science: Francis Bacon and the True Greatness of States," *Historical Journal* 35, no. 2 (1992): 279–305; *Classical Humanism and Republicanism in English Political Thought 1570–1640* (Cambridge: Cambridge University Press, 1995), chap. 4.

60. *DA, Works*, 9:293–94 = bk. 8, chap. 2; the quotation comes from a paper by Bacon, "Considerations Touching a War with Spain," *LL*, vol. 7:478.

61. See the citations and comments in Wormald, *Francis Bacon*, pp. 55, 155.

62. Orsini's statements, however, in his study of Bacon and Machiavelli, that Bacon's was a "piu raffinato machiavellismo" and that he was "piu machiavellico di Machiavelli," pp. 69, 70, are exaggerations; see also the comments of Felix Raab, *The English Face of Machiavelli* (London: Routledge & Kegan Paul, 1964), pp. 73–74. Raab deals only briefly with Bacon's relationship to Machiavelli, relying chiefly on Orsini's study.

63. Machiavelli, *Discourses*, preface to bk. 1.

64. *DA, Works*, 9:294, 295 = bk. 8, chap. 2.

65. *The Case of the Post-Nati of Scotland*, ibid., 15:196–99, 200–201, 227, 229. In this case Bacon also cited the well-known doctrine in English law of the king's two bodies, his body natural and his body politic and the capacities of each, in order to show how his politic capacity infused with its perfections his natural person and was inseparable from it; ibid., pp. 229–31.

66. These Latin aphorisms, *Aphorismi de Jure Gentium Maiore sive de Fontibus Justiciae et Juris*, were written during the reign of James I and left in manuscript. The text has been transcribed and included in Mark Neustadt's "The Making of

the Instauration: Science, Politics, and Law in the Career of Francis Bacon" (Ph.D. diss., Johns Hopkins University, 1987), app., pp. 255–60, 262–63; for further discussion of these aphorisms, see below, chap. 5.

67. *The History of the Reign of King Henry the Seventh, Works*, 11:240–41; the act in question, dealing with treason and often called the *de facto* act, was 11 H. 8, c. 1.

68. "Styx; or Treaties," *The Wisdom of the Ancients*, ibid., 13:90–91; cf. Machiavelli, *The Prince*, chap. 18.

69. "Perseus; or War," *Works*, 13:102–5.

70. "The Flight of Icarus; also Scylla and Charybdis; or The Middle Way," ibid., pp. 157–58.

71. "Diomedes; or Religious Zeal," ibid., pp. 126–28.

72. "The Cyclopes; or The Minister of Terror," ibid., pp. 87–88.

73. *The Prince*, chap. 7.

74. "Typhon; or The Rebel," *Works*, 13:84–87.

75. See "The Sister of the Giants; or Fame," ibid., pp. 107–8; Machiavelli, *Discourses*, bk. 1, chaps. 5, 58. Paolo Rossi, *Francis Bacon: From Magic to Science* (London: Routledge & Kegan Paul, 1968), pp. 110–16, discusses the political realism of some of Bacon's interpretations in *The Wisdom of the Ancients* and notes several resemblances to Machiavelli.

76. "Of Empire," *Works*, 12:140–46. The source of this statement may be Machiavelli, *Discourses*, bk. 1, chap. 41, on the imprudence of changing suddenly from gentleness to cruelty and the reverse; for a discussion of the type of revolution that results from the introduction of liberalization by repressive regimes, see Perez Zagorin, *Rebels and Rulers*, 2 vols. (Cambridge: Cambridge University Press, 1982), 1:51–53.

77. "Of Counsel," *Works*, 12:153–58.

78. "Of Seditions and Troubles," ibid., pp. 123–31.

79. Ibid., p. 127.

80. *DA*, ibid., 9:299–310; a much shorter version of this essay was included in the 1612 edition of the *Essays*; the text of the latter is printed in *Works*, 12:376–78.

81. Machiavelli, *Discourses*, bk. 1, chaps. 5, 6.

82. *LL*, 4:74.

83. "Of the True Greatness of the Kingdom of Britain," *Works*, 13:235, 237, 238.

84. Ibid., pp. 231–36, 241–42, 243–44, 250–51.

85. "Of the True Greatness of Kingdoms and Estates," ibid., 12:176–88.

86. This speech of 17 February 1607 is printed in *LL*, 3:307–25. For allusions to "considerations of estate," "principles of estate," and "reason of estate," see pp. 308, 312, 314; the quotation from Machiavelli is on pp. 323–24.

87. Ibid., pp. 313, 323, 325.

88. "Considerations Touching a War with Spain," ibid., 7:469–505. In an earlier and shorter paper on the same subject in 1619, Bacon proposed joint naval action by Britain and the Dutch republic with two fleets to blockade Spain in its home waters and its American empire; "A Short View to Be Taken of Great Britain and Spain," ibid., pp. 22–28.

89. "Considerations Touching a War with Spain," ibid., p. 500.

90. Pasquale Villari, *The Life and Times of Niccolo Machiavelli*, 2 vols. in 1 (London, n.d.), 2:511.

91. Ben Jonson, *Timber or Discoveries Made upon Men and Matters*, ed. Felix E. Schelling (Boston, 1892), p. 30. One wonders on what occasions Jonson heard Bacon speak. It could not have been in Parliament, whose meetings were closed to the public in Bacon's time and long afterward. Perhaps it was when Bacon spoke as an advocate in one of the courts or as lord chancellor.

92. *LL*, 4:279–80.

93. Ibid., pp. 73–74. I have extended Bacon's abbreviations in these notations, in accord with Spedding's reading of them in his footnotes. These private memoranda contain many other references to political problems and issues on which Bacon reminded himself to write something or take a particular action.

94. *The Case of the Post-Nati of Scotland*, *Works*, 15:198.

95. "A View of the Differences in Question betwixt the King's Bench and the Council in the Marches," *LL*, 3:371–72.

96. Ibid., pp. 373, 379. Bacon also appeared in this case as one of the counsel for the crown. Its historical background is discussed in the editor's preface to Bacon's argument. The latter was entirely technical and omitted the considerations described above, which he discussed in his observations; see *Works*, 15:95–118.

97. See "Of Judicature," *Essays*, ibid., 12:270.

98. See the discussion of the doctrine of the prerogative and Bacon's views in Francis D. Wormuth, *The Royal Prerogative 1603–1649* (Ithaca: Cornell University Press, 1939), chap. 4, and Margaret A. Judson, *The Crisis of the Constitution* (New Brunswick, N.J.: Rutgers University Press, 1949), pp. 168–70.

99. *LL*, 4:177.

100. Ibid., 7:171–72.

101. See his letter to the king in May 1612, ibid., 4:280, and his paper of 1613 entitled "Reasons for Calling a Parliament," ibid., p. 365.

102. Ibid., pp. 370–71.

103. "Of Judicature," *Essays*, *Works*, 12:269–70.

104. Machiavelli, *Discourses*, bk. 3, chap. 1.

105. *LL*, 4:372.

106. "Of Great Place," *Essays*, *Works*, 12:113.

107. Theodore K. Rabb, "Francis Bacon and the Reform of Society," in *Action and Conviction in Early Modern Europe: Essays in Memory of E. H. Harbison*, ed. Theodore K. Rabb and Jerrold E. Seigel (Princeton: Princeton University Press, 1969), brings out the conservative limits of Bacon's attitudes and actions as a reformer.

108. "An Advertisement Touching the Controversies in the Church of England" (1589), *LL*, 1:74–95; see above, chap. 1, for a discussion of this document.

109. "Certain Considerations Touching the Better Pacification and Edification of the Church of England," ibid., 3:103–27.

110. "Of Unity in Religion" (1603), *Essays*, *Works*, 12:86–92.

111. Machiavelli, *The Prince*, chap. 15.

112. See Rawley's preface to *New Atlantis*, *Works*, 5:357.

113. Among various discussions of *New Atlantis*, the following may be noted. Frank E. Manuel and Fritzie P. Manuel, *Utopian Thought in the Western World*

(Cambridge: Harvard University Press, 1979), chap. 9, contains a perceptive account of the work despite its tendentious Freudian comments on Bacon's personality. Frances A. Yates, *The Rosicrucian Enlightenment* (London: Routledge & Kegan Paul, 1972), chap. 9, esp. pp. 125–29, maintains that Bacon incorporated themes in the *New Atlantis* borrowed from the mysterious Rosicrucian manifestos that appeared in the first years of the seventeenth century, and that he depicted in it a commonwealth governed by the Rosicrucian brotherhood. No evidence can be found for this view, however. Since Bacon never mentioned them, it is impossible to tell whether he even knew the Rosicrucian publications, while if he did, he might well have dismissed them as fantasies, as he did other occultist writings. White, *Peace among the Willows*, chaps. 6–10 and passim, deals lengthily with *New Atlantis*, comparing it with Plato's *Critias* and *Timaeus*, and asserts without evidence that Bacon left the work unfinished because of his unwillingness to speak of certain secret matters. J. C. Davis, *Utopia and the Ideal Society: A Study of English Utopian Writing 1516–1700* (Cambridge: Cambridge University Press, 1981), chap. 5, deals with the work in the context of other English utopias of the early modern era. Faulkner, *Francis Bacon and the Project of Progress* pt. 3, chap. 11, presents an unreliable treatment that at times defies the plain sense of the text and states, for example (pp. 231, 241–42), that *New Atlantis* hints at a "politically ominous liberation of appetites," including seductive new sexual possibilities. Box, *The Social Thought of Francis Bacon*, chaps. 6–7, makes the interesting argument that the society shown in *New Atlantis* is basically incompatible with the pursuit and expansion of scientific knowledge at which Bacon aims in his natural philosophy. Charles C. Whitney, "Merchants of Light: Science as Colonization in *New Atlantis*," in *Francis Bacon's Legacy of Texts*, offers a prejudicial reading which claims that the work foreshadows the ideology of capitalism, racism, and imperialism. John E. Leary, Jr., *Francis Bacon and the Politics of Science* (Ames: Iowa University Press, 1994), pp. 231–58, includes some suggestive observations on the society pictured in the story.

    114. *New Atlantis, Works*, 5:369.

    115. Ibid., pp. 370–73.

    116. In the course of a conversation on some of the customs of the society, one of the strangers says that "the righteousness of Bensalem [is] greater than the righteousness of Europe"; ibid., p. 394.

    117. Ibid., pp. 385–95.

    118. Ibid., pp. 378, 380–84.

    119. Ibid., pp. 395–413.

CHAPTER 5
LANGUAGE, LAW, AND HISTORY

    1. Aristotle *Rhetoric* 1355b26–36 = bk. 1, chap. 1.

    2. See the historical surveys of rhetoric by George Kennedy, *A New History of Classical Rhetoric* (Princeton: Princeton University Press, 1994), and Brian Vickers, *In Defence of Rhetoric* (Oxford: Clarendon Press, 1988). Modern scholars have devoted a great deal of attention to the history and role of rhetoric in Renaissance culture. It is impossible to overestimate its importance as one of the disci-

plines of Renaissance humanism and a means of training students in eloquent speech and persuasive writing. For its place in Renaissance learning, see Brian Vickers, "Rhetoric and Poetics," in *The Cambridge History of Renaissance Philosophy*, ed. Charles B. Schmitt, Quentin Skinner, and Eckhard Kessler (Cambridge: Cambridge University Press, 1988), chap. 20, and Quentin Skinner's account of classical rhetoric in Renaissance England, *Reason and Rhetoric in the Philosophy of Thomas Hobbes* (Cambridge: Cambridge University Press, 1996), pt. 1.

3. As a part of his university education, Bacon read a number of classical works on rhetoric; see Brian Vickers, "Bacon and Rhetoric," in *The Cambridge Companion to Bacon*, ed. Markku Peltonen (Cambridge: Cambridge University Press, 1996), the most recent treatment of the place of rhetoric in Bacon's philosophy. An earlier discussion of the subject is Karl R. Wallace, *Francis Bacon on Communication and Rhetoric* (Chapel Hill: University of North Carolina Press, 1943), which surveys Bacon's ideas on rhetoric and their relation to classical rhetoric and to sixteenth-century writings on the subject. Although Bacon referred to Aristotle's and Cicero's works on rhetoric, he did not mention Quintilian. It seems highly probable, nevertheless, that he would have known the latter's treatise. George Puttenham's *The Arte of English Poesie* (1589), ed. G. D. Willcock and A. Walker (Cambridge: Cambridge University Press, 1936), contains a description (p. 140) of Bacon's father, Sir Nicholas Bacon, "a most eloquent man of rare learning," sitting in his gallery reading Quintilian's works. Other studies that discuss Bacon's involvement with rhetoric include Paolo Rossi, *Francis Bacon: From Magic to Science* (London: Routledge & Kegan Paul, 1968), chaps. 4–5; Lisa Jardine, *Francis Bacon: Discovery and the Art of Discourse* (Cambridge: Cambridge University Press, 1974), chaps. 9–12; B.H.G. Wormald, *Francis Bacon: History, Politics and Science, 1561–1626* (Cambridge: Cambridge University Press, 1993), chap. 4 and passim; John L. Harrison, "Bacon's View of Rhetoric, Poetry, and the Imagination," in *Essential Articles for the Study of Francis Bacon*, ed. Brian Vickers (Hamden, Conn.: Archon Books, 1968). Wilbur S. Howell, *Logic and Rhetoric in England 1500–1700* (Princeton: Princeton University Press, 1956), discusses the writings and ideas on rhetoric of Bacon's period and deals with Bacon on pp. 365–75.

4. See the discussion by Brian Vickers, *Francis Bacon and Renaissance Prose* (Cambridge: Cambridge University Press, 1968), chap. 2 and passim.

5. *NO, Works*, 8:86–99 = bk. 1, lix–lx.

6. *DA*, ibid., 9:111–12 = bk. 6, chap. 1.

7. *Preparative towards a Natural and Experimental History*, ibid., 8:359.

8. Richard F. Jones, *Ancients and Moderns: A Study of the Rise of the Scientific Movement in Seventeenth-Century England*, 2d ed. (Berkeley and Los Angeles: University of California Press, 1961), p. 91. Jones's pioneer studies of the scientific movement and its effect on language probably overstated its antirhetorical bias. For a corrective to his account, see Brian Vickers, "The Royal Society and English Prose Style: A Reassessment," in *Rhetoric and the Pursuit of Truth: Language Change in the Seventeenth and Eighteenth Centuries* (Los Angeles: William Andrews Clark Memorial Library, 1985).

9. See the discussion and citations in Barbara J. Shapiro, *Probability and Certainty in Seventeenth-Century England* (Princeton: Princeton University Press, 1983), pp. 227–46, which deals with language and communication in the

thought of Bacon, Wilkins, and others who were part of the contemporary scientific movement; the same author's *John Wilkins 1614–1672* (Berkeley and Los Angeles: University of California Press, 1969), pp. 46–48, 207–23, contains a fuller account of Wilkins's *Essay* and its relation to the work of other contemporary thinkers interested in the creation of a universal language. The aspiration to such a language was widespread in the seventeenth century and included philosophers like Descartes and Leibniz; see Stephen Gaukroger, *Descartes: An Intellectual Biography* (Oxford: Clarendon Press, 1995), pp. 200–202, and James Knowlson, *Universal Language Schemes in England and France, 1600–1800* (Toronto: University of Toronto Press, 1975).

10. Thomas Sprat, *History of the Royal Society of London* (1667), ed. Jackson I. Cope and Harold W. Jones (St. Louis: Washington University Studies, 1958), p. 113. See also Vickers's comments and contextualization of Sprat's statements on language, which were opposed not so much to rhetoric as to its abuses; "The Royal Society and English Prose Style: A Reassessment."

11. Plato attacked rhetoric in *Gorgias*, *Phaedrus*, and other dialogues. For his and the opposition of later philosophers to rhetoric, see Kennedy, *A New History of Classical Rhetoric*, pp. 9–10, 35–39; Vickers, *In Defence of Rhetoric*, chap. 3; on the attitude of Pico della Mirandola, ibid., pp. 184–92.

12. René Descartes, *Discourse on Method* (Harmondsworth: Penguin Books, 1968), p. 31 (discourse 1).

13. Thomas Hobbes, *The Elements of Law*, ed. Ferdinand Tönnies (Cambridge: Cambridge University Press, 1928), pp. 49–50; *Leviathan*, ed. C. B. Macpherson (Harmondsworth: Penguin Books, 1986), pp. 14–15, 136–37 = bk. 1, chaps. 5, 8.

14. John Locke, *An Essay concerning Human Understanding*, ed. Peter H. Nidditch (Oxford: Clarendon Press, 1975), p. 508 = bk. 3, chap. 5, sec. 34. These remarks occur at the end of a chapter on the abuse of words.

15. *AL, Works*, 6:120.

16. Ibid., p. 298; *DA*, ibid., 9:132 = bk. 6, chap. 3.

17. *DA*, ibid., 8:407 = bk. 2, chap. 1; for a discussion of this classification, see above, chap. 2.

18. Ibid., 9:60–62 = bk. 5, chap. 1.

19. Ibid., p. 134 = bk. 6, chap. 3; Cicero *Orator* 32.113; Quintilian *Institutio Oratoriae* 2.20.7; Cicero attributed the saying to the Stoic Zeno of Citium.

20. Aristotle *Rhetoric* 1356b1–10, 1357a14–34 = bk. 1, chap. 2.

21. *DA, Works*, 9:63 = bk. 5, chap. 1.

22. Cicero *De Inventione* 1.7.9. The five parts of rhetoric, according to Cicero and other Roman rhetoricians, were invention, arrangement, style, memory, and delivery; see the discussion in Vickers, *In Defence of Rhetoric*, pp. 62–67.

23. See Howell, *Logic and Rhetoric in England*, p. 15, and Jardine, *Francis Bacon*, pp. 32–33.

24. Besides invention, Bacon also took away memory and arrangement from rhetoric, leaving the latter merely as a subdivision of elocution or tradition; see below.

25. *DA, Works*, 9:64 = bk. 5, chap. 2.

26. Ibid., pp. 83–87 = bk. 5, chap. 3.

27. Ibid., pp. 93–108 = bk. 5, chap. 4, bk. 6, chap. 1.

28. Ibid., p. 108 = bk. 6, chap. 1.

29. Ibid., pp. 108–30 = bk. 6, chaps. 1–3.

30. Ibid., pp. 131–34 = bk. 6, chap. 3.

31. This faculty psychology derived from Aristotle's *De Anima* as its principal source; see Katherine Park, "The Organic Soul," in *The Cambridge History of Renaissance Philosophy*, chap. 14, and Vickers, "Bacon and Rhetoric," pp. 213–14. The only extended account of Bacon's psychological doctrines is Karl R. Wallace's *Francis Bacon and the Nature of Man* (Urbana: University of Illinois Press, 1967), which discusses his treatment of the various faculties and includes references to conceptions of the faculties by Bacon's predecessors and contemporaries.

32. *DA, Works*, 9:135–54 = bk. 6, chap. 3.

33. Ibid., pp. 155–82 = bk. 6, chap. 3.

34. Ibid., pp. 155, 182–83 = bk. 6, chap. 3.

35. Ibid., pp. 154, 182 = bk. 6, chap. 3.

36. Printed in ibid., 13:264–90.

37. See *Short Notes for Civil Conversation* and *Apophthegms New and Old*, ibid., vol. 13; *Promus of Formularies and Elegancies*, ibid., vol. 14.

38. Brian Vickers makes the suggestive observation that the Renaissance was fundamentally "a notebook culture" in which writers often presented tissues of quotations held together by threads of argument. He emphasizes Bacon's enormous debt to this "notebook culture" as manifest in the compilations of sayings, phrases, mottoes, metaphors, similes, etc., he made from an early age; *Francis Bacon: A Critical Edition of the Major Works*, ed. Brian Vickers (Oxford: Oxford University Press, 1996), pp. xli–xliv.

39. *DA, Works*, 9:122–23 = bk. 6, chap. 2.

40. See above, chap. 2.

41. *DA, Works*, 9:124 = bk. 6, chap. 2.

42. Ibid., pp. 124–25 = bk. 6, chap. 2.

43. Ibid., p. 123 = bk. 6, chap. 2.

44. Ibid., 8:407 = bk. 2, chap. 1.

45. This view has been expressed by, among others, L. C. Knights in his essay, "Bacon and the Seventeenth-Century Dissociation of Sensibility," in *Explorations* (London: Chatto & Windus, 1946). Although admiring Bacon, he held that Bacon had depreciated the imagination and the value of poetry. For criticisms of Knights's argument, see Harrison, "Bacon's View of Rhetoric, Poetry, and the Imagination"; Anne Righter, "Francis Bacon," in *Essential Articles*; Vickers, *Francis Bacon and Renaissance Prose*, pp. 142, 171, 290.

46. Eugene F. McCreary, "Bacon's Theory of Imagination Reconsidered," *Huntington Library Quarterly* 36, no. 4 (1973): 317–26, discusses Bacon's attitude toward the imagination; for other treatments of the same subject, see the excellent account in Harrison, "Bacon's View of Rhetoric, Poetry, and the Imagination"; John M. Cocking, "Bacon's View of Imagination," in *Francis Bacon: Terminologia e fortuna nel XVII secolo*, ed. Marta Fattori (Rome: Edizioni dell'Ateneo, 1984); Marta Fattori, "*Phantasia* nella classificazione Baconiana delle scienze," in ibid.

47. *Description of the Intellectual Globe, Works,* 10:404.

48. *AL,* ibid., 6:127.

49. *DA,* ibid., 9:62.

50. Ibid., 8:440–41 = bk. 2, chap. 13.

51. Ibid., p. 441 = bk. 2, chap. 13.

52. Ibid., pp. 442–69 = bk. 2, chap. 13.

53. Ibid., p. 441 = bk. 2, chap. 13.

54. Royal law officers were permitted to represent private clients, however, and Bacon did want to earn money by such representation. In his private memoranda of 1608, he speaks of "thinking of various courses" for "increase of practize"; *LL,* 4:48.

55. *AL, Works,* 6:389–90; *DA,* ibid., 9:311 = bk. 8, chap. 3.

56. The best study of Bacon's work as a lawyer is Daniel R. Coquillette, *Francis Bacon* (Edinburgh: Edinburgh University Press, 1992), despite its mistaken understanding of the relationship between Bacon's legal thought and his natural philosophy. An older, brief and authoritative survey of Bacon's achievement as a lawyer and writer on law is Sir William S. Holdsworth's *A History of English Law,* 2d ed., 13 vols. (Boston: Little, Brown, 1922–52), 5:238–54, 486–89. See also Paul H. Kocher, "Francis Bacon on the Science of Jurisprudence," in *Essential Articles,* and the comments in Wormald, *Francis Bacon,* passim. Julian H. Martin's recent work, *Francis Bacon, the State, and the Reform of Natural Philosophy* (Cambridge: Cambridge University Press, 1992), while it includes some interesting and useful matter, also introduces exaggerations and misconceptions arising from the author's thesis that Bacon's natural philosophy stemmed from his experience and ideas as a lawyer.

57. A number of Bacon's legal arguments and his *Reading on the Statute of Uses,* together with various other writings on law, are printed in *Works,* vols. 14–15. His unprinted argument in Slade's Case, an important case involving contract, is discussed with ample references in Coquillette, *Francis Bacon,* pp. 134–43. A legal paper attributed to him, *A Brief Discourse upon the Commission of Bridewell,* printed in *Works,* vol. 15, contains opinions and arguments based on Magna Carta which are so much at variance with his other writings that it seems to me most unlikely that he was the author.

58. Holdsworth, *A History of English Law,* 5:239.

59. *AL, Works,* 6:389–90.

60. *The Case of the Post-Nati of Scotland,* ibid., 15:225–26.

61. *Maxims of the Law,* ibid., vol. 14. This work was first published in 1630; the version printed in ibid. is based on a conflation of manuscripts. See Bacon's preface, pp. 180–85, for his account of the nature and purpose of the maxims. John C. Hogan and Mortimer D. Schwartz have briefly discussed Bacon's maxims and given a bibliography of treatises on legal maxims starting with the year 1546 in "On Bacon's 'Rules and Maximes' of the Common Law," *Law Library Journal* 76 (1983): 48–77; the same authors have also produced an English translation of the maxims in "Translation of Bacon's Maxims of the Common Law," ibid. 77 (1984–85): 707–18.

62. Sir John Fortescue, *De Laudibus Legum Anglie* (ca. 1468), ed. S. B. Chrimes (Cambridge: Cambridge University Press, 1949), pp. 21–23; Christopher St. Ger-

man, *Dialogue of the Doctor and Student* (1523), ed. William Muchall (Cincinnati, 1874), pp. 25–34.

63. Peter Stein, *Regulae Iuris: From Juristic Rules to Legal Maxims* (Edinburgh: Edinburgh University Press, 1966), discusses these rules in Roman law and in English common law; for the relationship of Bacon's maxims to this tradition, see ibid., pp. 170–74.

64. *Maxims of the Law, Works*, 14:182, 185.

65. Ibid., pp. 198–210.

66. Bacon's preface stated that he drew on the principles of Roman law when appropriate. He did so, for example, in rule 11, which says that rights founded on blood relationships cannot be extinguished by any civil law; ibid., pp. 182, 233.

67. Kocher, "Francis Bacon on the Science of Jurisprudence"; see Bacon's statement in *Reading on the Statute of Uses, Works*, 14:287.

68. Coquillette, *Francis Bacon*, pp. 45, 53, 102, 158, 256, and passim.

69. Harvey Wheeler, "The Invention of Modern Empiricism: Juridical Foundations of Bacon's Philosophy of Science," *Law Library Journal* 76 (1983): 78–120; the passages quoted are on pp. 81, 104, 107.

70. Kenneth W. Cardwell, "Francis Bacon, Inquisitor," in *Francis Bacon's Legacy of Texts*, ed. William A. Sessions (New York: AMS Press, 1990); Martin, *Francis Bacon, the State, and the Reform of Natural Philosophy*, chap. 4 and passim.

71. Bacon's conception of these rules did not differ from that of the Roman jurist Paulus, who was surely not thinking of induction when he wrote that "the law is not derived from the rules, but the rules from the law" ("Non ex regula ius sumatur, sed ex iure quod est regula fiat"); *Digest* 50.17.1, quoted by Stein, *Regulae Iuris*, p. 67.

72. *AL, Works*, 6:270–72; *DA*, ibid., 9:84–67 = bk. 5, chap. 2.

73. Ibid., pp. 86–87, 88–92 = bk. 5, chap. 3.

74. "Of Innovation," *Essays*, ibid., 12:160–61.

75. See Louis A. Knafla, *Law and Politics in Jacobean England* (Cambridge: Cambridge University Press, 1977), chaps. 5–6.

76. Bacon's work on the reform of the laws is discussed in detail by Coquillette, *Francis Bacon*, passim, and in a useful survey by Barbara Shapiro, "Sir Francis Bacon and the Mid-Seventeenth Century Movement for Law Reform," *American Journal of Legal History* 24, no. 4 (1980): 331–62.

77. *LL*, 1:339–40.

78. Ibid., p. 214, 3:19.

79. Ibid., p. 233; Bacon remarked on the similarity of such a court to the *grand conseil* of the king of France, which could draw causes from the French *parlements*.

80. Ibid., 4:94.

81. "A Proposition . . . Touching the Compiling and Amendment of the Laws of England," ibid., 6:61–71.

82. Ibid., p. 71.

83. Ibid., pp. 264–66.

84. Ibid., pp. 33–37. This letter to Villiers was written in 1616.

85. Ibid., pp. 18, 19.

86. Bacon's speech on becoming judge of the Court of Chancery is in ibid., pp. 182–93; his Chancery ordinances are printed in *Works*, 15:351–72;

Coquillette, *Francis Bacon*, pp. 192–211, contains a discussion and assessment of Bacon's work as a judge.

87. *LL*, 6:201–4.

88. See above, chap. 4. The *Aphorismi* were never printed and have been discussed and translated by Mark Neustadt, "The Making of the Instauration: Science, Politics, and Law in the Career of Francis Bacon" (Ph.D. diss., Johns Hopkins University, 1987).

89. Aphorisms 1–7, *DA*, *Works*, 9:311–13; the Latin original of the treatise on universal justice is in ibid., 3:135–71.

90. Aphorism 11, *DA*, ibid., 9:315.

91. Aphorisms 22–24, ibid., pp. 317–18.

92. Aphorisms 32–46, ibid., pp. 320–24.

93. Besides instituting proceedings on its own initiative, the Court of Star Chamber also heard suits between parties, something Bacon does not mention in describing the jurisdiction of the Censorian courts.

94. Aphorisms 52–64, *DA*, *Works*, 9:326–30.

95. Aphorisms 64–75, ibid., pp. 331–34.

96. Aphorisms 77–97, ibid., pp. 335–42.

97. Achsah Guibbory, *The Map of Time: Seventeenth-Century Literature and Ideas of Pattern in History* (Urbana: University of Illinois Press, 1986), discusses Bacon's idea of progress in the context of contemporary notions of time. For Bodin's intimations of a perception of progress, see his *Method for the Easy Comprehension of History* (1566) (New York: Norton, 1969), chap. 7, "Refutation of Those Who Postulate Four Monarchies and the Golden Age."

98. *Thoughts and Conclusions*, Farrington, p. 95; *NO*, *Works*, 8:109–11 = bk. 1, lxxviii–lxxix.

99. Ibid., p. 111 = bk. 1, lxxix; *Filum Labyrinthi*, ibid., 6:421; *Thoughts and Conclusions*, Farrington, pp. 77–78, 82.

100. Ibid., p. 94; *NO*, *Works*, 8:116–17 = bk. 1, lxxxiv.

101. *The Great Instauration*, preface, ibid., p. 29.

102. *Thoughts and Conclusions*, Farrington, pp. 94–95; *NO*, *Works*, 8:117 = bk. 1, lxxxiv.

103. Ibid., pp. 128–29 = bk. 1, xcii.

104. Bacon has always been recognized as occupying a central position in the emergence of the modern concept of progress; see the discussion in the classic work by J. B. Bury, *The Idea of Progress: An Inquiry into Its Origin and Growth* (New York: Macmillan, 1932), chap. 2. Paolo Rossi, "Bacon's Idea of Science," in *The Cambridge Companion to Bacon*, pp. 39–43, denies that Bacon held a progressive view of history and offers a definition of the idea of progress to which Bacon does not conform. It is evident, nevertheless, that he believed profoundly in the possibility of the progress of knowledge and that *The Great Instauration* is premised on a conception of progress.

105. The association of history with rhetoric derived from ancient authorities. In their writings on rhetoric, Cicero and Quintilian praised history and its contribution to oratory, and the former's *De Oratore* 2.15 contained statements, quoted repeatedly over the centuries, describing history's high office and its requisites in both substance and style.

106. Renaissance conceptions of history are discussed by Donald R. Kelley, "The Theory of History," in *The Cambridge History of Renaissance Philosophy*, chap. 21; Eric Cochrane, *Histories and Historiography in the Italian Renaissance* (Chicago: University of Chicago Press, 1981); Herschel Baker, *The Race of Time: Three Lectures on Renaissance Historiography* (Toronto: University of Toronto Press, 1967). Machiavelli wrote a *History of Florence* in 1532; Guicciardini was the author of two Florentine histories and a *History of Italy* written in the 1530s, which covered the period preceding the French invasion of 1494 to 1534. On their historical conceptions and writings, see Felix Gilbert, *Machiavelli and Guicciardini: Politics and History in Sixteenth-Century Florence* (Princeton: Princeton University Press, 1965), and Cochrane, pp. 165–70, 295–305, and passim.

107. *Artis Historicae Penus*, ed. Johann Wolf (Basel, 1579). On the *ars historica*, see the account by Girolamo Cotroneo, *I trattatisti dell'"Ars Historica"* (Naples: Giannini Editore, 1971). See also the remarks and references in Cochrane, *Histories and Historiography*, pp. 482–87; Kelley, "The Theory of History," pp. 753–58; Julian Franklin, *Jean Bodin and the Sixteenth-Century Revolution in the Methodology of History and Law* (New York: Columbia University Press, 1963), chaps. 5–9; and Giorgio Spini,"The Art of History in the Italian Counter-Reformation," in *The Late Italian Renaissance*, ed. Eric Cochrane (New York: Harper Torchbooks, 1970).

108. For surveys of developments in English historiography, antiquarian scholarship, and conceptions of history, see Lily B. Campbell, *Shakespeare's "Histories"* (San Marino, Calif.: The Huntington Library, 1947), chaps. 7–10; F. J. Levy, *Tudor Historical Thought* (San Marino, Calif.: The Huntington Library, 1967); F. Smith Fussner, *The Historical Revolution: English Historical Writing and Thought 1580–1640* (London: Routledge & Kegan Paul, 1962); Arthur B. Ferguson, *Clio Unbound: Perception of the Social and Cultural Past in Renaissance England* (Durham, N.C.: Duke University Press, 1979); D. R. Woolf, *The Idea of History in Early Stuart England* (Toronto: University of Toronto Press, 1990); Joseph M. Levine, "The Antiquarian Enterprise," in *Humanism and History: Origins of Modern English Historiography* (Ithaca: Cornell University Press, 1987).

109. See the quotations from Sidney's *Apology* and the discussion in Baker, *The Race of Time*, pp. 2–3, and Levy, *Tudor Historical Thought*, pp. 243–44. Sidney's differentiation between poetry and history went back to the well-known observation in Aristotle's *Poetics* which stated that poetry was thought to be more grave and philosophical than history on the ground that it dealt with the possible, the probable, and what might be, while history was limited to describing the thing that actually happened; *Poetics* 1451a36–b11 = chap. 9.

110. Tacitus *Annals* 3.65.

111. See Levy, *Tudor Historical Thought*, p. 251.

112. *The Ende of Nero and Beginning of Galba. Fower Bookes of the Histories of Cornelius Tacitus. The Life of Agricola* (Oxford, 1591). The paper Bacon wrote to Savile around 1604 or before, *A Letter and Discourse to Sir Henry Savill Touching Helps for the Intellectual Powers*, includes a testimony of their friendship; see *Works*, 13:295–304.

113. Whear's work originated as an inaugural lecture in 1623 and was later published in an enlarged form, *Relectiones Hyemales, De Ratione & Methodo Legendi*

Utrasque Historias Civiles et Ecclesiasticas (Oxford, 1637); on this work, see Woolf, *The Idea of History*, pp. 186–90.

114. William Camden, *The History of the Most Renowned and Victorious Princess Elizabeth Late Queen of England*, 3d ed. (London, 1675), "The Authour to the Reader." This is a translation of *Annales Rerum Anglicarum, et Hibernicarum. Regnante Elizabetha* (1615), with some later additions.

115. The plan of this history is printed in *Works*, 11:33–40.

116. *The Masculine Birth of Time*, Farrington, pp. 71–72; *Advice to Fulke Greville on His Studies* (ca. 1595), *LL*, 2:25. Although this letter to Greville has been attributed to the earl of Essex by Paul E. J. Hammer, "The Earl of Essex, Fulke Greville, and the Employment of Scholars," *Studies in Philology* 91, no. 2 (1994): 167–80, Brian Vickers has made a convincing case that it is by Bacon; see his "The Authenticity of Bacon's Earliest Writings," *Studies in Philology* 94, no. 2 (1997): 48–96. I am grateful to Professor Vickers for sending me a prepublication copy of this paper. He also discusses Bacon's authorship of this letter in his notes to its reprint in *Francis Bacon: A Critical Edition*, pp. 557–58.

117. "Of Studies," *Essays*, *Works*, 12:253; *Advice to the Earl of Rutland on His Travels*, *LL*, 2:112; see Vickers, "The Authenticity of Bacon's Earliest Writings," and the same writer's editorial notes to this composition in *Francis Bacon: A Critical Edition*, pp. 539–41, for evidence of Bacon's authorship of this work, which has been erroneously attributed to some of the secretaries of the earl of Essex by Paul E. J. Hammer, "The Use of Scholarship: The Secretariat of Robert Devereux, Second Earl of Essex, c. 1585–1601," *English Historical Review* 111, no. 430 (1994): 26–51.

118. *DA*, *Works*, 9:216–17 = bk. 7, chap. 3.

119. On Bacon's concept of history, the essay by Leonard F. Dean, "Sir Francis Bacon's Theory of Civil History" in *Essential Articles* is still of value; see also George Nadel, "History as Psychology in Francis Bacon's Theory of History," in ibid.; Judith Anderson, *Biographical Truth: The Representation of Persons in Tudor-Stuart Writing* (New Haven: Yale University Press, 1984), a perceptive treatment by a literary scholar; Wormald, *Francis Bacon*, chap. 3.

120. *DA*, *Works*, 8:407 = bk. 2, chap. 1.

121. Ibid., p. 453 = bk. 2, chap. 13; cf. the similar statement in *Description of the Intellectual Globe*, ibid., 10:403–4. Fussner, *The Historical Revolution*, pp. 256–57, criticizes Bacon's identification of history with memory for its failure to explain how history could be a discipline of knowledge; but of course, Bacon always conceived of memory as an aspect of thought and history as a type of thinking concerned with the past.

122. Bacon's approach on this point may be compared with Bodin's. The latter first classified history into human, natural, and divine; then, after pointing out how greatly divine and natural history differed from human, he quickly relegated the first two to the theologians and natural philosophers in order to concentrate on the third. According to Bodin, the distinctive feature of human history was that it flowed mostly from the will of mankind; *Method for the Easy Comprehension of History*, chap. 1.

123. *DA*, *Works*, 8:407 = bk. 2, chap. 1.

124. Ibid., pp. 409–18 = bk. 2, chaps. 3–4.

125. Bacon also called this history a history of literature ("historia literaria"). In an unpublished paper of 1996, "Writing Cultural History in Early Modern Europe," my friend and former colleague Donald R. Kelley has pointed out the groundbreaking character of a book published in 1551 by Christophe Milieu, a Swiss scholar, *De Scribendi Universitatis Rerum Historia Libri Quinque,* which posited cultural history as a field of study. One of the parts of history in Milieu's scheme was a "history of literature" ("literaturae historia"). His book was included in Johan Wolf's collection of *ars historica* of 1579. On the importance and influence of Bacon's concept of a history of learning and philosophical doctrines for the historiography of philosophy, see *Models of the History of Philosophy: From Its Origins in the Renaissance to the "Historia Philosophica",* ed. Giovanni Santinello; ed. C.W.T. Blackwell for the English edition (Dordrecht: Kluwer Academic Publishers, 1993), pp. 163–69.

126. *DA, Works,* 8:418–21 = bk. 2, chap. 4.

127. The Latin original expresses this thought as follows: "Etenim animum in scribendo ad praeterita retraheret veluti antiquum facere . . . denique verborum lumine sub oculos ponere, magni utique laboris est et judicii." Ibid., 2:201–2.

128. Ibid., 8:422–24 = bk. 2, chaps. 5–6.

129. Ibid., pp. 422–24 = bk. 2, chap. 6.

130. Ibid., pp. 424–26 = bk. 2, chap. 7.

131. Ibid., pp. 430–35 = bk. 2, chaps. 7–10.

132. Ibid., pp. 435–37 = bk. 2, chap. 1.

133. Ibid., pp. 437–38 = bk. 2, chap. 12.

134. Wormald, *Francis Bacon,* p. 61, asserts that when Bacon spoke of sympathy with the past, he did not mean the sympathetic penetration into alien past mentalities, but it is difficult to see what other meaning he could have intended.

135. *AL, Works,* 6:192–94. He reiterates this statement in *DA,* ibid., 8:426–28 = bk. 2, chap. 7. In a letter of 1606 to his friend Lord Chancellor Ellesmere, he also urged the need for a history of Great Britain that would provide a "just and complete history" of both England and Scotland; *LL,* 3:250.

136. *In Felicem Memoriam Elizabethae Angliae Reginae* (ca. 1608), printed with English translation in *Works,* vol. 11; *The Beginning of the History of Great Britain* (ca. 1610), ibid.; *Imago Civilis Julii Caesaris,* printed with English translation in ibid., vol. 12.

137. The surveys of the historiography of the period by Fussner, *The Historical Revolution,* and Woolf, *The Idea of History,* include a discussion of Bacon's *History.* F. J. Levy deals with it in the introduction to his reprint of the work, *The History of the Reign of King Henry the Seventh* (Indianapolis: Bobbs-Merrill, 1972). Other discussions include Edward I. Berry, "History and Rhetoric in Bacon's *Henry VII,*" in *Seventeenth-Century Prose,* ed. Stanley Fish (New York: Oxford University Press, 1971); Stuart Clark, "Bacon's *Henry VII:* A Case Study in the Science of Man," *History and Theory* 13, no. 1 (1974): 97–118; Anderson, *Biographical Truth,* chap. 10; Wormald, *Francis Bacon,* chap. 11. Jonathan Marwill, *The Trials of Counsel: Francis Bacon in 1621* (Detroit: Wayne State University Press, 1976), chap. 4, contains some interesting comments but takes a prejudiced view of the history. The

most recent treatment, by John F. Tinkler, "Bacon and History," in *The Cambridge Companion to Bacon*, claims that Bacon was "conventionally humanist" in his approach to history, and argues unconvincingly that his historical work is best understood in the context of classical and Renaissance rhetoric. The author takes no account of the fact that Bacon does not deal with history in his discussion of rhetoric and never connects rhetoric with his examination of the species of history.

138. *The History of the Reign of King Henry the Seventh, Works*, 11:43.

139. Even in this century, when historians were fully aware of Bacon's errors and dependence on preceding writers, it was difficult for them to free themselves of the picture he had given of Henry VII. S. B. Chrimes, *Henry VII* (London: Eyre Methuen, 1972), the best and most scholarly account of the king's government, retains little or nothing of Bacon's history. The latter is still cited in J. D. Mackie, *The Early Tudors* (Oxford: Clarendon Press, 1952), pp. 46, 52.

140. *Works*, 11:33.

141. *DA*, ibid., 8:441 = bk. 2, chap. 13.

142. Among the histories and chronicles on which he drew were those by Polydore Vergil, Edward Hall, Robert Fabyan, Bernard André, and John Speed, whose *History of Great Britaine*, published in 1611, was the latest of the works on which he relied. Wilhelm Busch, *England under the Tudors*, vol. 1, *Henry VII* (London, 1895), studied Bacon's literary sources and showed the extent of his dependence on them. Spedding's notes to the *History* draw attention to Bacon's use of some of these sources.

143. *Works*, 11:34–35.

144. Ibid., pp. 353–54.

145. Ibid., pp. 50, 51, 63.

146. See the illuminating discussion by Anderson, *Biographical Truth*, chap. 10, who stresses Bacon's use of the device of interior perspective. She suggests that Bacon's history employed some of the techniques of fiction: "thematic structuring and rigorous selectivity, coherent patterns of words and images, dramatized fictitious speeches, interior perspectives on character and causation, and complex but firmly conceived characterization" (p. 171).

147. *The History of the Reign of King Henry the Seventh, Works*, 11:181–82. We might note, incidentally, that the reference to the king's wise foresight is hardly consistent with the earlier opinion Bacon expresses about the king's inclination to short views and inability to think much about future events.

148. Ibid., p. 83.

149. Ibid., pp. 354–64.

150. Ibid., pp. 112–14.

151. Ibid., p. 234.

152. Ibid., p. 353. Polydore Vergil, *Anglica Historia* (1534), ed. Denys Hay (London: Royal Historical Society, 1950), pp. 126–30.

153. *The History of the Reign of King Henry the Seventh, Works*, 11:147–48.

154. Ibid., 54–55, 293–95, 300, 310, 315.

155. Ibid., pp. 143–45.

156. Ibid., pp. 354–64.

CHAPTER 6
CONCLUSION

1. *Of Love and Self-Love, LL,* 1:379; *AL, Works,* 6:168–69.

2. A. N. Whitehead, *Science and the Modern World* (New York: Pelican Mentor, 1948), p. 40. This well-known work was first published in 1925.

3. Antonio Pérez-Ramos makes this point among many other acute observations in his essay "Bacon's Legacy," the conclusion to *The Cambridge Companion to Bacon,* ed. Markku Peltonen (Cambridge: Cambridge University Press, 1996).

4. *NO, Works,* 8:115 = bk. 1, lxxxii.

5. Quoted in Joseph Needham, *The Grand Titration: Science and Society in East and West* (Toronto: University of Toronto Press, 1969), p. 43. All the essays in Needham's book relate to the problem of explaining why modern science emerged only in the West, despite the fact that in earlier centuries Chinese invention, technology, and some parts of science were more advanced than Europe's. It is worth noting that Needham, a distinguished biochemist as well as great historian of Chinese science, calls himself "more than half a Baconian" and contends that "controlled experimentation is surely the greatest methodological discovery of the scientific revolution . . . and it has never been convincingly shown that any earlier group of Westerners fully understood it"; ibid., pp. 49–50.

6. See *DA, Works,* 8:410–11, 415 = bk. 2, chap. 2, and the similar statement in the earlier *Description of the Intellectual Globe,* ibid., 10:407–8. For Aristotle's clear differentiation of nature and art, see *Physics* 192b8, 193a32–5, 194a21, 199a12–17 = bk. 2, chaps. 1, 2, and 8. Note the very interesting comments on this subject in Antonio Pérez-Ramos, *Francis Bacon's Idea of Science and the Maker's Knowledge Tradition* (Oxford: Clarendon Press, 1988), pp. 145–49.

7. *NO, Works,* 8:128, 145 = bk. 1, xcii, cxiv.

8. Max Weber, "Science as a Vocation," in *From Max Weber: Essays in Sociology,* ed. H. H. Gerth and C. Wright Mills (New York: Oxford University Press, 1946), pp. 142 and 143.

9. It should be pointed out that when Bacon spoke of nature as the book of God's works, he was relying on an old metaphor and familiar topos that went back to the Middle Ages and the twelfth century; see the discussion by Ernst Robert Curtius, *European Literature and the Latin Middle Ages* (Princeton: Princeton University Press, 1973), pp. 319–25. What distinguished Bacon's treatment from that of previous writers is that he used this *topos* and its counterpart, the book of God's word, in association with his argument that theology and natural philosophy needed to be kept separate and that their confusion did harm to both.

10. *NO, Works,* 8:161, 162 = bk. 1, cxxix.

11. *New Atlantis,* ibid., 5:415–16.

12. *The New Organon,* ibid., 8:117 = bk. 1, lxxxiv.

13. See Charles Webster, *The Great Instauration: Science, Medicine and Reform 1626–1660* (London: Duckworth, 1975), which traces out in detail the Baconian inspiration of many of the reformers and reforming projects of the revolutionary era.

14. This passage comes from a letter written by Rilke in November 1915, which contains many reflections on death; see Rainer Maria Rilke, *Briefe aus den Jahren 1914 bis 1921* (Leipzig: Insel-Verlag, 1938), p. 90.

15. *DA, Works,* 9:64 = bk. 5, chap. 2; *LL,* 1:137.

16. *The Wisdom of the Ancients,* ibid., 13:129–30.

17. *NO,* ibid., 8:162 = bk. 1, cxxxix.

18. Pérez-Ramos, "Bacon's Legacy," p. 330.

19. The passage in question comes from Kant's *Critique of Pure Reason,* preface to the second edition of 1787; see the translation by Norman Kemp Smith (London: Macmillan, 1929), p. 20. In this preface, Kant praises Bacon as the founder of empirical and experimental science and then goes on to say that to discover the laws of nature, reason "must approach nature to be taught by it. It must not, however, do so in the character of a pupil who listens to everything that the teacher chooses to say, but of an appointed judge who compels the witnesses to answer questions which he has himself formulated"; ibid. This is certainly a very Baconian sentiment, and there is nothing forbidding in it.

20. *The Great Instauration, Works,* 8:46. In his early work *The Masculine Birth of Time,* Bacon used a similar image, saying that from the union of the mind with things would spring "a blessed Race of Heroes to overcome the immeasurable helplessness and poverty of the human race. . . ."; Farrington, p. 72. Another version of it occurs in *The Refutation of Philosophies:* "Let us establish a chaste and lawful marriage between Mind and Nature, with the divine mercy as bridewoman. And let us pray God . . . that from that marriage may issue, not monsters of the imagination, but a race of heroes to subdue and extinguish such monsters, that is to say, wholesome and useful inventions to war against our human necessities and, so far as may be, to bring relief therefrom"; ibid., p. 131. *AL, Works,* 6:135, urged that knowledge should not be a courtesan for pleasure or vanity only, nor a bondswoman solely to acquire and gain for her master's sake, "but a spouse for generation, fruit, and comfort." Bacon also said in the preface to *The Great Instauration* that he had "established forever a true and lawful marriage between the empirical and rational faculty, the unkind and ill starred divorce and separation of which has thrown into confusion all the affairs of the human family"; ibid., 8:34. There is an odd contrast between these marriage metaphors in Bacon's writings on natural philosophy and the unenthusiastic view of marriage he expressed in his essay "Of Marriage and the Single Life."

INDEX